Britain in the Age of Arthur

Britain in the Age of Arthur

A Military History

Ilkka Syvänne

Vendel helmet. (Photograph by the author, Historiska Museet, Stockholm)

Pen & Sword
MILITARY

First published in Great Britain in 2019 by
Pen & Sword Military
An imprint of
Pen & Sword Books Ltd
Yorkshire – Philadelphia

Copyright © Ilkka Syvänne 2019

ISBN 978 1 47389 520 1

The right of Ilkka Syvänne to be identified as Author of this work has been asserted by him in accordance with the Copyright, Designs and Patents Act 1988.

A CIP catalogue record for this book is available from the British Library.

All rights reserved. No part of this book may be reproduced or transmitted in any form or by any means, electronic or mechanical including photocopying, recording or by any information storage and retrieval system, without permission from the Publisher in writing.

Typeset by Mac Style
Printed and bound in the UK by TJ International Ltd, Padstow, Cornwall.

Pen & Sword Books Limited incorporates the imprints of Atlas, Archaeology, Aviation, Discovery, Family History, Fiction, History, Maritime, Military, Military Classics, Politics, Select, Transport, True Crime, Air World, Frontline Publishing, Leo Cooper, Remember When, Seaforth Publishing, The Praetorian Press, Wharncliffe Local History, Wharncliffe Transport, Wharncliffe True Crime and White Owl.

For a complete list of Pen & Sword titles please contact

PEN & SWORD BOOKS LIMITED
47 Church Street, Barnsley, South Yorkshire, S70 2AS, England
E-mail: enquiries@pen-and-sword.co.uk
Website: www.pen-and-sword.co.uk

Or

PEN AND SWORD BOOKS
1950 Lawrence Rd, Havertown, PA 19083, USA
E-mail: Uspen-and-sword@casematepublishers.com
Website: www.penandswordbooks.com

Contents

List of Plates vii
List of Maps ix
Acknowledgements xi
Introduction xii
Abbreviations xiii

Chapter 1   A Bit of Polemics   1

Chapter 2   The Introduction   10

Chapter 3   The Main Narrative with Geoffrey of Monmouth Included: The Creation of the British Commonwealth, 406–445   51

Chapter 4   Vortigern and the Rise of the Saxons   76

Chapter 5   Ambrosius Aurelius/Aurelianus, the *Dux Bellorum* and the Boar of Cornwall in 451/452–462   82

Chapter 6   Ambrosius Aurelius/Aurelianus, the Utherpendragon (A Dragon's Head/The Dragon Pennon Head) in 462–464   96

Chapter 7   Aurelius/Aurelianus Ambrosius, the Arthur/Arthurus (The Bear) 464–466   104

Chapter 8   The Reorganization of the Realm in 465/466   120

Chapter 9   Ireland, the Orkneys, Iceland and Gothland/Götaland in 466/467   122

Chapter 10   Norway and Jutland/Denmark in 468   125

Chapter 11   Campaigns in Gaul in 469/470 (Geoffrey 9.11ff.)   131

Chapter 12   The Crowning as High King/Augustus in 471 (Geoffrey 9.12–15)   140

Chapter 13   The War in Gaul in 471/472 (Geoffrey 9.15ff.)   143

Chapter 14	The Revolt of Mordred and Arthur's Last Campaign in 472	169
Chapter 15	Arthur's Immediate Successors	179
Chapter 16	Arthur the Once and Future King	182

Appendix I: The Reign of Frothi III the Magnificent   184
Appendix II: Swedish Rock Carvings and Naval Tactics   214
Appendix III: Odin the Man   216
Appendix IV: Saint Patrick and the 'Spiritual' Conquest of Ireland   229
Bibliography   242
Notes   245
Index   259

List of Plates

1. The Romantic image of Arthur, drawn by N.C. Wyeth.
2. Author's interpretation of King Arthur in period Roman equipment.
3. King Arthur at the apex of his cavalry wedge.
4. A Briton legionary/heavy-armed footman equipped with a ridge helmet, scale armour, a large *scutum* shield, *hasta*-spear and *spatha*-sword.
5. A Briton legionary/heavy-armed footman equipped in the standard equipment of the period.
6. A foot archer equipped in the typical period equipment.
7. A group of late Roman soldiers as depicted by the Polish re-enactor group Vicus Ultimus.
8. A Finnish re-enactor depicting a late Roman front rank fighter. (© *Jyrki Halme*)
9. Various types of equipment worn by the late Roman and Britons. (*With permission of Vicus Ultimus*)
10. Late Roman soldiers and women as depicted by re-enactors. (*With permission of Vicus Ultimus*)
11. Re-enactor in period dress in readiness to use his knife. (© *Jyrki Halme*)
12. Jyrki Halme in late Roman/Briton equipment on the frozen surface of a lake. (© *Jyrki Halme*)
13. A draco-banner, which would have been used by the Britons and by their enemies. (© *Jyrki Halme*)
14. Jyrki Halme depicting a late Roman soldier as he could have appeared during a leave of absence in summer. (© *Jyrki Halme*)
15. Jyrki Halme depicting a late Roman soldier with a hood to protect him from the elements on the dark autumn day. (© *Jyrki Halme*)
16. Typical Pictish warrior showing his tattoos and bravery.
17. Typical Irish warrior in his equipment.
18. Saxon spearman.
19. Saxon swordsman armed with a *seax* (figure drawn after Richard Underwood).
20. Saxon foot archer armed with a wooden self-bow.
21. An Anglo-Saxon elite warrior, chieftain or king in Britain according to Gamber and Alclud.
22. A Vendel helmet decoration of two footmen engaged in combat.
23. A Valsgärde 7 helmet illustration of two warriors equipped with spears that have thongs to assist in throwing.

24. Author reconstructions of elite warrior equipment.
25 and 26. Helmet illustrations from the graves of Vendel in Sweden (ca. 600–700 AD).
27. Author reconstruction of rider helmet.
28. Author reconstruction of a North European elite warrior on horseback based on the finds at Vendel and elsewhere in North of Europe.
29. Valsgärde 8 helmet decoration.
30. A Scandinavian elite warrior of the Vendel Period attacking.
31. Author illustration of typical Finnish warrior using skis and a bow.
32. Contesti-helmet used by the late Romans. (*With permission of Vicus Ultimus*)
33. Worms-helmet used by the late Romans. (*With permission of Vicus Ultimus*)
34. A fifth century Finnish elite warrior on the basis of grave finds.
35. A typical fifth century Lithuanian warrior.
36 and 37. Traditional images of Finnish crossbowmen.
38. A Finnish hill-fort as it would have appeared during the so-called Viking Age.
39. Jyrki Halme depicting fifth century equipment used by the Romans and Britons. (© *Jyrki Halme*)

List of Maps

British Isles, Locations and Cities	xiv
British Isles, Countries and Provinces	xv
Gaul	xvi
Northern Europe	xvii
Irish and Pictish Fortifications	19
Silchester	59
London	60
Chester/Deva	67
Battle of Mold and Britain	68
Alan Settlements in Gaul 1	73
Alan Settlements in Gaul 2	73
Totnes and Torquay	84
Dinas Emrys	85
Battle of the Field of Maisbeli in 452	88
York	90
Caerleon	94
Dimilioc	99
Dark Age Tintagel	100
Verulamium (St Albans)	102
Lindum (Lincoln)	106
Battle of the Caledon Wood in 462	108
Movements of Arthur and Saxons	110
Possible location of the Battle of Badon 1	112
Possible location of the Battle of Badon 2	114
Arthur's Movements after the Battle of Badon	116
Dumbarton Rock and Loch Lomond	117
Loch Lomond	118
Organization of the Kingdom in 465	121
Lone/Osterøy	125
Scandinavian Iron Age Forts	127
Arthur's Scandinavian Campaign	129
Bourges	132
Arthur's Campaign in Gaul 469/470	134
Paris	136

Bononia (Boulogne)	137
Soissons	138
Mont Saint Michel	146
Saussy (Siesia)	151
Castrum of Dijon	154
Battle of Siesia 1, 2, 3, 4, 5, 6	156, 157, 158, 160, 161, 163
Langres	165
Autun	166
Cabillonum	167
Rutupiae/Richborough	172
Landing Beach at Richborough	173
Winchester	174
Battle of Winchester	175
Battle of the Camblam River	176
Fort of the Wends	189
A Naval Battle in the Baltic Sea	192
Stenby and Birka	201
Tiurinlinna and Nakolinna	204
Odin's Odyssey	222
St Patrick's First Movements in Ireland	233
Northern Ireland	234
Tara	239

Acknowledgements

I want to acknowledge the support of my family and friends. The patience of my wife Sini deserves particular thanks. It is not easy to be in a household where the husband spends so much time in front of a laptop and piles of books, and who also occasionally travels to far-flung places.

Friends like Perry Gray have once again contributed to the study by reading a chapter or chapters, and they all deserve big thanks. I would also like to thank those who kindly commented on my Appendix 3 posted on academia.edu. These include John Matthews and Halstein Sjølie. None of them, however, bears any responsibility for the mistakes that remain. Those are the sole responsibility of the author. It should also not be assumed that those who have commented on my material would always agree with my conclusions. I know for a fact that some of them do not.

The members of the Polish re-enactor group *Vicus Ultimus* deserve great thanks for their stellar photos of Late Roman equipment. They helped me with the *MHLR* Vol. 2 and have also given me additional photos for use in the *MHLR* Vols. 3–5, so it goes without saying that they have contributed greatly and I owe them a big thanks. I also owe a very big thanks to the Finnish re-enactor Jyrki Halme, who has gone to great lengths to provide me with still more photos, this time for this monograph and for three other books simultaneously. He has even acquired additional pieces of equipment so that his impressions of Late Romans would be accurate representations of the fifth century Late Romans and Britons. Jyrki Halme has also contributed to the book project(s) in another way. He has kindly made several suggestions regarding the typology of the equipment used by the Romans. Please note, however, that he does not bear any responsibility for the remaining mistakes in this or the other books.

The Commisioning Editor Philip Sidnell, Matt Jones and the staff of Pen & Sword Publishing once again deserve thanks for their stellar work.

I dedicate this book to the brave inhabitants of the British Isles and to their ancestors, regardless of their origin, background and religion. Cheers.

Introduction

This book began as an article project to shorten the third, fourth and fifth volumes in the *Military History of Late Rome* series by analyzing the Arthurian Era in Britain as a separate study, but it grew up into a full-scale study of Dark Age Britain when I noted a definite need for a reassessment of the evidence.

Abbreviations

ASC	Anglo-Saxon Chronicle
Geoffrey	Geoffrey of Monmouth
Gildas	Gildas, *De excidio Britanniae*
MVM	*magister utriusque militiae*
Nennius	Nennius, *Historia Britonum*
PLRE1	*The Prosopography of the Later Roman Empire*, A.H. Jones and J. Morris. Cambridge 1971.
PLRE2	*The Prosopography of the Later Roman Empire*, J.R. Martindale. Cambridge 1980.

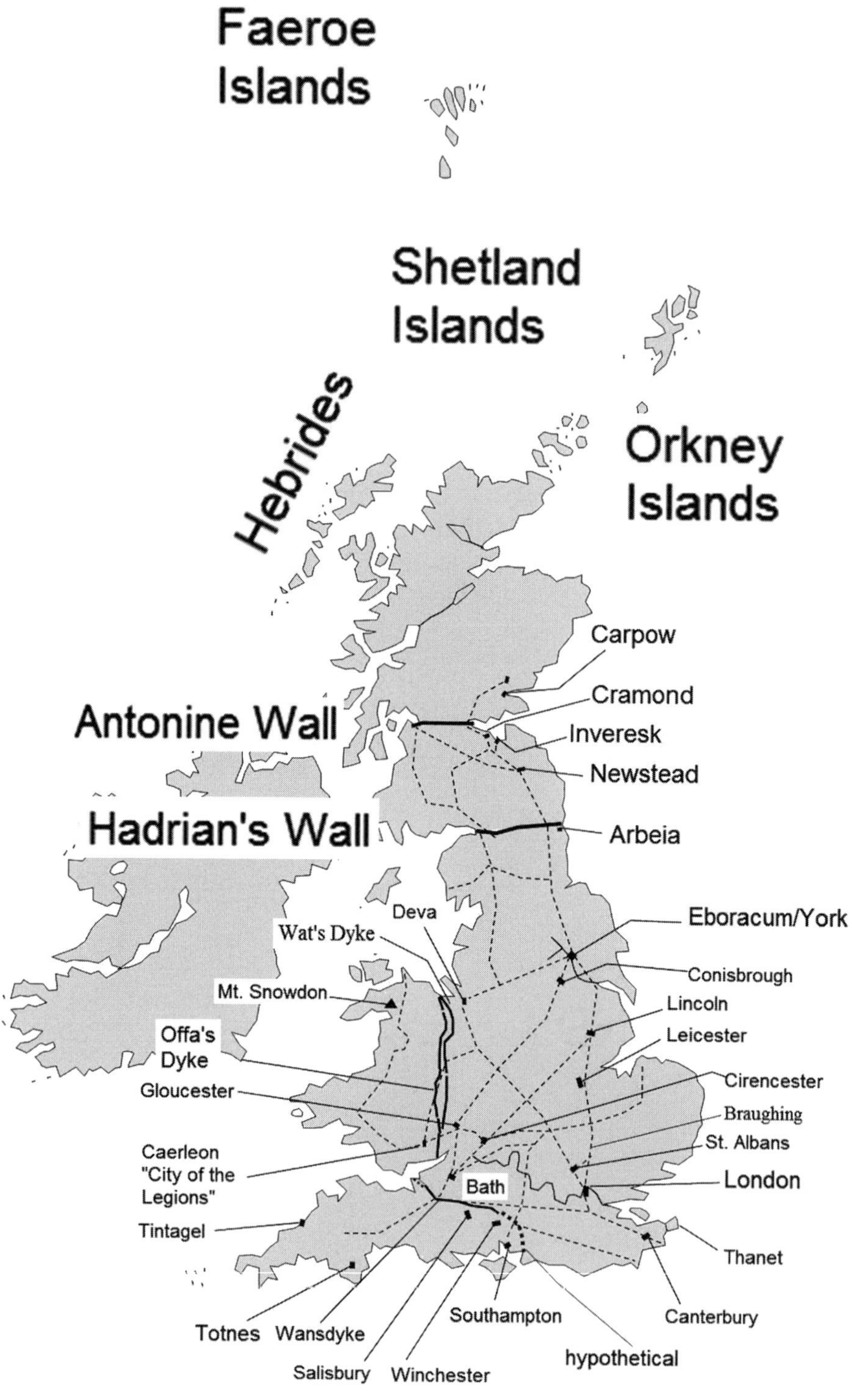
Faeroe Islands
Shetland Islands
Hebrides
Orkney Islands
Carpow
Cramond
Antonine Wall
Inveresk
Newstead
Hadrian's Wall
Arbeia
Deva
Eboracum/York
Wat's Dyke
Conisbrough
Mt. Snowdon
Lincoln
Offa's Dyke
Leicester
Gloucester
Cirencester
Braughing
Caerleon "City of the Legions"
St. Albans
Bath
London
Tintagel
Thanet
Southampton
Canterbury
Totnes
Wansdyke
hypothetical
Salisbury
Winchester

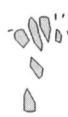

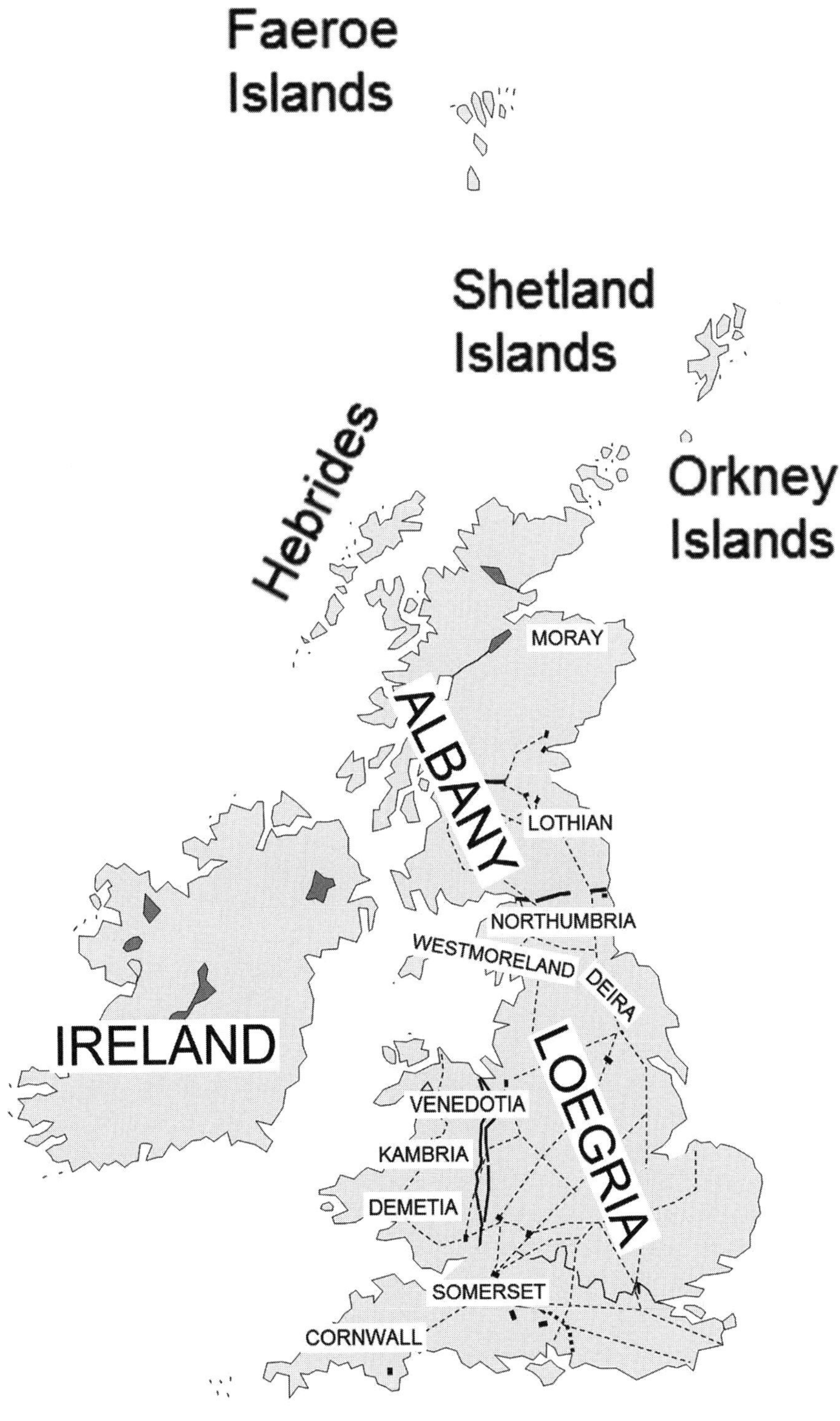
Faeroe Islands
Shetland Islands
Hebrides
Orkney Islands
MORAY
ALBANY
LOTHIAN
NORTHUMBRIA
WESTMORELAND
DEIRA
IRELAND
LOEGRIA
VENEDOTIA
KAMBRIA
DEMETIA
SOMERSET
CORNWALL

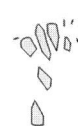

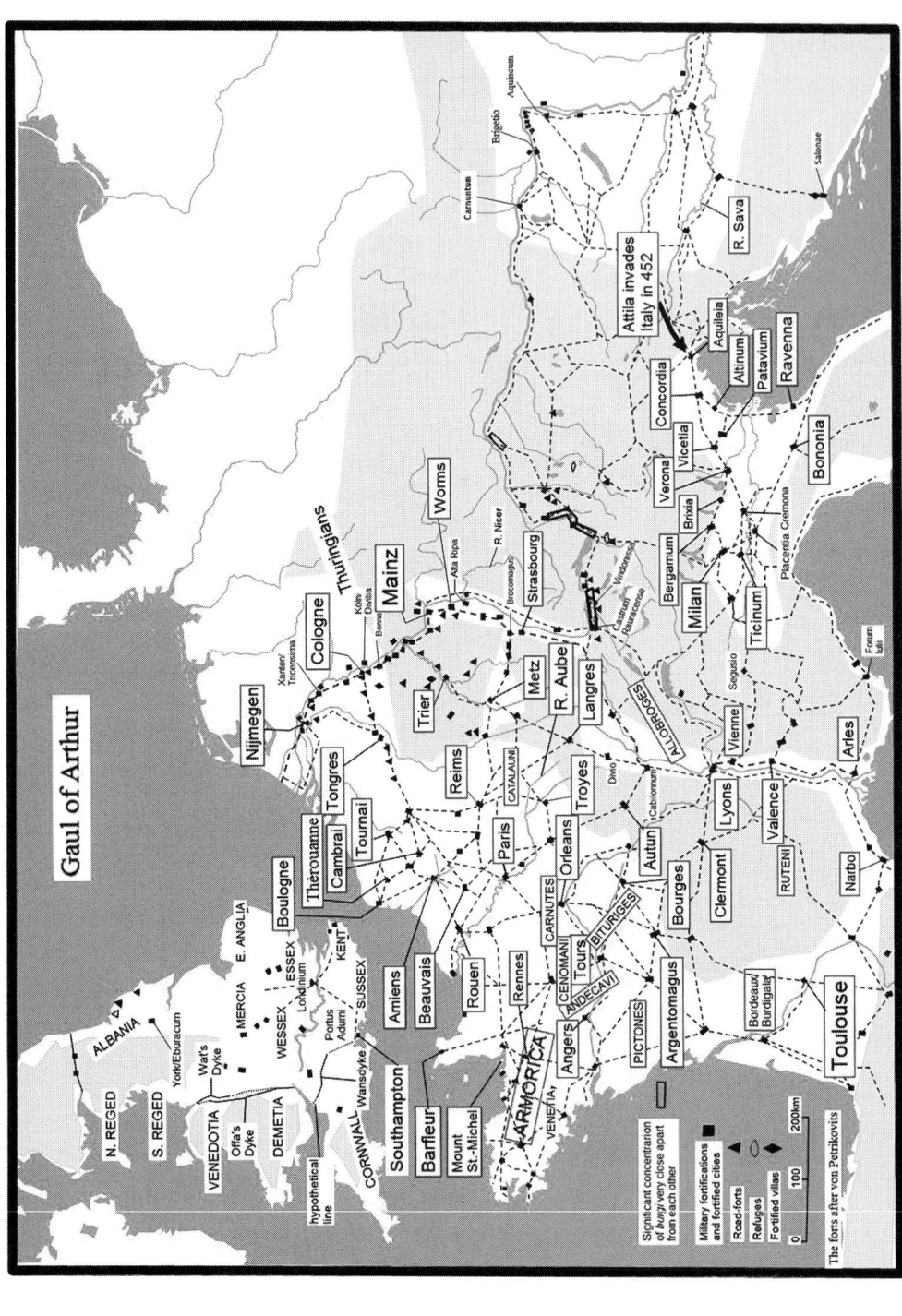

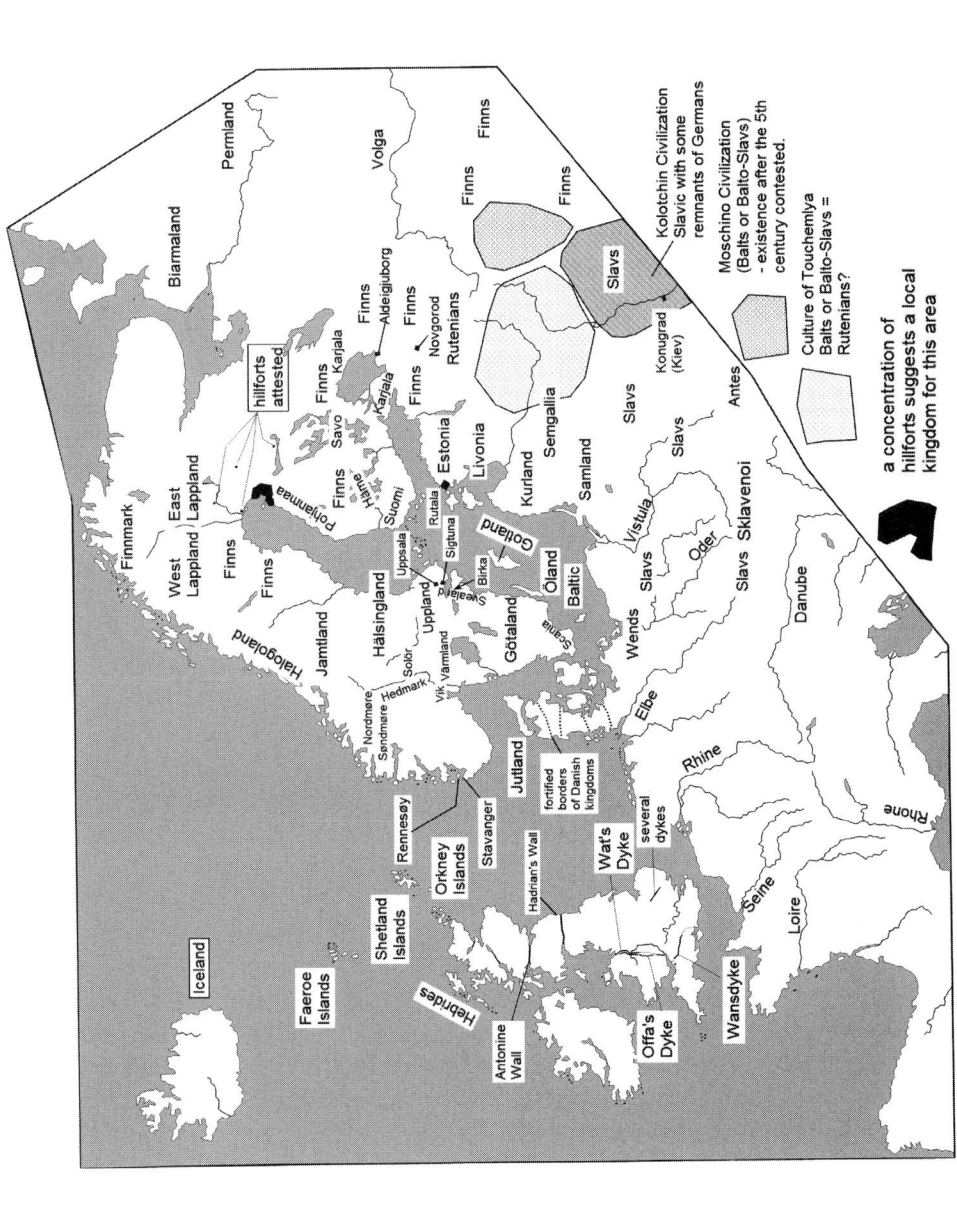

Chapter 1

A Bit of Polemics

The purpose of this chapter and monograph is threefold: 1) to criticize the methodology employed by ultra-conservative historians in their reconstruction of the past; 2) to demonstrate with very controversial topics that one can find new insights into the past if one just abandons the faulty methodology followed up by the ultra-conservative, pompous brand of the Classicist and Medievalist schools, which consider their own very subjective conservative view of the past superior to the actual evidence provided by the sources, and in some cases do this even by following an approach to the sources that can only be called racist; 3) to entertain and titillate the imagination of the readers.

This study is a sort of follow-up to my *The Age of Hippotoxotai*, Melitene article and other studies that criticize the way this certain but ever smaller group of ultra-conservative historians approach the source material – the passage of time will take care of the problem, I guess. The following discussion includes some tongue-in-cheek expressions because I do not believe that the censorship of language, such as the politically correct approach, would serve any good purpose, but it is still intended to be serious in the topics it raises. My intention has been to show that the analysis of history needs not be as serious-minded as it too often is. Historians should be able to laugh at themselves and criticize their own trade and way of doing things.

As background information, I need to state that I began my university studies in the field of modern history and obtained my MA in 1997. It was only after this that I changed my field of specialization to ancient history in 2001, with the result that I received my PhD in 2004. This has given me an outsider's perspective into the study of antiquity and the Middle Ages. The reason for the change of specialization was that I considered modern history to be a potentially dangerous field, as people (who had participated in many a murky operation) were still often in positions of influence and were/are considered 'untouchables'. I was already highly critical of the methodology employed by the modern historians in their so-called attempt to find the 'truth', but the methodology employed by the ultra-conservative Classicists/Medievalists (henceforth I mean both brands of these ultra-conservative historians, regardless of which of the terms I use) is even worse in the fields of political, economic and military history. There are, of course, some very notable open-minded and vocal exceptions, just as there are those who agree with me but have chosen to conform with the accepted way of conducting research

2 Britain in the Age of Arthur

or just choose not to raise the topic publicly. It is certainly high time to raise a more open revolt against the ultra-conservative approach to the sources, because I am not alone in my views. Note, however, that the following discussion concentrates mainly on the topic of military history, because I am first and foremost a military historian.

The principal faults of the Classicists – quite obvious to those whose specialty is the modern era – are that they in general tend to ignore the terrain and the so-called military probabilities in their analysis of warfare, and instead concentrate almost solely on a grammatical analysis of the language used by a particular source (this is often based on earlier interpretations of the words and grammar, which are all too often based on an incomplete understanding of the material) and not on an analysis of its contents, that directly affects the way the words should be translated in each case,[1] and to seek to find out the *topoi* (the commonplaces) and quotations or other possible sources, the assumption being that if something is found out to be a *topos* or a quote from some earlier source, then it follows that it is not a reliable piece of text for the period it describes. It is considered an anachronism or a fictitious story. The result of this is that some studies become studies of the sources that are actually analyses of the textual sources supposedly used by the source under scrutiny, or of similarities between different sources that are then assumed to have led the author to copy the story, that would not have any period relevance. This means that such studies usually include or become long lists of quotes (or supposed quotes) and commonplaces supposedly used by the source, all of which are then condemned as unreliable because of this. These studies have all too often forgotten to include any real analysis of the actual contents, or if there is any analysis then it is restricted to the claims that such and such parts of the text in the original sources are supposedly unreliable because these contain the above-mentioned *topoi* or quotes from other sources. This is to say that the Classicists have all too often forgotten that the purpose of historical analysis is to arrive at a probable reconstruction of the past on the basis of the analysis of the various types of sources (narrative texts, archival/official evidence, archaeology, terrain, weather, human psychology, military probability, general probability etc.), in which the analysis of the text and textual sources is only one of the methods employed and not the only one! It should also be understood that the level of probability varies from case to case.

As is obvious to any modern historian, or any author who has written anything, the commonplaces and quotations are used (when this is done conscientiously) because these describe (according to the opinion of the author/historian) the event particularly well. The use of quotes and linguistic expressions (sentences, figure of speech, metaphors etc.) borrowed from earlier texts – either consciously or unconsciously – is also common to all eras, and merely reflects the influence of education and culture upon all of us. To put it plainly, if I use a piece of text borrowed from some earlier author to describe the actions of, let's say, Presidents Obama or Putin, it doesn't mean that a later historian should discard that piece of text in its entirety because it includes a quote from an earlier source, as is often done by Classicists when they analyze the ancient sources. This is particularly relevant for the analysis of military information. It is thanks to this horrible mistake that most Classicists have failed to understand the basic continuities in warfare from antiquity until the advent of firearms. It doesn't matter what was the name/title of the unit or file or rank. What mattered is that the men were deployed in ranks and files. Similarly, it does not matter if the frontier troops are called *limitanei* or just legions and auxiliaries. What matters is their deployment pattern. It is this that most of the Classicists have failed to understand in their claim that when the Byzantines copied ancient military treatises, or included long quotes from those in their own treatises, that it follows that this piece of text would not have any period significance. It is precisely because of continued relevance that these pieces of text were included.

The Classicist approach also includes one unbelievably idiotic phenomenon, which is that in order to prove one's credentials as a historian, one needs to show critical thinking in the form of the dismissal of extant evidence, merely on the basis of subjective opinion. This can be seen most clearly in the dismissal of all evidence which doesn't suit one's own pre-conceived ideas (which are usually based on the ultra-conservative consensus opinion, formed as a result of the opinion presented by some influential historian of the past) and the acceptance of evidence which does suit this. The most glaring example of this is the dismissal of all evidence which includes large numbers of troops for late antiquity, in support of which is then used the smaller numbers of troops in the very same sources. The source is either trustworthy or it is not! One should not just pick and choose such evidence as fits one's own preconceived ideas. Obviously this doesn't mean that one should not dismiss an impossibly large figure consisting, for example, of millions of men, but it does mean that the historian should analyze the sources for their content on the basis of military probability (how large forces were logistically feasible to be for the theatre of war on the basis of what we know of the economy), which is not accepted as a valid tool by the Classicists at all.[2] When one brings this tool into use, it is easy to dismiss the figures running into millions, but then the figures of tens or hundreds of thousands are plausible if the forces were spread out to facilitate supply, being close to major population centres or close to a major logistical route. On the basis of knowledge of how militaries have operated through the ages, it is also easy to understand that there were many different types of operations (according to the current needs), from special operations (commando strikes, assassinations, guerrilla operations etc.) to guarding and patrolling, that included only small numbers of forces, all the way up to major campaigns with large forces – and every kind of operation between these extremes. When one realizes this, it is no longer possible to dismiss all the larger figures in the sources by using the smaller figures as evidence to the contrary. It is in light of this that one should see the problems relating to the usual Classicist practice (and often also among the Medievalists) to use the smaller numbers in the source to dismiss the larger numbers in the very same source – as is obvious, this is problematic on so many levels.

When one realizes the above, it is easier to seek explanations for the larger figures in the sources. For example, historians have been in the habit of dismissing Procopius' claim that the Goths besieged Belisarius in Rome with 150,000 men. As evidence against this, the historians point out the small numbers of forces supposedly fielded by Belisarius. This doesn't take into account the fact that Procopius actually doesn't mention the entire armed strength under Belisarius, which also included thousands of marines and sailors, and tens of thousands of Roman civilians. On top of that, the historian should remember that the length of the Roman walls would have required truly sizeable forces to either defend or besiege them. When one realizes this, it is quite easy to understand that the Goths may indeed have needed 150,000 men for the task.

It should also be stressed that the value of a source does not entirely disappear, even when it is judged to be unreliable, as is usually done by the Classicists. The best example of this faulty approach is the general frowning towards the so-called *Historiae Augustae*, which has been claimed – but not conclusively proven – to be a late fourth-century forgery. It is a situation in which the historian dismisses the only source that he has of certain events of the past without any attempt at analysis, and replaces it with their own pre-conceived ultra-conservative prejudices, ending up with the statement that the events of this era cannot be reconstructed because the only source is unreliable. It is the same if a modern intelligence operative would dismiss as worthless a specific referral by a terrorist in custody to a forthcoming terrorist attack, when this inherently unreliable person provides an incoherent and muddled account thanks to sleep deprivation, torture and/or use of drugs. The Classicists' approach to this would be to reject the information in its entirety, because the source is unreliable and the information has been obtained in a situation in which the person doesn't necessarily speak the truth. This is a faulty approach. One has to act on the basis of that one specific referral to an existing threat, even if that person were the only source. The same is true of the analysis of the ancient and Medieval sources in which the source in question is the only one for the period or events in question, as is the case for example with the *Historiae Augustae*, al-Tabari, Armenian and Georgian chronicles, and Nordic sagas. If one has only a single source of evidence available, one has to use and analyze it, and not dismiss it in its entirety. If we do that, all that we have left is our own modern opinion. Fortunately, we historians/Classicists/Medievalists are in a better position in that we do not have to act immediately on the basis of the information available, but can assess the reliability of the information in a timely manner.

The Classicist method of the study of the sources also includes other preconceived assumptions, some of which are actually common to most historians – historians of the modern era included. The worst of these is the assumption that if a source is a contemporary one, then it follows that it must be more reliable than a later source. This is certainly not always the case. It suffices to note that a contemporary historian (or a person in charge of making the official records) is sometimes constrained by the circumstances in which they live. This is especially true when the person lives under a dictatorship, but can also be true in circumstances in which the person belongs to a particular political grouping or because the person has to take into account the opinions of his contemporaries in other ways (in today's world, libels or the threat of being ostracized or otherwise sidelined). The evaluation of the worth of each piece of evidence should always be a judgment call by the historian, and not based on the pre-existing assumptions as to the veracity of the source or evidence. This is equally true for the narrative sources (the principal source material for the Classicist) and for official records. It is a mistake to classify the reliability of the source solely on the basis of its closeness to the period under scrutiny. Similarly, it is a grave error to believe that the majority opinion is always correct. It should be a judgement call on the part of the historian if they choose to rely on the evidence presented by a period source rather than that provided by a later source, and if they choose to rely on the majority opinion and not the sole opposing view. It is the historian's job to make those judgement calls case by case.

It should also be stressed that the official records are by no means as reliable as a source category as is often assumed. In order to be able to assess the reliability of a record (even modern records produced in supposedly corrupt-free environments can be very unreliable, as the common view of grades of lie – a lie, an utter lie, statistics – so well attests), one needs to know the exact circumstances in which the record was produced and for what purpose, and this is usually impossible even today. In order to achieve a relatively high probability, one would always need to interview/ interrogate/cross-examine the staff in charge of the making of the record, but even this is still unlikely to be entirely reliable. Ideally, one should be able to interview persons who have left the workplace in anger or been sacked in order to obtain the other side of the story. Another good source is a retired employee who has a grudge against his former employer. One would of course need to assess the reliability of each source, because the person who has a grudge is not always speaking the truth. Regardless, it is this phenomenon that can make the later source more reliable than the period one (or a group of sources that present one and the same version of the events), and this has all too often been left out of the consideration. Once again, the historian should make a judgment call on whether the record is to be trusted on the basis of all the evidence they have.

It is also in this light that the historians of antiquity and the Medieval period should assess the relative reliability of the sources they use. The official record is not necessarily as reliable as usually thought. It is entirely possible that the official record contains purposeful falsification(s) or has purposefully left out some material, while the period or later historian has had access to more reliable sources (e.g. a whistleblower) that tell of what has not been included in the official records, histories or chronicles. Therefore, we should not pre-classify the reliability of the evidence on the basis of some preconceived ideas put forth by the Classicist School of analysis, but make our own judgements case by case.

6   Britain in the Age of Arthur

The above is also true of court cases of the past. It is entirely possible that a court of law has convicted an innocent man/woman or found a guilty man/woman innocent. Courts are not infallible, and are also subject to being manipulated, even in modern Western societies. Each society has its own untouchables. In other words, we should not blindly trust court rulings to be correct when we analyze the events of the past. As historians, we have greater freedoms when we seek the truth than the courts, which are at least officially bound by law. It is the duty of any historian worth their mettle to present their case regardless of what a court of law has ruled, or has not ruled. As historians, we are not bound by law, but by our duty to seek the truth based on the extant evidence, whatever the result or however subjective our truth is – and the truth is always subjective, even when courts of law make their judgments. We are all fallible as humans.

The Classicist approach of favouring one's own personal, subjective view over the evidence presented by the ancient/Medieval sources has also caused other strange phenomena, including statements that ancient/Medieval warriors could not have performed such feats of arms as stated by the sources. Good examples of this are the traditional claims that armoured knights needed help to mount their horses, that horses could not be ridden well without the help of stirrups or that archers could not shoot as fast and accurately as claimed by the sources. Fortunately, these silly claims have now been refuted by the past two generations of re-enactors, who have shown that such feats were and are quite feasible. The reason for the reluctance of the typical Classicist to accept the manly feats of ancient/Medieval warriors is that the typical Classicist has been a physically weak bookworm who has been barely able to lift a pen let alone a sword (an exaggerated figure a speech on my part)!

Similarly typical for the ultra-conservative brand of Classicists is to dismiss evidence on the grounds that it is gossipy and full of material fit for a modern soap opera. Such dismissals of evidence are purely based on the person's own pompous, hypocritical views of what is fitting or appropriate to be told or printed, and what can have happened according to their own sensibilities. It doesn't take into account the fact that humans have behaved in this way as long as they have existed, and will do so in the future. Such gossipy matters have often played decisive roles in the past, the best examples being assassinations of rulers by those whose wives, daughters or sons they had foolishly seduced or raped – and the topic of cheating is obviously very relevant when one analyzes the career of Arthur. One should not forget that extramarital affairs have led to the downfall of many a politician and general, even today (e.g. US general and CIA director David Petraeus).[3] It is this ultra-conservative approach to history that has brought to us the very strange concept of Platonic love; whereas in truth Plato was a gay paepdohile[4] who certainly ravished any pretty boy he could lay his hands on as required by his pederastic teaching methods – most now recognize this, even if there still remain those who deny it.

Another mistake perpetuated by the Classicists and many Medievalists is their readiness to dismiss all evidence presented by a source if it includes any elements of supernatural or supposedly legendary material. The latter can often mean a prejudiced attitude towards manly feats of arms, which are too often dismissed as legends without taking into account the fact that warrior societies saw such deeds as particularly important things to record. This approach is particularly odd because the very same historians are often ready to accept Procopius' descriptions of single combats as accurate. In short, they do not accept that some other person would have made a similar record of a memorable single combat that has found its way to some later piece of evidence. The readiness to dismiss the entire source as evidence of past events on the basis that it includes supernatural elements is extremely silly and takes no account at all of the period culture. It is like claiming that the Bible cannot be used as evidence of the history of the Jewish people because it includes supernatural elements, or that Jesus Christ cannot have existed because the New Testament is full of supernatural elements. This is actually what has been done with King Arthur, and I will attempt to prove that there really existed a person who was called King Arthur. There is actually only one independent period source that confirms the existence of Jesus Christ, and it would be possible to dismiss this as evidence on the grounds that it may be a later addition to the original text made by a later copyist, as has been done in the case of Arthur. This would be incredibly foolish. In my opinion, there is no reason to suspect that Jesus Christ lived and died, and that Arthur also lived and died, even if their later influence on humanity cannot be compared. It is quite obvious that Jesus Christ has influenced history to a far greater degree than Arthur ever did. However, one of the topics of my research in this book is the career of the legendary King Arthur: one cannot dismiss his central role when discussing the history of Dark Age Britain.

There is also another way to criticize the Classicist dismissing of so-called legendary Medieval material in its entirety. Every Classicist is aware of the fact that ancient authors invented relevant speeches which they put into the mouths of their characters, but in spite of this they do not dismiss the entire source as worthless, but attempt to find out what pieces of evidence are credible according to their biased opinion. In other words, every Classicist understands that the ancient authors followed certain conventions of writing that do not make the whole source worthless. However, they do not extend this same approach to other sources, which they dismiss as legendary inventions. They do not take into account the particular conventions of these narrative sources (sagas, poems, epics, hagiographies, Christian chronicles and other chronicles). These conventions include supernatural beings (dragons etc.) and intervention by various gods (if the source is pagan) or by the God, saints or angels on behalf of humans. These conventions are no less reliable than the ancient/classical ones. Should we discard the classical sources solely on the basis that they often present long series of omens that foretold the future? It is the historian's job to see past these conventions and attempt to piece together what

8   Britain in the Age of Arthur

really happened. The historian who dismisses such evidence does their job very poorly. They do not even follow the same criteria towards all of the sources they use: this is racism, pure and simple.

The average ultra-conservative Classicist appears to classify the value of the source according to the prevailing racist view arising from the greater appreciation of a classical education (I, like the Classicists, have been educated according to this system, and it tends to produce excessive pride in one's own learning), in which the Greek and Roman sources in the classical tradition and letters are the most valued, after which come the poems of those Romans with a classical education, which are followed in the hierarchy by the Christian Chronicles and other chronicles. At the very bottom of the hierarchy are the so-called legendary sources, the sagas and poems of the Germanic peoples and historical works of Georgians, Armenians, Iranians and Arabs. The chronicles and poems produced by those without classical education can also be classified according to other racist categories, in which the researchers value the credibility of the sources of their native land (or their own field of specialty) more highly than those of other countries. A good example of this is the claim that the poem *Beowulf* contains more reliable evidence of the events taking place in the Frisian Islands than the Nordic sagas describing the same era. This kind of classification of sources should be condemned by all. The value of every source for each particular piece of evidence should be judged according to its particular merits and defects on a case by case basis, and not according to some preconceived value system that is in truth racist in the extreme.

The following analysis makes the assumption that Geoffrey of Monmouth's *History of the Kings of Britain* includes valuable pieces of evidence regarding the career of Arthur that must have come from a lost source or sources. Geoffrey's account includes all of the above-mentioned points of criticism in one single source. It has all too often been dismissed as a possible source of evidence, and not used at all by Leslie Alcock and John Morris, both of whom believed that Arthur existed. Geoffrey's reputation has been so bad that no self-respecting modern historian has been courageous enough to base his account on this version. This is about to change. I am making the *a priori* assumption that Geoffrey's account is based on some unknown earlier source, which has preserved important snippets of information missing from other sources. By making this assumption, I am breaking away from convention. I am not attempting to analyze once again the possible reliability of each of the sources, which is impossible to achieve thanks to the very poor survival of period material. Rather, I am checking the information included in the source against the other extant evidence.[5]

Readers should be aware that what follows is not 'sober history' as described by Guy Halsall in his *Worlds of Arthur. Facts & Fictions of the Dark Ages* (Oxford, 2013), but history that seeks to bring to light possible new ways to connect existing evidence and new avenues of thinking through novel approaches to the Medieval sources – I am making the bold suggestion that we should attempt to analyze the sources for their content and not dismiss those parts that do not fit our preconceived ideas of the past. If Halsall's way of writing is called sober history, then my way of writing history can perhaps be called a 'pint of bitter please'. The important point here is that Halsall has purposefully dismissed as fictitious all evidence in the sources that mention Arthur, because the Welsh would have wanted to invent such a hero who would come to save them, and accepted as valid only those sources which do not include references to him. It can actually be argued that the exact opposite is true. It is equally valid to claim that the Anglo-Saxon sources would have had every reason to hide the existence of such a figure, so they falsified the evidence. My personal view is that since there are referrals to Arthur in the sources in Ireland, Great Britain and Bretagne, it is very unlikely that he would have been invented universally in all of those regions.[6]

In the following discussion, I will at least partially stick to the *topos* of academic historical writing when I give a brief overview of the sources and include explanations and endnotes to back up my analysis – but I have inserted some of the notes into the text itself. I do this only to back up my argument. After all, I am still a historian who has been taught to do this, despite all my ranting! It is funny that no-one has paid any attention to these *topoi*. As regards the far developed legendary material included, for example, in the texts of Chrétien de Troyes or Sir Thomas Mallory, I have not attempted to include those. However, I firmly believe that it would also be possible to find traces of the real Arthur in those by examining each of the instances in detail. The following analysis is based on Geoffrey of Monmouth and earlier material. The dates are my best educated guesses based on the very few known dates in the sources, and should be seen as such. The evidence for the fifth century is so sparse, and sometimes so contradictory, that it would be possible to date certain events in another way. All I can say is that the events that I describe in this book took place approximately at the time I have dated them, give or take a couple of years.

Chapter 2

The Introduction

2.1 The Background 1: The Belligerents

2.1.1 The Britons

The military forces fielded by the Britons were based on their Late Roman inheritance. Their forces therefore consisted of the remaining regular Roman units and naval detachments, the federate forces that had remained on the island, the newly organized citizen levies and the retinues/mercenaries (*bucellarii, comitatus*) employed by the wealthy. The regular units, federate forces and *bucellarii* were well-equipped and efficient, but since there were not enough regular units/naval detachments and private retinues available, the actual defence of the island fell on the citizen levy, which was organized according to the Roman manner. As we shall see, in the initial stages of the fifth century this paramilitary force of civilians was quite inefficient. It was undoubtedly numerically sufficient, but its morale was very low because its members had no experience of combat, it was apparently not well-equipped and was inadequately indoctrinated and trained. The lack of adequate equipment is proven by the fact that the Romans paid particular attention to this fact during their second intervention in the affairs of the island. The continual fighting and desperate situation brought about a marked improvement in the fighting quality of the citizen militias, and eventually tilted the balance back in favour of the Britons when they also obtained a charismatic new leader called Arthur.

In about 410, the British realm appears to have been organized around a council consisting of representatives of the city councils and magnates, some of which held titles such as *duces*/kings or consuls and were called tyrants by those who despised them. The magnates/kings appear to have consisted of the old Celtic nobility, who had never lost in their entirety their tribal connections. It is probable that these men were seated around the famous round table, so that none were considered superior to the others. However, one of them was still considered by mutual agreement to be the *primus inter pares* (*princeps*). He also had the title of king, or rather high king (Vortigern, Riothamus) or emperor/*imperator*/*dux bellorum* to separate him from the other kings. The first known *princeps* is Vortigern, and the most famous Arthur. Geoffrey of Monmouth's list of notables allows us to reconstruct some sort of hierarchy for them at the peak of Briton fortunes. At the very top was obviously the high king/emperor (who ruled England proper), and immediately after him were the five kings (of Scotland, Reged, North Wales, South Wales and Cornwall). The next in ranking were the three archbishops. During the reigns of Vortigern and Vortimer, the pagan priests would obviously have held higher rank that the bishops. Below the clergy were the eleven *duces* with the dignity of consul. Six of these ranked higher (Gloucester, Worcester, Salisbury, Cargueit/Warguit/Warwick, Leicester/Legecester and Kaicester) than the rest (Dorobernia, Roffensis, Bath, Dorchester and Ridoc/Oxford). The lesser worthies below these had titles which may indicate a membership of a city council or something similar. In addition to this, there were client kings, consuls and *duces* outside Britain (e.g. in Bretagne) who recognized the supreme position of the British high king and were required to contribute forces for campaign purposes.

It is not entirely clear whether the British Council consisted solely of the eleven consuls/*duces* and the first consul/*princeps*, or whether it also included the five kings and perhaps the Primate of England. The former actually appears likelier, and would explain why Aurelianus Ambrosius was called *dux bellorum*. The five kings would have been rulers of the surrounding semi-independent Celtic areas that recognized the authority of the council of Britain.

The devastation of the British countryside, towns and cities by the invading Saxons, together with the simultaneous collapse of the Roman Empire and its administrative and military organization and trade networks, caused severe deterioration of living conditions and standards in what remained of Roman Britain. The high end villas were abandoned and local nobles resettled their families, followers and property in rebuilt Iron-Age hill forts, which became local centres of power. In such turbulent times, the nobles and their followers sorely needed the protection provided by these forts. However, according to the latest archaeological analysis, the Britons did not completely abandon the towns and cities, but continued to live in them, occupying humbler abodes that incorporated the old Roman stone buildings as parts of the new wooden ones. This is not surprising. The towns usually possessed walls, which made them good places of refuge for the population. Furthermore, the bishops required cities and towns to serve as their sees as long as the Britons held the upper hand in the conflict with the barbarian invaders.

The British Fleet
The core of the British fleet apparently consisted of the naval detachments left behind in their naval stations. The bulk of these ships would have consisted of the so-called small to medium-sized *liburnae/dromones* and naval scouting ships (*scafae/pictae/picati*) painted blue. We do not know the name of the commander of the British fleet, but one may make an educated guess that he would still have been called Fleet Prefect (*praefectus classis*), while his assistant would have been called *subpraefectus*. The *navarchi* appear to have been in charge of several ships (classed as tribunes or *centuriones classiarii*, according to the number of ships). The *trierarchi* in their turn were captains of individual ships (classed as *optiones navaliorum* and

12   Britain in the Age of Arthur

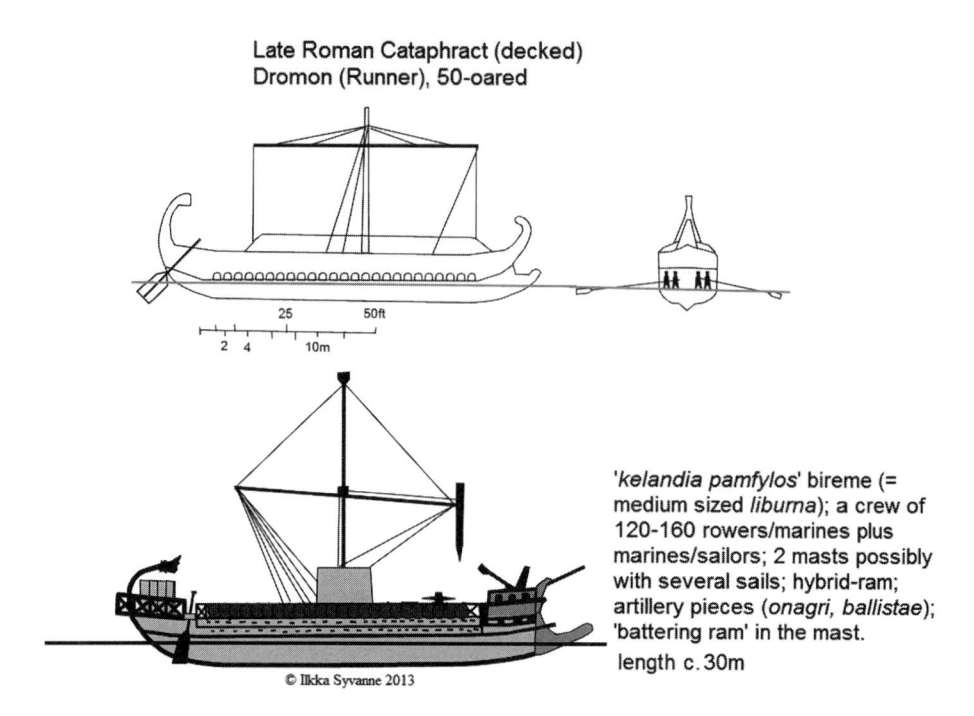

Late Roman Cataphract (decked)
Dromon (Runner), 50-oared

'*kelandia pamfylos*' bireme (= medium sized *liburna*); a crew of 120-160 rowers/marines plus marines/sailors; 2 masts possibly with several sails; hybrid-ram; artillery pieces (*onagri, ballistae*); 'battering ram' in the mast.
length c. 30m

© Ilkka Syvänne 2013

suboptiones, depending upon the size of the vessel). In addition to this, the fleets would have had administrative staff, artisans, workmen, rowers, sailors and marines. Everyone would have been paid in kind and not by any money.

The British fleet would therefore have consisted of the scout ships, *monoremes* (2 x 25 oars, with one to two men per oar) and *biremes* (2 x 25 oars per side with one rower per oar; 2 x 20 oars, upper deck 80 rowers and lower deck 40 or 80 rowers). It is just possible that the flagship of the fleet would have been the so-called *dromon trieres/dromon/dromonion* (a *bireme* with three rowers per oar on the upper deck, so that the upper had 200–230 rowers plus other crew, including seventy soldiers). The *bireme* had varying numbers of oars and rowers per oar, but always three rowers per oar on the upper deck to make the ship a '*trireme*'. The ships were presumably equipped with bronze rams or hybrid-ram/spur-spikebow, a transitional version of the spur. The ships could also be equipped with *onagri* stone-throwers and *ballistae* dart/spear-shooters.

The illustrations above show some examples of the ships (a scouting ship, small *monoreme* and *bireme dromons*) used at this time.

The standard naval battle tactics was to array the ships into three divisions – the left, centre and right – which in turn were used to form the following battle formations: line abreast; two lines abreast; crescent (used for outflanking); crescent with two lines; convex with one line (used for breaking through the enemy middle);

convex with two lines; and the defensive circle. The Romans could also post separate reserves on the flanks and in the centre. The merchant and transport ships corvéed for service when not used as fighting vessels were kept out of harm's way by placing them behind the battle line.

The Land Forces
The analysis of the referrals to the military organization, modes of combat and tactics in the *Mabinogion* and Geoffrey of Monmouth's *History of Kings of Britain* find corroboration from the third- to sixth-century Roman sources, and can therefore be considered to contain reliable material. The most important of these are the referrals to the size of the legion and tactics employed in Geoffrey's *History*, but incidental details, such as can be found in the *Mabinogion*, shed additional light on the period practices. For example, in the *Dream of Maxen* (pp.118–27), the *Mabinogion* refers to thirty-two horse-mounted 'kings' accompanying Maxen (Maximus),[1] who created a shade for the sleeping Maxen by placing shields on spears – the spear/shield combination was the standard practice at least until the twelfth century. The thirty-two horsemen were actually a *turma*, which accompanied its leader. These horsemen were usually deployed for combat in rank-and-file array. If these were then united with another thirty-two horseman *turma*, then they could form a wedge of sixty-four horsemen, and then if another sixty-four horsemen were added, the array could be formed into a 128-horseman *rhombus*.

The legions and auxiliaries the British inherited consisted of five different varieties. Firstly, there were the traditional legions and auxiliaries. Their principal building blocks were the files (eight fighters, one recruit and one servant), centuries (eighty fighters, ten recruits and ten servants) and cohorts (480 fighters, sixty recruits and sixty servants; milliary cohorts, 800 fighters, 100 recruits and 100 servants). The cavalry was organized into units of 512 or 608 horsemen, plus the supernumeraries.

The second variety consisted of 6,000 footmen and 732 horsemen legions, which appear to have been created under Septimius Severus and then reinstated by Diocletian. Its principal building blocks were also files, centuries and cohorts (regular cohorts, 550 men; milliary cohorts, 1,100), but these were slightly stronger than the previous ones (see below).

The third variety of units had been created presumably during Constantine the Great's reign. These were modelled after the Greek practice so that the units followed the principle of dividing the army into multiples of four (four, eight, sixteen, thirty-two, sixty-four, 128, 256, 512 etc.). The most important organizational change was that Constantine the Great separated the legionary cavalry into separate units. For practical purposes, the actual differences in the size of the basic fighting blocks, the infantry cohorts (standard cohort 480 vs 512 vs 550; milliary cohort 800 vs 1,024 vs 1,100), were quite meaningless.

The fourth variant is included in the sixth-century author John Lydus' *De Magistratibus* 1.46. According to him, the professional Roman army consisted of units (*speirai*) of 300 *aspidoforoi* (shield-bearers)[2] called cohorts (in truth 320 legionaries making up the cohort, plus 160 light-armed); cavalry *alae* (*ilai*) of 600 (= 608) horsemen; *turmae* of 500 (= 512) horsemen; *vexillationes* of 500 (= 512) horsemen; and legions of 6,000 footmen and the same numbers of horsemen. Lydus' list of different types of legionaries suggests that there was also a variant legion in which there were 6,000 footmen and 1,600 horsemen (*turma, ala, vexillatio*). There were also the supernumeraries, which consisted of the officers, bodyguards, standard-bearers and musicians. The 6,000 footmen included artillerymen and artisans, so the actual combat strength of the infantry portion was about 4,800 men, plus the supernumeraries. The existence of this type of legion is confirmed by fifth-century sources (*MHLR* vols.3–4) and by Geoffrey.

In addition to this, there were detachments and units of irregular size, which consisted mainly of the former *numeri* and *foederati* and of the detachments that had become separated from their mother units.

It was thanks to this great variety of unit sizes that the Romans could either divide or unite these units as needed for combat purposes, so the actual combat units consisted of blocks of 200–500 men, 1,000–3,000 men and 6,000–7,000 men. All of these units were divided into ranks and files.[3]

The following example of the composition of the traditional legion by Vegetius (source: Syvänne, *MHLR* Vol.1) gives a good indication of how the traditional legions were organized in practice:

Vegetius' Legion (Epit. 2.6ff.) with additional comments in brackets.
- 1 *praefectus legionis* formerly *legatus*; commander of the legion.
- 1 *tribunus maior*; appointed by the emperor in charge of one cohort (probably the 1st; second-in-command of the legion).
- 1 *Praefectus Castrorum* (camp, medics, siege equipment etc.).
- 1 *Praefectus Fabrorum* (workmen, construction etc.).
- *tribuni minores* from the ranks (6 tribunes? put in charge of the cohorts and cavalry along with the *praepositi*).
- 5 centurions of the 1st Cohort (Vegetius' list differs from the other known lists of officers and is also 100 men short of the 1,100 men he gives for the 1st Cohort).
    primus pilus in charge of four centuries/400 men (this probably means that there were 440 men, which consisted of 4 centuries each with 110 men).
    primus hastatus 'now called *ducenarius*' in charge of two centuries/200 men (probably 220 men).
    princeps 1.5 centuries/150 men (probably 165 men).
    secundus hastatus 1.5 centuries/150 men (probably 165 men).
    triarius prior 100 men (probably 110 men).
- 5 centurions for the cavalry.
- 45 centurions of the 2nd – 10th Cohorts each in charge of 100 men, 'now' called *centenarii*.

- 1st Cohort: 1,105 footmen (this probably means that there were 720 heavy infantry deployed four deep and 360 light infantry deployed two deep with 10 *optiones*, 10 standard-bearers and 5 centurions).

  132 horsemen (128 horsemen and four decurions; in truth the decurions may have been part of the 128 horsemen, in addition to which came one centurion, two musicians and one standard-bearer; when trained to do so, the 128 horsemen could form up a rhombus so that at each apex stood one decurion).
- 2nd – 10th Cohorts: 9 x 555 footmen (this probably means that there were 360 heavy infantry deployed four deep and 180 light infantry deployed two deep with 5 *optiones*, 5 standard-bearers and 5 centurions).

  9 x 66 horsemen (sixty-four horsemen and two decurions; as noted above, the decurions should probably be included as part of the sixty-four horsemen, who could be formed either as a wedge or two rank-and-file oblongs).
- artillerymen (fifty-five *carroballistae*, each with eleven men and ten *onagri* per legion), 'squires', servants and various kinds of standard-bearers and musicians and other specialists like clerks, medics, wood-workers, masons, carpenters, blacksmiths, painters, siege-equipment builders, armourers etc. (*aquiliferi, imaginarii/ imaginiferi, signiferi/draconarii, tesserarii, optiones, metatores, librarii, tubicines, cornicines, buccinators, mensores, lignarios, structores, ferrarios, carpentarios, pictores* etc.).
- My above hypothesis regarding the organization behind Vegetius' figures suggests that a possible overall fighting strength of Vegetius' legion may have been: 4,400 heavy infantry; 1,100 light infantry; 726 cavalry; at least 660 artillerymen, with fifty-five *carroballistae* and ten *onagri*; at least 550 recruits left to defend the marching camp, together with the servants and workmen. The extra men on top of the older paper strengths may actually represent the recruits not normally included in armed strengths. The obvious problem with Vegetius' information and my reconstruction based on it is that we have practically no evidence to corroborate it, but at least if one presents the information in this manner it does make sense and is therefore plausible. Vegetius notes that the legion could also include several milliary cohorts, which probably refers to the Praetorians or refers to the practice of his own day to group together different units to form 'temporary legions' that were later called *mere* by the East Romans (sing. *meros/ division*).

The Roman combat doctrine was based on the expectation that the Romans would fight all of their wars in the most advantageous way. This meant that the Roman generals were required to pay particular attention to intelligence gathering so they would always possess timely and accurate intelligence of each potential or real enemy and its intentions, allowing them to formulate the best possible response. In addition to this, the Romans expected their generals to pay particular attention to the provisioning, training, equipment and morale of the army. The general was also required to ensure the safety of the army by surrounding it with layers of spies, scouts and patrols during marching, and by using safe marching formations and fortified marching camps whenever necessary.

Surprise attacks and ambushes were considered the best ways to deal with the enemy, but when this was not possible, the Romans sought to engage the enemy in advantageous terrain at the most advantageous time (e.g. when the sun shone or wind blew from behind the Romans). The standard combat tactics were based on the use of joint (all arms of service) and combined (allies included) operations, so the standard combat formations consisted of the different varieties of the phalanx array. The principal phalanx arrays the Romans used were: lateral phalanx with reserves; oblique formations to outflank one enemy wing; forward-angled half-square; rearward-angled half-square; double phalanx when the rear was not protected by baggage train, marching camp, city or terrain; crescent; convex; mixed infantry and cavalry formation; and hollow square or oblong. The cavalry was usually placed on the wings and in reserve, but when the Romans used the mixed array then the cavalry was placed between the infantry units. Roman generals were required to use reserves, which they were to place wherever needed; this was also true of the cavalry, so cavalry arrays always had a second support line and flank units to protect the flanks.

Unit manoeuvres were designed to give them and their officers greater operational freedom than would have been possible with the above-mentioned grand tactical formations. Unit manoeuvres included: shallowing/widening of the array to outflank the enemy or prevent outflanking; deepening of the array to create weight for the attack or withstand enemy attack; forming of a double front (*orbis/amfistomos*) to withstand attack from the rear/flank; forming of a double phalanx to protect the rear and flanks or outflank the enemy; forming of a wedge to crush the enemy formation; forming of a hollow wedge as a counter tactic against a wedge; opening of the formation to let enemy cavalry, elephants or chariots through; forming of a forward-angled half-square to outflank the enemy; and forming of a crescent to outflank the enemy.

The *Mabinogion* (e.g. 157, 160, 169, esp.173, 174) includes very important references to the use of dogs by horsemen. The breed is not usually mentioned, but since one shepherd had a mastiff (p.150), which was used as a war dog by the Romans, it is possible that the Britons employed mastiffs for the same purpose. The British cavalry appear to have unleashed their packs of dogs just before the charge to disorder the enemy cavalry (or possibly even infantry), just like the Finns did during the Thirty Years' War in the seventeenth century. This was certainly a very effective tactic against those cavalries that had not trained their horses to ignore the barking and biting dogs.

When the Romans had a significant numerical advantage, they sought to outflank the enemy on both flanks (lateral phalanx, crescent, forward-angled half-square). The Romans sought to outflank the enemy on one flank (lateral phalanx, oblique arrays) when they had slightly more men than the enemy or parity. If the Romans had fewer men than the enemy, they could still attempt to outflank the enemy on one flank by using the oblique array, or by sending one wing forward while the rest stayed behind. If the enemy outnumbered the Romans, they could also attempt to break the enemy array in the centre while reconnecting their wings (lateral phalanx with a wedge or deep formation in the middle; mixed formation with heavy cavalry in the middle; convex; rearward-angled half-square). The hollow square/oblong array could be used in all circumstances when the commander thought it necessary to provide the foot formations with a 360° defensive perimeter. The hollow square/oblong was the standard Late Roman tactical formation after the reforms of Valentinian and Valens, and was also used by Arthur, as I will show.

The hollow square/oblong had three different varieties: 1) the entire army could be deployed as one massive hollow square/oblong; 2) ca. 2,000–3,000 strong units (*moirai*) could be deployed as hollow squares/oblongs; 3) legions/mere/divisions of ca. 6,000–7,000 men could be deployed as hollow squares/oblongs. The cavalry could be deployed on the flanks, inside the squares, behind the squares, in front of the squares or in the intervals between the squares, as required by the situation. All of these varieties saw use in the fourth and fifth centuries.[4]

For illustrations of standard Briton equipment, see the Plates section. The illustrations are based on information obtained from the period sources and other sources used in the main narrative. The key piece of information is that before they left, the Romans taught the Britons how to construct Roman military equipment, which means that the Britons used standard Roman fourth- and fifth-century equipment.[5]

2.1.2 The Enemies

The Romans
As strange as it may sound, the Romans formed one of the principal enemies of the Britons, thanks to the fact that the Roman Empire was in an almost constant state of civil war. For the military system employed by the Romans, see the above chapter on Britons who were also Romans.

The Picts and the Irish[6]
The Picts of Scotland and Scots of Ireland formed the principal threat to Roman Britain until the early 450s, after which their place was taken by the Saxons (Saxons, Angles, Jutes etc.). It should be noted, however, that the Picts and Scots sometimes also cooperated with the Saxons, just as they had done in the 360s.

Scotland under the Picts consisted of seven kingdoms, each of which was ruled by a king. These seven kingdoms were further grouped together to form two separate peoples/confederations called Verturiones and Dicalydones (northern and southern Picts). Both of these had a High King. It is usually speculated that the Dicalydones were the senior branch, which means that its ruler could command

18   Britain in the Age of Arthur

both confederacies. The hierarchy below the king consisted of his designated heirs (second-in-command) of the tribal chieftains, each in charge of their own clan and several sub-clans.

The so-called 'higher men' formed the core of the armed forces, while the free farmers formed the general levy. The commoners (subjects?) and slaves were forbidden to carry weapons. We do not know the armed strength of the Pictish armies, but on the basis of their ability to take cities, one may estimate a minimum of 20,000 young warriors and 10,000 older ones, in addition to which one should count the general levy. The standard battle formation appears to have consisted of an infantry centre and cavalry wings. The infantry consisted of line infantry armed with spears, javelins, axes and swords, and light infantry archers armed with bows and crossbows. The cavalry was equipped with spears, swords and shields.

On the basis of later documents, we can make a better estimate of the size of the Pictish fleet. It was divided into northern and southern fleets, each of which consisted of 150 longboats and curraghs, each with a minimum crew of 14 rowers and one steersman. The probable offensive strength of the Pictish fleet was therefore in the neighbourhood of 150 ships (perhaps about 2,100–4,500 men), because it would seem probable that the Picts would have usually left half of their ships behind to protect their homes. The Pictish raiders usually bypassed Hadrian's Wall by ship and attempted to raid the coastal areas. The British response to this had been to establish guard towers and military ports with ships along the coast to intercept the raiders. After successive British usurpers had transferred a significant proportion of the regular forces to the mainland, the Britons lacked adequate forces for this, which eventually resulted in the loss of Wales to the Scots and Picts, then significant portions of the north to the Picts.

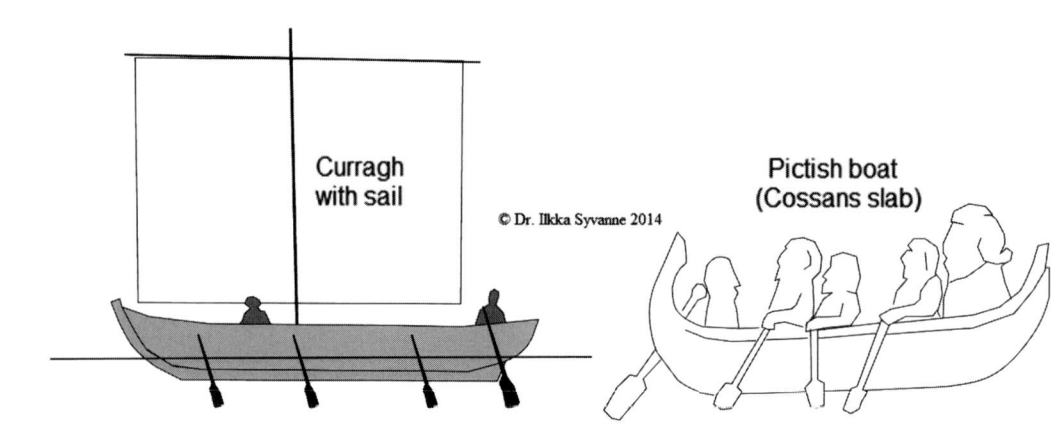

Curragh with sail

© Dr. Ilkka Syvänne 2014

Pictish boat (Cossans slab)

Ancient Ireland under the rule of the Scots (Scotti) was divided into about 150 tribal kingdoms. The tribes in their turn formed five to seven provinces called Fifths. Each of the kingdoms had a king who commanded its tribal army, calledthe *Tuath*. The *Tuath* consisted of noble families and their clients. The higher-ranking kings consisted of kings of several *Tuaths* (including his own), and of the kings of Fifths. At times the Irish were ruled by a single high king. Later evidence suggests that the average strength of one *Tuath* was about 700 men, which means that the Irish could theoretically put into the field a truly sizeable force. This military potential explains well why the Irish Scots were subsequently able to conquer Scotland/Caledonia from the Picts and Wales from the Britons. The principal target of Irish piratical activity was naturally the coastal lowlands of Wales. Events prove that their seagoing currachs/curraghs were quite well suited for this task. The largest of these had crews of about 30–50 men per ship. The tactics on land naturally followed the same principles as everywhere in the barbarian west, and were therefore based on the use of close-quarters weapons (spears/javelins, swords) in melee and the use of the infantry phalanx. Swords employed by the Irish were double-edged, the length of which was close to that of the Roman *gladius*.[7] The Irish were lightly equipped and prone to flee if they faced strong resistance. Their particular specialty was to then pepper their pursuers with javelins and wrest victory out of the jaws of defeat.

The defensive systems employed by the Irish (Scotti and others) were quite rudimentary by Roman standards, and consisted mainly of fortified hill forts and manors. For examples, see the following illustrations, drawn after Nicolle:

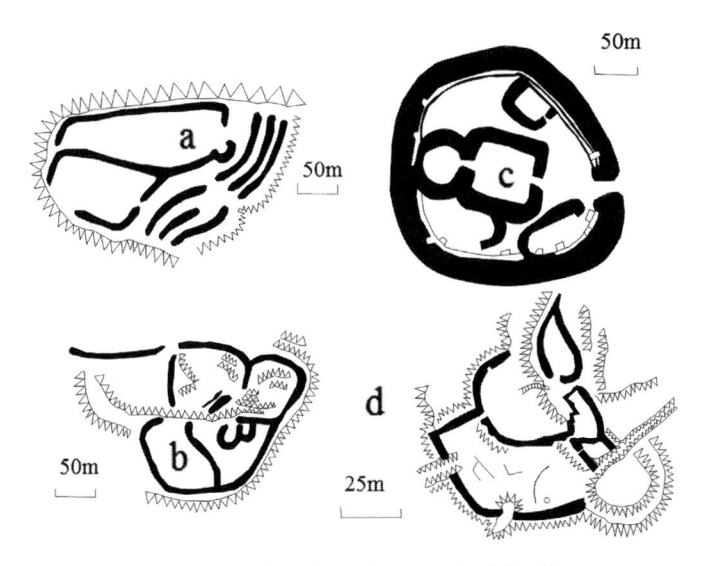

Irish and Pictish fortifications drawn after Nicolle
a) North Pictish ramparts at Burghead 4th–5th century.
b) Pictish fort at Dundurn 7th century.
c) Irish fortified farmstead at Leacanabuaile in Country Kerry, early medieval.
d) Dal Riata fort at Dunadd, Argyll, early medieval.

The 'Saxons': The Saxons proper, Angles, Jutes, Danes, Frisians, Heruls, Franks and Others[8]

Period sources use the Saxons as a generic term to mean the Saxons proper together with the Angles and Jutes, and to lesser extent splinter groups of Heruls, Frisians, Franks, Danes, Norwegians and others. Henceforth, when I refer to the Saxons, I will mean all of the above unless I specify otherwise, even if it were the Angles (Anglii) who ultimately gave their name to the country. The Saxons had received their name from their favourite weapon, the *seax/scramasax* (short single-edged sword).

The Saxons posed various threats to the Britons: 1) they raided the coasts of Britain and Bretagne in ships; 2) the Saxons settled on British soil, or in Gaul raided Briton territories with land and naval forces; 3) the Saxons could join forces with the Picts, Scots, Franks and Romans against the Britons; 4) there were also the rebel Saxons who had been invited to Britain by the locals.

The martial equipment of the Saxons consisted of the single-edged *seaxes/scramasaxes*, double-edged *spatha*-swords, spears and shields. Only the wealthy elite wore armour and helmets. In addition to this, the Saxons employed long bows, thrown stones, spears, javelins, barbed javelins and to a lesser extent hand axes and thrown *francisca*-axes. Despite the use of missiles, Saxon tactics on land were solely based on close-quarter fighting in melee. The use of missiles was usually restricted to naval battles and sieges.[9] For illustrations of the Saxon warriors, see the Plates section.

According to Heinrich Härke, it is possible to suggest on the basis of archaeological finds of weapons that the Saxon battle formation may have been more open in the fifth and early sixth centuries than during later centuries, with each Saxon warrior fighting as an individual. The reasons for Härke's conclusion are: 1) the earlier graves have greater quantities of *spatha*-swords and *francisca*-axes than the later ones, which have a preponderance of *seaxes*; 2) the fifth- and early sixth-century shields are smaller (usually with diameters of 0.4–0.5 metres), with a flat thin board, and have shield-bosses with a rod or spike apex, which together with the use of the *spatha* suggest a fighting formation in which the warriors fought as individuals and in which the shield was used for 'bashing'. During the late fifth and early sixth centuries, the shield began to change. At first only the boss became heavier, but in the course of the sixth century the boards became thicker, the diameter increased to 0.6m and the bosses became lighter and taller, while some shields even started to have curved boards. In the seventh century, the same trend continued, so that the bosses became taller and the boards thicker and larger (0.90m in diameter). Härke's conclusion is that the later equipment suggests the use of group combat in a shield-wall, because larger shields were clearly meant for more static combat.[10] In my opinion, this conclusion is incorrect. The reason for this is that the archaeological finds suggest that the fifth- and early sixth-century Saxons were employing pikes (Härke, p.99), while the Saxons of later centuries used spears that could either be used as slashing weapons with their broad blades or as thrown javelins. The length of these spears/pikes would in all probability have been close to those found in the Nydam bog,[11] which were 8–11½ft (2.4–3.5m) long. When one takes into account the contraction of wood over time, it is probable that the actual lengths had been close to the equivalent Roman standard lengths, which were ca. 2.5–3.74m.

In short, the fifth-century Saxons employed the pike phalanx in which their small shields were deployed shoulder-to-shoulder, while the later Saxons used the Roman/Frankish tactical system, based on the use of thrown javelins and close-quarter fighting with the *seax* (essentially a short sword akin to *gladius/machaira*) and larger shield. The probable reasons for these differences are that during the fifth century, the Britons appear to have used cavalry to great effect – the best means to counter that threat would have been the pike phalanx. The long *spatha* would also have been better suited for use against horsemen than the short *seax*. The subsequent change to weaponry that was better suited to infantry warfare suggests that the principal threat to the Saxons in the sixth century consisted of footmen and archers; hence the use of larger shields and the javelin/spear with the short sword.

On land, the Saxons employed typical infantry-based West Germanic battle tactics, which were based on the use of the shield-wall/phalanx, defensive hollow square/circle and infantry wedges. Siege tactics were very rudimentary. The Saxons appear to have employed only ladders, battering rams, blockade and ruses. There is also some scattered evidence for the use of *ballistae* and stone-throwers, but these played only a very small role. Contrary to popular opinion, this does not mean that the Saxons would only have ridden to the battlefield and fought on foot. I agree with Mortimer's conclusion regarding the use of cavalry. Referrals to the use of true cavalry forces in a Danish and Swedish context are proof enough, as the Saxons were originally inhabitants of Denmark (I mention the modern nations of Denmark, Norway, Sweden or Finland etc., for want of a better term; all these nations at this time consisted of several kingdoms, whose borders varied). It is just that the Saxons had too few true horsemen for these to play any significant role on British battlefields. The Saxons who arrived in Britain were primarily seamen/pirates who fought on foot, mainly because they could not transport enough horses and were apparently unable to obtain sufficient additional mounts from the Britons.

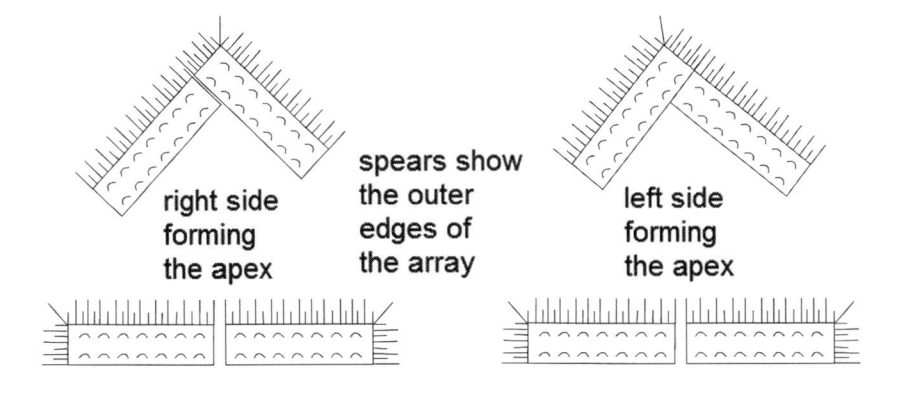

right side forming the apex

spears show the outer edges of the array

left side forming the apex

It appears probable that there actually existed three different forms of infantry wedges: one which was almost certainly invented by the Germanic/Scandinavian peoples, another which had probably been invented by the Greeks – or at least it is mentioned for the first time in Greek sources – and a third which may have been invented by the Greeks as its structure corresponds closely with Hellenic troop strengths. The last mentioned, with possible Greek provenance, had a wedge protruding out of the infantry line, the purpose of which was to break up the cohesion of the enemy line at that point. This wedge consisted of 64 men. The Germanic/Scandinavian wedge was an independently operating separate wedge (actually a rhombus/*globus*)[12] that was sent forward from the main battle line to break through the enemy formation, or which just operated as an independent array (see Appendix 3). This wedge consisted of 1,110 men and one chiliarch. The Greek version consisted of two phalanxes which were placed obliquely for the purpose of breaking through the enemy formation. It was meant to be used by forces of thousands of men, which in Greek military theory meant at least 8,192 men. Despite its probable Greek origins, the Germanic peoples also used this array, as is proven by several sources, the most important of which is a detailed description of the Frankish wedge by Agathias (see Syvänne, 2004; Syvänne, 2010). It is probable that this wedge was invented independently by several peoples. See the illustration for an example of this type of wedge.

Saxo Grammaticus's *Gesta Danorum* includes two different variants of the infantry wedge (Book 1, p.32; Book 7, pp.248–49) used by the Danes and Swedes, both of which were therefore definitely used by the Saxons, Angles, Jutes, Frisians, Heruls, Danes, Swedes and Norwegians. This information has been needlessly considered suspect. It has been claimed that Saxo merely copied a Roman tactical manual. The truth appears to be the exact opposite of this – none of the extant Roman treatises includes the *Svinfylking* (rhombus wedge). It is very likely that the rhombus wedge described by Saxo was actually Germanic in origin and had been copied from them by the Romans, if the Late Roman *caput porci/porcinum* did indeed resemble it. Regardless of this, there are actually very strong reasons to suspect that the Romans did indeed have direct influence upon Germanic tactics, just as the Germans had influenced Roman tactics. It is not without reason that Tacitus had noted that the Germans of Arminius and Maroboduus fought like the Romans. It would also be surprising if the many generations of Germans who had served in the Roman army had not brought back home any Roman influences. It is strange that modern historians generally accept that the Germanic peoples adopted Roman military titles like *magister*, *comes*, *dux*, chiliarch, *centenarius*, *bucellarius* etc., and many of Rome's institutions (systems of taxation and administration, church organization, *annonae*-payments etc.), but would not have copied Roman military organization and tactics when the sources state otherwise.

It is also quite clear that Roman culture and military practices had reached Scandinavia. Michael Olausson lists several examples of Roman influence in

Late Iron Age/Migration Period Sweden. The Scandinavian peoples had already adopted Roman units of measurement for their farming systems as early as the Early Iron Age, but this process received a further boost in the Late Roman period. It is from AD 300–500 that one recognizes a deliberate architectural building programme of hill forts and buildings which employ a Roman system of measurement and the portcullis. The hill forts were a native development, but these were now strengthened with probable Roman features. The new types of hill fort were smaller than previously and had massive ramparts, sometimes double ones, with fortified manors placed at the highest point of the hill. The ramparts employed an improved shell construction technique, which resulted in narrower and higher walls. Olausson suggests that these new features had been introduced thanks to the Roman influence on building techniques. The houses, manors and reception halls were built according to the standardized Roman system of measurement. Olausson claims on the basis of this that the Scandinavians must have served in the Roman army, as a result of which they had adopted Roman weaponry and may have also copied Roman military organization and tactics. I agree.

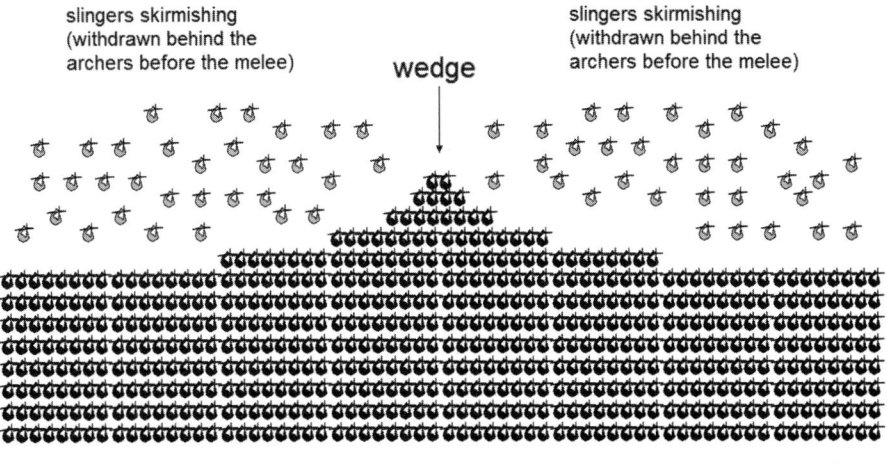

As noted above, the two wedge variants given by Saxo were clearly meant for different purposes. The first of these had two men in the front rank, four in the second rank, eight in the third rank and so forth. The slingers were deployed on the flanks of the wedge, then withdrawn behind the infantry phalanx, all the way past the archers forming the rear ranks. On the basis of sheer probability, it is likely that the last rank of this wedge consisted of thirty-two men, because after that the width of the wedge would have been too great for its purpose. This means that the wedge portion of the array consisted of about sixty-four men. It is quite obvious that this sort of array had three purposes: 1) to place the best fighters in front; 2) to restrict the fighting to the apex of the array, where the best fighters were; 3) to force the enemy to bend and disorder their array if they wanted to engage the rest of the army, which could cause it to break up at the point where the wedge was placed.[13] The fact that this wedge array was based on multiples of two, four, eight, sixteen etc., together with the structure of the array, suggests a connection with Greco-Roman tactical theory. In light of this, it is probable that the actual phalanx also followed the same structure, and consisted of eight ranks of heavies and four ranks of light infantry.

In the second variant given by Saxo, the entire front was divided into three *turmae* (units/squadrons),[14] each of which was to have a density of twenty men, but with the centre extending twenty men forward from the wings (*alae*), while the wings were to bend back in oblique manner from the centre. The rear of the array consisted of three similar divisions deployed in like manner, except that they faced the rear. The resulting formation would therefore have been a rhombus/rhomboid. The men of the actual wedge were arranged so that there were two men in the first rank, three in the second, four in the third and so forth, until the twentieth rank. The centre would therefore have consisted of 185 men, and if the wings consisted of the same amount of men, then the overall strength of the wedge was 555 men, which is incidentally the same number of men as Vegetius' ideal regular cohort.[15]

Following this, Saxo states that each of the wings was to contain ten ranks; behind them were to be the young men armed with javelins, and after them a 'cohort' of older men as a rearguard. This suggests a standard depth of sixteen ranks for the phalanx proper, but Saxo adds behind them the slingers (*funditores*), which would apparently add up to the twenty ranks already mentioned. This array was not based on the Greco-Roman tradition in its entirety, because the standard depth for the phalanx would actually have been twenty-four ranks (sixteen heavy infantry and eight light foot) and not twenty. It should also be recognized that a wing consisting of 185 men cannot be deployed in the same manner as the centre, but includes five supernumerary men (two centurions or optios, a standard-bearer, trumpeter and cape bearer). This array is the famous boar's head formation: the *Svinfylking* of the Vikings and the *Caput Porci/Porcinum* of the Romans. Even if it is considered as one of the wedge formations, strictly speaking it is not. It is an independently operating rhombus/*globus* that had in all probability been invented by the Germanic peoples.

If the Germanic command structure followed the Roman one, as is very probable, then the overall commander of the entire 1,110-man cohort/rhombus would have been the *tribunus maior* of Vegetius (*chiliarchos* = a commander of a thousand), the commander of a thousand men, the existence of which is attested for almost all Germanic peoples, while each of the *turmae* would have been commanded by two centurions, one of whom (*ducenarius/primus hastatus*) would have been superior to the other centurion (*centenarius/hekatontarchês*). Once again, it is well known that Germanic peoples had combat units called hundreds. The centurions would also have been classed further, with the commander of the rear half of the rhombus ranked as *primus pilus* (*vicarius/ilarchês*, second-in-command of the entire rhombus). It is probable that the *tribunus maior* commanded the front half in person.

The first evidence for the adoption of this unit structure dates from the reign of Septimius Severus. The referral to the use of the 550-man group (a cohort?) is in the period source Dio (86.12.5) and should therefore be acceptable, even to the sceptics who follow the standard flawed methodology used by the ultra-conservative Classicists. This is clearly the same number of men that can be found in Vegetius and in Saxo. One may make the educated guess that this structure had been introduced by Septimius Severus for his new Parthian legions.[16] What is particularly notable about this is that this unit structure is at odds with the earlier system followed by the Romans until then, which was based on the unit structure in which a *decanus* (commander of ten) commanded an eight-man file, one recruit and one servant. In other words, it followed the same principles as were used by the Macedonians. This begs the question what had inspired this change? Could it be that this was one of the results of the Marcomannic Wars? One possible reason for such a change could be that the Germans had used the *caput porci* array to great effect against the Romans, and that it was this that inspired Septimius to adopt the same structure and tactics for his new elite units. It is of course possible to use the *caput porci* array with different sized units, but if the array was already of the right size then the process of imitation would have been even easier. However, the other and likelier possibility is that the new larger cohorts and legions of Septimius and the rhomboidical wedge date from different periods. This is more likely, because the first sources (Vegetius, Ammianus) that lend any support for the use of the rhomboid wedge by the Romans are considerably later than Severus' reign and the migration of Odin's people (see Appendix 3), with the implication that the Romans copied it from the Germans, while the Germans presumably copied the unit organization from the Romans so that it was still used a few centuries later in Scandinavia, just as it was used in the Germanic successor states, but all of this is obviously speculative because there exists no firm evidence for the dating of the rhomboidical array.

The counter tactic against this *globus*-wedge was called the 'small crow array/ horned array' (Saxo 8.262–264: '*cornicula acie*'), which means a hollow wedge, crescent or the forward-angled half-square; all of which could be employed in this case, so it is difficult to be certain which was meant. All of these were also used by the Greeks and Romans, and were equally useful against the larger Greek wedge and possibly against the small sixty-four-man wedge.

There is also the problem of how the ranks and files of these men were deployed obliquely. Were the light-armed deployed inside the rhombus or in the flanks/middle? I have given here the two likeliest alternatives, but in my opinion 'Alternative 1' with the light-armed placed in the middle would be the likeliest, on the grounds that it would have been easier to use the light-armed for skirmishing if deployed in that manner.

26   Britain in the Age of Arthur

ALTERNATIVE 1

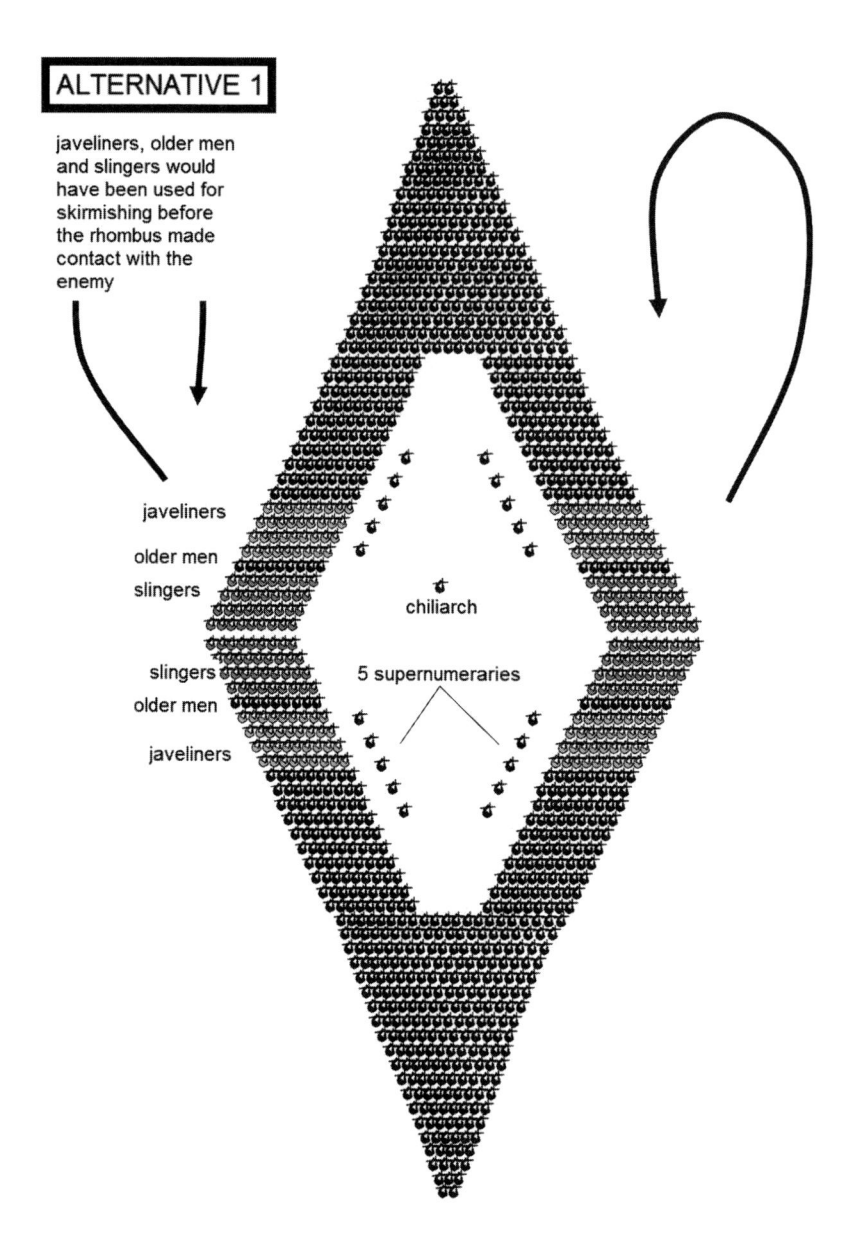

javeliners, older men and slingers would have been used for skirmishing before the rhombus made contact with the enemy

javeliners
older men
slingers

slingers
older men
javeliners

chiliarch

5 supernumeraries

It is probable that the Saxon ships resembled closely the clinker-built ships of the Vikings. See also the reconstructed Sutton Hoo and Nydam ships included in this book. These ships were powered by both sails and oars, so that on average the crews would have probably consisted of about thirty to sixty men, while the smallest warships had twelve rowers and the largest ships had about 100–120 men on board.

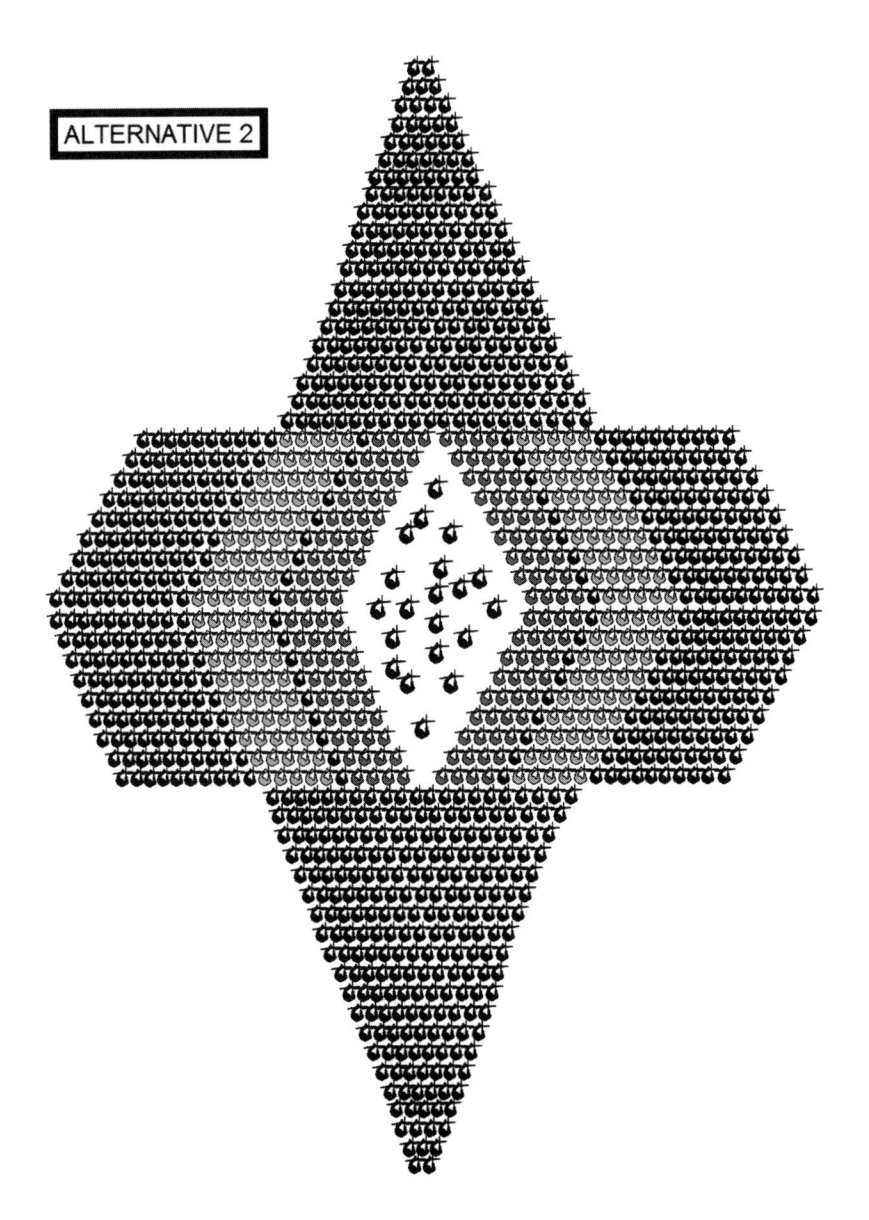

The date for the adoption of the sail by Scandinavian and Saxon ships is contested. For example, Crumlin-Pedersen suggests that this change took place in the sixth century. He bases his conclusion on the fact that the Nydam ship and other Nordic ships had round bottoms, which were better suited to rowing than for sailing. In order for the ship to have kept a steady course during sailing, it would have needed a proper keel and a large lateral plane of the kind that can be seen in the so-called

Hedeby, c. 985, 54-62 men, c. 30.9 x 2.7 x 1.5m

Fotevik 1, c.1100, c. 16 men, 10.3 x 2.4 x 1.0m

Ladby, 900-950, c. 35 men, c. 22 x3.2 x 1.0m

Skuldelev 5, c. 1050, 26 men, 17.4 x 2.6 x 1.1m

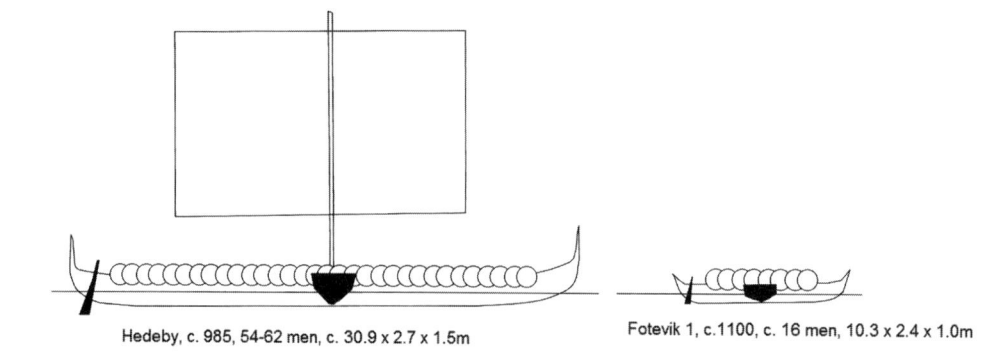

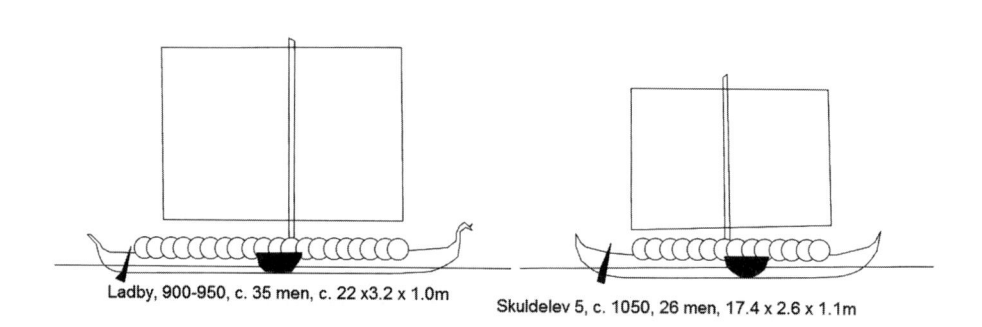

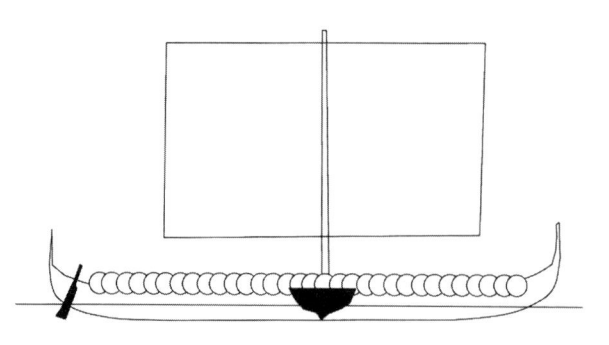

Skuldelev 2, c. 1060, c.60-70 men, c. 30 x 3.8 x 2.1m

These later Viking ships are likely to be representative of the various types and sizes of ships used by the Saxons and other Scandinavians during this era. Note that the ships could carry more passengers/marines than the crew mentioned here.

(Drawn after Crumlin-Pedersen with additions and one correction to the information regarding Skuldelev 2)

Gokstad and Ladby ships (from the early Viking Age). The opposite view is held by Haywood, who points out that the sources state in no uncertain terms that the Saxons sailed in stormy weathers by using the sail. I agree with the latter view. The warships were longships/boats because their primary function in war was to be a galley, but this does not mean that they would have lacked sails. The structure of the ship was a compromise between two different demands. Even Crumlin-Pedersen notes that the Gokstad ship had a very broad length-to-breadth ratio in comparison with the much later Viking Age warships from Ladby and Skuldelev. In other words, the Vikings preferred to make their warships longships.

Myhre's study of the boathouses of Norway confirms that these longships were the warships employed by the Iron Age Norwegians. According to his study, the Iron Age boathouses of Norway (meant for warships rather than for the boats that could have sheds as short as 10m) were large, narrow buildings, 25–35m long and 5–6m wide at the entrance. The longest attested boathouses from this era were the 37m-long boathouse of Sømme, Sola, and the almost 40m-long boathouses of Flesland, Bergen, and Obrestad, Hå (see also Chapter 10). This means that the typical Iron Age warships were narrow in breadth, 2.6–4.4m, and that most could easily attain the length of the 27m Sutton Hoo ship. However, it is quite probable that the Northmen could also build much larger ships than this, as is demonstrated for example by the extant carvings of ships.

The overleaf illustration shows my reconstruction of the Sutton Hoo ship, which is based on the reconstructions included in the second edition of John Haywood's outstanding monograph *Dark Age Naval Power*. It has often been suspected that the Sutton Hoo ship would have been unsuited to the use of sails, but I agree with John Haywood that the Sea Wylfing Project has proven that it was. The evidence in the period sources should have been enough to prove this, but since the ultra-conservative branch of Classicists/Medievalists continually and needlessly suspects the evidence, it is practically always necessary to prove them with experimental archaeology or re-enacting. This ship can be considered to be representative of the typical Saxon ship. It had forty oars (twenty per side), which means that it had a crew of fifty to sixty men.

On the basis of Saxo Grammaticus' text (7.249), the likeliest tactical formation employed by the Nordic fleets (including the Saxons) consisted of a front line deployed line abreast, behind which stood a separate reserve. In addition to this, the Saxons also knew how to place a naval ambush, tie up the ships to serve as a fighting platform and array the ships as a defensive circle.

The typical naval raiding force appears to have consisted of anything from about 150 men up to several hundred, while the major raiding forces consisted of 1,500–2,500 men. The Saxons did not need large forces, because they attacked places which were poorly defended. The Saxons attacked the coasts of southern Gaul in stormy weather so that they could surprise their enemies. This speaks volumes of the high quality of Saxon ships and sailors. It was not easy to sail and navigate in the stormy Atlantic Ocean. However, when the Saxons grouped together for a major campaign with the intention of conquering some province, it is probable that the army would have had at least 10,000–15,000 men, because in those cases the Saxons needed to overcome significant enemy forces who were expecting them. The Saxons were certainly brave fighters, but even they needed to possess at least a quarter or third of the numbers they faced. They did employ terror tactics to scare the enemy, but this was not sufficient alone. It is probable that the knowledge that the Saxons would sacrifice every tenth prisoner to their pagan gods would have stiffened the will to resist among those who could not flee to any safe locale. The Britons could not be sure who would be killed and who would survive if they surrendered. See *MHLR* Vol. 4.

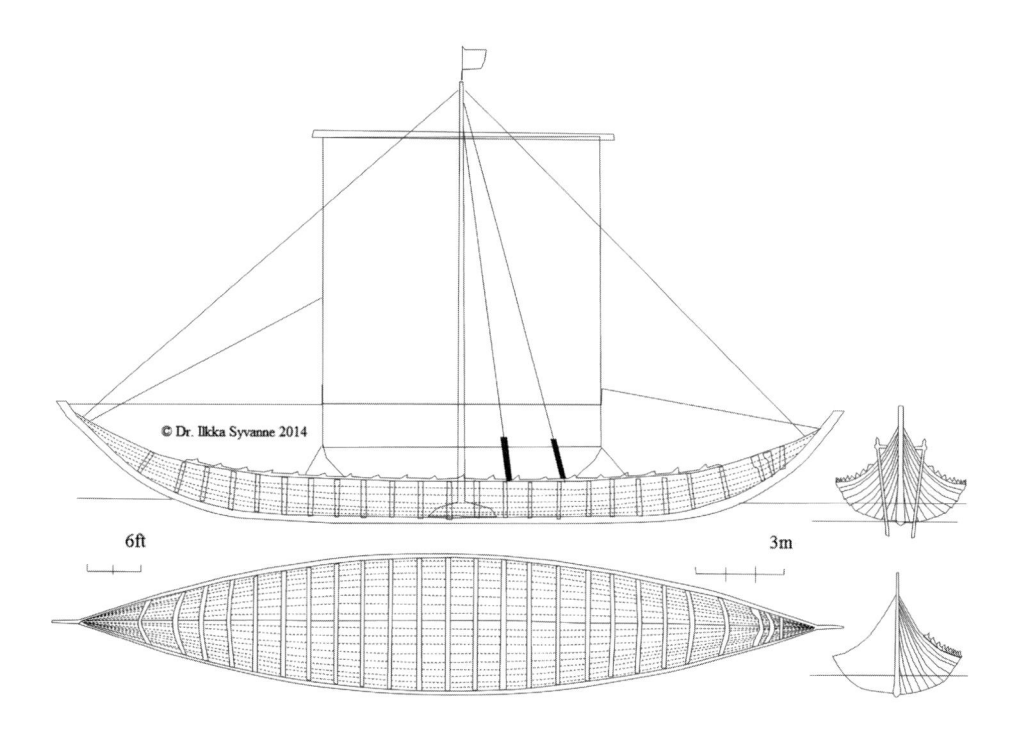

The Saxons were a particularly difficult enemy to counter because their homeland was originally located far away from the Romano-Britons and Romans. As a result of this, the first information the Britons/Romans received of their naval invasions and raids often occurred only after the fact. The fortifications built in the third and fourth centuries against the Saxons became gradually meaningless in the course of the fifth century, because the Saxons occupied land directly across the Channel and obtained land in Britain in return for service as mercenaries. The principal problem for the Britons was that the Saxons were able to flee to safety across the Channel if they lost a war in Britain, and then return later, meaning that the Saxons always had the initiative. It was difficult for the Britons to conduct campaigns of punishment against Saxon territories because these lay across the sea. This required a sizeable fleet, but such could exist only under a unified leadership. As we shall see, Arthur changed the rules.

The Franks
The first referral to the existence of the Frankish Confederacy of tribes dates from the third century, but by the fourth century it had once again broken up. In the fifth century, the Frankish Confederacy consisted of three different groupings: the Salii/Salians in modern Belgium and Netherlands; the Ripuarians along the Rhine, roughly between Cologne and Mainz; and the Thuringians east of the Ripuarians. During this era, the loyalty of the different groupings of Franks towards the Roman Empire varied greatly from one year to another; at times they served the Romans loyally as federates, while at others they were in revolt. However, in the periods during which the Britons campaigned in Gaul, the Franks served the Romans loyally, which means that whenever the Britons fought the Romans, they also faced the Franks and Saxons.

The Frankish way of fighting was based on the West German tradition, in which primacy was given to close-quarter fighting in tight infantry formations. The Franks had received their name from the use of the famous *francisca*-throwing axe, which was their national weapon. The other weapons employed by the Frankish footmen consisted of the wooden club, sword, short sword (*scramasax/seax*), dagger, spear, javelin, harpoon javelin (*angon*) and bow. The horsemen were typically equipped with lances and swords. Defensive equipment consisted usually only of the round shield, because the Franks preferred to fight in light equipment, but the wealthier warriors could also wear some armour and helmets. The standard infantry tactic was to throw the *angon* or *francisca* at the enemy and then engage them with swords at close quarters. The maximum throwing range for the *francisca* was about 10–12m, and 30m for the *angon*. The Franks did on occasion employ archery to soften the enemy's will to resist, but this was not their typical way of fighting as they did not possess large numbers of archers. The standard cavalry tactic was to impetuously charge straight at the enemy at full gallop, which the Romans considered a disorderly way to fight. By Romano-Briton standards, their siege tactics were rudimentary and consisted of the use of blockade, assault with ladders and battering rams. There is also some evidence for the use of siege artillery, but this arm of service was underdeveloped by Roman standards.

The Franks had the potential to raise truly large armies when they cooperated; in the sixth century, they could despatch armies of 75,000–100,000 men to Italy. This was a rare phenomenon, but it did also happen in the fifth century.[17] It was still far more typical for the Franks to use small raiding forces running from hundreds to thousands, but even so it is possible that when Arthur fought against the Roman armies in Gaul that these contained very significant numbers of Franks.

The Franks also employed ships, but apparently only along the Rhine during this particular era, because the mouth of the Rhine appears to have been under Saxon-Herul control. It is unfortunate that we do not know what types of ships the Franks used, but it is possible that their warships resembled the Roman riverine scouting ships (crews of twenty to twenty-six oarsmen) discovered at Mainz and the so-called Bruges boat (Haywood, 45ff.). It is not known whether the Franks employed these in any capacity against Arthur when he was fighting in Gaul.

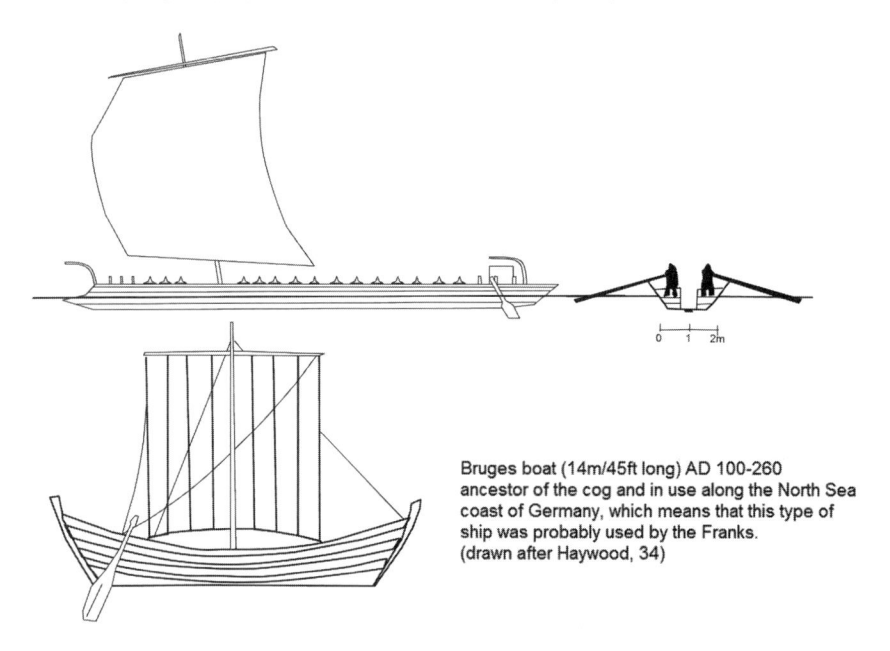

Bruges boat (14m/45ft long) AD 100-260 ancestor of the cog and in use along the North Sea coast of Germany, which means that this type of ship was probably used by the Franks. (drawn after Haywood, 34)

The Other Enemies
Other enemies included the Britons who supported some other candidate for the throne and the various Scandinavian kings. The Scandinavians resembled the other Germanic peoples of the era, with the exception that they employed all arms of service – the fleet, infantry and cavalry – simultaneously and were more fully armoured than was typical for the other Germans. The illustrations opposite and in the plate section show the type of equipment worn by the Swedes of the Vendel period. For a fuller discussion, see Mortimer's *Woden's Warriors* with the narrative and appendices.

2.2 The Principal Sources for Arthur
The sources for the Arthurian era include the following: Christian chronicles, Gildas, Gregory of Tours HF, Gallic Chronicles, East Roman sources, Jordanes'

Getica, Nennius HB, the *Anglo-Saxon Chronicle*, Bede, Welsh sources, Irish sources, Geoffrey of Monmouth and Saxo Grammaticus. However, I will here pay particular attention only to those British sources that are relevant specifically to Arthur. The readers should also note that there are several editions and translations of these sources, in which headings/chapters vary slightly. I have not attempted to streamline these, as it is easy to find out the exact location for each of my notes/footnotes in the text, even when one uses a different edition (I have used several and all of those have variations), if one checks the chapters close to that given by me.

Gildas was a British monk who lived either at the turn of the sixth century or during the sixth century. There are two different versions of his life, but both claim that he was a son of a king who chose the life of a monk. According to his own words, he was born on the same day the Battle of Badon was fought, which makes him roughly contemporary with Aurelius Ambrosius and Arthur. It is because of this that his account of the exploits of Aurelius Ambrosius is of particular importance. The referrals to Aurelius can be found in Gildas' polemic *De Excidio et Conquestu Britanniae*, which was highly critical of the rulers of Britain. He appears to have used mainly period sources for his polemic. Towards the end of his life, Gildas moved to Brittany, where he founded a monastery called St Gildas of Rhuys and where he was buried.

Nennius was a Welsh monk who lived in the ninth century. He has traditionally been considered as the author of *Historia Brittorum*, but several eminent modern historians contest this, probably needlessly. He compiled a history of the Britons from many sources, one of which was apparently Gildas and another the *Life of St. Germanus*. When compiling his sources, Nennius made a number of mistakes so that he includes some events twice and misdates evidence. At the heart of the problem is the misdating of the transferral of British forces from Britain to Gaul to the reign of Maximus, which is common to all British sources. This has led to other serious problems, the most important of which is the misdating of St Germanus' trips to Britain. However, his account is still very important, because it preserves an account of Arthur and his twelve battles. As a Welshman, Nennius was apparently attempting to preserve the traditions of Roman Britain so that the heroic deeds of the Welsh-Britons would not be lost amid Anglo-Saxon propaganda, which omitted referrals to Anglo-Saxon defeats.

Bede has been considered the father of British history, but he was not an impartial witness. He lived from 672/3 to 26 May 735. Bede wrote extensively on many topics, but for this study the most valuable of his works are *Historia ecclesiastica gentis Anglorum* (*Ecclesiastical History of the English People*) and *Chronicon*. Bede was not an impartial historian, but a man with a strong Northumbrian bias, to the extent that he omitted important events and persons when he felt hostility towards them. He used as his sources Eusebius, Rufinus, Saint Jerome, Orosius, Gregory of Tours, Constantius' *Life of St Germanus*, Gildas, Cassiodorus and Anglo-Saxon oral traditions, among others.

The Anglo-Saxon Chronicle is among the most important sources for Dark Age Britain. The original manuscript was created during the late ninth century, probably at the instigation of King Alfred the Great. It survives in many slightly different manuscripts, but the original is lost. The *Chronicle* is a compilation and contains information drawn from Anglo-Saxon sagas, Bede's texts, lists of kings and bishops, and other annals and chronicles. The annals contain a number of mistakes and omissions, the most important of which are the defeats suffered by the Anglo-Saxons.

Geoffrey of Monmouth[18] is justifiably famous as the author of the *History of the Kings of Britain* (*Historia Regum Britanniae*). However, there are historians who do not accept this and call him therefore Pseudo-Geoffrey. In my opinion, there is no reason to doubt his authorship. Geoffrey of Monmouth lived in twelfth-century Britain. His work became highly popular and was used as a source by subsequent generations of historians. In spite of this, his work was not accepted as genuine by everyone, even during his lifetime, being condemned as fiction.

There exist five major theories regarding the sources used by Geoffrey: 1) he used a 'little book' given to him by Walter of Oxford written in the Welsh language that he then translated into Latin; 2) Geoffrey's main source was the oral tradition through Walter the Archdeacon; 3) some pseudo-Geoffrey wrote (this theory is based on a variant version of the text) an earlier text which Geoffrey then used; 4) Geoffrey simply invented the story and mixed true events taken from other sources into his narrative; 5) Geoffrey used some variation of the above. My own view is that Geoffrey used a combination of sources, which included at least the following: some little book written in the Welsh language (this introduced most of the supernatural events and was probably based on a mixture of oral traditions and literary sources), Gildas, Nennius, Bede and the Welsh oral traditions preserved by Walter of Oxford. Geoffrey embellished these with cross-references to the Bible and several Latin writers, along with his own narrative style. It is probable that the ancient book written in Welsh included some of the elements often thought to be among the inventions of Geoffrey. These would for example include the elements usually associated with histories written in the Classical tradition, such as invented speeches by commanders and probably also the references to real Roman combat units (see the Battle of Saussy/Siesia between Arthur and Lucius Tiberius in Chapter 13) that had been converted into kingdoms by the unknown Welsh author. As regards Geoffrey's use of sources, he seems to have used the little book written in Welsh as the narrative core, into which he has inserted excerpts from other sources. This means that the order of events has sometimes become mixed, so that some events described by Geoffrey should be dated backwards and others forwards. I will include a fuller analysis of the different sections in the main narrative. Of note is that Geoffrey also includes the same account in summary form in his *Vita Merlini*.

Readers should take note that when I use the period source Gildas as the basis on which to build my case for the rehabilitation of Geoffrey, that this follows the traditional approach adopted by historians. In my opinion, this is validated by the generally accepted reliability of Gildas' polemic text to his own era, which in my opinion is OK so long as one remembers that Gildas did still have his own views and goals, and has in all probability made some mistakes as well.

2.3 Dating the Arthurian Age
We can date the Arthurian Age on the basis of two relatively secure dates. The first of these is the British embassy to Aetius in his third consulship, which can be dated to 446. The second of the roughly secure dates is the campaign of the king of the Britons, Riothamus, as an ally of Anthemius against the Visigoths, which can roughly be dated to the period 468–471. This latter date can be pinpointed even more accurately thanks to the following analysis of the narrative sources. This alliance must have taken place at a time when the Britons had defeated the Saxons and re-established the Roman Empire in the British Isles and Armorica/Bretagne/Brittany.

The *Annales Cambriae* mentions two battles of Badon, the first of which is dated to 516 and the second to 665. According to this text, it was in the former battle that Arthur carried the Cross of Jesus Christ to the glorious victory over their enemies. I would suggest that the *Annales* has actually grossly misplaced the dates and battles, so that it was actually the second of the battles in which Arthur achieved his famous victory and that it took place roughly 150 years before 665, which means that the Battle of Badon dated to 516 was actually the second of the battles. To those who think that one should trust the dating in the *Annales*, it suffices to note that the *Annales* are known to have misplaced several battles and events,[19] which should make one suspicious of other dates as well, the battles of Badon included.

2.4 The Background 2: Summary of the Usual Sources Used
In order to build my case, I will start with the accounts of Gildas, Nennius, the *Anglo-Saxon Chronicle* and Bede, because their evidence is usually accepted with greater ease than that of Geoffrey of Monmouth.

Gildas
Gildas (*De excidio Britanniae* 12ff.) claims that Maximus took most of the British troops with him when he usurped power in 383, with the result that the Scots and Picts attacked. This is a mistake, and should be Constantine III, as will be made clear later, even if it is still clear that both Maximus and Constantine III took away forces with them when they sailed across the Channel. It is also very probable that Constantine III did not take with him the frontier forces belonging to the *Dux Britanniae*, because the presence of garrison troops along Hadrian's Wall can be attested for the early fifth century through archaeology. The Romans also appear to

have already organized the natives between the Antonine Wall and Hadrian's Wall into federate forces in the fourth century[20] so that the Picts were unable to make any significant impression against them. As a result of this, the Picts sought to bypass both areas of heavy concentration of troops with their ships, and use their forces against the soft underbelly of Britain.[21]

After having suffered terribly for many years, the Britons sent urgent calls for help. It is unfortunate that Gildas fails to pinpoint the date for this call for help. Consequently, it is possible that this happened when Stilicho wielded power, after the British usurper Constantine III had taken most of the forces into Gaul in about 408, after Honorius had regained control of Gaul in about 414/415 (I prefer this date) or that it took place in about 428.

The Romans sent one of the legions back to Britain, and it was with the help of this legion that the enemies were driven out. Gildas claims that the legionaries then instructed the Britons on how to build a turf wall from sea to sea as protection. It is usually suggested that this is mistaken for repairs of the existing Antonine Wall or Hadrian's Wall. The likeliest alternative is that the Britons still tried to hold on to their northern territories, so that the repairs were indeed made on the Antonine turf wall. The other possibility is that the Britons did build a new wall on some other location, for example in Wales or Cornwall (Wansdyke/Woden's Dyke), but this is less likely than the renovation of the Antonine Wall. Regardless, it is still possible that the Britons also built turf walls facing Wales, because on the basis of radio carbon dating some sections of Wat's Dyke may have been built during the period 411–561, while the lowest layers of Offa's Dyke have been dated to ca. 430. These dates are contested, but on the basis of this it is entirely plausible to suggest that several turf walls were built during this period. Wansdyke/Woden's Dyke in Cornwall may also have been built during the fifth century, but it is probable that this was not the wall meant by Gildas because it faced north, and therefore was to keep out the Saxons.

There also exist other dykes and ditches in Cambridgeshire and Suffolk possibly dating from this era. These ditches were meant to block the so-called Icknield Way, and are usually supposed to have been built by the Anglo-Saxons against the Britons. The so-called Cambridgeshire Dykes consist of the Bran Ditch in the west and Devil's Ditch in the east (both usually dated post-Roman), with the Brent Ditch (possibly post-Roman) and Fleam Dyke (fifth century) between them. Behind the Fleam Dyke stands another wall, Grim's Dyke/Ditch, which is dated to the fifth or sixth century, but which may originally date from pre-Roman times. For additional details, see the English Heritage website and other websites. East of the Devil's Ditch in Suffolk there is still another line of walls, the Black Ditches of Cavenham, which are usually supposed to be Anglo-Saxon in origin. The dating of these walls is contested because there exists some evidence that suggests a continued use from pre-Roman until Anglo-Saxon times, with the dykes repaired whenever there was a need. In other words, the local populace renovated/rebuilt those dykes when threatened, and the fifth century was certainly such a period.

After the invaders had been defeated and the turf wall built, the legion returned to the continent, with the result that the Pictish and Scottish oarsmen invaded again in sailing ships and boats. The Britons once again sent urgent pleas for help. The Romans responded by dispatching cavalry (*equites*) and sailors/marines (*nautae*), who mowed down the enemy. This must have happened at some point in the 420s or 430s, probably in about 429/430, when St Germanus visited the island. In return for their service, the defenders taxed the country, after which they informed the Britons that they would have to take care of their own defence from that day onwards. The Romans would no longer dispatch any armies to help them. The Picts and Scots were not considered 'worthy' enemies. Before leaving, however, the Roman soldiers instructed the civilians on how to build a better turf wall from sea to sea between fortified cities (presumably one of the above-mentioned walls between Chester and Caerleon, or the Antonine Wall). The building project was financed from public and private funds. In order to secure the southern coastline, the soldiers and sailors also built towers at regular intervals. It is usually thought that this refers to the towers of the Saxon Shore, but it is possible that new towers were built from perishable materials which have left no traces in the archaeological record. In addition to this, the soldiers gave to the Britons patterns from which they could manufacture arms, and then instructed them in the use of the *pelta* (small shield), *ensis* (sword) and *hasta* (spear) so that they could form paramilitary forces to defend the wall. After this the Romans left, never to return. Note that this means that the Britons continued to use typical Roman-pattern equipment!

When the Picts and Scots learnt of this, they invaded immediately and apparently occupied the north of England up to the wall. Casey suggests the Antonine Wall, but Hadrian's Wall is more likely in my opinion. The defenders of the wall did not dare to make a move, but hid inside their forts, with the result that the invaders could pillage the land with impunity. The peasant and urban militias were not up to the job, and abandoned their cities and the wall and just ran away. On top of this, the Britons started to fight against each other. This invasion appears to have started in about 441/2. According to Gildas, the last remaining pockets of resistance sent envoys to Aetius 'thrice consul'. It is usually thought that this refers to Aetius's third consulship in 446, which would mean that the plea for help was sent when it was known that Aetius would be nominated as consul for 446, or immediately after it. However, it is possible that P.J. Casey is correct in that the 'thrice consul' was only meant to separate Aetius the Western *magister utriusque militiae* (*MVM*) from his Eastern namesake, which could place the plea for help to an earlier period. But at the same time it assumes that the audience would have been quite knowledgeable of the office-holders in the eastern half of the empire. The *Anglo-Saxon Chronicle* actually dates the embassy to Rome to 443. However, on the basis of the manner in which Gildas refers to the third consulship, I would still prefer the date 446.

According to the envoys sent to Aetius, the barbarians threw the Britons into the sea, after which the sea threw the Britons back towards their foes! Aetius's cold response was that the Britons would have to look after themselves. We know that at the time, in 446, he was facing the prospect of having to fight against Attila. As noted above, on the basis of the *Anglo-Saxon Chronicle*, it is possible that the Britons actually sent two embassies to Aetius in the 440s; the first in 443, when they begged help against the Picts, which was not forthcoming because Aetius was fighting against the Huns, and then again in 446, which was not successful because there was a threat of war against Attila (see *MHLR* Vol. 4). According to the *Anglo-Saxon Chronicle*, the Britons also sent envoys to the Angles in 443 to seek their assistance.

According to Gildas, when the Britons obtained no help, they sought refuge in the mountains, caves and woods, and finally managed to defeat the enemy for the first time on their own. The peace did not last long, because the British kings once again started to fight against each other, and the enemies returned. Each murdered king was followed by an even more cruel and brutal king. The Picts settled permanently in some unnamed extremity of the island. There was a period of rest during the winters, and it was then that the desperate Britons engaged in all kinds of fornication and vice, because they knew that they would once again have to fight during the following summer. After this, the Britons finally managed to assemble a council to discuss what to do. It was then, under the leadership of the tyrant Guthrigern (presumably Vortigern), the British king, that the councillors agreed to invite the Saxons to protect them.[22] According to the *ASC*, this took place in 449, but on the basis of the *Gallic Chronicle* 452, which dates the start of the Saxon dominance to 441, it is possible that this took place in about 441–444.

The first Saxons arrived in three warships called *cyulis* (keels), presumably to negotiate, unless this refers only to the ships of the leaders of three different tribes. These forces landed on the eastern side of Britain (according to the *ASC* in the Wippidsfleet) and were soon followed by others (the *ASC* says Angles, Old-Saxons and Jutes). The Saxon leaders, says the *ASC*, were Hengist and Horsa. The Saxons were given monthly subsistence in return for their military service, but soon started to complain that this was insufficient, the reason obviously being the arrival of ever more Saxons. The Britons appear not to have agreed to the extortion of more supplies, with the result that the Saxons pillaged neighbouring towns and lands, then marched to the other side of the island. The Saxons pierced the defences with the help of battering rams, then killed, pillaged and burned. Some Britons took refuge in the wildernesses and mountains, while others fled to Bretagne or surrendered as slaves to the invaders. The survivors of this carnage grouped together under the leadership of Ambrosius Aurelianus. His parents had assumed the purple and been killed in the same tempests. My own guess is that

Ambrosius' father or grandfather had been Constantine III. After Ambrosius took charge of the defence, the Britons fought with varying success until the siege of Mons Badon/Badonis ('*obsessionis Badonici montis*') and the slaughter of the invaders at that battle. It is important to keep in mind this referral to Ambrosius Aurelianus as the man who won the Battle of Mons Badon when one starts to unravel the information provided by Geoffrey. The enemy had been defeated, but regardless of the recovery of the island, many of the cities were still in ruins at the time when Gildas wrote forty-four years and one month after the Battle of Badon Hill. Gildas claims that thereafter, kings, public magistrates, private persons and clergy followed wiser policies than before, but after they had died and been succeeded by those who were ignorant of the troubles, the people once again started to fight amongst themselves. In light of Geoffrey's account, this appears to be a moralizing statement. Also of note is the statement of Gerald of Wales (Wales 2.2), who claims that Ambrosius Aurelianus was so successful that even Eutropius praised him. Just like Gerald's translator Lewis Thorpe (p.257 n.584), I do not know the source of this claim, but all the same this proves that some Eutropius (not the famous historian) had recorded Aurelius Ambrosius' deeds and that this text was still extant when Gerald wrote.

Gildas described the kings and people who followed Ambrosius in his *Epistle* 1ff as variously tyrants with many wives; judges who acted like criminals; wives who were adulteresses; commoners who were perjurers; Britons who fought against each other in civil wars; and so forth. Gildas reserved his particular ire towards five kings: 1) Constantine, the king of Damonia, who killed two royal youths on the altar while wearing the habit of an abbot, and who was also an adulterer and sodomite; 2) Aurelius Conanus, who was a filthy murderer, fornicator and adulterer; 3) Vortipore, who married his own daughter; 4) Cuneglasse, who was a butcher of his own countrymen and an adulterer; 5) Maglocune, who was the king of kings when Gildas wrote and therefore the object of particular ire as a sodomite, liar, adulterer and killer of his own relatives. Despite Maglocune's personal failings, Gildas still acknowledges that he controlled most of the island, which means that the Saxons had not yet been able to make a major comeback at the time this tirade against the kings was written by Gildas.

Nennius
According to Nennius' account (26ff.), 'Maximianus' withdrew all military forces from Britain and settled in Armorica/Bretagne with his British followers, who were given British wives. As will be made clear later, this Maximianus/Maximus was actually Constantine III. It is also clear that Nennius has mixed Maximianus (reigned 285–305) and Maximus (383–388) with each other. After 'Maximianus' and his son Victor had been killed, the Romans dispatched deputies three times to take control of the island, but all of these were killed. It was only when the Scots and Picts exploited the absence of Roman forces and raided Britain, that

the Britons asked the Romans to assist them. The Romans dispatched a powerful army, defeated the enemy, appointed a new ruler, organized the administration and then again returned home. However, the Britons rebelled again, leading to the same results: the Picts and Scots invaded again and the Britons were forced to ask help. The Romans again threw out the invaders, took plenty of booty and then returned back home once more.

Nennius states that between the death of 'Maximianus' (Maximus) and the above-mentioned war, and the termination of Roman power by Vortigern, was a period of forty years, and that it was Vortigern (Guthrigern) who called Horsa and Hengist in three ships to the island. This would date Vortigern's reign to 428.[23] It is quite possible that Vortigern began his rule in that year, but he did not invite the Saxons to the island then. The name Vortigern actually means 'Over-king' (Morris, p.55), which I would connect with his position as *Princeps* of the British Council. According to Nennius, it was also at about this time that St Germanus arrived in Britain to chastise a tyrannical king called Belinus. This date is roughly accurate as far as the arrival of St Germanus is concerned, because it has usually been dated to 428/9. We know that St Germanus was called to root out the Pelagian heresy, which can perhaps be connected with the chastising of the tyrant Belinus. We also know from Constantius' *Life of St Germanus* that he fought against the Picts and Saxons during this same trip. This brings to the fore the problem of whether the Roman troops arrived before St Germanus' trip or with him. If the Romans had defeated the invaders before the arrival of St Germanus, then his subsequent presence in Mold and the Alleluia Victory would have taken place in the neighbourhood of the dykes of Wat and Offa, which would either mean that the Picts and Saxons had attempted to prevent the building of the dyke or that they had tried to penetrate it after it had already been built, with the result that they were defeated by St Germanus. The other alternative is that Constantine has left out of his *Life of St Germanus* the fact that St Germanus was actually acting as a commander for the Roman troops dispatched to the island, and that it was St Germanus who, with the help of these forces, defeated the invaders, built one of the dykes (either Wat or Offa) and re-established religious orthodoxy in Britain.

However, instead of dealing with the events of the Alleluia Victory, which is covered in the later chapter 47, Nennius (32–33) includes an account of St Germanus' dealings with the king Belinus/Benli. This incident is not recorded in the *Vita*, but in light of the role St Germanus played in Britain as military commander, it is entirely plausible that this event took place. According to Nennius' version, St Germanus and his attendants/retinue (*comites*, i.e. his *bucellarii*) appeared before the gate of a city in the country of Powys (Pouisorum/Ial), aiming to chastise the king for his behaviour. The king, however, refused to let him in. It was then that one of the king's servants, Catel Drunluc (Catellius), gave St Germanus his own suburban house to use. On the next morning, St Germanus once again asked for an audience, but in vain. It was then that one of the locals prostrated before St Germanus and recited his belief in the Holy Trinity. When this man then entered the city, he was killed by the king's prefect. St Germanus and his retinue stayed before the gates for the whole day, after which St Germanus advised his host to bring out all his friends from the city. Then 'fire fell from the heaven' during the night and burned the entire city, together with its inhabitants and king. A more prosaic account of this would of course be that St Germanus' military retinue burned the city to the ground with the help of his local host, who betrayed his native city. St Germanus duly rewarded Catel with the dukedom of Powys, and his descendants were still governing the area when Nennius wrote. In my opinion there is every reason to believe that this is actually one of the events that took place during St Germanus' trip to Britain in about 429, and that he provided not only religious but also military leadership to back up his preaching. It is the presence of the military retinue that his hagiography has left out on religious grounds. The fact that St Germanus killed a *rex* and replaced him with a *dux* suggests that he restored the area to Roman control. It was presumably after this that St Germanus was informed of the Saxon threat to the northern portion of the dyke near Chester and Mold. In light of this, it is probable that St Germanus fought the Alleluia battle only after the dyke had already been built.

The so-called Pillar of Eliseg, set by the king of Powys in about 800, claims that Vortigern had created the kingdom and placed Brittu (Bruttius) as its ruler, and that Germanus blessed this Bruttius. This suggests that the person blessed by Germanus was Catellius Bruttius (Catel Drunluc). The text also claims that Vortigern was son-in-law of Maximus. According to Morris, Powys was a Welsh spelling of the Latin *pagenses*, the populace of rural areas. In this case, it implied that the upland territories of the Cornovii had been separated from the city of Wroxeter. In other words, it appears probable that Vortigern, as Over-king, had dispatched Germanus to the border regions of Wales, where Germanus implemented Vortigern's military programme to subdue those who resisted the authority of the British Council and posed a potential threat if they formed an alliance with the invading hordes of Picts and Saxons. These potential deserters apparently consisted of the Irish settlers of Cornovia. Notably, the hill fort of Moel Fenli in this region preserves the name of Benli/Belinus, and may have been the scene of Germanus's operations against Belinus. Germanus' military/religious mission was followed up by two military/religious missions against Ireland. Palladius was dispatched to Britain in 431. He strengthened the orthodoxy, first among the Britons, and then sailed to Ireland to convert them, but was forced to return to Britain, where he died shortly afterwards. In 432, his mission was taken over by the famous Briton monk Patrick (educated and trained in St Germanus' monastery), and, as is well known, his mission met with great success.[24]

It is possible that there were actually two or more Over-kings after 428. The reason for this is that the Vortigern of 428–430 appears have supported orthodox beliefs, while the later Vortigern is better known as a staunch pagan. The claim that the earlier Vortigern was a son-in-law of Maximus (the usurper of 383–388) can also be used in support of this theory. However, none of this is conclusive, because it is possible that there was just one Vortigern who had married Maximus' daughter (who could also be daughter of the other usurper Maximus of 408–411) and then became a pagan towards the end of his life to court the views held by the Saxon mercenaries.

One may make the educated guess, on the basis of Nennius' confused details (36ff.) regarding the arrival of the Saxons under Hengist and Horsa on the island of Tenet, that Vortigern actually considered their force to be too small to be of use rather than that there would have been too many of them, with the result that Hengist promised more troops to support him. This would have happened at some point between 447 and 450. Vortigern gave permission and sixteen ships carrying troops arrived from 'Scythia'. With them was Hengist's daughter, whom he intended to marry to the lusty king in order to secure his own position. Hengist's plan worked like a dream. Vortigern married Hengist's daughter, in return for which the Saxons were given Kent and Hengist became the king's principal advisor. The *regulus* of Kent was forced to give up his territory, which presumably means that the *regulus*, together with his followers, fled to Bretagne.

Hengist then managed to convince Vortigern that it would be wise to call in ever more of his relatives, who in return for their services against the Scots (apparently actually the Picts) were promised all the territory in the north near the wall of Gual. Hengist's son Octha and brother Ebissa brought with them forty ships (*chiulis*). They pillaged the Orkneys and captured some territories belonging to the Picts. After this, Hengist continued to call more of his countrymen to Kent, with the result that some of the islands (Frisian Islands?) became deserted.

According to Nennius (39, 48), while this went on, Vortigern became ever more degenerate and married his own daughter, who gave birth to a son called Faustus. It is possible that Nennius has mixed two different people in this case, Vortigern and Vortipore. Nennius claims (39ff.) that St Germanus then forcibly adopted and re-educated Faustus, but unless this refers to the period prior to ca. 441, this must be a mistake. Nennius claims that it was because of St Germanus' intervention that Vortigern fled and attempted to build a new fort to serve as his place of refuge. It seems preferable to connect this with the revolt of the Saxons and revolt of Vortigern's son, Vortimer. If Vortigern did indeed marry his daughter, then it is possible that this would have been the straw that broke the camel's back and caused Vortimer's revolt against his father. Nennius has actually confused several entirely separate events in this context, and has also created doublets of the same. His mistakes include: 1) the connection of the flight of Vortigern with St Germanus' visit unless it means his second visit (39–42, 47–48); 2) the creation of doublets of the flight and building of the fort (39–42, 47–48); 3) the confusion of the revolt of Vortigern's son Vortimer against his father with other events (39–48); 4) the confusion of the legends of Merlin, Ambrosius Aurelius and Arthur with each other (39–50).

The most reasonable reconstruction for this confused mess is that we should discard all referrals to St Germanus in this context and follow the text of Geoffrey, so that the reconstructed version of subsequent events would be as follows: 1) the revolt of the Saxons, who forced Vortigern to flee; 2) Vortimer's revolt against his father Vortigern (Nennius has confused Vortimer and his son Guorthemer with each other, see 43–45, 48); 3) the flight of Vortigern to a new place of refuge after his body of advisors, consisting of twelve wise men, had recommended this (presumably the round table/Council of Britain that I have speculated to have already existed by 406); 4) Vortimer's campaigns against the Saxons and his death; 5) Vortigern's return to power; 6) the revolt of the Saxons; 7) the rise of Ambrosius Aurelius.

On the basis of Nennius' account, there also exists the possibility that Ambrosius Aurelianus and Ambrosius Merlin were actually one and the same person, so that Ambrosius Aurelianus/Merlin would have actually served as *dux* and *architectus* (i.e. as architect/philosopher/siege engineer) for King Arthur or that Ambrosius Aurelianus/Merlin/Arthur are the same person. Nennius' statement that Vortigern made Ambrosius ruler of the western provinces of Britain as a reward for his witty argumentation against being killed can actually be used to support the idea that it was thanks to this that most of the known locations of the battles fought by Ambrosius Aurelianus lay in the border region with Wales. It is of course equally possible that it was actually Ambrosius Merlin who became ruler of this region, because he too is associated with the area in question – he is supposed to have been in charge of the school of philosophers in the City of the Legions (associated either with Chester or Caerleon, with the latter being my preference) during the reign of Arthur. My own educated guess is that Nennius' Ambrosius is the Ambrosius Merlin of Geoffrey of Monmouth, so that Merlin was actually also a duke of the area. When Merlin had then been given in my opinion Caerleon, Vortigern went to a region called Gueneri in the Kingdom of Dimetae, where he built a city called Cair-Guorthigirn on the River Tivis to serve as his base of operations against the Saxons and his son Vortimer.

Nennius states that Vortimer revolted against his father and took charge of operations against the Saxons. He also claims that Vortimer's son Guorthemer (Nennius 43–44) commanded the Britons, but then contradicts himself in chapters 45 and 48. The end result was that Vortimer drove Hengist, Horsa and the Saxons to the Island of Tanet. The Saxons brought reinforcements from the mainland and attacked again. Vortimer then fought a first battle against them upon the river Derwent/Derevent; a second battle at the ford of 'Episford' ('Set thirgabail/Sathenegabail') where Horsa and Vortimer's brother Catigirn fell; and a third battle on the shore of 'the Gallic Sea', which resulted in the flight of the Saxons to their ships. The result proved ephemeral, because Vortimer died soon after his victory. He instructed his followers to bury his body at the entrance of the so-called Saxon Port so that his ghost would prevent the Saxons from ever making a landing, but his instructions were not followed. This suggests that Vortimer, just like his father Vortigern, was actually a pagan.[25]

The death of Vortimer meant the rise of Vortigern back to power (45ff.). Vortigern needed supporters, and Hengist was quite prepared to promise him his aid if he and his Saxons would be readmitted to Tanet and the rest of Britain, but this was only a ruse. Vortigern was foolish enough to accept his father-in-law's conciliatory message. The treaty was to be signed at a banquet attended by 300 British nobles and an equal number of Saxons. The Saxons had hidden daggers and used these to butcher the Britons after Hengist shouted '*Nimader sexa*'. Hengist subdued Vortigern, some of the Britons managed to flee, but most were massacred. Vortigern purchased his freedom from Hengist by granting him three provinces – Eastsex, Southsex and Middlesex – together with other territories. After this, Nennius includes three versions for the death of Vortigern, one of which is a doublet, with the arrival of St Germanus to force the pagan Vortigern to convert and the flight of Vortigern, which is now connected with the Alleluia Victory. Nennius then claims that St Germanus caused fire to fall from heaven and kill Vortigern, his wife and all his followers at a castle called Cair Guorherngirn. The second of the versions is that Vortigern just disappeared or that the ground swallowed him when his castle was burned.

This is followed up by the first extant account of the exploits of King Arthur. Nennius first states that Vortigern had four sons: Vortimer, Cathigirn, Faustus and Pascent. Faustus was supposed to be the incestuous son of Vortigern, who was raised by St Germanus and later became founder of a monastery. Pascent was granted the provinces of Buelt and Guorthegirnaim by the new High King Ambrosius (*rex inter omnes reges Britanniae*). It is unfortunate that Nennius fails to specify who this Ambrosius was. Was he Aurelianus/Aurelius, was he Merlin, or are these one and the same person? It is probably not the latter, because Nennius' description (50, or 56, or 63–64) of subsequent events suggests that he probably considered Ambrosius and Arthur to be the same man, which would mean that he could not have been Merlin.

There was also one important change in the Saxon kingdom, which was that Octha succeeded as king of the Saxons of Kent after his father Hengist died. According to Nennius, Arthur was nominated as commander of all British armies ('*ipse dux erat bellorum*') against the Saxons twelve times, despite there being many other commanders/kings of more noble birth than he. The name Arthur supposedly meant a horrible bear. The first battle was fought at the mouth of the River Glein/Glem. The second, third, fourth and fifth were fought on the River Duglas in the region of Lunius/Linnius (this location is unknown, but there are several theories), and the sixth on the River Lussas/Bassas. The seventh was fought in the wood of Celidon/Calidonis/Cacoit Celidon, and the eighth near the castle of Guinnion/Gunnion, where Arthur carried the image of the Madonna on his shoulder and pursued the fleeing Saxons for an entire day. The ninth battle was at the City of the Legions (*in urbe Legionis*)/Cair Lion (Caerleon?). The tenth was on the banks of the River Ribroit/Trat Treuroit, with the eleventh on the mountain of Agned Cathregonnon/Breguoin/Cat Bregion. The twelfth battle was the famous hard-fought battle of the hill of Badon ('*monte Badonis*'), where Arthur reputedly killed either 840 or 940 men by his own hand. This referral to the Battle of Badon connects Arthur with the Ambrosius Aurelius of Gildas. Arthur won all of these battles, but every time he defeated the invaders, they called more men from every province of Germania. The Saxons kept on calling for reinforcements until they established their first kingdom in Bernech and Cair Affrauc under Ida.

Nennius ended his history with the dating of events, which included St Patrick's journey to Ireland, and a list of Saxon kings.

The Anglo-Saxon Chronicle
The best way actually to summarize the Anglo-Saxon Chronicle is to include a list of excerpts from the translation of Giles (1914) with some comments. My own comments are inside brackets.

> AD 381. This year Maximus the emperor obtained the empire: he was born in the land of Britain and went thence into Gaul. And he there slew the emperor Gratian (*date should be 383*). … In these days the heresy of Pelagius arose.
>
> AD 382–408. [No entries]
>
> AD 409. This year the Goths took the city of Rome by storm, and after this the Romans never ruled in Britain (*the date is one year off, and the claim that the Romans never ruled Britain after this is a common mistake in all sources, as we shall see*).
>
> AD 410–417. [No entries]
>
> AD 418. This year the Romans collected all the treasures that were in Britain, and some they hid in the earth, so that no one has since been able to find them; and some they carried with them into Gaul (*this proves that the Romans had not abandoned Britain in 409, but had returned. This probably refers to the first occasion on which the Romans dispatched legions back and then returned with the loot to cover their expense; I would suggest that the Roman forces landed in about 414/415 and then returned to Gaul in 418, as stated by the* ASC; *see MHLR Vol. 3*).
>
> AD 419–422. [No entries]
>
> AD 423. This year Theodosius the younger succeeded to the empire (*Theodosius II became emperor of the East in 408; and then after the death of Honorius also the legitimate emperor of the West in 423. In the West, power was usurped by John in 423, but Theodosius installed Valentinian III on the throne through force in 425; see MHLR Vol. 3*).

46   Britain in the Age of Arthur

AD 424–429. (*The* Anglo-Saxon Chronicle *leaves out the second Roman intervention, presumably by St Germanus, which included a campaign against the Picts and Saxons. This is typical of the* ASC, *which tends to hide the setbacks suffered by the Saxons.*)

AD 430. This year Palladius the bishop was sent to the Scots by pope Celestinus, that he might confirm their faith (*the Scots are the Irish Scotti*).

AD 430. This year Patrick was sent to the Scots by pope Celestinus to preach baptism to the Scots.

AD 443. This year the Britons sent over the sea to Rome and begged for help against the Picts; they had none, because were themselves warring against Attila, the king of the Huns (*Aetius was indeed at war with the Huns in 443–44, as he was in 446*). And then they sent to the Angles, and entreated the like of the ethelings of the Angles (*the* Gallic Chronicle 452 *dates the beginning of Saxon dominance of Britain to 441–442, which means that it is entirely plausible that the Britons would have sent the first plea for help to the Angles in 443, as stated here; it is actually quite possible that the Britons under Vortigern first asked help from Aetius in 443, and then from the Angles and then again from Aetius in 446. It seems probable that the ASC has left out the participation of the Saxons in the Pictish invasions of 441–443 so that the proposed alliance between the Britons and Angles was meant to direct the latter against their neighbours; see MHLR Vol. 4*).

AD 444. This year St Martin died.

AD 445–447. (*The* ASC *leaves out the plea to Aetius in 446.*)

AD 448. This year John the Baptist …

AD 449. This year (*in truth 450*) Martianus (*Marcian / Marcianus*) and Valentinus succeeded to the empire and reigned seven years (*this means Marcian*). And in their days (*inaccurate expression, which could actually mean the 440s in general*) Hengist and Horsa, invited by Vortigern king of the Britons, landed in Britain on the shore which was called Wippidsfleet; at first in aid of the Britons, but afterwards they fought against them. King Vortigern gave them land in the south-east of this country, on condition that they should fight against the Picts (*i.e. as federates*). Then they fought against the Picts, and had the victory wheresoever they came. They then sent to the Angles; desired a larger force to be sent and caused them to be told the worthlessness of the Britons, and the excellencies of the land. Then they soon sent thither a larger force in aid of the others. At that time there came men from three tribes in Germany, from the Old Saxons, from the Angles, from the Jutes. From the Jutes came the Kentish-men and the Wightwarians (*this actually suggests that Hengist and Horsa belonged to the Jutes rather than to the Angles or Saxons*), that is, the tribe which now dwells in Wight, and that race among the West-Saxons which is still called the race of Jutes. From the Old-Saxons came the men of Essex and Sussex and Wessex. From Anglia, which has ever since remained waste betwixt the Jutes and Saxons, came the men of East Anglia, Middle Anglia, Mercia, and all North-humbria. Their leaders were two brothers, Hengist and Horsa; they were the sons of Wihtgils; Withgils son of Witta, Witta of Wecta, Wecta of Woden; from this Woden sprang all our royal families, and those of the South-humbrians also.[26] (*It is possible that the invitation of the Saxons by Vortigern should be placed to the year 447/8.*)

AD 449. And in their days Vortigern invited the Angles thither, and they came to Britain in three ceols, at the place called Wippidsfleet.

AD 450–454. [No entries]

AD 455. (*means 448–449?*) This year Hengist and Horsa fought against King Vortigern at the place which is called Aegels-threp (*Aylesford*) and his brother Horsa was there slain (*this would presumably mean the battle against Vortimer*), and after that Hengist obtained the kingdom, and Aesc his son (*this hides the Saxon defeat underneath the matters of succession*).

AD 456. (*still 448–449 or later?*) This year Hengist and Aesc slew four troops of Britons (*presumably generic legions*) with the edge of the sword, in the place which is named Creccanford (*Crayford*).

AD 457. (*still 448–449?*) This year Hengist and Aesc his son fought against the Britons at the place which is called Craeganford (*Crayford*) and there slew four thousand men (*this can be a doublet of the above*); and the Britons forsook Kent, and in great terror fled to London (*it is also possible that this actually refers to the instance in which Arthur was forced to retreat to London and to call for reinforcements from Armorica*).

AD 458–464. (*The ASC is silent here about the great successes of the Britons under Aurelius Ambrosius. Its technique is to spread out the successes of the Anglo-Saxons throughout the years, so it is very likely that the events of the following years should be placed to occur between 456–464.*)

AD 465. This year Hengist and Aesc fought against the Welsh near Wippidsfleet (*Ebbsfleet?*), and there slew twelve Welsh ealdormen, and one of their thanes was slain there, whose name was Wipped.

AD 466–472. (*The ASC is again silent here on the great successes of the Britons under Aurelius Ambrosius.*)

AD 473. This year Hengist and Aesc fought against the Welsh and took spoils innumerable; and the Welsh fled from the Angles like fire.

AD 474–476. (*The cover-up of the ASC continues.*)

48   Britain in the Age of Arthur

AD 477. This year Aella, and his three sons, Cymen, and Wlencing, and Cassa, came to the land of Britain with three ships, at a place which is named Cymenes-ora, and there slew many Welsh, and some they drove in flight into the wood that is named Andreds-lea. (*This account actually proves the cover-up of the* ASC, *because it no longer includes Hengist and large numbers of Saxons. Instead of this, the Saxons are no longer residing on the island, but are actually raiding the Welsh lands with a mere three ships. This proves that Aurelius Ambrosius had already expelled the Saxons. As noted above, the* ASC *spreads out the claimed successes of Hengist over many years so that it could cover up the successful counter-attack by the natives, but incidental details like this prove that the Saxons had in the meanwhile suffered a complete defeat, as stated by the many extant sources written by the Britons.*)

AD 478–481. (*The* ASC *is once again silent on the successes of the Britons.*)

AD 482. This year the blessed Benedict, by the glory of his miracles, shone in this world, as the blessed Gregory relates in his book of dialogues.

AD 486–487. (*The* ASC *again covers up the successes of the Britons.*)

AD 488. This year Aese succeeded to the kingdom, and was king of the Kentish-men twenty-four years (*it is quite possible that some of the Saxons etc. remained on the island as federates, even after their defeat*).

AD 489–490. [No entries]

AD 491. This year Aella and Cissa besieged Andredscester, and slew all that dwelt therein, so that not a single Briton was there left (*this suggests that the Saxons had once again started to raid in strength*).

AD 492–494. [No entries]

AD 495. This year two ealdormen came to Britain, Cerdic and Cynric his son, with five ships at the place which is called Cerdics-ore, and the same day they fought against the Welsh (*this is clearly a piratical raid and not an attempt to conquer territory*).

AD 496–500. [No entries]

AD 501. This year Port, and his two sons Bieda and Maegla, came to Britain with two ships at a place which is named Portsmouth, and they soon affected a landing, and they there slew a young British man of high nobility (*this is a very small-scale raid on British coastal areas*).

AD 502–507. [No entries]

AD 508. This year Cerdic and Cynric slew a British king, whose name was Natan-leod, and five thousand men with him. After that the country was named Natan-lea, as far Cerdicsford (*Charford*) (*this is the first recorded full-scale operation by the Saxons after they had been defeated by Aurelius Ambrosius, and may actually be dated close to the time it occurred*).

AD 509. This year St Benedict the abbot, father of all monks, went to heaven.

AD 510–513. [No entries]

AD 514. This year the West-Saxons came to Britain with three ships, at the place which is called Cerdic's-ore, and Stuf and Whitgar fought against the Britons, and put them to flight (*this is a mere raid*).

AD 519. This year Cerdic and Cynric obtained the kingdom of the West-Saxons; and fought against the Britons where it is now named Cerdicsford.

AD 520–526. [No entries]

AD 527. This year Cerdic and Cynric fought against the Britons at the place which is called Cerdic's-lea (*another instance of large-scale operations*).

AD 528–529. [No entries]

AD 530. This year Cerdic and Cynric conquered the island of Wight, and slew many men at Whit-garas-byrg (*Carisbrooke on the Isle of Wight*) (*Cerdic and Cynric continue their major operations*).

AD 531–533. [No entries]

AD 534. This year Cerdic, the first king of the West-Saxons, died, and Cynric his son succeeded to the kingdom, and reigned from that time twenty-six years; and they gave the whole island of Wight to their two nephews, Stuf and Wihtgar (*this suggests that the only possession of the West-Saxons at this stage was the island of Wight*).

AD 535–537. [No entries]

AD 538–543. [No entries]

AD 544. This year Wihtgar died, and they buried him in With-gaa-byrg (*Carisbrooke*).

AD 545–546. [No entries]

AD 547. This year Ida began to reign, from whom arose the royal race of Northumbria; and reigned twelve years, and built Bambrough, which was at first enclosed by a hedge, and afterwards by a wall. Ida was the son of Eoppa, Eoppa of Esa, Esa of Ingwi, Ingwi of Angenwit, Angenwit of Aloc, Aloc of Benoc, Benoc of Brond, Brond of Beldeg, Beldeg of Woden (*Odin as an ancestor; see Appendix 3*); Woden of Frithowald, Frithowald of Frithuwulf, Frithuwulf of Finn, Finn of Godwulf, Godwulf of Geat.

AD 548–551. [No entries]

AD 552. This year Cynric fought against the Britons at the place which is called Searo-byrig (*Old Sarum*), and he put the Britons to flight (*it is clear that the Saxons were now well established in Britain and no longer marginalized as they were after Aurelius's victories, which means that the Arthurian Age was over. Consequently, I will include only a summary of the rest of the story in the main narrative*).

Chapter 3

The Main Narrative with Geoffrey of Monmouth Included: The Creation of the British Commonwealth, 406–445

3.1 Britain and Armorica in 406–413[1]

The Britons voiced their disapproval of the way in which Honorius and Stilicho ruled in late 406 or early 407 by revolting under Marcus. We do not know what the reasons were, but we can make an educated guess that the Irish (*Scotti*), Picts and Saxons were ravaging Britain and no help was forthcoming from the continent. What is notable is that Marcus was a low-ranking soldier, which suggests that the soldiers were dissatisfied with the corrupt officers in charge of the defence. The local magnates/tribal leaders may also have preferred a low-ranking man, because they could influence his decisions with greater ease. However, Marcus proved unable to satisfy the high hopes placed in him, and he was killed. His replacement was Gratian, a local townsman. This shows that the civilians (the city councils, city dwellers and peasants) were equally dissatisfied with the situation, which is unsurprising considering the widespread corruption of the imperial authorities and officer cadre. Gratian was killed after having ruled for only four months, which suggests that he was also too slow in his actions. The people and soldiers wanted fast results and the ousting of the incompetent Honorius. Consequently, the Britons elevated Constantine III (Flavius Claudius Constantinus) from the ranks to the throne in very early 407, because he had an auspicious name. According to Zosimus (6.3.1), the reason for the raising of the usurpers Marcus, Gratian and Constantine in Britain was the invasion of Gaul by the Vandals, Alans and Suevi in 406, but I would suggest that the real cause still lay in the local circumstances of Britain and that the invasion of Gaul in 406 was only the last straw for those forces that may have been temporarily stationed in Britain.

In my opinion, this series of usurpations was the first sign of the love of freedom demonstrated by Roman Britons in the fifth century, which eventually led to their full independence from Rome under King Arthur. It is highly probable that the Britons had already formed a council (*consilium*) consisting of councillors (*consiliarii*), which is mentioned for the first time by Gildas (22–23) during the reign of King Vortigern. It is unlikely to be a coincidence that the West Romans attempted to retain the support of the Gallic nobility by convening the Gallic Council at Arles in 407. The later legends of King Arthur and the Round Table are probably a reflection of this. The round shape of the table expressed equality among the people seated at it, even if one of them was considered first among equals (*Princeps*). It would have been this *Princeps* who would eventually become high king. The *posessores* of the city councils must have played a very important role in the nomination of the city councillor Gratianus as emperor. It seems unlikely that the military would have accepted a civilian ruler unless the local councils had already assumed a far greater role through mutual cooperation as a Council of Britain. The local kings/ magnates would have exercised their rule through patronage, their tribal forces and their personal *bucellarii*. It is also probable that many of the landlords had become patrons to the soldiers who had been levied from their lands. After all, the families of these soldiers still lived on those estates. The other soldiers would have followed their example. Hence the appointments of the low-ranking soldiers (Marcus, Constantine) as emperors.

3.2 Constantine invades Gaul: The birth of independent Armorica and Britain in 407–411

The new emperor, *Augustus* Constantine III, sought to strengthen his own (probably?) fictitious connection with the former dynasty of Constantine the Great by taking the imperial name of Flavius Claudius and renaming his sons as Constans and Julian (Iulianus).[2] Constantine may also have sought support simultaneously from both pagans and Christians through using these names.

The usurper landed his forces in Bononia/Boulogne in the spring of 407. He stayed there for several days and, according to Zosimus (6.2.2), won over to his side all the forces down to the Alps that divided Gaul from Italy. After this, he defeated the invading barbarian hordes (Suevi, Vandals, Alans, Saxons, Heruls, Burgundians and Alamanni) somewhere in Gaul. This gave him effective control of most of Gaul and Spain. After this initial success, however, things did not go as planned, the usurpation ending in failure. Constantine III was beheaded in September 411. Before his death, however, he had set in motion the events that were to lead to the downfall of West Rome and the birth of the successor states. The civil war he initiated enabled the barbarian invaders to start the carving up of the Western empire. Honorius' government had been unable to make any response because he foolishly killed his commander Stilicho and persecuted his barbarian followers. On top of this, Honorius alienated Alaric and his Visigoths. As a result, Honorius faced hostile Visigoths, who were supported by the former Roman soldiers of barbarian origin on Italian soil, while Constantine III threatened him from Gaul.[3]

The re-conquest of Gaul and Britain initiated by Constantius on behalf of Honorius from ca. 411 onwards brought both areas back under imperial rule. Honorius had already sent letters to the cities of Britain in 410, in which he urged them to defend themselves (Zos. 6.10.2). The Roman government was unable to send any troops to assist them. This proves that the Britons had already overthrown all representatives of Constantine III and that Britain was ruled by members of the city councils. It is clear that some sort of central governing body must have existed, because any organized defence against Constantine's supporters and barbarians would have otherwise been quite impossible. As noted above, the sequence of usurpations in 406 suggests that such a body (the Council of the Round Table?) already existed by that date. It is unfortunate that we do not know the exact date from which the leading members of this body started to call themselves kings in order to obtain the support of the native Celts/Romans.

Geoffrey's (5.12ff.) account allows one to reconstruct the events in Armorica and Britain in greater detail. Geoffrey, just like Gildas, claims that it was Maximianus/Maximus who invaded Gaul with British forces, with the result that the island was denuded of defenders. A somewhat similar version of events can also be found in the Welsh *Mabinogion* (pp.118–27). This is partially true, because the *Notitia Dignitatum* does not mention any forces for the *Comes Britanniae* (Occ. 29) while it still does mention some for the *Comes litoris Saxonici per Britanniam* (Occ. 28). These forces must have been transferred to the continent by the real Maximus or, after him, Constantine III. What is certain, however, is that Constantine III must have had an army – the last officially Roman field army of Britain – with him when he landed in Gaul. It is possible that this army did not consist of the regular forces of the *Comes Britanniae*, if the *Notitia Dignitatum* dates from the period before 407, but of such forces that had been transferred temporarily from the continent by Stilicho to Britain, along with federate/native units not mentioned by the *Notitia Dignitatum*.

This raises the question why both sources claim that it was Maximus/Maximianus who removed the defenders from Britain. It is possible that Gildas, who was clearly the principal source for all later writers, just made a mistake or used a source that included the mistaken information. For example, it is possible that King Arthur was related to Constantine III,[4] which then caused a muddling of the evidence. It is also possible that the British authors have confused Gerontius' puppet emperor Maximus (*Augustus* in 409–411) with the earlier Maximus, or that this puppet emperor removed the last field forces from Britain. Another possibility would of course be that Constantine III's original name was Maximianus and that he changed his name to obtain support, which would mean that the British tradition would have preserved for us Constantine III's original birth name. Since we know that Gildas wrote in the sixth century, it is clear that the falsified/muddled version of events probably dates from the reign of Arthur, and that it was this chronicle/history that was used as a source by Gildas and by the source or sources used by Geoffrey. The redating of the removal of troops from Britain from 407 to 383 has also resulted in the mix-up of other events and persons, and it is by no means surprising that the Medieval historians have despaired of even attempting to piece together real events from the confused mess. For example, it is quite clear that the exploits of Bishop Germanus in Britain have been misplaced by at least about forty years in some of the extant accounts. Other similar mistakes abound.

Geoffrey claims that Maximianus (in truth Constantine; I use here both names synonymously) landed his forces in Armorica/Bretagne, where he fought a battle against the Gauls under Imbaltus. When most of Imbaltus' forces were in danger (presumably of being encircled), they had to flee. They left Imbaltus dead on the battlefield, together with 15,000 killed. It is possible that these Gauls were in truth the barbarian invaders known to have been defeated by Constantine in 407, but more likely that they were the army of the *Tractus Armoricani* under its *dux*. Constantine Maximianus' army included Celtic forces under Conanus/Conan, whose army appears to have consisted of men of Albany. It is probable the Albany in question refers to the area between Hadrian's Wall and the Antonine Wall, which appears to have been left in the hands of Celtic federates under the Severans.[5] Conan and Maximianus had previously fought an inconclusive war, which had been ended on terms which appear to have included the requirement that Conan fight as a federate for Maximianus. In order to secure Conan's continued loyalty, Constantine had evidently promised Armorica/Bretagne to him. After the victorious landing, both marched to Rennes and took the city on the same day. The local men fled in such haste that they even left behind their families. The Britons killed all the men they found in the other cities and towns of the area, leaving only the women alive, then garrisoned the area. Geoffrey claims that Maximianus published a decree in which he ordered 100,000 British commoners and 30,000 soldiers to be resettled in Armorica, after which he continued his march to the rest of Gaul and Germany. The fact that the *Notitia Dignitatum* (Occ. 37) includes a list of *praefecti* under a *dux*, with units of Moors and Dalmatae for the *Tractus Armoricani*, suggests that Conan came to the region with Constantine rather than with Maximus. Geoffrey claims that following this, Maximianus conquered Gaul and Germany and set up his capital at Treves (Trier). This appears to have been an accurate description of what happened. Constantine took charge of the defence of Trier in person and inflicted a defeat on the invading barbarians, while his generals secured the Italian frontier. It was only later that Constantine settled his headquarters at Arles. Geoffrey then claims that Maximianus attacked Gratian and Valentinianus, killing one and expelling the other from Rome. These exploits were performed by the real Maximus and not by Constantine.

If one combines the above with the names of the cities sacked by the invading barbarians in Gaul after 406, it is possible to speculate that in truth Constantine landed at Boulogne (Zosimus), from where he advanced against the invading barbarians. After having defeated these somewhere between Boulogne and Paris, Constantine advanced to Rennes and from there to Armorica, which was given to Conan. This would also explain what Constantine did while his *magistri* Justinian and Nebiogast advanced towards south-east Gaul in 407 and occupied Lyon, Vienne and Arles – a question that has caused a fair amount of speculation. In other words, Constantine subdued the forces posted to protect the *Tractus Armoricanus* in order to secure his supply lines to Britain, while his generals secured the rest of

The Main Narrative with Geoffrey of Monmouth Included   55

Gaul. The list of cities (in the narrative histories and hagiographical works) sacked by the barbarian invaders in 406–409 proves that they did not manage to pillage Armorica. It should be noted that the main part of the invasion started only in 408, when Stilicho is claimed to have invited the barbarians into Gaul for use against Constantine.[6] The timing of the major invasions and the list of cities lend credence to Geoffrey's claim that Conan was given control of Armorica. There had to be some sizeable, centrally organized military presence in Armorica/Bretagne for the barbarians to avoid it. It was during the 408 invasion that the Saxons gained control of the Gallic coast from the Seine up to Boulogne, and the Heruls north of that possibly up to the Rhine. At the same time, the Saxons also took control of Jersey, Guernsey and other islands.

Geoffrey (6.15ff) claims that the Gauls and Aquitanians harassed Conan and the Britons of Armorica, but with no success. One possibility would be that this refers to the situation after the settlement of the Visigoths in Aquitania, but since the circumstances fit better the situation in about 408/9 I have adopted this interpretation. In other words, Conan would have been harassed by the barbarian invaders soon after having settled in the area. It was after his victory over these that Conan decided to seek wives from Britain so that his men would not become mixed with the locals. The probable reason for this would have been to retain tribal 'purity', so it would form a separate entity in the area. The other reason would obviously have been the lack of marriageable women in the area after the ethnic cleansing by Conan and Constantine. Conan's forces needed women to procreate. The *Mabinogion* (126–127) includes very interesting additional information regarding the situation facing Conan (Kynan in the *Mabinogion*). According to this version, Armorica was conquered by Conan and Avaon, and when they had accomplished their mission Avaon decided to return home while Conan opted to stay. Conan ordered the tongues of the women captives cut out so that they would not contaminate the language of the resulting offspring, as usually happened in such cases. In light of this, Conan's decision sounds quite logical, as does the information provided by the *Mabinogion*. The Briton conquerors of Brittany/Bretagne kept their 'racial purity' and language better than many other conquerors.[7]

Consequently, according to Geoffrey, Conan asked the king of Cornwall, Dionotus, to dispatch women for his forces. It is probable that this Dionotus was another Romanized Celtic noble who retained control over his own tribe and had effectively become a federate leader of them. Dionotus was acting as a sort of governor general for Britain in the absence of Constantine. It is quite probable that this message to send the women to Bretagne had been delivered by the above-mentioned Avaon of the *Mabinogion*. The title of king for Dionotus may be anachronistic, but it is also possible that he, like many other British nobles, had assumed it in order to control the local populations and tribal mercenaries with greater efficiency. This was not a new phenomenon. For example, Constantius I appears to have appointed the king of the Alamanni, Crocus, as his *Comes Domesticorum*, just as Gratian used the king of the Franks, Mallobaudes. It was quite possible for people to occupy two positions simultaneously.

Dionotus collected the women (11,000 belonging to the upper classes, meaning the Roman settlers, and 60,000 belonging to the commoners) and ships in London, and then dispatched them to Conan. Unsurprisingly, this measure was highly unpopular. It is quite possible to think that the revolt of the city councils of Britain against Constantine III in 409 would have been caused by this. Dionotus would have been one of its first victims. The trip along the Thames was uneventful, but then the ships were dispersed in a storm when approaching Armorica. Some of the ships were sunk with all hands, while others were shipwrecked on 'strange islands', which must mean Guernsey and Jersey, where they were killed by forces under the command of Guanius and Melga.

According to Geoffrey, Gracianus (emperor Gratian/Gratianus) had formed an alliance with Wanius, king of the Huns, and Melga, king of the Picts, and dispatched them to harass everyone who supported Maximianus (i.e. Constantine) along the coastline of Gaul and Germany (the coastline in Saxon hands).[8] This may suggest that the Huns were federate forces that had been put on board the Pictish vessels. What is obvious is that the federates in question cannot have been dispatched by Gratian, but by either Honorius or Gerontius/Maximus. The obvious goal would have been to cut off the supply route leading from Britain to Gaul. It was these forces that encountered the shipwrecked women and then butchered them on the Channel Islands. On this occasion, Geoffrey gives them the collective name Ambrones, who were a Celtic people who had joined the Cimbri and Teutones. This suggests that the Ambrones may have come from the same general region as the Saxons (were they actually Saxons inhabiting the islands?), or that they were Picts. I would suggest that the Ambrones (including the so-called Huns) were probably one of the tribes that made up the Saxon nation. The 'Huns' in question would indeed have been originally one of the tribal groupings that made up the Hunnic Empire, but had sought its fortunes elsewhere, like so many other so-called Huns of unknown origins had.

When these forces learnt that Maximianus (Constantine) had denuded Britain of its defenders, they decided to exploit the situation and formed an alliance with the Picts and Scots, landing their forces in Albany (Scotland), after which they invaded. The invasion was a great success. One may guess that the transferral of the federate forces of Conan from Albany to Bretagne was the cause of this disaster. Constantine's response was to dispatch two legions under Gracianus the Freedman (Gratian) back to Britain. It is easy to see that if there really existed a freedman called Gratianus, as is probable, while Gerontius' puppet emperor was Maximus, that this could have caused plenty of confusion among later writers, just as the existence of the two Theodosii for the Eastern empire has. The two legions should be considered to mean 'generic' legions of the period military theory (*mere* in Greek), each consisting of about 5,000–7,000 men. These professional legions, containing several units and including a mix of infantry and cavalry in varying proportions, were more than a match for the enemy and forced them to flee to Ireland.

Meanwhile, according to Geoffrey's version, the friends of Gratian had killed Maximianus in Rome, with the result that the Britons accompanying him were also either killed or scattered. The remnants of this force fled to Armorica, which became a second Britain (Brittany/Bretagne). This appears to be a very muddled memory of the end of Constantine, who surrendered to Honorius' *MVM* Constantius at Arles in 411 and was then sent to Honorius, but was killed en route somewhere in Italy. According to Geoffrey, when Gratian the Freedman learnt of the news in Britain, he declared himself king (*Augustus*?), but acted in so high-handed a fashion that the local plebs assassinated him. This would suggest the possibility that it was Honorius' letter that incited the local plebs to kill Gratian. Another less likely possibility is that Gratian had already declared himself emperor while Constantine was alive in about 409 (presumably at about the same time as Gerontius revolted in 409), and that he had been killed in about 409/410, so it was only after his death that Honorius dispatched his famous letter to the British cities in 410.

Geoffrey follows this with material that combines Gildas' account with his Welsh source. When the death of Gratian was reported to the barbarians, Wanius and Melga returned from Ireland with the Irish Scots, Norwegians and Danes. The Norwegians and Danes would presumably have consisted of mercenaries and adventurers from Norway (there were several kingdoms at this time) and Denmark (Danes, Jutes, Saxons and Angles). Gildas, on the other hand, states that the Picts invaded from the north and the Scots from the west. These were certainly the principal invaders at the time, even if one cannot exclude the possibility that there would have been adventurers from elsewhere present, as stated by Geoffrey. The Britons dispatched envoys to Rome to beg for help. The Romans responded by sending a single legion. Once again, one should understand this to refer to a combined force of infantry and cavalry consisting of 5,000–7,000 men. The Romans met the invaders in hand-to-hand combat and drove them out. I would date this roughly to 413–415, because Honorius confirmed the Burgundians as Roman federates in *Germania Prima* in 413 (Prosper 413) and Exuperantius (probably as *Dux Tractus Armoricani et Nervicani*; see PLRE2, Rutilius Namatianus 213ff.) pacified the Bacaudae of Armorica before 417. This does suggest Roman operations in the neighbourhood, the goal of which must have been to re-establish imperial control over these areas, Britain included.[9]

According to Geoffrey, the Romans ordered the local population to divide Albany from Deira by constructing a wall from one sea to another. The inhabitants were made to pay for the construction. Since Geoffrey notes that the previous war had devastated Albany completely, this must mean that the Antonine Wall was repaired. At the same time it is possible that Geoffrey (and other sources) have mistaken the wall-building to mean the walls facing north, while the new wall would have been built to face Wales, or that the Britons rebuilt the Antonine Wall to protect Albany against the Picts, renovated Hadrian's Wall and/or built a new turf wall between

Chester and Caerleon as protection against the Scots and their allies. My own educated guess is that the Britons either refortified the Antonine Wall and left its defence in the hands of the local federate tribesmen, as had been the practice ever since the days of Caracalla,[10] or that they renovated Hadrian's Wall. The Romans then announced that they would leave the defence of Britain in local hands, in return for which the Romans no longer taxed the islanders. The men of military age were then assembled in London, where they were conscripted as levies into the army. According to Geoffrey (6.1), the Archbishop of London, Guithelinus, encouraged the new conscription of recruits. Before leaving, the Romans showed them how to construct weapons and recommended that additional towers be constructed at intervals along the southern coast.

3.3 The House of Constantine Returns (?) to Britain in about 418/419 (Geoffrey 6.4ff.)

When the legion had returned home, presumably in 418 (*ASC*), the previous enemies sailed back from Ireland, accompanied by the Scots, Picts, Norwegians and others under their command. This time the invaders occupied Albany all the way up to the wall (presumably Hadrian's Wall). The peasants were useless as defenders of the walls and cities; they simply fled. In this case, Geoffrey follows Gildas and continues his account all the way to the British appeal to Agicius (Aetius), three times consul. It is obvious that the insertion of Gildas at this point has caused a dislocation of the real sequence of events, into which Geoffrey returns when he starts once again to use his Welsh source. When the invaders had crushed the peasant levy, the Britons convened their council. It was decided that Archbishop Guithelinus would attempt to seek help from Bretagne. According to the dating provided by the *ASC*, the Bacaudae of Armorica had, in about 417, been pacified by Exuperantius, which means that it was now under Roman control.[11] If true, it should be noted that on the basis of Geoffrey's account and the subsequent revolts in this area, this control was only superficial. According to Geoffrey, Bretagne was now ruled by Aldroenus, who was the fourth king after Conan.[12] Guithelinus told Aldroenus that the Romans were no longer prepared to assist them, so the Britons were now prepared to make Aldroenus the king of Britain. Aldroenus replied that he was not interested in obtaining the throne because he could govern his own kingdom in Bretagne in complete liberty, while as a king of Britain he would lose this freedom because Britain was under Roman rule. This suggests the possibility that the *ASC* has made a mistake in dating the return of the legion to 418. Geoffrey's account suggests that Aldroenus was still an independent ruler of Bretagne at the time Guithelinus arrived. Aldroenus suggested that his brother Constantine would come to help the Britons. The archbishop agreed and Constantine sailed, together with 2,000 soldiers, to Totnes (see map on page 84). The smallness of this force also implies that Aldroenus needed most of his forces for some other purpose, the likeliest of which would have been the defence of his kingdom against the Romans.

On his arrival, Constantine levied the local youth, and advanced against and defeated the enemy. Now the Britons flocked to his army and a council was assembled at Silchester, where Constantine was enthroned as king. Constantine married an unnamed woman of noble birth who had been raised by Guithelinus. According to Geoffrey, she gave birth to three sons: Constans, Aurelius Ambrosius and Utherpendragon. Constans was placed in the church of Amphibalus in Winchester to be raised as a monk, while Guithelinus was given the task of raising Aurelius and Utherpendragon. As noted by Thorpe (p.151), Geoffrey gives Utherpendragon the name he only took later in his life. However, this is not all that is amiss. As will be made clear later, Aurelius Ambrosius and Utherpendragon and Arthur are likely to be one and the same person. Constantine's rule secured ten years of relative peace, but it ended in disaster when a Pict in his staff stabbed him to death with a dagger, presumably in about 420–428. Geoffrey doesn't name the reason for the murder, nor the likely man/men behind it. Perhaps it was the ultra-ambitious Vortigern.

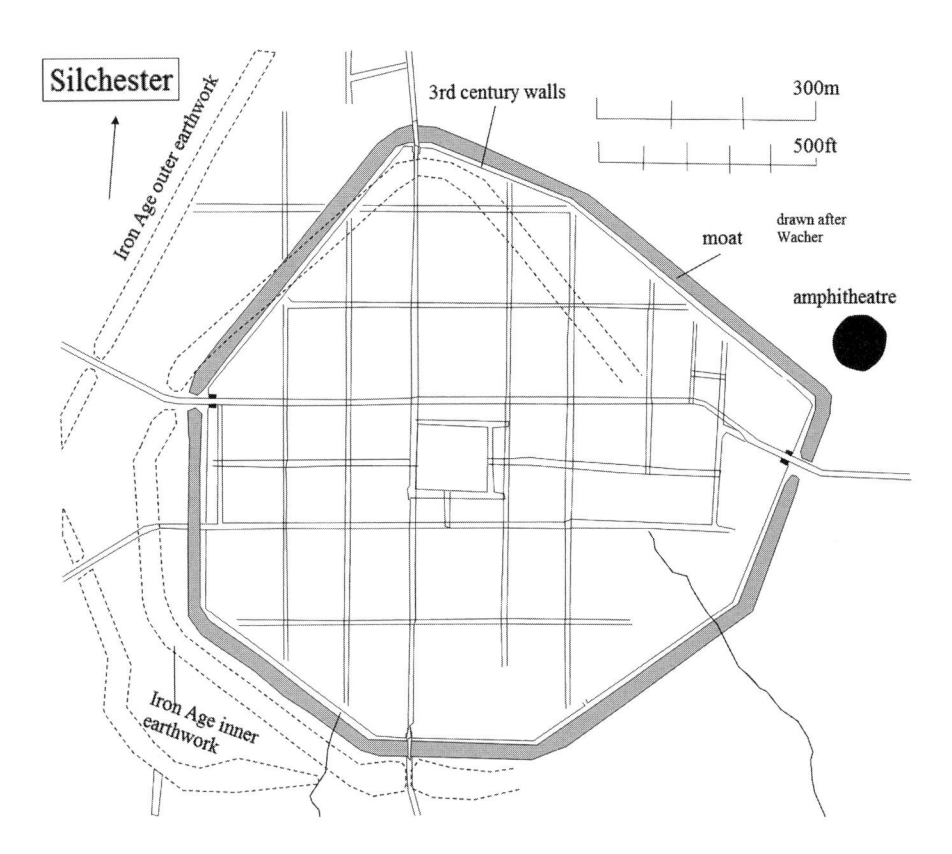

Modern historians have usually considered Constantine, the king of Britain, and his sons Constans, Aurelius Ambrosius and Utherpendragon to be confused memories of the usurper Constantine III (Constantinus III, *Augustus* in 407–411) and of his sons Constans II (*Augustus* in 409/410–411) and Julianus, because the names resemble each other and because Constans II was also a monk like Geoffrey's Constans. It is possible that this is so, but it is equally possible that there were actually several people with the same name and that the Armorican-Briton Constantine exploited his supposed/claimed bloodline by associating himself and his sons with the usurper Constantine III and with Constantine I the Great. It is even possible that Constans was made a monk in imitation. The names and circumstances would have added legitimacy for the new ruler, and I have here made the assumption that this was indeed the case and that Geoffrey has retained a muddled memory of this. It is not a coincidence that the name of Constantinus etc. abounds in the PLRE2.

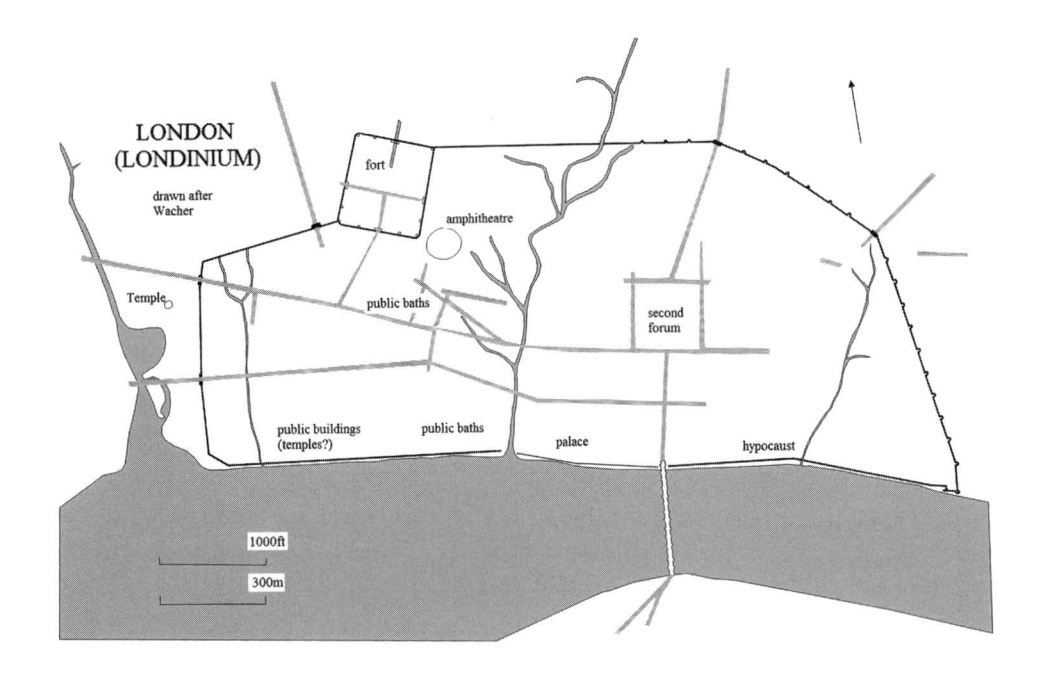

After the death of Constantine, the British leadership was at loss what to do. Some favoured Aurelius Ambrosius and others Utherpendragon (note that this is likely to be a mistake) or other relatives of Constantine. Vortigern, the leader of the Gewissei, exploited the situation, brought Constans to London and crowned him as king, then ruled in his name. Vortigern had *de facto* usurped power. He immediately started using the royal treasury to increase the size of his own retinue and buy the loyalty of the cities and garrisons.

After this, Vortigern moved on to remove Constans with the help of the Picts. He told Constans that the Picts intended to bring the Danes and Norwegians against the Britons, and that it would therefore be a good idea to use Picts as Constans' bodyguards so that Constans could use them as his spies. Note that Saxo Grammaticus claims that the Danes and Norwegians fought against the Britons under Frothi III, and that this event can be dated roughly to 429/430. It is therefore possible that Frothi did indeed attack the Britons rather than the Picts. However, the circumstances in the British Isles actually suggest that the object of Frothi's attack were the Picts (the Picts and their Saxon mercenaries had fleets that could threaten Denmark), so Frothi acted as an ally of the Britons and Romans (see Appendix 1). However, there still existed the danger that the Picts could ally with the Danes and it was this that Vortigern exploited. On the other hand, it is also possible to think that the Danes in this case actually meant the Saxons.

According to Geoffrey's version (6.7–8), Vortigern managed to convince the Picts that it would be in their best interest to kill Constans because, as a king, Vortigern could offer them greater advantages. The drunken Picts duly murdered Constans, with the result that Vortigern assembled the citizens of London to kill the traitors. Those in charge of Aurelius Ambrosius and 'Utherpendragon' (Guithelinus had died in the meanwhile) took them to Bretagne, where its king, Budicius, gave them a place of refuge. Since there was no-one to oppose him, Vortigern crowned himself as king of Britain. When the Picts learnt of Vortigern's treachery, they, together with the peoples that they had brought to Albany, revolted against him. It was then, according to Geoffrey, that Hengist and Horsa arrived in three ships. Since, with the exception of Nennius, all other sources (Gildas, the *Anglo-Saxon Chronicle* and Bede) date the arrival of Hengist and Horsa to the period after 441, or more precisely to 449–450,[13] and Geoffrey of Monmouth has left out the exploits of St Germanus against the Saxons and Picts and has not included Gildas' second instance in which the Romans brought forces to Britain, it seems probable that Geoffrey's account has jumped straight from 420–430 to 447–449.

This leaves open several possibilities, of which I list here the three likeliest. Firstly, it is possible that Geoffrey has just left out the exploits of St Germanus in about 429 and has then jumped to the period 432–441, when Vortigern would have murdered Constans with the help of the Picts.

Secondly, it is possible that Constans was already murdered in about 420–430 because it is clear that Aurelius Ambrosius was still a child when the murder took place and the circumstances would fit that timeframe. If the murder occurred in about 428–430, it would explain Geoffrey's referral to the imminent arrival of the Danes and Norwegians in Albany/Scotland as allies of the Picts and the subsequent murder of Constans by the Picts. In this case, the reason for the murder of Constans would have been Vortigern's double betrayal. He would have betrayed the Picts in the north (evidently at peace with the Britons; note their subsequent revolt against Vortigern) with his alliance with the Danes of Frothi III, and also betrayed the Picts in Constans' retinue by having them beheaded by the Londoners. This alternative also receives support from the claim of Geoffrey (6.9) that Aurelius Ambrosius was coming to a man's estate at the time of the arrival of Hengist and Horsa, which on the basis of the Gallic Chronicle 452 would take place in 441/442 or after.

The third alternative is that Frothi III attacked the Picts and Saxons as Vortigern's ally in about 429/30, and it was then the memory of this very recent invasion that Vortigern exploited in about 432–434 to convince Constans that the Danes and Norwegians were now planning to invade Britain. Vortigern claimed that the presence of Picts in Constans' unit of bodyguards would enable him to convince the Picts to side with him against the Danes and Norwegians. The invasion did not materialize because it had been invented by Vortigern merely to convince Constans to hire the Picts. The Danes and Picts continued to be allies of Vortigern. When the Picts then duly killed Constans on behalf of Vortigern in about 432–434, the Armoricans (i.e. the relatives of Constans) demanded that the West Roman government act against Vortigern, and when this did not happen, the Armorican Bacaudae revolted under the charismatic Tibatto in 435. At least this would seem the likeliest reason for the revolt of Tibatto mentioned by the Gallic Chronicle (a. 435, 437). Vortigern appears to have returned Britain into the bosom of the Roman Empire. This alternative receives further support from the claim of Geoffrey (6.9) that Aurelius Ambrosius was coming to a man's estate at the time of the arrival of Hengist and Horsa, which other sources date to 449/450. However, this would seem a rather late date.

The likeliest alternatives are the second and third ones, but it is ultimately impossible to know which of the possible versions is the correct one (if any). However, what appears certain is that the Picts and Saxons invaded Britain in about 427–430, and that it was the success of this invasion that caused Vortigern to ask help from the Romans in about 428. Vortigern and the local bishops faced double trouble. The desperate local population had started to seek comfort from the Pelagian heresy and the invaders had achieved considerable success. The Romans answered by sending a fleet and cavalry (according to Gildas) in about 429/430. It is probable that these forces were placed under the leadership of St Germanus, the Bishop of Auxerre. As noted previously, it was either in 429 or 430 that Frothi's fleet arrived in Albany, where his forces inflicted a defeat on the Picts and Saxons, the other alternative being that Frothi did indeed defeat the treacherous Vortigern somewhere in the north while St Germanus was in London with reinforcements. The former is more likely on the grounds that none of the extant sources mention any piratical raids against the Danes by the Britons at this date, which was the stated reason for Frothi's attack. Could it be that the Roman fleet which intervened was actually Frothi's fleet, while their cavalry force consisted of St Germanus' *bucellarii*? Consequently, I propose to complement Geoffrey's account at this point with information taken from Saxo Grammaticus (see Appendix 1), Nennius, Bede, Prosper and from Constantius' *Life of St Germanus*.[14]

3.4 The Alleluia Victory in 429/430

According to the *Life of St Germanus* (Constantius, *Vita S. Germani* 12ff., with Bede, *Eccl.* 19ff.; Prosper a. 429), the Britons sent a deputation to Gaul to ask help from the Catholic bishops against the Pelagian heretics. This was an important question because the Romans at this time controlled the population through religion. According to the *Vita*, the bishops gathered a great synod in Gaul and decided to dispatch Germanus (bishop of Autissiodorensis/Autessiodurum, mod. Auxerre) and Lupus (bishop of Tricasses/Trecassina/ Augustobona, mod. Troyes) to Britain. Prosper contradicts this by stating that the men were sent by Pope Celestius, but one may reconcile the versions if one presumes that the synod was convened by the Pope. It would actually be very surprising if the Pope had not been consulted. The Church, in its turn, must have coordinated its activities with the earthly authorities, because these operated hand-in-hand during this period. In light of this, it is not surprising that many of the bishops (like St Germanus) had military background or were former civil servants. Administrative and military backgrounds were particularly useful in Gaul and Britain, where the central administration had collapsed. It enabled the Roman government to guide the populace/flock through the bishops, who could also act as administrators and generals if necessary. At this time the Catholic Church was not really an independent entity but part of the imperial administration.

The distances between Britain, Gaul and Italy suggest that the British ambassadors probably arrived in Gaul in early 429 (the date given by Prosper for the arrival of St Germanus in Britain). It seems probable that St Germanus and Lupus then embarked on ships at Bononia very early in 429, which would explain the storm their ship faced.

Even though Constantine fails to mention this, it seems very probable that St Germanus was accompanied by cavalry. This would be the personal retinue of St Germanus mentioned by Nennius. There are four pieces of evidence to back up this suggestion. Firstly, St Germanus leads soldiers at the Alleluia Battle. Secondly, Nennius mentions St Germanus' retinue in connection with military activity. Thirdly, it is probable that St Germanus' campaign is the instance mentioned by Gildas in which the Romans dispatched cavalry and a fleet to assist the Britons against the Picts, after which the Britons built a better wall. Fourthly, it is possible to connect St Germanus with Wat's and Offa's Dykes because the Alleluia Battle was fought in Mold, which is located close to those dykes. Consequently, I would suggest that St Germanus, as a former military man, acted as the military brains of the expedition, while his fellow bishop, Lupus, offered him advice on religious matters. The reason for the use of St. Germanus' retinue rather than 'legions', as previously, would have been the vast problems the West Romans were facing at the time (see *MHLR* Vol. 4).

The Synod had made the right choice. Both of these bishops were charismatic figures, and St Germanus was also a gifted military commander. Constantius, in his *Life of St Germanus* (1–2) states that Germanus had risen to the rank of *dux* of more than one province before his election as bishop, which took place in about 418. M.E. Jones (pp.369–370) suggests that Germanus had the rank of *Dux Tractus Armoricani et Nervicani*. In fact, it was the local populace that had forced Germanus to become their bishop and protector against the imperial tax gatherers and officials. Germanus conceded, sent his wife to a nunnery and became a bishop.[15] Germanus had the presence of mind and the right connections to protect the populace. Regardless, it is still clear that he did not become the tool of the local populace, but rather an instrument of the imperial authorities. In essence, the imperial administration outsourced the governance of the area to St Germanus and the Catholic Church. St Germanus acted very wisely and sought to spread the Catholic faith and imperial control among the barbarians (mainly Goths) settled in Aquitania (*Vita* 6ff.) by establishing a new monastery. He also acted as a mediator between the locals, imperial administration and Church, which enabled the Roman government to retain its grip on North-West Gaul and Britain. In fact, Constantius (7, 9) claims that Germanus performed his role as bishop as if he was still a *dux*, and in this capacity also acted as a sort of detective, interrogator and social worker (he cured many thieves, much like G.K. Chesterton's modern fictitious character Father Brown).

The bishops crossed the Channel in a storm, possibly because they did not have to fear Saxon pirates in such weather. When the bishops reached Britain, the populace greeted them enthusiastically. Their arrival strengthened the position of the Catholic Church immediately, but more was needed. The bishops gathered a public debate, which was probably held somewhere near London. The hagiography naturally claims that the Pelagians lost their debate with Germanus, but this was apparently not enough, because St Germanus was forced to stage a miracle to convince the doubters. Consequently, while the debate was still going on, a tribune, his wife and 'blind' 10-year-old daughter approached the bishops. Germanus duly performed a miracle and cured the girl's eyes. The gullible populace was duly impressed and abandoned the false doctrine. It is quite obvious that the 'miracle' had been orchestrated for this purpose.[16] It is even possible that Germanus was the tribune's old commander. After the Pelagian problem had been solved satisfactorily, the bishops travelled to the shrine of St Alban/Albanus, which was probably located in modern St Albans (Verulamium, see map on page 102).

According to Constantius, St Germanus was then forced to remain in some unnamed locale for some time because he had suffered an injury. It was there that another 'miracle' took place. When several houses were burned down, the bishop's house was 'miraculously' saved. Could it be that the Pelagians had attempted to murder St Germanus through arson? Or should we connect this fire with the torching of the city of King Belinus/Benli mentioned by Nennius? It is obviously quite impossible to know.

Constantius follows this with the story of the famous Alleluia Victory, which places St Germanus in Mold close to the dykes in the area, which is also close to the area where St Germanus chastised King Belinus/Benli. The order of events in Nennius is that St Germanus destroyed Benli years before the Alleluia Victory, which is clearly a mistake, while Constantius does not even mention the Benli incident. This means that it is impossible to say with absolute certainty whether St Germanus had already moved against the rebel Benli in 429, as implied by the order of events in Nennius, before his fight against the Picts and Saxons, or the other way around. If the former is true, then St Germanus moved against Benli during the winter/spring of 429, because Benli had revolted against Vortigern and it was necessary to destroy Benli before the enemy arrived in the region. It is quite possible that Benli had even invited the Saxons and Picts to help him against Vortigern. If the latter is true, then St Germanus engaged Benli because he had refused to cooperate in the defence of the area against the Saxons and Picts. The former appears more likely.

It is notable that the Romans did not send a legion in this case but cavalry forces, and from Nennius' account we know that St Germanus was accompanied by his companions/cavalry retinue. In other words, this force would have been St Germanus's personal retinue, which he would have formed while he was still a *dux*. It was his private army. It is also probable that the Romans did not dispatch a regular fleet, but an allied fleet provided by Frothi (see Appendix 1), hence the need to cross the Channel during a storm. It was also easier to correct the Pelagian heresy during the winter when there was a break in hostilities. It is therefore probable that St Germanus' next mission would have been to engage the foreign invaders when they arrived in the following spring, but this mission was interrupted by the revolt of Benli.

As noted above, instead of dealing with the events of the Alleluia Victory, which is covered in the later chapter 47, Nennius (32–33) includes an account of St Germanus's dealings against King Belinus/Benli. This incident is not recorded in the *Vita*, but in light of the role St Germanus enjoyed in Britain as military commander, it is entirely plausible that this event also took place during his stay. According to Nennius' version, St Germanus and his attendants/retinue appeared before the gate of a city in the county of Powys (Pouisorum/Ial). He aimed to chastise the king for his behaviour. The king, however, refused to let him in. It was then that one of the king's servants, Catel Drunluc (Catellius), gave St Germanus his own suburban house for use. The next morning, St Germanus once again asked for an audience, but in vain. It was then that one of the locals prostrated before St Germanus and recited his belief in the Holy Trinity. When this man then entered the city, he was killed by the king's prefect. St Germanus and his retinue stayed before the gates for the entire day, after which St Germanus advised his host to bring out all his friends from the city because 'fire would fall from the heaven' during the night and would burn the entire city, together with its inhabitants and king. A more prosaic reason for this would of course be that St Germanus did arrive before the city with his military retinue, consisting of his *bucellarii*, and that his host betrayed his native city to this force to be burned to the ground. St Germanus rewarded Catel with the dukedom of Powys, which his descendants still governed when Nennius wrote his treatise. In my opinion, there is every reason to believe that this event actually took place during St Germanus' trip to Britain in about 429, and that he provided not only religious but also military leadership to back up his preaching. It is the presence of the military retinue that his hagiography has left out on religious grounds. The fact that St Germanus killed a *rex* and replaced him with a *dux* suggests that he restored the area to Roman control. It was presumably after this that St Germanus was informed of the Saxon threat to the northern portion of the dyke, near Chester and Mold. In light of this, it is probable that St Germanus fought the Alleluia Battle only after the dyke had already been built.

The so-called Pillar of Eliseg set up by the king of Powys in about 800 claims that Vortigern had created the kingdom and placed Brittu (Bruttius) as its ruler, and that St Germanus had blessed this Bruttius. This suggests that the person blessed by St Germanus was Catellius Bruttius (Catel Drunluc). The text also claims that Vortigern was the son-in-law of Maximus. According to Morris, Powys was a Welsh spelling of the Latin *pagenses*, the populace of the rural areas. In this case it implied that the upland territories of the Cornovii had been separated from the city of Wroxeter. In other words, it appears probable that Vortigern had dispatched St Germanus to the border regions of Wales, where St Germanus implemented Vortigern's military programme to subdue those who resisted the authority of the British Council (the so-called '12 wise men') and posed a potential threat if they would form an alliance with the invading hordes of Picts and Saxons. These potential deserters apparently consisted of the Irish settlers of Cornovia. Notably, the hill fort of Moel Fenli in this region preserves the name of Benli/Belinus, and may have been the scene of St. Germanus' operations against Belinus.[17]

According to Constantius' account, the Saxons and Picts had joined their forces and invaded Britain while St Germanus was still suffering from his injury. The Britons had been forced to withdraw their army into their camp (presumably in Chester). One cannot preclude the possibility that the Pelagians and the invaders would have cooperated, even if this is not mentioned. The British soldiers asked St Germanus and Lupus to help them, and the bishops hastened to the scene of operations. Constantius fails to mention the place where St Germanus had rested, but my guess is that it was the city of Benli.

The traditional location for the subsequent battle is near Mold in Flintshire, but Hoare (p.300) notes that it is possible that the St Germanus of Auxerre has been mixed with the St Germanus of Man in the Celtic tradition (the Celtic name for Germanus being Garmon). It is also odd to find the Saxons cooperating with the Picts on the west coast, but not impossible. If the identities have been mixed, then the subsequent battle would have taken place somewhere north of London, probably

Chester/Deva
(drawn after Bishop)

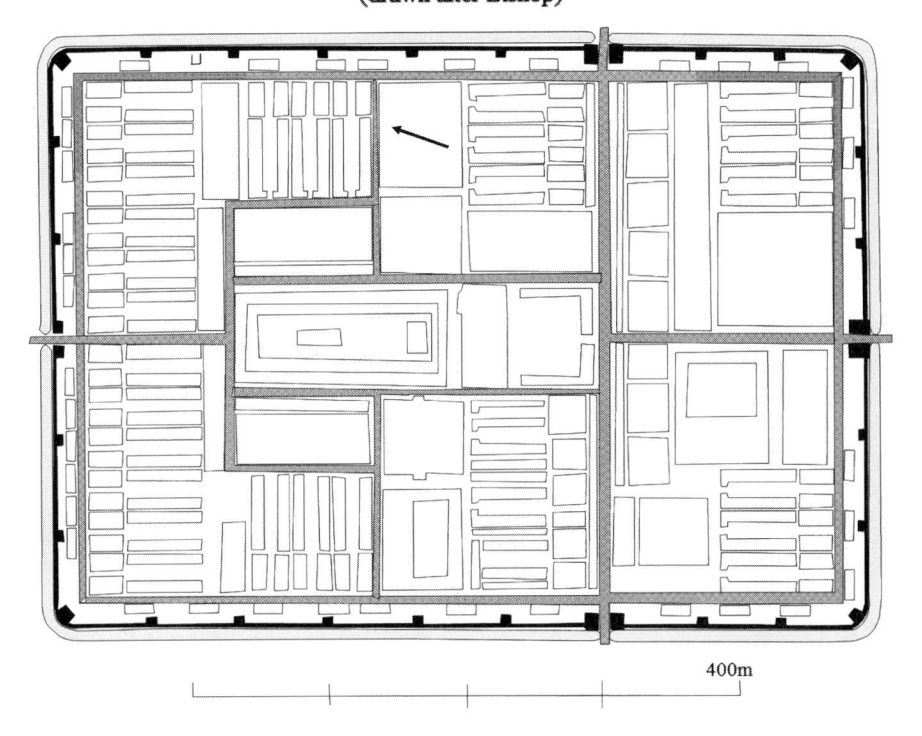

400m

near Braughing. However, if the traditional locale for the battle is correct, and I would suggest that it is, then it is clear that the Picts had formed an alliance with the Saxons (perhaps these Saxons are the Ambrones of Geoffrey, who would have stayed in the north or alternatively the Danes). This was very advantageous because the Saxons possessed bigger ships that could transport more men to the objective. The attackers also appear to have attempted to surprise the Britons by invading early in the spring – the season of Lent in 429 (or at the latest in 430). Consequently, the local forces would have been completely surprised and hopelessly outnumbered when the invaders landed their forces. It is not at all surprising that the defenders chose to retreat to their camp and call for help.

The sources do not give any army sizes, but one can make some educated guesses based on the location of the battle and circumstances in the area. The Saxons very rarely employed large fleets, so an invasion force of about 10,000–15,000 men would already have been a truly major campaign. The Picts appear to have employed even smaller naval forces, with an approximate upper limit of about 4,000–5,000 men (see *Military History of Late Rome*, Vols.1–2). This means that the maximum size for this invading force would have been no more than 15,000 footmen, but it is probable that the Romans had even fewer men to oppose them, because most of their regular forces were in the north. One may make the educated guess that the local paramilitary forces had no more than 4,000 to 5,000 men based at Chester/Deva in the old legionary camp of *Legio XX Valeria* to oppose them. In addition to these, one should also count the cavalry retinue of St Germanus, which cannot have been smaller than 1,000–2,000 horsemen for it to have made the difference it apparently did. Just before the battle on the Easter Day in about 429, St Germanus encouraged the troops with religious ceremonies that were held in the temporary church built inside the marching camp. After this he placed some lightly-equipped expediti troops in ambush on the higher ground along the enemy's route of approach.

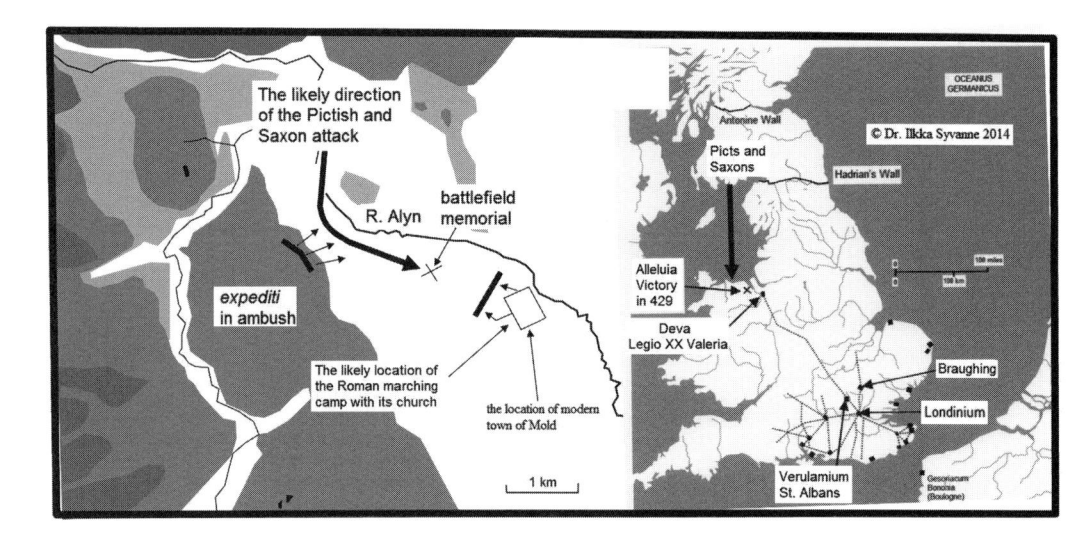

Being well versed in military matters, St Germanus intended to magnify the effect of his ambush by ordering all troops to shout in unison the battle-cry 'Alleluia' when he and Lupus gave the signal. The unsuspecting enemies crossed the river and marched towards the Roman camp. When they had passed the ambush, St Germanus and Lupus shouted together the 'Alleluia' three times, which was repeated in unison by the entire Romano-British army. The shout echoed loudly back and forth in the confined space and magnified the sound, with the result that the surprised and surrounded barbarians panicked, threw away their weapons and ran. Some of them were drowned in the river. Constantius claims that the rout of the enemy had been achieved without any bloodshed. This may be true as far as the Romans are concerned, but it is clear that the pursuing Romans would not have spared any of the fleeing barbarians whom they managed to catch. It is quite probable, as noted by M.E. Jones, that Constantius was at pains to exonerate the bishops of the guilt of having shed blood when he claimed that it was a bloodless victory. The bishops had achieved a complete victory over the invaders and the Britons were able to collect the booty scattered around the field. According to Constantius, this victory over the barbarians had secured Britain and its wealth, and so it remained until 441.

There is no doubt in my mind that M.E. Jones is correct in stating that St Germanus' Alleluia Victory proves that the essential features of Roman military organization, civil government, cities and Christianity had survived almost intact in Britain. I would actually go so far as to claim that Britain remained securely part of the Roman Empire and that several of the old Roman units remained stationed on the island in the north. The only real difference with the past was that the British field army had been replaced by a paramilitary citizen militia and that local magnates and their cities possessed field forces of their own consisting of a mix of citizen militias, mercenaries and private retinues. On the basis of the accounts of Gildas, Bede, Nennius and Constantius, the Britons considered themselves part of the Roman Empire at least until 446/447, and probably even beyond that, as the legend of Arthur proves.

According to Gerald of Wales/Giraldus Cambriensis (Wales, 2.4, 2.18), Germanus of Auxerre and Lupus of Troyes were so successful in their endeavour to put a stop to the Pelagian heresy in Wales that the Welshmen were still following their teachings in the twelfth century. The only lapse back into the Pelagian heresy appears to have taken place in about 471.

St Germanus' military/religious mission to Britain was followed by another religious mission by Palladius, who was dispatched by Pope Celestine to Ireland in 430 or 431. Palladius strengthened the orthodoxy among the Britons and then sailed to Ireland to convert them, but was forced to return to Britain where he died shortly afterwards. In the following year, 431 or 432, his mission was taken over by British monk Patrick (who was educated and trained in St Germanus' monastery), and as is well known his mission met with great success (see Appendix 4).

There also exists a tradition according to which St Germanus took with him Vortigern's incestuous son, Faustus, and raised and educated him in the Christian doctrine so that he eventually became a bishop and founder of a large monastery on the banks of the River Renis (Nennius 47–48). The problem with this is that it is possible that Nennius has confused Arthur's successor, Vortipore, who married his daughter, with Vortigern. In addition to this, Nennius has clearly confused the exploits of St Germanus and Aurelius Ambrosius with each other, so that St Germanus becomes the man who chases Vortigern, the daughter of Hengist and Vortigern's other wives (including his daughter) to his last hideout, the castle of Cair Guothergirn in the kingdom of Dimetae, and then burns the castle with heavenly fire that fell from heaven. I believe this man was actually Aurelius Ambrosius and the heavenly fire consisted of fire-bombs shot by stone throwers. This also raises the possibility that Faustus was actually the son of Belinus/Benli, because we can definitely connect St Germanus with that siege. However, one cannot entirely rule out the possibility that there was a germ of truth behind the story. The reasons for this are: 1) Vortigern was definitely a lusty old man; 2) there really existed a British bishop Faustus in Gaul who was educated by St Patrick.

Ashe has noted an interesting possibility regarding the bishop Faustus, which may suggest that the man was indeed Vortigern's son who was born between 405 and 410, and that he had a nephew from Britain called Riocatus. Sidonius, the famous Bishop of Clermont, corresponded with this Faustus and on one occasion, after having become bishop in about 470, noted that Riocatus had been staying with Faustus. In light of this, it is not surprising that Sidonius also knew the British High King Riothamus, as we shall see.[18]

The missions of Palladius and St Patrick to Ireland are recorded by several sources. The *Irish Annals*[19] usually place the mission of Palladius to 431 and St Patrick to 432, but in light of the tendency for the Irish sources to place events too late, it is possible that Bede is correct in placing both missions a year earlier.

It is very difficult to see how Palladius could have convinced the pagan rulers of Ireland to convert without the threat or use of force, just as was the case when the southern Baltic coasts and Finland were converted to Christianity through force.[20] It is far more likely that Palladius' mission to Ireland resembled those Crusades, and that he landed his army in Ireland in about 430/431 and then forced the local rulers to convert, or at least to allow the presence of priests in their territory. The fact that Palladius did not remain in Ireland, but returned to Britain, supports the same conclusion, as does the above-mentioned entry in the *Irish Annals* if it is interpreted as I do. Another possible reason for the campaign would have been to force Irish High King Loegaire to acknowledge Roman supremacy, if he had not expressed this after the death of his father Niall in Roman service. In fact, it is possible that Frothi's invasion of Ireland is connected with this effort (see Appendices 1 and 4). On the basis of this, it is clear that St Germanus' religious and military operations in Britain in 429/430 were very effective. It was thanks to this campaign that the Britons were able to turn the tables and start threatening the Irish coasts. As I have already shown in the case of St Germanus, we should be far more sceptical regarding the miracle stories of the saints than is usually the case. It is inherently more likely that most of the conversions resulting from the so-called 'miracles' were either the result of tricks performed by professional 'magicians' (in this case the bishops) or were forced on the populace by the presence of armed retinues (see also Appendix 4) – or are there any historians around who still believe that the miracles really took place?

In my opinion, it is probable that the entry dated to 434 in the *Irish Annals*, which states that the Saxons plundered Ireland for the first time, refers to a British raid of the Irish coast, and that we should connect it with the letter of St Patrick which he sent to the soldiers of Coroticus. The other possibility is that St Patrick's letter referred to some unknown instance that took place at a later time. According to Charles-Edwards, the Saxons in the *Irish Annals* usually meant the English (i.e. Anglo-Saxons), which in this case probably meant the Saxons. My view, however, is that we should rather consider the 'Saxons' of this era to be the Britons, despite the appearance of the Saxons in the Irish Sea. The other alternative is that the Saxons really did raid Ireland for the first time in 434, but if they did so, they saw no immediate benefit in continuing their raids, which suggests that the Irish defended their territory quite effectively. The unknown Coroticus commanded Romano-Britons who had killed and captured Christian Irishmen and then sold them as slaves to the Scots and apostate Picts – and this when even the pagan Franks were prepared to sell their Christian captives back to the Roman Gauls in return for a ransom. St Patrick naturally demanded that the Christian captives be set free. If St Patrick managed to obtain this, he obviously strengthened his own standing among the Irish. It is unfortunate that we do not know what the result of this request was (see also Appendix 4).

3.5 The Revolt of Armorica 435–437 (see *MHLR* Vol. 4 with the PLRE2 for further details)

As noted above, it seems probable that the revolt of the Armorican 'Bacaudae' against the imperial authorities under the charismatic leader Tibatto should be connected with the murder of Constans by Vortigern, and the refusal of Aetius to assist the Armoricans against Vortigern. We do not know why Aetius would have chosen to do so, and whether the revolt of the Burgundians against Aetius took place before, at the same time or after the revolt of Armorica. The reasons for the Burgundian revolt are also unknown, but the two likeliest possibilities are that they resented the favouritism shown by Aetius towards the Huns, their traditional enemies, or that they exploited the revolt of Armorica. What is known is that the Burgundians revolted in *Germania I* and invaded the neighbouring *Belgica*.

Aetius' response to the double revolt was to divide his field forces in two. He sent the *comes* Litorius with the Hun cavalry against the Armoricans, while he himself marched against the Burgundians. The sources do not state the numbers involved, but one can make some educated guesses on the basis of the enemy numbers and territory to be occupied. On the basis of this, it is clear that Litorius must have had at least 30,000–40,000 men. This is a bare minimum because he was later able to engage the much more numerous Visigoths with the same army. Aetius must have had at least 50,000–60,000 men for him to be able to face the Burgundian army of 50,000–80,000 men.[21] The rest of the soldiers would have been left to secure both Italy and southern Gaul against possible hostile action by the Visigoths. Aetius defeated the Burgundians, but they revolted almost immediately after he had left the scene. Litorius was similarly successful against the Armoricans, but had a harder time than Aetius because it took until 437 for him to crush the revolt. Tibatto was captured and the rest of the rebel leaders either killed or captured, but as a result of peace negotiations they appear to have been released on condition that they would henceforth remain loyal to the imperial government. Aetius had undoubtedly ordered Litorius to reach some sort of accommodation with the Armoricans because the revolt of the Burgundians and Visigoths in Gaul in 436 and the revolt of the Suevi in Spain required the transfer of all available forces against them. In these circumstances, Aetius was forced to adopt a defensive posture for 436, and it was only after the Armoricans had been pacified that Aetius was able to resume the offensive. Litorius was ordered to relieve the city of Narbonne, which was besieged by the Visigoths, while Aetius and his Huns advanced against the Burgundians. Narbonne was relieved and the Burgundians crushed. However, it took until 440 for Gaul to be fully pacified. Armorica enjoyed a short respite from hostilities after 437, but difficulties restarted in 441 when the Picts and Saxons started to raid Britain.

3.6. Britain, Armorica and Bishop St Germanus in 441–445 (see *MHLR* Vol. 4 for further details)

The sources provide too few details of the events between 441 and 445 to make any certain conclusions, but the following is my attempt to shed light on the events of these years.

According to the *Gallic Chronicle* (ca.441), the Britons were subjected to the authority of the Saxons in 441. This presumably meant that the Saxons had invaded, so the Britons once again dispatched an urgent plea for help to Rome. This was answered as previously with the dispatch of the Bishop St Germanus to Britain (*Constantius* 25ff.). St Germanus' second trip to Britain has usually been dated to 448, but in my opinion 441/442 or 444/445 are more likely.[22] This time St Germanus' religious advisor was the Bishop of Trier, Severus. In other words, the roles were the same as previously. St Germanus took care of the military side of the campaign with his personal retinue, and performed some fake miracles to convince the populace to adopt the orthodox doctrine, while Severus advised St Germanus on matters of religious doctrine. According to the *Vita*, the official reason for the visit of St Germanus was the need to crush the Pelagian heresy on the island. I would suggest that the resurfacing of this heresy on the island should be connected with the simultaneous Saxon invasion. The people were just seeking some consolation from the heretical version of Christianity, which official Roman policy considered tantamount to treason.

When the bishops arrived in Britain, they were greeted by Elafius, one of the leading men of the country. He had brought with him his 'crippled' son so that the bishops could perform a staged miracle/show for the crowds that had gathered to witness the arrival of the holy men. Unsurprisingly, St Germanus healed the son and the superstitious populace was once again impressed by the 'miracle', which enabled the bishops to hold fiery sermons against the heresy. The authorities rounded up the Pelagian preachers and exiled them to the continent, presumably mainly to Armorica. The fact that the Pelagians were banished to Gaul proves quite

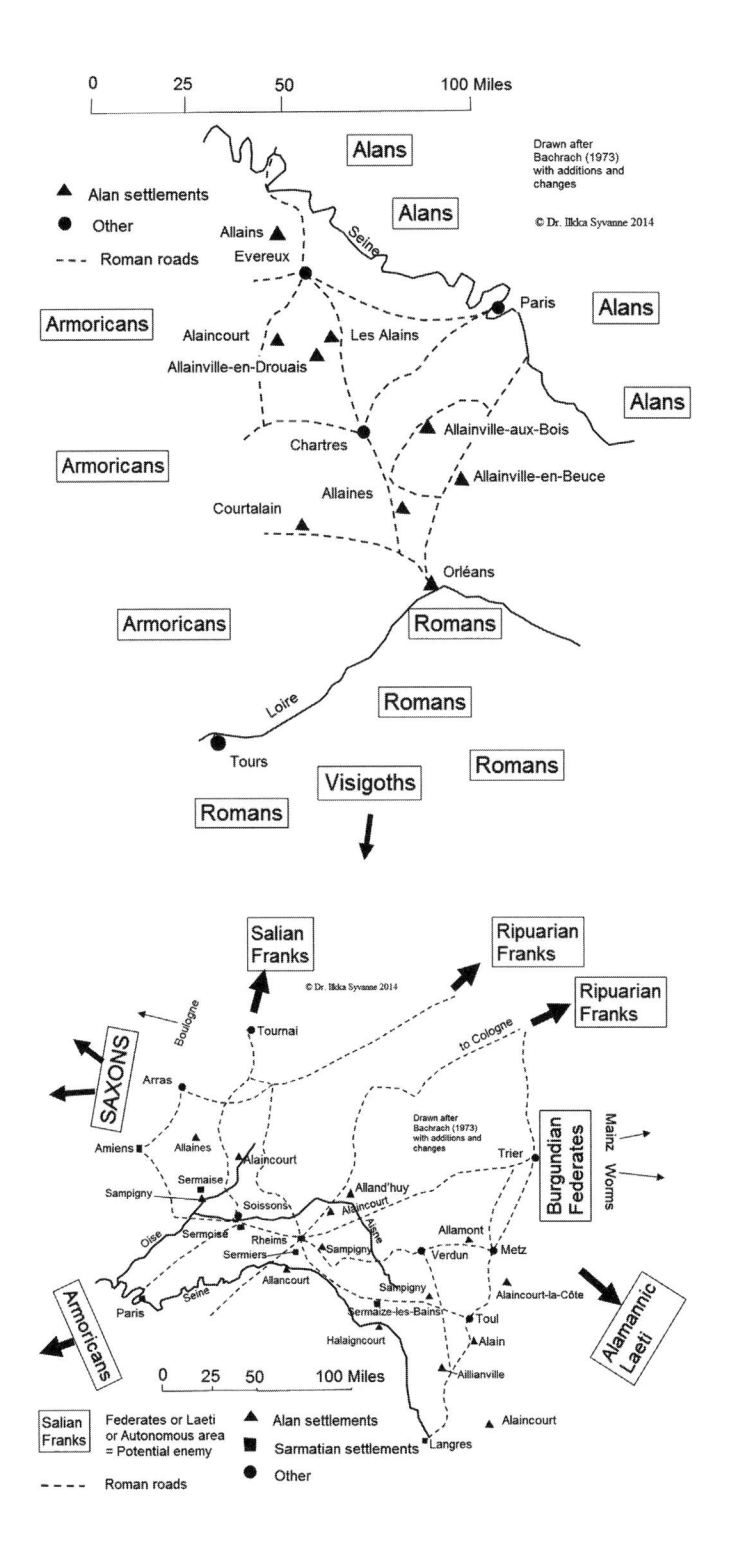

The Main Narrative with Geoffrey of Monmouth Included   73

nicely that Britain was still considered part of the Roman Empire. According to Constantius, the Pelagian heresy was so thoroughly uprooted from Britain that it was still staunchly Catholic at the time when Constantius wrote his hagiography of St Germanus in the 480s.

St Germanus' operations in Britain appear to have brought only a temporary respite from the worst ravages, because the Britons dispatched envoys to Rome to seek help again in 443 and/or 446. St Germanus and Severus returned to Gaul in 442, but had a new crisis on their hands. A delegation of Armoricans confronted St Germanus when he set foot on Armorican soil. The envoys begged his help in an effort to avert a war. We do not know what the reason for the disturbance was, but the usual suggestion is that the revolt of Armorica against Aetius was caused by the settlement of Alans south-west of the Seine. This view appears to be true, because the *Gallic Chronicle* states that the Alans took over the land by force and drove out the owners in 442. The first map by Bachrach of the Alan settlements lists the known locations of the Alan settlers in the areas previously dominated by the Armoricans. Kouznetsov and Lebedynsky (106ff.), however, suggest that there may have also been settlements of Alans further west.

The second of the maps drawn after Bachrach shows the territories from which the Alans advanced to the areas occupied by the Armoricans. It is very probable that some of the Alans remained there and did not move further west. The Seine region clearly possessed a very significant concentration of Alan cavalry. Note that the Burgundians were later resettled by Aetius in 'Burgundy', where we shall meet them when King Arthur makes his appearance.

This begs the question why the *Patricius* Aetius ordered such a move, the likeliest answer being that he wanted to reward the loyal Alans of King Goar by settling his men on territory held by the disloyal Armoricans, which also weakened the latter. The natural result of this was the revolt, but it had not yet started at the time St Germanus arrived and Goar's forces had not yet started full-scale hostilities to drive out all of the inhabitants from the areas promised to them. The reason for this conclusion is that when St Germanus had heard of the trouble, he immediately advanced to block the route of advance of the iron-clad cavalry forces of the Alans by riding forward to meet King Goar, who was surrounded by his *catervae* of cavalry. Germanus requested through an interpreter that the king should not invade, but to no avail. After this, St Germanus chastized the king, seized Goar's bridle and stopped him and the army with his bold gesture. St Germanus was clearly an old campaigner ready to resort to any trick. The surprised Goar lost his composure. He dismounted, pitched camp on the spot and agreed to the demands, on condition that St Germanus obtained a pardon for the Armoricans from the emperor or Aetius. He promised to wait until St Germanus obtained the pardon. St. Germanus set out for Italy in secret, but his cover was blown and his mission ended in failure. The Armoricans had meanwhile revolted again under Tibatto, with the result that Goar had launched a full-scale attack. On top of that, St Germanus contracted an illness and died on 31 July 442 or 444/445. We know only one detail of the resulting war between Tibatto's Bacaudae and Romans: the Armorican rebels attacked Aetius' lieutenant Majorian (Maiorianus) at Tours.[23] It is usually assumed that the revolt was quashed primarily by the Alans in about 445, but it is possible that resistance continued at least until 448. The reason for this conclusion is that the *Gallic Chronicle* mentions that the physician Eudoxius fled to the Huns in 448. The *Chronicle* claims that he had perverse talents as a Bacaudae leader, which may imply that resistance continued at least until that date. In my opinion, it is less likely that the revolt restarted in 448. Attila undoubtedly entertained the possibility of using Eudoxius as his puppet, but in this he was to be disappointed because the Armoricans united as one man behind Aetius against the invading Huns in 451. The Huns were a threat of an entirely different calibre than the Roman authorities.

Two decisions undertaken by Aetius during those long years were to have a profound effect on the course of British and European history. The first of these was the settlement of Burgundians in Sapaudia (Savoy) in 443. The second was Aetius's refusal to help the Britons when they pleaded their case before him in 446. It is also possible that he may have refused a similar request in 443 (*ASC* 443).

Chapter 4

Vortigern and the Rise of the Saxons[1]

According to the *Gallic Chronicle 452*, the Saxon dominance of Britain began in AD 441/442, which would date it to the period just after the trip of St Germanus in about 441. This is problematic because Gildas 19 claims that the Britons dispatched a plea for help to Aetius in late 445 or early 446, and Geoffrey and other sources date the arrival of Saxon mercenaries to the period after that. It is also clear that the Saxons did not start their hostiles against the Romans at that time, because according to Gildas the invaders in 445/446 were the Picts and Scots who disembarked their army just south of Hadrian's Wall. It is of course possible to think that the Saxon dominance meant merely their arrival as mercenaries. Another way to reconcile the sources would of course be to assume that the Ambrones of Geoffrey (Saxons?) had remained in the north and would have formed part of the invading force. This would also explain the plea for help in 443 which is included in the *Anglo-Saxon Chronicle*. The garrison on Hadrian's Wall (this must mean collectively all of the garrisons) was a useless bunch of cowards, according to Gildas. When the garrison then abandoned the wall, the frightened Britons abandoned their cities and dispersed in flight, but the 'Saxons' pursued them relentlessly. The situation was aggravated by the fact that the Britons started a civil war. It was at this moment that the last few remaining defenders decided to seek help from Aetius (Gildas 20–23, tr. by Giles):

> 'Again, therefore, the wretched remnant, send to Aetius, a powerful Roman citizen, address him as follows: – "To Aetius now Consul for the third time [i.e. in 446]: the groans of the Britons." ... "The Barbarians drive us to the sea; the sea throws us back on the barbarians: thus two modes of death await us, we are either slain or drowned." The Romans, however, could not assist them, and in the meantime the discomfited people, wandering in the woods, began to feel the effects of a severe famine, which compelled many of them without delay to yield themselves up to their cruel persecutors, to obtain subsistence; other of them, however, lying hidden in mountains, caves, amid woods, continually sallied out from thence to renew the war. And then it was, for the first time, that they overthrew their enemies, who for so many years had been living in their country, [it is not known with any certainty what number of years this means, but it is clear that the Britons who offered effective resistance consisted mainly of the least Romanized Celtic tribes of Wales and Cornwall. The old Caesarian

view that the more civilized the tribesmen became as a result of their contacts with Roman civilization, the less warlike they became, appears to be true. The likeliest reasons for this are that the least civilized tribes were more used to hardships and were also more prepared to organize themselves militarily, because they did not expect the central government to act on their behalf] for their trust was not in man, but in God; … The boldness of the enemy was for a while checked, but not the wickedness of our countrymen: the enemy left our people, but the people did not leave their sins. … The audacious invaders therefore return to their winter quarters, determined before long again to return and plunder. And they too, the Picts for the first time seated themselves at the extremity of the island, where they afterwards continued, occasionally plundering and wasting our country. During these truces, the wounds of the distressed people are healed, but another sore, still more venomous, broke out. No sooner were the ravages of the enemy checked, than the island was deluged with … every kind of luxury and licentiousness. … Kings were anointed, not according to God's ordinance, but such as showed themselves more cruel than the rest; and soon after, they were put to death by those who had elected them, without any inquiry into their merits, but because others still more cruel were chosen to succeed them. … For a council was called to settle what was best and most expedient to be done, in order to repel such frequent and fatal irruptions and plunderings of the above named nations [this would be the famous Round Table, which would have been modelled after the older provincial council]. Then all councillors, together with that proud tyrant Gurthrigern [Vortigern], the British king, were so blinded, that, as a protection to their country, they sealed its doom by inviting in among them (like wolves into the sheep-fold) the fierce and impious Saxons, a race hateful both to God and men, to repel the invasions of the northern nations.'

Aetius clearly decided not to send any help to the Britons in 446, but this was not such a great disaster as often thought because the Britons could defeat the invaders on their own, which means that Aetius' decision was the correct one. The damage caused by the invaders, however, was such that very large numbers of Britons, who considered living conditions on the island to be intolerable, fled to Armorica, with the result that it came to be called Brittany/Bretagne. The real disaster for the Britons was Vortigern's decision to employ Saxons as his mercenaries which happened probably either in 441 or 443/4 or in 446/7.

The fact that Armoricans, Saxons and probably also Britons[2] fought under Aetius against Attila the Hun in Gaul in 451 proves that the rulers of Britain and Armorica still acknowledged the Romans as their overlords. Since both Armorica and Britain were clearly governed by their own rulers, it is probable that these had formed similar *foedera* (treaties) with Rome as the barbarians. The threat posed by Attila to all in the West was such that all *foederati* and subjects of the emperor were quite ready to show their loyalty and unite their forces against the common enemy.

In sum, the pacification of Britain and Armorica meant that both areas continued to recognize the Roman emperor, even if both areas – especially Britain – had become autonomous or even independent states which no longer paid any taxes to the emperor.

It was about this time, in 441–446 or 446–449, that the exiled Aurelius Ambrosius had come into adulthood and had become a real threat to Vortigern's rule.[3] In 441 or 443 Vortigern faced a real problem. He did not receive any support from the Romans while the Armoricans (including Aurelius Ambrosius) were his enemies. The arrival of three ships in Kent bearing Saxons and the brothers Hengist and Horsa must have felt like a godsend. Vortigern met the brothers in Canterbury and agreed to hire them. The Saxons were very useful allies against the Armoricans and Picts (and Ambrones?). This would have happened at some point during 441/442 or 443/444. Soon after this, a huge army of Picts advanced from Albany to ravage the north. Vortigern assembled his army and met the enemy north of the Humber. The Saxon mercenaries distinguished themselves in combat and defeated the Picts. It is quite clear that there were now more Saxons in the army than those carried in the three ships. The grateful Vortigern gave Hengist and his men lands in Lindsey. When Hengist realized that Vortigern was entirely reliant on the Saxons, Hengist suggested that he could invite even more soldiers from Germany/Scythia in return for a title (earl or prince) and a city. Vortigern agreed to enlarge Hengist's domains, but did not agree to grant him a title or city. Either sixteen (Nennius) or eighteen (Geoffrey) ships arrived from Germany/Scythia fully laden with men. On board one of them was Hengist's daughter, Renwein, whom he planned to marry to the lusty king. Vortigern swallowed the bait and married Hengist's daughter. The Saxons were given Kent in return for the marriage pact and Hengist became the king's principal advisor. Gorangonus, the Earl (*Regulus*/minor king) of Kent was forced to give up his territory and presumably fled to Bretagne.

After this, Vortigern agreed to invite more of Hengist's relatives to settle as defenders near the wall (Wall of Gual in Nennius = Hadrian's Wall) between Deira and Scotland. Hengist's sons, Octa/Octha and Ebissa, brought with them forty ships (*chiulis*, keels) of warriors. They were joined by a man called Cherdic so that their entire force consisted of 300 ships. Since the average crew size of the Norwegian warship was between thirty-five and seventy men, one can estimate a minimum of 10,500 men and a maximum of 21,000, with an average figure of 15,750. En route, they pillaged the Orkneys and captured some territories belonging to the Picts. After this, Hengist continued to call ever more of his countrymen to Kent, with the result that some of the islands (Frisian Islands and/or islands off the coast of Gaul?) became deserted.

The influx of Saxons worried the other Briton leaders, with the result that they asked the king to put a stop to it. Vortigern refused because he knew that his own position depended on Saxon support – the fact that he was in love with Renwein was not unimportant either. This did not satisfy the Britons, who revolted and nominated Vortigern's son, Vortimer, as their new king. Vortimer had no reason to love his father – he had abandoned Vortimer's mother in favour of the pagan Saxon. Vortimer attacked the Saxons and defeated them in four pitched battles. The first of the battles was fought along the River Derwent/Derevent. The second battle took place above the ford at Epiford/Episford. It was there that Horsa fought hand-to-hand against Vortigern's son, Katigern/Catigirn, and both fell in action. The third battle was fought on the coast of 'the Gallic Sea' (Kent). The Britons drove the Saxons to their ships and they duly fled to the Isle of Thanet. Vortimer besieged the Saxons with his fleet, with the result that the Saxons dispatched Vortigern to his son to ask his permission for the evacuation of the island so that they could return to Germany. This was only a ruse. As the negotiations continued, the Saxons embarked on their longships, left their local families behind and sailed back to Germany. This enabled Vortimer to redistribute the land to its rightful owners. According to Geoffrey, Vortimer also restored the churches at the request of St Germanus. This may actually suggest that Germanus' second trip to Britain took place at the same time as Vortimer's operations, and that everything mentioned here should be dated back roughly to the years 442–446.

Vortimer's victory proved ephemeral because he died soon after. Renwein had stayed behind and managed to convince one of Vortimer's servants to administer a poison to his drink. When Vortimer realized that he would die, he gave presents to his soldiers and instructed them to build a bronze pyramid as his grave at the entrance of the so-called Saxon Port, so that his ghost would prevent the Saxons from ever making a landing. Vortimer's instructions were not followed, his men burying him in the town of Trinovantum. This suggests that Vortimer, just like his father Vortigern, was actually a pagan,[4] despite the lip service he paid to the Catholic Church.

The death of Vortimer enabled Vortigern to retake power, and he asked Hengist to bring his Saxons back, but only a small number of them and not an army. Hengist, however, had other plans. This time he intended to conquer all of Britain and not be satisfied to play second fiddle to anyone. Geoffrey claims that Hengist assembled an army of 300,000 men and shipped them to Britain, but this figure is clearly exaggerated.[5] A figure of about 30,000 men is quite plausible in light of later Viking armies. The figure of 300,000 could only be believable if Hengist also shipped their families at the same time, but this is unlikely because it would have taken a long time to transport such a huge number of people. It is likelier that Hengist arrived with a large naval force carrying only warriors so that he could surprise the Britons. When Vortigern and the other princes of the realm heard of this they were angry and frightened, and decided to attack the Saxons. Hengist proposed a compromise, in which Vortigern would allow a certain number of Saxons to stay and send the rest back to Germany. Vortigern and the princes accepted this. Vortigern sent a message which stated that the Saxons and Britons were to choose either 300 (Nennius) or

460–480 (Geoffrey) nobles and meet each other without arms at the Cloister of Ambrius near Salisbury/Kaercaradduc on 1 May. Hengist had no intention of keeping his word. He ordered his followers to hide daggers in their boots and then attack the unarmed Britons when he shouted '*Nimader sexa*' (or '*Nimet oure saxes*', which roughly translates as 'get your knives'). At the banquet, Hengist subdued Vortigern in person and then shouted the order. Most of the Britons were massacred, but some managed to flee. Geoffrey names one Briton in particular for his bravery, Eldol, the *Dux/Comes* of Gloucester. He managed to grasp a wooden stake with which he attacked the Saxons, breaking limbs, shoulders and skulls, so that seventy lay dead after he fled to Gloucester. Contrary to the popular view among your average modern historian, the seventy killed in one encounter is actually a credible figure for a martial arts expert (which Eldol clearly was, according to this story) if he faced enemies equipped with mere knives. History is full of examples of men who had exceptional fighting skills, killing enemies far in excess of anything that sounds credible.[6]

Hengist used the imprisoned Vortigern to obtain control of most of Britain. According to Geoffrey, Vortigern obtained his freedom by handing over London, York, Lincoln and Winchester to the Saxons. According to Nennius, Vortigern purchased his freedom from Hengist by granting him three provinces – Eastsex, Southsex and Middlesex – together with some other territories. Both versions are roughly the same. The Saxons took control of all these cities and ravaged and pillaged the surrounding countryside like wolves. The freed Vortigern fled to Wales, where he assembled his 'magicians'. This proves that in his hour of greatest distress, Vortigern became publicly pagan. The 'magicians' advised Vortigern to build a strong tower on Mount Erith (Snowdon) to serve as his last place of refuge if all the other fortresses were lost to the invaders. It appears probable that this mountain holdout was built on the tribal lands controlled by Vortigern's Gewissei. However, the building of foundations for the tower failed because the earth swallowed them up. The 'magicians' advised Vortigern to sacrifice a fatherless boy to the gods. Human sacrifices were also a typical answer for the pagans of Rome whenever the city was threatened, despite the abhorrence most Romans had always felt towards the followers of Baal. The superstitious have always felt a desperate need to buy the goodwill of their god or gods with various kinds of sacrifices, including the sacrifice of humans, animals, property, food or personal pleasures (the alternative version is to indulge in sexual pleasures for the god or gods, which I guess is preferable to the former if one has to choose!), or the inflicting of personal pain by various means.

The chosen victim was Ambrosius Merlin, a bastard son of the daughter of a king of Demetia. Merlin managed to convince the king to abandon his plan by demonstrating that the real reason for the faltering of the foundations was that there was a pool beneath it, and that there were two stones on the bottom of the pool which had dragons inside. This account is entirely believable. This would not have been the first or last time that superstitious people have resorted to human sacrifices in their distress, and have been fooled by a wise person. The mixing of the supernatural with the rational was also in keeping with period practices, in which the skilled manipulators of the human psyche (both pagans and Christians) convinced their followers that they possessed supernatural knowledge. In this case, Merlin had clearly had a good philosophical education that had included engineering and architecture, so he realized that the foundations faltered because the ground was not strong enough to support them. His claim that there were sleeping dragons inside the stones was just meant to create awe among superstitious fools, including Vortigern.

Chapter 5

Ambrosius Aurelius/Aurelianus, the *Dux Bellorum* and the Boar of Cornwall in 451/452[1]

The Arrival of the Rightful Heir Ambrosius Aurelius/Aurelianus in 451/452[2]

According to Geoffrey's version, Merlin prophesied to Vortigern that he would meet his end at the hands of the 'sons' of Constantine, who were already fitting out their ships in Armorica for a campaign against Vortigern. Consequently, Vortigern faced the very unwelcome dual threat of the returning Aurelius Ambrosius 'with' Utherpendragon, as well as the Saxons. The prophecy claimed that both Aurelius Ambrosius and Utherpendragon would be poisoned and succeeded by the latter's son, Arthur. Again, I would suggest that Geoffrey's account hides, behind the three names Aurelius Ambrosius, Utherpendragon and Arthur, only one person who had three nicknames at different periods of his rule. A more prosaic version would be that Aurelius Ambrosius was just exploiting the opportunity to exact vengeance against Vortigern at a time when Vortigern had lost support among the natives thanks to his disastrous dealings with the Saxons. The attack would have taken place immediately after the Huns had been expelled from Gaul, either in 451 or 452, and it may have included units of Britons that had taken part in that campaign. Aurelius would also have been the champion of the Roman cause against the pagan Vortigern and Saxon invaders, and this was to be reflected in his title *dux bellorum*.

It is also possible to reconcile Geoffrey's version of the three different individuals – Aurelius Ambrosius, Utherpendragon and Arthur – with the extant record in another way, if one accepts the date 441/442 for Saxon dominance in the *Gallic Chronicle 452*. According to this timetable, Vortigern would have first murdered Constans in about 428 or 433 so that the Picts and Scots invaded. Hengist and Horsa, with their Saxons, would have arrived immediately after this and balanced the situation in favour of the Britons. The revolt of Vortimer against his father and the expulsion of the Saxons would then have taken place in the late 430s, and the return of Vortigern to power in about 440/441. The Saxons would then have returned to Britain in about 441/442, so the *Gallic Chronicle 452* could claim that their dominance started then. For other alternatives, see the previous text. The conquest and pillaging of most of Britain would then have continued during the following years, with the Britons first dispatching envoys to the Romans in 443 and then again in 446 when they had already lost most of their territories, with Vortigern seeking safety from his mountain hideout in Wales. In this scenario, the Britons were saved by the timely arrival of Aurelius Ambrosius in about 447, who then started the process of recovery for Briton fortunes. He would then have been poisoned in about 449/450 and succeeded by his brother Utherpendragon. Utherpendragon in his turn was then poisoned in about 464/465 and succeeded by his 15-year-old-son, Arthur. The problem with this reconstruction is that it is at variance with the accounts of Gildas and Nennius. Firstly, according to Gildas, Vortigern hired the Saxon mercenaries only after the Britons had dispatched a plea for help to Aetius 'thrice consul'. Once again, it would be possible to reconcile this version by claiming that the referral to 'thrice consul' Aetius was meant to separate this Aetius from the Eastern Aetius who was active at the same time, so that it would be possible to date the plea for help to take place before the third consulship in 446, but this would suggest considerable awareness from a Briton of the affairs of East Rome in the fifth century. Secondly, Nennius claims that it was Arthur who fought twelve times against the Saxons until he obtained the final victory at the Battle of Badon, and Gildas says that the revival of British fortunes began under Aurelius Ambrosianus. Therefore, Aurelius Ambrosianus and Arthur are likely to be the same person, and the nickname Utherpendragon was probably used to hide his treacherous behaviour towards his benefactor – which would definitely have been in the best interests of the twelfth-century Welsh to hide if they expected Arthur to return to rule them. This means that my conclusions are based on the assumption that Gildas as a Briton was better informed of the affairs that had taken place in Britain than the *Gallic Chronicle*, but ultimately one cannot be absolutely certain and we are here just dealing with varying degrees of probability.

The Siege of Dinas Emrys in 451/452
Aurelius Ambrosius embarked slightly more than 10,000 soldiers (Geoffrey 8.4) on ships in Armorica and sailed to 'Totnes' in Cornwall (mod. Devon). The scattered Britons flocked to the scene and Aurelius Ambrosius was crowned as king by the assembled clergy (Nennius: *rex inter omnes reges Britanniae*). The Britons' leadership urged Ambrosius to attack the Saxons first, but Ambrosius managed to convince the Britons to deal with Vortigern first. In this Ambrosius was following in the footsteps of most emperors, who always dealt first with Roman enemies and only after that with foreign enemies. In this case Ambrosius obviously had a personal grudge against the killer of his father and brother, and this played its own role too, but his decision also made perfect strategic sense. By eliminating Vortigern first, Ambrosius was able to remove a potential threat to his lines of communication while also uniting all Britons under his banner. Secondly, the route taken to destroy Vortigern enabled Ambrosius to unite his forces with the tribal contingents of

84   Britain in the Age of Arthur

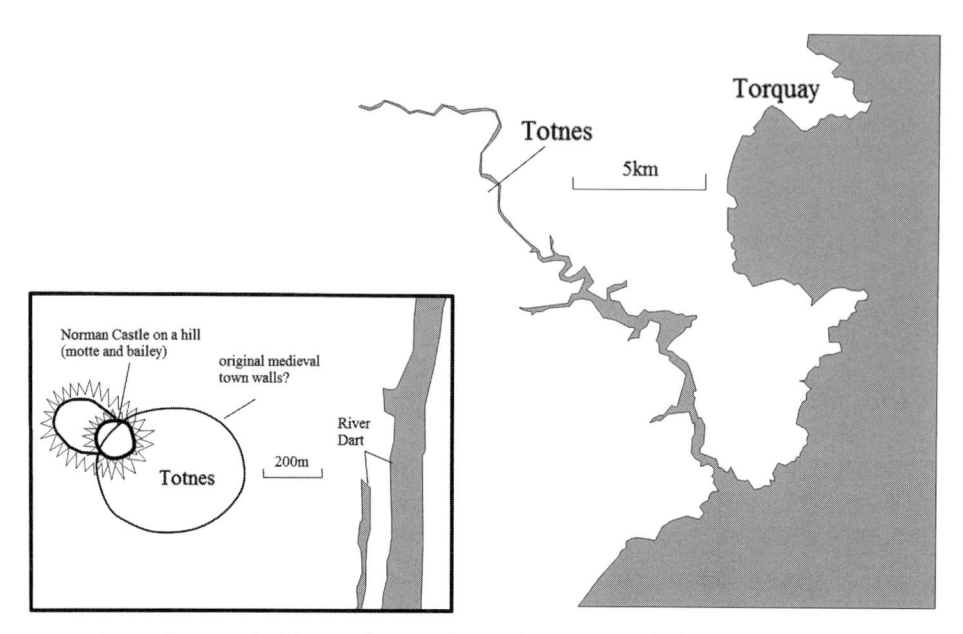

Despite the fact that the history of Totnes during the Roman period is largely unknown there are no reasons to suspect Geoffrey's account, because Geoffrey's location for the landing is actually quite logical in light of what we know of the period warfare. Totnes was ideally located inland along a river and it was well-suited to act as a landing place. It had also a hill which was well-suited to the type of defensive structures favoured by the Dark Age Britons and this was also later recognized by the Normans who built a castle on the hill.

Wales. This also allowed Aurelius to add the paramilitary forces of the the city of Deva to his army and advance from there along the old Roman road to Eboracum/York against the Saxons.

Consequently, Ambrosius' first object was to put Vortigern under siege in his hideout, which is traditionally considered to be the Dinas Emrys (Fortress of Ambrosius) in Snowdonia. See the illustrations.

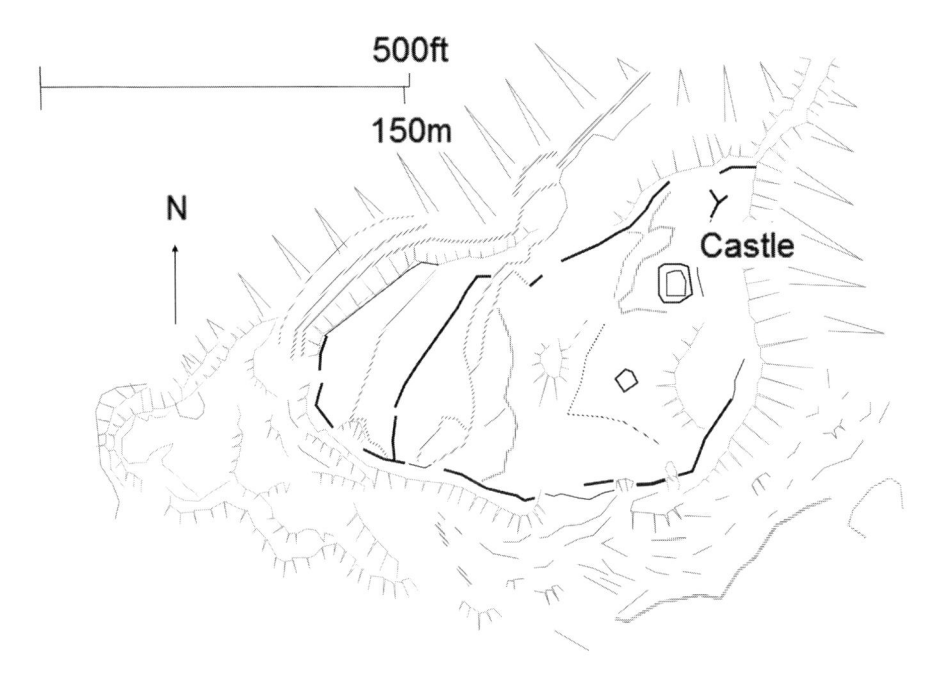

The Dinas Emrys (Fortress of Ambrosius) in Snowdonia is usually associated with Vortigern, Merlin and Aurelius Ambrosius. The historians usually suspect this association, but there are several things that support this association. I am quite prepared to accept the identification of the locale with these persons and events. Firstly, it was built during the fifth century at a location in which Vortigern is claimed to have built his last place of refuge. Secondly, it does have an underground cistern/pool in the centre of a plateau as claimed by the legend. According to Geoffrey, Merlin stated that there were two dragons underneath the foundations locked inside stones in the pool in question. The location was well chosen. The crag is located 75 metres above the river Glaslyn. It has 3-metre thick walls to protect the vulnerable sections and it was approachable only from two directions. The fort was practically impregnable despite the fact that the two approaches were left without gates. It was easy enough to protect those with men posted on both sides. The fort was not large even by the standards of the day and could have housed at most 1,500 to 2,000 men if the men were packed in crowded conditions. It is easy to see that the place was really the last place of refuge for Vortigern and his personal followers. He did not possess enough men to face Aurelius on the battlefield and the place was not quite as impregnable as it looks because it was taken. This is not surprising in light of the Roman siege engineering skills and was not the last impregnable place taken with these means. For additional details concerning the fort of Dinas Emrys, see Konstam 20–23. The accompanying illustration is drawn after it.

The siege machines were put in position and every effort was made to destroy the walls, but to no avail. It was then that the Britons tried fire, which worked like a dream. The tower, including Vortigern, was burned down in a blaze of fire. This suggests the use of fire-bombs with stone throwers or the use of bellows to bring down walls, as shown in the illustration below. The Britons and Armoricans had clearly maintained their old Roman military traditions. This is the siege Nennius falsely attributed to St Germanus.

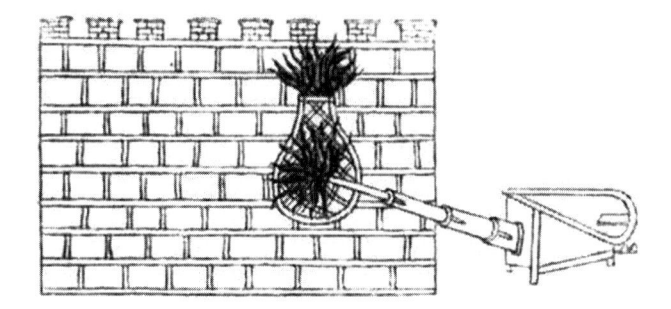

In this instance it is important to pay attention to Geoffrey's claim (10.3) that King Arthur fought a single combat against the giant Retho on Mount Arvaius. Mount Arvaius is identified by Thorpe (after Tatlock) as Mount Snowdon, which suggests the probability that the incident referred to took place at the time when Aurelius (i.e. Arthur) was fighting against Vortigern, because this is the only occasion when Aurelius/Arthur was fighting on the mountain. According to Geoffrey, the giant Retho (a Saxon?) had a fur cloak made out of the beards of the kings he had killed, and sent a taunting message to Arthur in which he ordered Arthur to rip off his beard so that he could add it to his cloak. This only angered Arthur and made him ready to accept the challenge to a duel that Retho next proposed. Arthur won the duel and took the giant's beard as a trophy, but only with great difficulty, as Retho was the strongest opponent Arthur ever met. Note that the taking of beards – and presumably other body parts, scalps or even heads – was considered not only acceptable, but a sign of manhood. People and their body parts could be trophies, like animals, the best example of this being the stuffed Emperor Valerian in the Persian court.

Geoffrey claims that Hengist became very frightened when news of the arrival of Aurelius Ambrosius was brought to him, because Ambrosius had gained great fame in Gaul as an unbeatable duellist, both on foot and horse, and was known as a very skilled army commander. He was also famous for his modest behaviour, observance of religion, liberality with gifts and honesty. The Saxons were therefore facing a man who was not only the rightful heir of the British throne, but also an incorruptible religious man who had a superb military record. It was impossible to bribe him or turn his followers against him. The Saxons decided to abandon the south of Britain and retreat north of the Humber, so that they could – if need be – unite their forces with the Picts, Scots, Danes, Norwegians and others. When news of this was brought to Ambrosius, he assembled and reinforced his army, presumably by adding the paramilitary forces of the city of Deva to his army, and then continued his march from Deva towards Eboracum/York. When reports of this were brought to Hengist, he collected a hand-picked force, which supposedly consisted of 200,000 soldiers – 20,000 would be closer to the truth. According to Geoffrey, Hengist attempted to encourage his men with the claim that their adversaries numbered hardly more than 10,000 Armorican Britons. Even if there is no evidence for this speech, it does ring true because the Saxons had already faced other Britons, but not the Armoricans.

The Battle of the Field of Maisbeli in 451/452
Hengist knew that Ambrosius would have to march through the Field of Maisbeli and decided to attempt to surprise the Britons there. This bid failed because Aurelius learnt of it either from his spies or scouts in a timely manner, but this did not deter him and he still decided to march straight forward to engage the enemy. When the Saxon array came in sight, Aurelius deployed his forces. The Demetian Welshmen were stationed on the hills, which must have been located on the left, and the Venedotian Welshmen were in the encircling woods, which must have been on the right. Three thousand Armoricans were ordered to take their battle stations with their horses, and the rest of the Armoricans were distributed among the Britons. The centre of the army would presumably have consisted of the rest of the Britons (men of Cornwall, Somerset and other remnants of the Briton military). The distribution of the reliable Armoricans among the rest of the divisions was clearly meant to bolster their self-confidence with the veterans of continental wars. It is probable that at least the centre was deployed as hollow square/oblong divisions, as was customary at the time, but the wings may have been arrayed either as loose hollow squares or in an irregular fashion suited to such terrain. I have here made the guess that the Welshmen consisted mostly of light foot archers and would have had some heavy infantry to protect them, so the result would have been the hollow square/oblong array for each division, which was one of the Late Roman ways to use light infantry.[3] Eldol, the *Dux* or *Comes* of Gloucester (*Claudiocestriae*), sought permission from Aurelius Ambrosius to engage Hengist in a single combat to exact vengeance against him, which was granted. Eldol apparently fought on foot in this and in the following battle.

The terrain of the chosen battlefield suggests that Hengist's intention had been to avoid the threat of being outflanked, either by the numerically superior enemy force (in Geoffrey 8.8, the force under Aurelius is called a multitude) or the numerically and qualitatively superior cavalry force, so that he would be able to defeat the Britons with a frontal attack. With this in mind, Hengist arrayed his men as wedges (*cunei*).

We do not know whether he used the Greco-Roman (*cuneus/embolos/embolon*) or Scandinavian version (*Svinfylking/caput porcinum*), but I have made the educated guess that, as a Scandinavian, Hengist would have adopted the latter. The infantry wedge and pikes were particularly well-suited to breaking the cohesion of attacking cavalry.[4] It is probable that Aurelius had at least 30,000–35,000 men. He exhorted his men to rely on God, while Hengist urged his men to put their trust in their gods, and both armies joined combat. Eldol sought to engage Hengist, but to no avail, because when Hengist saw that his men's attack had failed and they had lost the battle, he fled to the *Oppidum* of *Kaerconan/Cunungeburg/Cunegeburc* (mod. Conisbrough). The attached illustration shows the principal features of the battle. I have added cavalry units to the intervals between the hollow oblongs because it is probable that the Britons had cavalry too. I have made the educated guess that, as Scandinavians, the Saxons would have used the standard Nordic version of the wedge, which was the rhombus, rather than the Greek-Roman-Germanic variant, and that there was one reserve unit under Hengist. It would have been the use of the rhomboids that enabled the Saxons to retreat from the battlefield after their attack had failed.

The Battle of the Field of Maisbeli in 451/2

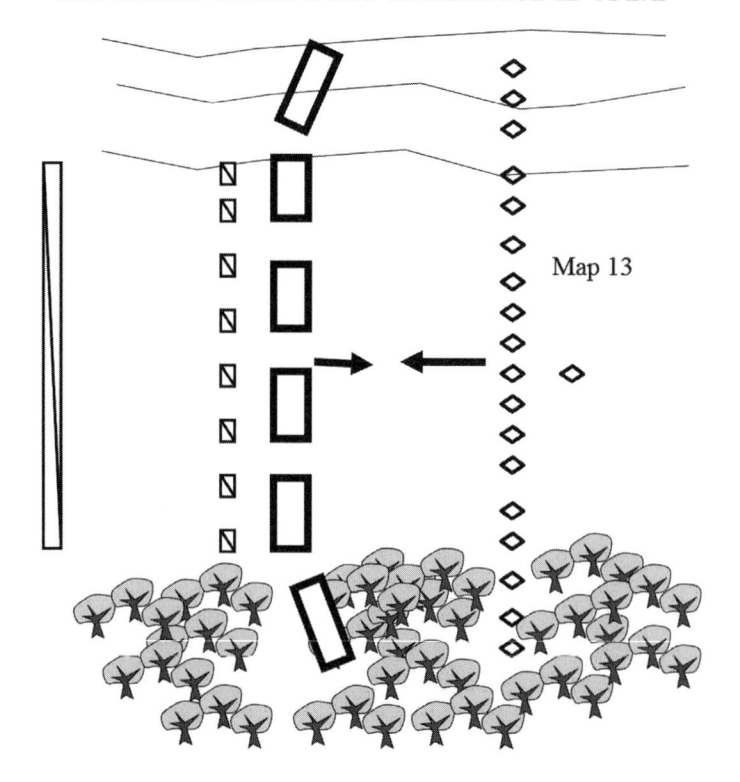

Map 13

The Battle of Conisbrough in 451/452
When Hengist saw that Aurelius pursued him to Conisbrough, he decided that it was more advantageous to engage the Britons in the field of battle rather than be besieged by them, so he led his men outside the town. Both sides arrayed their forces as previously, but this time the Saxons fought with such desperate determination that the Briton foot was forced to retreat and the Britons came close to losing the battle. However, the timely arrival of Aurelius with his 3,000 Armorican horsemen saved the day. The Armorican cavalry forced the Saxons to retreat, which turned into rout when an attempt to reform the lines failed. When the Britons saw this, they rushed at the enemy as one man. Aurelius and Eldol both galloped around the battlefield, issuing orders and killing enemies. In the midst of the fighting, Eldol and Hengist came face-to-face and started to fight against each other with swords. This definitely implies that Hengist fought at the apex of his wedge, and may also imply that Hengist used reserves. The fight was even, with each fighter forced to concede ground in turn, but then Gorlois, the *Dux* of Cornwall (*dux Cornubiae*), advanced his phalanx and forced the Saxon *turmae* (this means infantry, despite the use of the word *turma*) to retreat before it. The use of phalanx to describe Gorlois' array is problematic, because on the basis of the standard tactic used by the Britons, one would expect him to have led the cavalry reserve, but the word phalanx implies the use of infantry (perhaps the rear half of the hollow oblong or another hollow infantry oblong). My educated guess is that this is just another example of imprecise use of military terms, and that Gorlois did lead a cavalry phalanx after all. The arrival of Gorlois revived Eldol's hopes; he grasped the nasal part of Hengist's helmet and dragged him by it back to his Britons. This may imply that Eldol and Hengist fought on foot but not conclusively so because the dragging could also have been from the saddle. The incident may also suggest that Hengist had managed to stop the Briton cavalry charge under Gorlois after which the regrouped Briton infantry under Eldol had advanced again against him. The capture of Hengist naturally demoralized the Saxons and energized the Britons. However, even before this had happened, the Britons had kept up the pressure by charging repeatedly at the enemy. This attack continued until Saxon morale collapsed and they were routed, which probably happened after Hengist had been captured. This description indicates that the Britons' tactical doctrine was to use the infantry oblongs as safe bases for their cavalry, which charged through the intervals at the enemy and then if needed retreated, to the flanks of the infantry unit, behind it or inside the hollow oblongs. The footmen in their turn were brought forward when their cavalry was unable to retreat and needed help.

The Saxons were scattered in flight. Some fled to nearby towns, others to the wooded mountains and some to their ships, but most regrouped under Hengist's son, Octa, and his kinsman, Eosa, in York. Aurelius advanced to Conisbrough, where he halted for three days. The dead were buried, the wounded tended and the men rested. The leaders were assembled to decide what to do with Hengist. Eldadus, the Bishop of Gloucester and brother of Eldol, said that he would kill the Saxon leader if nobody else would, with the result that Eldol led Hengist outside the city and cut off his head. Aurelius ordered that Hengist be buried with full pagan honours.

It is possible that this battle represents Nennius' eighth battle of Arthur near the *castello Guinnion/Gunnion*, where Arthur carried the image of the Madonna on his shoulder and pursued the fleeing Saxons for an entire day.

The Siege of York and the Restoration of Peace in 451/452
After events at Conisbrough, Aurelius led his army against York. The Saxons decided to seek peace. The first to approach the Britons was Octa, who begged for mercy, which was granted. After him followed Eosa and the rest of the Saxons, who were settled as *foederati* near Scotland.

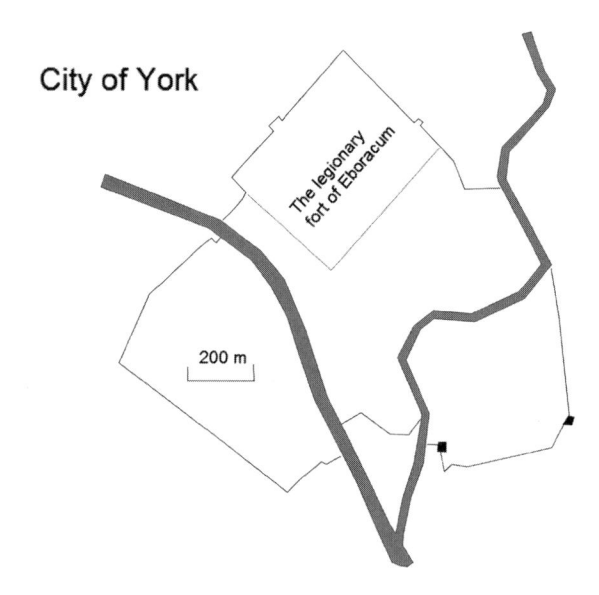

City of York

The legionary fort of Eboracum

200 m

Aurelius ordered the churches of York rebuilt, and after having spent fifteen days at York he left for London, which was rebuilt to serve as Aurelius' capital. All estates that had no surviving rightful heirs were distributed among Aurelius' followers. After this, Aurelius went to Winchester, which he also restored. He visited the monastery of St Ambrius near Salisbury (Kaercaradduc), where the Saxons had murdered the Britons' leaders, to show his respect for them. He wanted to build a mausoleum for the dead, and collected carpenters and stonemasons for this project. It was then that the Archbishop of the City of the Legions (Caerleon), Tremorius, advised Aurelius to use Merlin as his architect, because he was skilled in prophesying and engineering. Merlin was found in the territory of Gewissei

(Vortigern's tribal home). According to Geoffrey, Merlin told Aurelius that he was to use the stones of the Giants' Ring of Mount Killaraus in Ireland as the building blocks of his monument if he wanted to build a fitting memorial for the murdered men. Aurelius laughed, but agreed to carry out the plan when Merlin claimed to be able to bring the giant stones to Britain. The Irish were to be presented with an ultimatum: deliver the stones or be punished. It is clear that there is once again a germ of truth behind this account. The Irish were ordered to deliver to the Britons a monument they considered to be religiously particularly valuable, which would then become a visible sign of their submission to the rule of Aurelius. The intention was to punish the Irish for their previous campaigns and force them to become tribute-paying subjects. This also means that St Patrick's mission had not brought a complete cessation in hostilities, as had been hoped.

The Irish Campaign of Aurelius Utherpendragon in 452/453
According to Geoffrey, Aurelius sent 15,000 men under his brother Utherpendragon to Ireland to carry out the plan. As previously noted, it is probable that Geoffrey has confused three different titles of one man, with Aurelius, Utherpendragon and Arthur actually just Aurelius Ambrosius with two different nicknames. The size of the army suggests a fleet of at least 150–200 galleys, with the Armorican fleet consisting of about 100–150 ships and the Briton west coast fleet of about 50–100 ships. Note that there is a significant consistency in the size of the expeditionary army with the size of the fleet employed. Aurelius arrived with more than 10,000 men, he led 15,000 to Ireland and later led 12,000 to Gaul as Riothamus. This suggests that the size of the fleet remained static.

Merlin accompanied Utherpendragon to act as his advisor. This pairing of philosopher/magician and military leader was not unique to Roman Britain; similar pairings of philosophers and rulers can be found in use elsewhere in the fifth-century Roman Empire. In Dalmatia, there was the pagan *Magister Militum* Marcellinus, who was known as a skilled soothsayer, whose pair was the cynic Sallustius of Emesa. The fact that Sallustius was known to ridicule the gods suggests that Marcellinus was similarly disposed, and only used soothsaying as a means to encourage his soldiers. In the East, there was the pair of the Orthodox Christian Praetorian Prefect Anthemius and Hellene philosopher Troilus, and Orthodox Christian *Magister Militum* Illus and Neo-Platonist soothsayer Pamprepius (born in Thebes, Egypt, and apparently black). This suggests a practice in which the generals encouraged superstitious men with the right kind of prophecies, while they also used the knowledge of the philosophers in things that were both practical (siege engineering etc.) and morale-boosting (magical gimmicks used to encourage the men, much akin to the 'miracles' employed by St Germanus). Fifth-century Rome was facing a crisis, and the men in charge needed both practical advice and suitable gimmicks to encourage their superstitious men. It is probable that this was the reason for the looting of Irish stones. Merlin claimed that the stones possessed supernatural qualities (baths placed at the foot of the stones would cure the sick) similar to the Christian miracles resulting from the touching of holy relics of martyrs, which were also used for similar purposes during this era. Ireland was a poor country and it would have been quite difficult to encourage the men to exact vengeance against the Irish over the Irish Sea, when the only things that were worth looting were cattle and prisoners/slaves. However, when one claimed that the stones had supernatural qualities, foolish and superstitious men could be encouraged to do what was demanded of them. For additional comments, see my *MHLR* vols.3–4.

The arrival of the British fleet came as a surprise to the Irish, but they still managed to collect an army to face the invaders under their brave young High King, Gillomanius. If Mount Killaraus means Kildare in Leinster, then the object of the attack lay in an area that was largely Christian and usually allied with the Romans. There are two possible explanations. Firstly, it is possible that the Leinstermen had raided Britain and were really the target of the operation. Secondly, Geoffrey's source may have meant some other locale. There are many other places which would fit the bill. In this case, the target of the attack would have been the elderly Loigaire/Loegaire (see Appendix 4).

When Gillomanius learnt of the demand, he laughed at the stupidity of such request and ordered his men to arm themselves for a fight. When Utherpendragon saw this, he deployed his men for battle and attacked. The Irish were crushed in the first attack and forced to flee.

The *Irish Annals* contain information that can be made to fit the above. Firstly, the *Annals* mention that in 452 a great number of Leinstermen were slaughtered. It is possible that they were killed by Britons. Secondly, it is possible that the *Annals* have misdated the events. In this case, the target of the attack would have been Loagaire, who would have then broken his agreements with St Patrick. According to entry a.458, Loegaire/Loigaire was defeated and taken prisoner by the Leinstermen at the Battle of Ath Dara and then released in return for a promise to deliver cattle-tribute. This promise was sealed with an oath (ca.462) that stated that Loegaire would die if he travelled to the area between Eriu (Ireland) and Albu (Albany, mod. Scotland). This oath would be out of place if it meant Leinster, but would be quite in order if Loegaire promised not to invade Wales via the Irish Sea, which was located between Ireland and Albany. If this was true, then the Leinstermen would have also included Britons. The problem with this is that it requires the redating of events and includes the making of educated guesses. Consequently, I prefer the first alternative. The destruction of Leinstermen by Britons in 452 would in its turn have weakened the hold of St Patrick on Loegaire, which he evidently exploited by revolting against him in the following year (see Appendix 4).

The Britons advanced to Mount Killaraus, and Merlin challenged the men to use whatever mechanical device or means at their disposal to move the stones, but all of these measures proved useless. It was only then that Merlin intervened and used his own gear to dismantle the monument and transport the stones to the ships. His aim was clearly to demonstrate his superior knowledge of engineering, which he undoubtedly claimed to be supernatural. The bishops, abbots and notables were also assembled on Mount Ambrius, where the burial place was consecrated. After this, Aurelius celebrated the feast of Whitsun for three days, after which he rewarded his landless followers with lands, and appointed Samson as Bishop of York and Dubricius as Bishop of the City of the Legions. The stones brought from Ireland were erected around the burial place of the martyrs of the Saxon treachery. These stones are usually associated with the stones of Stonehenge, but it is quite probable that this is a mistake and that the stones brought from Ireland are no longer extant, or that these really form only a part of the monument, which had been built in the distant past, or that these are now part of some other monument.

Pascentius vs. the Britons in ca. 462/463 (Geoffrey 8.13ff.)
Meanwhile, according to Geoffrey, the son of Vortigern, Paschent/Pascent (Pascentius),[5] had managed to buy the support of many young men in Germany with promises of great wealth if they would restore him to the throne. When Paschent had assembled a large fleet, he landed his forces in Scotland, which he began to ravage. When the news reached the king, he assembled his forces and marched to meet the invaders, who were duly defeated and forced to flee to Ireland. Gillomanius received the fugitives with open arms. The previous defeat made him more than eager to join forces with Paschent and his Germans. Consequently, the Irish fitted out their ships and, together with the Germans/Saxons, landed near the town of Menevia in Kambria in about 462/463 (date according to the *Irish Annals*).

Geoffrey claims that Aurelius was bedridden in Winchester (*Gwintonia urbe*) at the time of the landing, and it was thanks to this that military operations were put into the hands of Utherpendragon. I would suggest that this is a mistake that has crept into the Welsh tradition at some point to explain the appearance of Utherpendragon in the sources, and that it was Aurelius Ambrosius Utherpendragon who was in Winchester. According to Nennius (HE 48), it was Aurelius Ambrosius who was the contemporary of Pascent. According to Geoffrey's version, when Pascent and Gillomanius learnt that Aurelius was ill, they were delighted because they thought that in the absence of its leader the kingdom was ripe for conquest. They also employed a Saxon called Eopa/Capa as an assassin to kill Aurelius. He was to pretend to be a monk and doctor so that he could gain entrance, and according to this version he was successful and managed to administer a poison to the king in the form of a drug. When the king then died, Utherpendragon supposedly saw a star of great brilliance, with a single beam with a dragon at each end. Merlin interpreted this to mean that Aurelius had died in Winchester and that he would be succeeded by Utherpendragon. Menevia and the enemy were at a distance of half a day's march, and Merlin's advice to Utherpendragon was to attack them immediately. Another possibility is that the star of great brilliance with dragons was a public vision by Aurelius Ambrosius (now Utherpendragon), used to encourage men in the same manner as Constantine the Great encouraged his men with the Chi-Rho sign (one of the earliest forms of christogram) in the sky.

The Battle of Menevia or Caerleon in ca. 462/463
When Gillomanius, Pascent and Octa learnt of the imminent approach of the Britons, they deployed for combat and marched to meet Utherpendragon. After a battle that lasted most of the day, the Britons were victorious, killing Gillomanius and Pascent, with the result that the enemy fled to their ships. According to the version given by Nennius (HE 48), Pascent was not killed in this battle, but was given by Ambrosius two provinces, Buelt and Guorthegirnaim, to rule. Nennius calls Ambrosius the great king among the kings of Britain. This version definitely suggests that the person in charge of the British armies was Aurelius Ambrosius and that the victory over the Saxons and Irish was achieved through the desertion of Pascent, who had been bribed with the twin provinces, one of which was his father's native territory, and that Utherpendragon was just his new nickname, obtained as a result of his vision and the use of the dragon banner to encourage the men.

The *Irish Annals* have evidence to support this. The entry in the *Annals* (ca.462 or 463) states that Loegaire/Loigaire, son of Niall, died at Grellach Dabaill by the side of Cass in Mag Lifi, between two hills called Eriu (Ireland) and Albu (Albany/Scotland). He was supposedly killed there because he had broken the oath given to the Leinstermen in the name of the sun and wind. This is clearly a muddled memory of a battle which was fought in a place between Ireland and Albany, which in this case is clearly Wales. The account which is preserved in the *Annals* (already in muddled form) becomes even more muddled in later stories, so that in the *Borama*-saga Loegaire thought that he would be safe from the oathbreaking if he did not sail out into the Irish Sea, but was then killed when he went between two hills with the names Ireland and

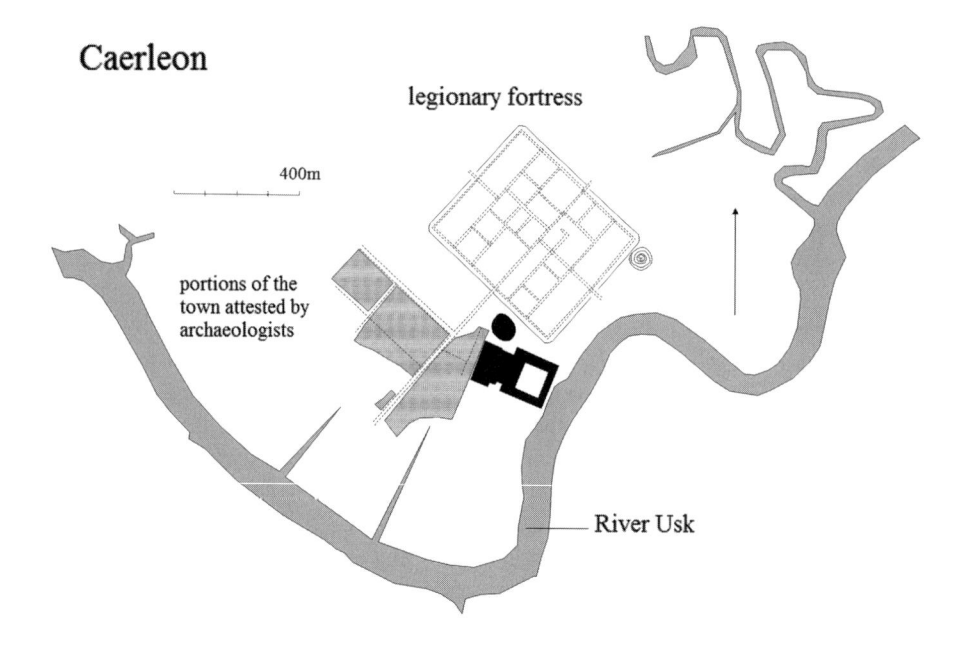

Albany located in northern Leinster.[6] In my opinion, we should take the reference to the area between Ireland and Albany literally, so that Loegaire died in Wales in 462/463.

It is probable that we should identify this battle with Nennius' ninth battle of Arthur, which Nennius placed at the City of the Legions (*in urbe Legionis*)/Cair Lion (Caerleon), because this is actually the only occasion on which such a battle could have taken place. In this case, the Saxons would not have stayed at Menevia in Kambria, as stated by Geoffrey, but would have marched towards the Britons, whom they would then have fought somewhere near the city of Caerleon. This actually makes more sense than for the Saxons to have stayed where they had landed, and my own educated guess is that the armies indeed fought a battle somewhere near Caerleon.

According to Geoffrey, 'Utherpendragon' turned back to Winchester after his victory, and when messengers told of the death of Aurelius, he convened the clergy and people to appoint a new king, who was none other than Utherpendragon. Utherpendragon ordered two golden dragons to be fashioned, one of which was left at the cathedral of Winchester, while he kept the other for himself. This was the reason why it came to be called Utherpendragon (a Dragon's Head). In other words, the golden dragon was installed as a helmet crest.

There are two different possible explanations for the above. Firstly, there is the explanation which I have already given, which is that Geoffrey – or his source – has purposefully attempted to find explanations for the appearance of different names for the leader of the Britons, and has created three different people out of one man. In this case, one possible explanation would be that Aurelius Ambrosius had resorted to a ruse in which he purposefully pretended to be ill, and then advanced secretly against the enemy in an effort to surprise them, but which failed thanks to the presence of Saxon scouts around the town of Menevia. The second possible answer is that there really were two separate people, Aurelius Ambrosius and Arthur, and that the former died now, because it is immediately after this that Nennius introduces Arthur, who fights against Octa. According to Geoffrey, the death of Aurelius made void the previous pact between Octa and the Britons, with the result that Octa revolted. This could be used to support the separate existence of Aurelius and Arthur. However, the list of battles fought by this Arthur in Nennius (HE 50) rather suggests that we are once again dealing with the same man, and not with separate individuals. Therefore, I suggest that Aurelius Ambrosius, Utherpendragon and Arthur are one man, and that the Britons attempted to play a ploy against the invaders, which failed. However, I would still suggest that Aurelius Ambrosius obtained his victory over the Saxons and Irish, in this case by bribing the son of Vortigern to switch sides, as suggested by Nennius.

It is possible that the appearance of the new name Utherpendragon as a ruler of Britain coincided with Aurelius' tenth year in power, when he distributed a donative to the troops. It is also possible that the soldiers named their ruler and commander Utherpendragon as a form of recognition of martial achievements, or that Aurelius was given a British title similar to the official titles of the Roman world such as *Augustus* or *Imperator*.

Chapter 6

Ambrosius Aurelius/Aurelianus, the Utherpendragon (A Dragon's Head/ The Dragon Pennon Head) in 462–464[1]

Octa and Eosa vs Utherpendragon in 462/463
The next to revolt, or rather to continue their revolt, were Octa and Eosa/Cosa, because the 'death' of Aurelius had released them from the treaty they had made. It is probable that they simply exploited the situation because, as I have noted, it is improbable that Aurelius died. The Saxons formed an alliance with those Saxons Pascent had brought, and sent messengers to Germany to obtain even more mercenaries. Octa assumed command and invaded the northern provinces, destroying towns and forts from Albany as far as York, which he put under siege.

The Battle of York in 462
Meanwhile, Utherpendragon had assembled all available forces and arrived before York just as the Saxons began their siege. He did not waste time, but advanced against them immediately. The Saxons deployed opposite him. The Britons attacked repeatedly, but with no result. In the end, the Britons were forced to abandon their attempt to lift the siege and withdraw. This suggests that the Britons employed similar tactics as before, which consisted of the use of infantry hollow squares/ oblongs and cavalry, with the cavalry conducting repeated attacks against the enemy, infantry providing support or a place of refuge. The Saxons pursued the defeated Britons to Mount Damen.

The Battle of Mount Damen in 462
Mount Damen was a steep hill with a summit full of hazel wood which was protected by jagged rocks halfway up the hill. The Britons occupied the top of the hill and slept among the rocks and hazel bushes. Utherpendragon called a meeting of his leaders to decide how to proceed in this situation, in which the Britons had just suffered a defeat and were besieged by a numerically superior enemy. Gorlois, the *Dux* of Cornwall/Cornubiae, suggested that the Britons should make a surprise attack during the night and attack the Saxons in their camp. This suggestion was accepted by all; the leaders armed their men, deployed their *turmae* for combat and advanced against the enemy. The Saxon sentinels (*vigiles*) were too late observing the approach of the Britons. They woke their comrades by blowing their cornets,

but the Britons attacked the Saxon camp in their dense *turmae* arrays with drawn swords before the Saxons could organize their defence properly. The Saxons panicked. The Britons' use of drawn swords was a sign of desperation which had the double intention of forcing the men to attack at close quarters while showing the enemy that they were facing desperate foes willing to fight to the death. It is also quite probable that the Britons had used most of their missiles in the previous battle before the city of York, so that they could not have used missiles had they wanted to. The Britons butchered the Saxons by the thousands, capturing Octa and Eosa. It is possible that this battle represents Nennius' eleventh battle of Arthur, which was on the mountain Agned Cathregonnon/Breguoin/Cat Bregion.

Utherpendragon exploited his victory by marching to the town of Alclud, where he restored order and then advanced to Scotland, where he similarly restored order and punished those who had rebelled against the Britons. After the Northern provinces had been pacified, Utherpendragon moved to London, the capital of his realm. Octa and Eosa were imprisoned there and the nobles of the kingdom were ordered to assemble at London the following Easter.

Gorlois vs Utherpendragon and Sieges of Tintagel and Dimilioc in 463 (Geoffrey 8.19ff.)
The nobles did as asked by their overlord, and Utherpendragon was able to celebrate Easter with due pomp. Utherpendragon's aim was clearly to demonstrate the unity of the nobles under the Christian banner. According to Geoffrey, Gorlois' wife, Ygerna, was the most beautiful woman of the realm, and Utherpendragon was unable to control his lust towards her. When Utherpendragon's approaches became untolerable, Gorlois decided to leave without receiving permission. Utherpendragon was enraged and ordered Gorlois to return to court to be punished for his insolence. Then Utherpendragon threatened to destroy Gorlois's land unless the latter returned, which he refused. This resulted in a war over a woman. Contrary to the common view among the prudish branch of ultra-conservative historians, this is quite believable as a motive. The sexually depraved behaviour of rulers has caused several wars, and has usually also resulted in the downfall of these same men. Roman history is full of such instances, and the same phenomenon can also be detected in more modern times, as for example the behaviour of Henry IV of France proves. Consequently, if this story has any basis in truth, and we can assume that it has, Uthependragon's inability to control his sexual behaviour had important political and military consequences. It is in fact quite probable that the earlier Welsh narrators or Geoffrey of Monmouth hid Aurelius Ambrosius/Arthur's crime beneath the name of Utherpendragon so that their hero's reputation would not become tarnished with treachery caused by lust.

It should also be noted that it is possible that the war between friends resulted from a series of misunderstandings. It is quite possible that Gorlois could have misinterpreted the overly polite behaviour of the king towards Ygerna to mean that the king was attempting to seduce his wife, with the above-mentioned results.

However, there is another possible ulterior motive for Utherpendragon's actions. It is possible that the traditional story hides the real reason for the war, which was Utherpendragon's plan to destroy Gorlois because his position vis-à-vis the king was too powerful. Aurelius Utherpendragon owed his power to Gorlois. Gorlois had received Utherpendragon at Totnes with open arms, had saved the Britons at the Battle of Conisbrough with his timely counter-attack, and had with his correct advice brought about the victory at Mount Damen. It is therefore possible that (assuming Geoffrey's story has some basis in truth) Utherpendragon purposefully made quite visible advances towards Ygerna so that Gorlois would commit some angry blunder that would enable Utherpendragon to destroy him without appearing ungrateful to his benefactor. It should be remembered that Utherpendragon only paid close attention to Ygerna by conversing with her and smiling at her, and stopped at that. This gave Utherpendragon the reasonable excuse of not having committed anything serious.

Consequently, he led a huge army against Cornwall and therefore repaid Gorlois' kindness and support with treachery. Utherpendragon's army pillaged and burned Cornwall almost at will, as Gorlois' forces were too small to stop them. Gorlois' strategy was to garrison strongpoints and conduct a guerrilla campaign against the attackers until he could obtain help from Ireland. Consequently, Gorlois left his wife Ygerna in the impregnable *oppidum* of Tintagel and himself occupied the *castellum* at Dimilioc/Damelioc, 5½ miles south-west of Tintagel. Dimilioc is located near the village of Pendogget and consists of three concentric ramparts and ditches with a diameter of 448 yards, according to Thorpe. It is known locally as Castle Dameliock.[2] The purpose of these actions was apparently to force Utherpendragon to concentrate his army against Gorlois so that he would be unable to attack Tintagel. When Utherpendragon learnt of this, he marched his army there and blockaded Gorlois inside Dimilioc.

According to Geoffrey (8.19ff.), the king became desperately lusty after a week and sought the advice of Ulfin of Ridcaradoch, one of his familiars (friends forming the advisory body) on how to conquer the impregnable Tintagel. Ulfin's advice was to seek advice from Merlin. Consequently, Utherpendragon ordered Ambrosius Merlin to present himself before him. Merlin then gave him a drug which changed his appearance into that of Gorlois, Ulfin's into that of Jordan and Merlin's into that of Britaelis. Then the three men went to Tintagel in the twilight hours and managed to gain entrance as they looked like the lord of the castle and his friends. Utherpendragon then slept with the queen and Arthur was conceived. Meanwhile, Utherpendragon's men attacked Dimilioc on their own initiative, with the result that the *Dux* sallied out and was among the first to be killed. Gorlois' army was routed and his camp pillaged. The initial attack against Gorlois' camp would have been a stratagem in which the besiegers first made a feint assault, which

Map 16

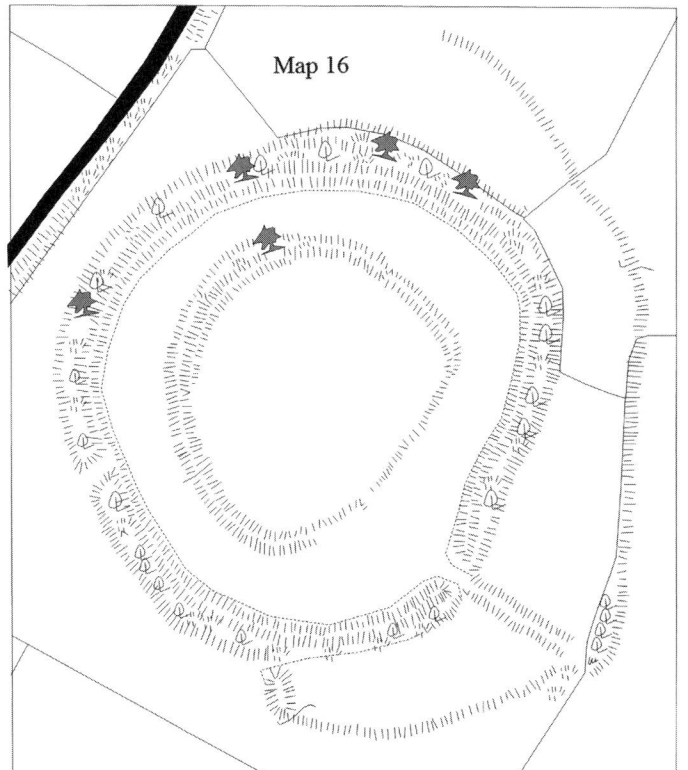

Damelioc/Dimilioc Castle according to Dickinson (p.69) based on the 25-inch Ordnance Map.

drew the besieged out in pursuit. When news of this was brought to Tintagel, the messengers saw the '*Dux*' beside Ygerna, with the result that they thought they had made a mistake. The false *Dux* then stated that he would go out and make peace with Utherpendragon, after which he returned to his army. Tintagel was then captured, together with Ygerna. Geoffrey claims that henceforth Utherpendragon and Ygerna lived together as equals. She duly gave birth to Arthur and Anna. Cador was appointed as new *Dux* of Cornwall; he was clearly a loyal supporter of his lord.

This is clearly a distorted memory of the lusty behaviour of Aurelianus/Aurelius Ambrosius Arthur, and of his treacherous behaviour towards his friend and the rape or seduction of his wife after the death of Gorlois. It is probable that Ygerna became the concubine/mistress of Aurelius Utherpendragon, rather than his equal. Furthermore, it is quite obvious that Anna was Aurelius Ambrosius' sister and Arthur would be Aurelius Ambrosius Utherpendragon's new untainted name. It is no coincidence that Geoffrey later (9.9) calls Anna Aurelius Ambrosius' sister. This is the real version which has become so distorted over the course of time that Geoffrey could claim that Anna was actually Aurelius' niece.

DARK AGE TINTAGEL

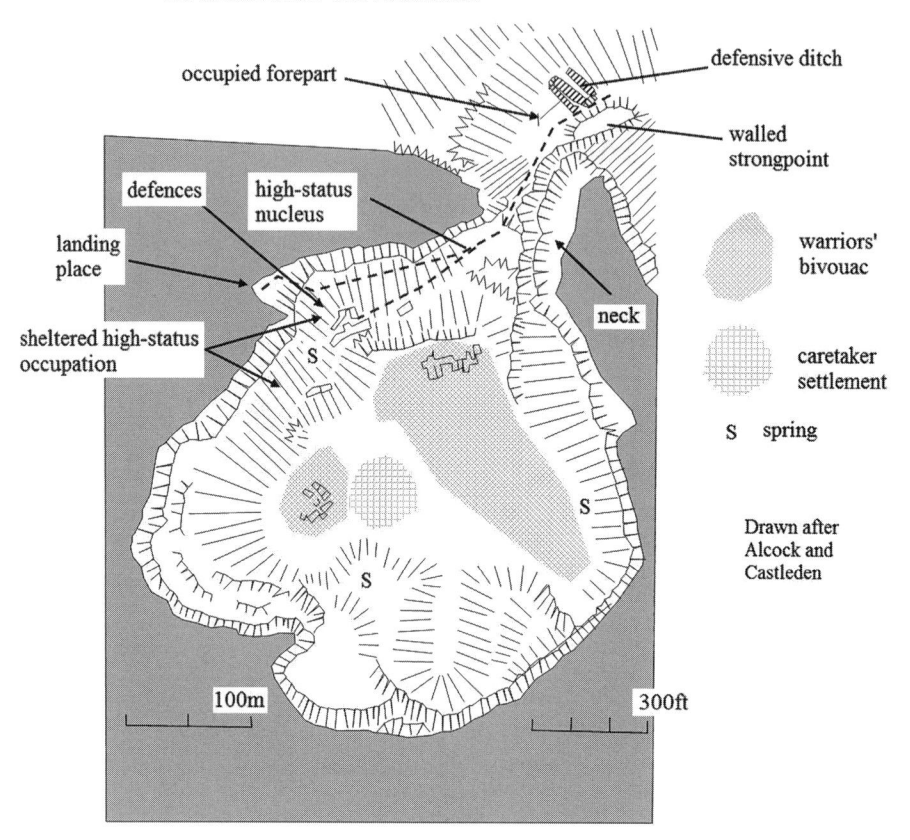

Map labels: occupied forepart; defensive ditch; walled strongpoint; defences; high-status nucleus; landing place; neck; sheltered high-status occupation; warriors' bivouac; caretaker settlement; S spring; Drawn after Alcock and Castleden; 100m; 300ft

One possible way to make sense of the story is that Aurelianus used a disguise to gain entrance to Tintagel, or that Ygerna betrayed her husband, after which the angered and desperate Gorlois sallied out of Dimilioc and was killed in combat. The other possible explanation is that Gorlois was killed in a desperate sally and that it was after this that Utherpendragon managed to gain entrance with the above-mentioned ruse or simply by assault or surrender. The latter alternative is the more likely of the two, because the death of Gorlois as a result of a foolish sally resulting from a stratagem would have enabled Utherpendragon and his men to don the distinctive equipment previously worn by Gorlois and his friends. If he wore Gorlois' dress and equipment in the twilight hours, as stated by the legend, it is quite possible that he could have passed initial inspection by the guards at the gates. The two stratagems used to conquer Tintagel and Dimilioc would have undoubtedly been devised by Ambrosius Merlin, who was an expert at engineering skills, which included knowledge of siege methods and stratagems used in sieges. As noted, Aurelianus Arthur and Ambrosius Merlin were a similar general-philosopher pair to the West Roman general Marcellinus (a pagan who acted as if he could foretell the future) and the cynic philosopher Sallustius of Emesa, and the East Roman general Illus and Neo-Platonist Pamprepius (born in Thebes, Egypt). The philosopher friends of these generals acted as if they could foretell the future. The aim was clearly to make the superstitious people believe that their masters, the generals, possessed magical powers thanks to their connection with these philosopher-magicians. This was clearly one of the major phenomena of the fifth-century Roman world, even if Arthur and Merlin are the only commonly known pair. In the chaotic circumstances, it was wise to attempt by any means possible to make the men follow their leaders. It should be noted, however, that the philosophers in question did not only employ trickery to frighten their enemies, but also possessed actual scientific knowledge of matters associated with siege techniques, architecture and chemistry. This practice had always been followed. It is no coincidence that Julius Caesar and Augustus had expert architects and philosophers in their service, or that Trajan was accompanied by Apollodorus (an architect and engineer), or that it was a philosopher who introduced the fire-bomb hand-grenades into the East Roman navy at the beginning of the sixth century or Greek Fire in the seventh century against the Muslims (see Syvänne, 2004). All wise commanders knew the value of good advice.

Octa and Eosa vs Utherpendragon and the Battle of St Albans in 463
Geoffrey claims that Ygerna and Utherpendragon were united in love and that the realm was at peace for years, until one day the king fell ill. It was then that the guards who had grown bored released the Saxon chieftains and fled with them to Germany. The fugitives fitted out a huge fleet and sailed to Albany. Since the king was bedridden, he appointed Loth of Lodonesia (*de Lendeseia*) to be in charge of the army, with instructions to contain the enemy in the north. Geoffrey claims that Utherpendragon had married his daughter Anna to this Loth, but as noted above it is probable that this is a mistake resulting from the multiplication of persons in Geoffrey's source. Anna was the sister of Ambrosius Aurelius Utherpendragon Arthur. This Anna had previously been married to Budicius, the king of the Armorican Britons, with whom she had at least two sons, of whom Hoel had now become king. Aurelius appears to have remarried Anna with Loth after the death of Budicius in order to unite the two noble houses, while keeping his nephew in power in Armorica. According to Geoffrey, Anna gave birth to two sons for Loth, Gawain and Mordred. This means that the remarriage of Anna must have happened in about 453–456 for Mordred to be eligible to act as a regent in the absence of Aurelius Arthur in 471. However, it is actually probable that Geoffrey has here made a mistake, because it is more than likely that Mordred had been born out of the previous marriage with Budicius, so he would have been brother of Hoel of Bretagne. The other alternative is that Geoffrey has made a mistake in calling the rebel leaders of 472 sons of Mordred, but the former is the likelier. The third alternative is that Loth was remarried to Anna in about 442.[3]

Fourth-Century Verulamium (St. Albans)

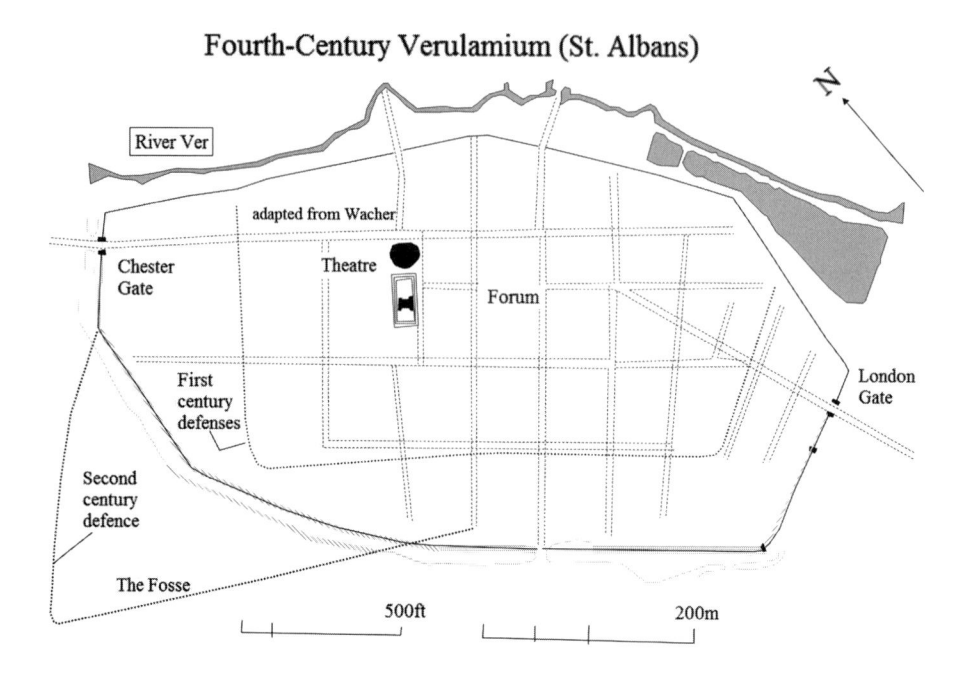

adapted from Wacher

- River Ver
- Chester Gate
- Theatre
- Forum
- First century defenses
- Second century defence
- The Fosse
- London Gate
- 500ft / 200m
- N

Loth marched north, but was worsted by the Saxons in most encounters due to the unwillingness of the Britons to follow his orders. The Britons were forced to seek shelter in the cities, leaving the Saxons free to pillage the surrounding lands. Even on those occasions on which Loth managed to rout the Saxons and forced them to flee into the forests or ships, the Saxons quickly regrouped so that Loth was forced to continue his fighting retreat southwards. When the Saxons finally reached the neighbourhood of St Albans (*Verulamium*), the king had to act. Utherpendragon took command of the army in person and ordered himself carried on a litter to St Albans. When news of this was brought to the Saxons, they claimed that there was no honour in fighting against a half-dead man and retreated inside the town. I would suggest that this means that the Saxons were surprised by the presence of the king and decided to seek shelter behind the walls. Utherpendragon ordered an immediate assault and came close to taking the town, but the fighting ended in a stalemate. The Saxons realized their folly of seeking shelter inside the town and decided to sally out.

At daybreak, the Saxons deployed in their *catervae* for combat, and the Britons arrayed their army in *turmae* (in this case this means both cavalry and infantry) and attacked. The Britons were victorious, Octa and Eosa were killed and the Saxons fled. Utherpendragon did not pursue the fleeing enemies, which enabled them to regroup and continue their pillaging in the northern provinces. Geoffrey (8.24) claims that the Saxons then sent spies/commandos disguised as beggars to St Albans while Utherpendragon lay ill there, and when the spies noted that there was a spring close by they poisoned it, with the result that the king and 100 other Britons died after having drunk the water. Utherpendragon was then buried inside the Giants' Ring.

I believe that this account is a confused memory of the situation following the killing of Gorlois. Firstly, I would suggest that the desertion of the guards guarding Octa and Eosa would have resulted from the treacherous behaviour of Aurelius Ambrosius Utherpendragon towards his friend Gorlois. Secondly, I would suggest that Aurelius Ambrosius Utherpendragon was forced to stay in the neighbourhood of London to crush the rebels there. These were the persons who had released Octa and Eosa. Thirdly, I would suggest that the poor discipline of the forces and their unwillingness to follow Loth's orders resulted from the general dissatisfaction of the soldiers towards their commander and Aurelius Ambrosius Utherpendragon. Fourthly, I would suggest that Aurelius Ambrosius Utherpendragon's orders to Loth had been to conduct a guerrilla campaign against the invaders while he crushed the revolt of the Londoners. Fifthly, I would suggest that the poisoning of Utherpendragon and 100 men did actually take place near St Albans, but did not cause the death of the king, as claimed by Geoffrey. Sixthly, I would suggest that the Saxon withdrawal inside St Albans was a ruse, which they had used to draw the king and the Briton army to the poisoned spring. Finally, I would suggest that the poor health of the king resulting from the poisoning enabled the Saxons to regroup, with the result that the Britons were forced to retreat to Silchester to regroup. The fact that the Britons did not attempt to hold on to London suggests that Utherpendragon had not managed to fully pacify the area before the Battle of St Albans.

Chapter 7

Aurelius/Aurelianus Ambrosius, the Arthur/Arthurus (The Bear) 464–466[1]

The Britons Regroup in 464–466

Readers should note that from this date (464–466) onwards, all events may have taken place one year later than I have stated thanks to the uncertainties in the dating of Arthur's Gallic campaigns.

According to Geoffrey's version of history, after the death of Utherpendragon, the leaders of the Britons assembled in the town of Silchester to choose a new king. They suggested to Dubricius, the Archbishop of the City of the Legions, that he should crown Arthur, the 15-year-old son of Utherpendragon, as the next King of Britain. The reason for the urgency of the matter was that the Saxons had appointed Colgrin as their new leader and had received reinforcements from Germany. The Saxons had already devastated the lands from the Humber to the Sea of Caithness (north of Scotland).

As noted above, it is more or less certain that Geoffrey's version has purposefully muddled the real persons and events so that we should rather see the new name of the king of the Britons to signify his robust health, which was bear-like. He had survived the poisoning and was now ready to lead the Britons against the enemy. The fifteen years of Geoffrey's version is probably a confused memory of a donative given in the fifteenth year of Aurelius Ambrosius' rule. This means that we can date this event roughly to 464/465. For the sake of convenience, I will henceforth call Aurelius/Aurelianus Ambrosianus Arthur, and use the other names only occasionally.

Arthur called to arms all the young men of the realm and assembled the remnants of the army. He distributed gifts freely to everyone in an effort to encourage the men to fight with greater eagerness. There were so many soldiers that Arthur ran out of gifts to distribute, but he solved the problem by promising the wealth then in the Saxon hands as a reward for his own retainers. Geoffrey claims these to be the crowning gifts (donative), and while it is certain that the gifts in question were a donative, they were not the ones given at the time of crowning, but the crown-money given every five years, or on every family occasion of the imperial family or whenever the soldiers needed encouragement. In this case, it is probable that the crown-money/donative was given to officially celebrate the fifteen years in power.

Aurelius/Aurelianus Ambrosius, the Arthur/Arthurus (The Bear) 464–466

Battle of the River Douglas in 464/466

Arthur's first objective was again the city of York, which appears to have formed the centre of operations for the Saxons in the north of England. In the final stages of the march the probable route taken by Arthur would have once again followed the Roman road from Gloucester to York.

When Colgrin learned of this, he assembled his Saxons and united with his allies, the Scots and Picts, after which he advanced to meet Arthur. The armies made contact with each other beside the River Douglas somewhere near the city of York. The modern name of the river is not known with certainty; it may be one of the smaller rivers in the area or a branch of the Ouse. The Britons won the engagement and Colgrin fled to York, where he was duly besieged by Arthur.

It is probable that Nennius has grouped all battles fought by Arthur near York as his second, third, fourth and fifth battles, so that all of these were fought on the river Douglas in the region of Lunius/Linnius.

Siege of York in 464/466

As soon as Baldulf, the brother of Colgrin, who had been left behind on the coast to await the arrival of *Dux* Cheldric with reinforcements from Germany, heard of the situation, he decided to bring relief to his brother. It is probable that Baldulf's fleet was located at the mouth of the River Ouse, so that he advanced from the south towards York. When Baldulf was 10 miles from York, he decided to attempt to surprise the Britons with a night attack, but this failed thanks to the good intelligence apparatus of Arthur. It was thanks to this that Arthur was able to place Cador, the *Dux* of Cornwall, with 3,000 foot and 600 cavalry, in an ambush along the route taken by the enemy. Cador placed his men on both sides of the road and surprised the Saxons. The Saxons were cut to pieces and the survivors fled in complete panic. Baldulf was at a loss what to do, but since he knew that help would shortly arrive from Scotland, he wanted to make contact with his brother so that the desperate Saxons inside York would not surrender.[2] Consequently, he dressed himself as a minstrel with a harp and managed to get inside the city in this disguise. Geoffrey claims that the messengers from Germany appeared only after this, but it is more likely that they had actually arrived before Baldulf took the personal risk to achieve contact with his brother.

The Britons retreat and obtain reinforcements from Armorica in 465/466

When the Britons learnt of the arrival of Saxon reinforcements, Arthur assembled his council of advisors, who duly advised him to abandon the siege and retreat to London. The Saxons had overwhelming numerical superiority; their fleet consisted of 600 longships, all of which were loaded with soldiers. Since the typical Norwegian shipsheds were designed for ships of thirty-five to seventy men, we can estimate that the fleet consisted of a minimum of 21,000 men and a maximum of 42,000, with an average of 31,500. This was clearly a major army, whose intention was nothing less than the total conquest of Britain. The readiness of the Saxons and other Germans to sail to Britain in large numbers must have resulted from their previous successes. It seemed as if the island, just like the rest of the Roman Empire with its richnesses, was ripe for conquest. The lure of booty was just too much for most to resist.

Geoffrey claims that Arthur assembled the bishops and clergy in London to discuss what to do next, and that they decided to ask for help from the Armoricans. The inclusion of the bishops and clergy suggests two things: 1) the Britons needed religious guidance to revive morale; 2) Arthur considered members of the clergy to be among the wisest in the realm, which was undoubtedly true because they consisted of the wealthy and literate. Messengers were sent to the King of Armorica, Hoel, the son of Arthur's sister, Anna, and previous king, Budicius. When Hoel heard the news, he assembled 15,000 warriors and sailed to Southampton at the first fair wind.

The Siege and Battle of Lincoln in 465/466

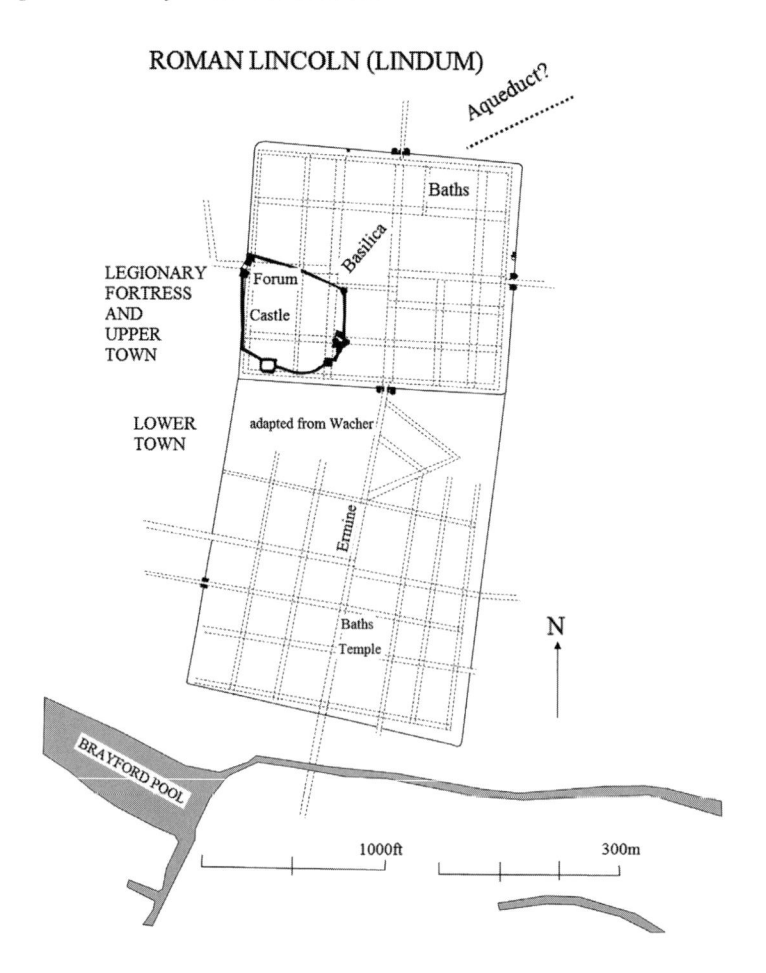

The armies were united, and after a few days' rest Arthur ordered them to begin their march towards Kaerluideoit/Kaerwydcoed/Lincoln/Lindicolium, which was besieged by the Saxons. It is probable that the Britons marched along one of the Roman roads, but it is not known whether they used the Cirencester-Lincoln road or the London-Lincoln road. The Britons inflicted a very serious defeat on the Saxons, with 6,000 of them killed in combat or by drowning in the rivers surrounding Lincoln, and the Saxons were forced to abandon their siege. This implies that the Britons had managed to surprise the besiegers so that they had not been able to form a battle array against the Britons. It is also probable that the Britons' attack was supported by a sally of the garrison/paramilitary forces of Lincoln against the Saxons besiegers. The 6,000 killed would have represented the majority of the besiegers on one side of the city. This is probably Nennius's sixth battle of Arthur on the River Lussas/Bassas.

The Battle and Siege of the Caledon Wood in 465/466
Arthur pursued the fugitives up to the Caledon Wood, which is either the Celidon Wood near Lincoln or a Caledonian Wood somewhere in Caledonia/Scotland. This battle would be Nennius' seventh battle of Arthur in the wood of Celidon/Calidonis/Cacoit Celidon. The Saxons regrouped there and defeated the pursuers. The trees provided shelter against the Briton missiles (*tela Britonum*). This proves that the Britons used large numbers of archers, just like the other Late Roman armies. The woods would obviously have also provided safety against javelins, but not to the same extent as against arrows or darts, the use of which is implied here with the *tela*. This is the reason for the recommendation in the sixth century *Strategikon*[3] to use larger numbers of javelin throwers in the woods and not archers. It is also probable that the British archers included mounted archers, because it would be strange if the armament of Briton armies would not have resembled the other Roman armies of the fourth and fifth centuries, when their tactical systems and equipment (note Gildas) were clearly the same.

Arthur adopted a very ingenious solution to this problem, which was to cut down a part of the wood around the Saxons so that they were surrounded by a circle of felled trees, which effectively formed a barricade or abatis around them and prevented the Saxons from leaving the forest. This was one of the standard tactical ploys that had been used by the Germans against the Romans. The accompanying two images on the previous page from Olaus Magnus' history show how the Finns employed similar tree abatis defensively in the sixteenth century.

Arthur's plan was to besiege the Saxons and force them to surrender through famine. The stalemate continued for three days, after which the Saxons offered to surrender on the following terms: 1) they offered to surrender all their gold and silver; 2) they promised to hand over hostages; 3) they promised to return to Germany; 4) they promised to start paying tribute to Arthur. Arthur convened his advisors to discuss the terms. He agreed to let the Saxons go back to Germany in return for their treasure and hostages. The hostages were naturally meant to ensure

Arthur besieges the Saxons inside the forest. The felled trees form an abatis through which the Saxons could not advance easily. If the Saxons attacked they faced the prospect of being subjected to missile attacks when attempting to go through the obstacle and if they managed to get through they faced the prospect of having to fight the well-ordered Britons while they themselves were scattered and disordered. The Saxons knew that the situation was hopeless. This demonstrates well Arthur's tactical genius. Not to scale.

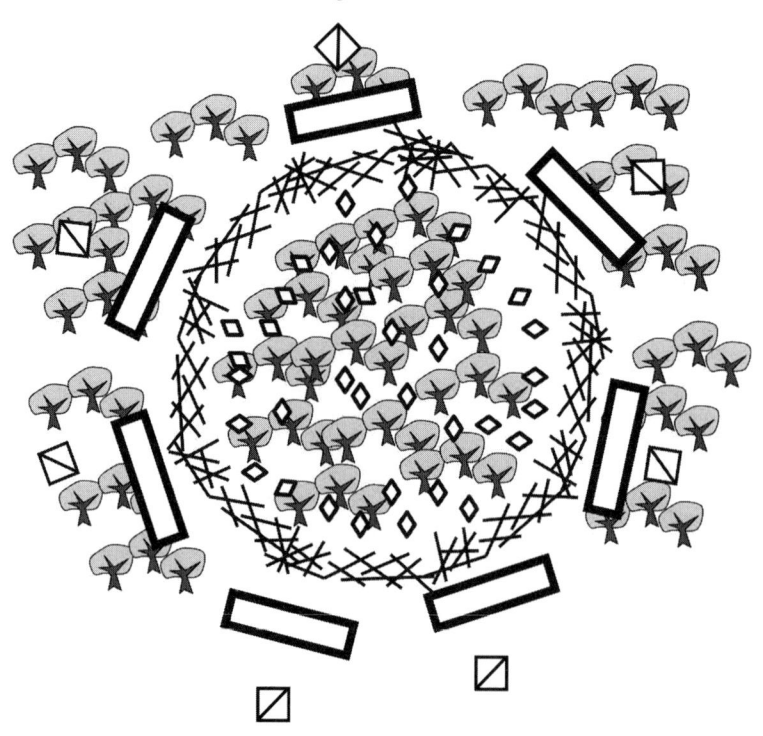

that the Saxons would also honour their promises. Consequently, the Britons opened up a route for the Saxons and let them go to their ships. Arthur and his advisors clearly followed the ancient dictum that it was not wise to fight against desperate enemies. This suggests that the Saxon army was still considered mighty and powerful by the Britons, but as we shall see, what seemed like a good idea at the time proved to be a mistake. Geoffrey fails to tell how the Britons and Saxons dealt with the Picts and Scots which were present in the Saxon army. The likeliest answer is that the Britons allowed them to leave with the Saxons. Otherwise, the Saxons would have been forced to fight against their allies, who would have felt betrayed if left inside the siege.

Consequently, it is probable that after the Saxons had embarked, Arthur marched north to pursue the retreating Picts and Scots. Arthur's goal appears to have been to destroy those who had fought with the Saxons so that they could not reinforce the defence of their homelands, and to prevent the two enemies from uniting so that he could subdue their homelands more easily. It seems probable that Arthur divided his army into two corps, so that Hoel (who ended up in Alclud/Dumbarton) advanced against the Scots along the western coast of Albany/Scotland while Arthur attacked the Picts along the eastern coast.

The Battle of Mount Badon (Mons Badonicus/Badonis) in about 465/466[4]
The Saxons, however, did not keep their word, but attempted to strike at the very heart of Roman Britain by landing their ships near Totnes. Arthur had made the mistake of not shadowing the retreating Saxons with a fleet and army, but we should remember that his choices were limited. The North was still in the hands of his enemies, and if he had shadowed the Saxons, he would have left northern England undefended. He trusted that the hostages would ensure that the Saxons would keep their word. When the Saxon fleet sailed towards the coast of Gaul and the city of Boulogne it appeared as if they were keeping their word. In truth, they were exploiting the opportunity provided by the absence of Roman troops from Cornwall and Somerset by attacking it from the sea. The Saxons depopulated all the countryside up to the Severn Sea, then reached the neighbourhood of the town of Bath with a forced march and besieged it.

When Arthur learnt of the Saxon betrayal, he had the hostages hanged, abandoned his campaign against the Picts and Scots, and then marched south as fast as possible to relieve Bath. He was forced to leave behind Hoel in the city of Anclud because he had contracted a serious illness. Arthur reached Somerset and faced the Saxons somewhere near Bath. Gildas calls the subsequent Battle of Badon the siege of Badon; the exact location of the battle is contested.[5] If the Saxons left their ships near Totnes, then it is impossible to present any definitive theory regarding the location of the battle, because it could have taken place in almost any hilly location in Somerset. However, if one makes the assumption that the Saxon fleet followed the land forces and met them on the coast of the Severn Sea to load

110   Britain in the Age of Arthur

captured booty, then it is possible to think that the fleet would have sailed upstream along the River Avon and have been anchored just west of Bath. This in turn would mean that Arthur's army would have marched from the direction of Gloucester towards the Saxon fleet, so as to force the Saxons to abandon their siege. However, even if the Saxons had left their fleet near Totnes, it is still highly likely that the battle took place very near Bath, and that Arthur used the Gloucester road for the approach. The reason for this is that the sources unanimously place the battle in the neighbourhood of Badonis/Bath, and because the Saxons retreated eastwards after the battle.

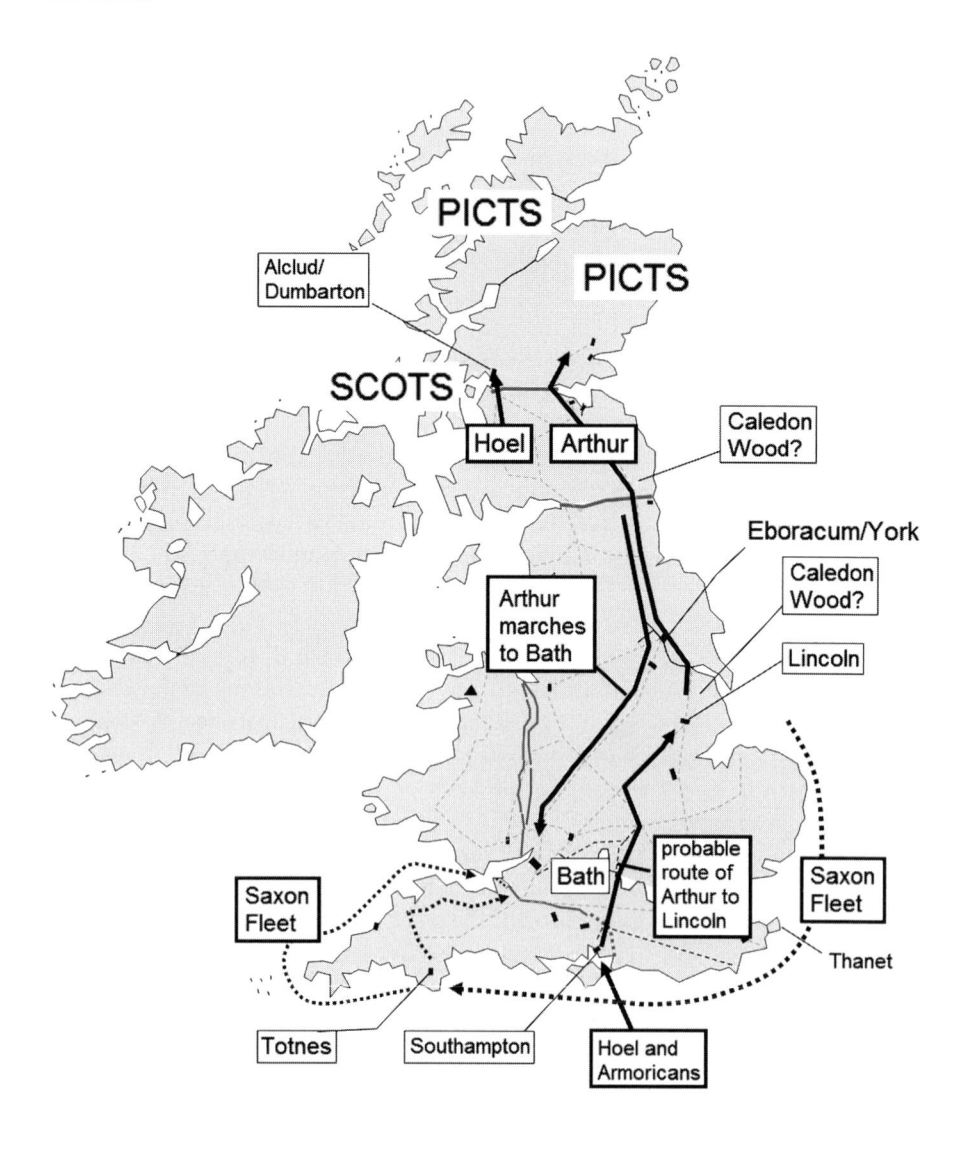

Notably, *The Dream of Rhonabwy* (*Mabinogion*, 178–191) supports my conclusion regarding the route taken by Arthur. According to this story, the Britons advanced from the direction of the Havren/Severn (i.e. from the north-west of Bath) to the Battle of Baddon close to the Caer Vddon (Fortress of Baddon), and, just like in Geoffrey, the Duke of Cornwall played an important role (in the *Mabinogion*, Cadrw Earl of Cornwall). The *Dream* also claims that the Saxons attempted to negotiate a truce (in the *Mabinogion*, twenty-four horsemen arrived as envoys of Osla Big Knife), but at the advice of Kay (Kai in the *Mabinogion*), the Britons attacked and advanced to Cornwall. It is by no means impossible that the Saxons could have attempted to negotiate once again, possibly to find out the size of the enemy force they were facing, but that it came to nothing as it was not in Arthur's interest to prolong the conflict. It is possible that information regarding the fight between Arthur's forces and Twrch Trwyth at the mouth of the Havren/Severn, and then in Cornwall, is also a distorted memory of the Battle of Bath (*Mabinogion* 173–175). Of note is that this story refers to the use of two cavalry lines in combat, which is in agreement with the period Roman cavalry tactics and can therefore be used as another possible piece of evidence of distorted memories of early Dark Age Britain in the *Mabinogion*.

Consequently, it was probably somewhere near Bath that Arthur's forces came face-to-face with the Saxons, who had taken defensive positions in wedge-shaped formations. I would suggest that this was very close to the town (see map overleaf), as stated by the sources. The other alternative would be that the battle was fought at a distance of about one day's march north of Bath (see map), so the Saxons would have used the Jurassic Way, which would have given them the advantage of terrain together with a central position between the Roman roads. The Saxons had at least 20,000–25,000 warriors; considering Arthur's readiness to engage them, he must have had more than that.

Arthur opted to engage the Saxons head-on because he had learnt that the Picts and Scots had attacked and besieged Hoel in Alclud. Arthur ordered his men to arm themselves for combat, after which Dubricius, Archbishop of the City of the Legions (Caerleon), encouraged them by stating that all those who died in combat against the infidel invaders would receive absolution of their sins. Contrary to popular belief these religious concepts were adopted well before the Crusades and are therefore not anachronistic to this era. The origins of these concepts lay in the fourth century Christianity as it was interpreted by the imperial authorities for use in the armed forces. For further details, see Syvänne (2016).

After this, Arthur donned his *lorica*-armour fit for a king, and placed on his head a golden helmet adorned with a crest in the shape of a dragon. Then he took his *Prydwen/Pridwen clipeus* (round shield),[6] which featured a painting of Mary, and girded his *Caliburnus gladius* (*Excalibur* sword) that had been forged on the Isle of Avalon.[7] Lastly, Arthur took his *Ron lancea* (spear/lance) with a long and broad blade in his right hand, which shows that it was meant to be used for thrusts and cuts, not

112   Britain in the Age of Arthur

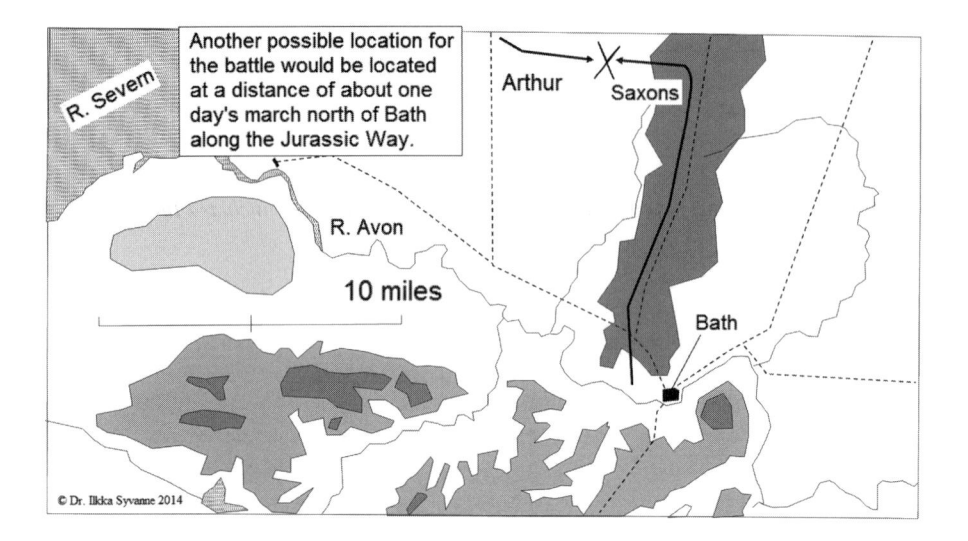

Another possible location for the battle would be located at a distance of about one day's march north of Bath along the Jurassic Way.

© Dr. Ilkka Syvänne 2014

for throwing.⁸ Then he arrayed his men for combat and ordered them to launch an attack against the Saxons. The Saxons resisted bravely and the Britons were forced to launch a series of attacks, all of which ended in withdrawal and regrouping of their forces. Close to sunset, the Saxons finally withdrew towards a neighbouring hill, where they pitched their camp for the night. If my line of reasoning is correct, then the hill was located east of the road leading from Gloucester, which meant that Arthur's army was now in possession of the most direct route leading to the anchoring place of the Saxon fleet.

On the following morning, Arthur ordered his men to attack the Saxons on the hill. Burne has noted that there were certainly good reasons for Arthur to repeat his attack against the Saxons, despite the fact that the Saxons possessed an advantageous defensive position. The previous day had left the Britons in possession of the battlefield, which signified victory. The fact that the Saxons had been forced to take refuge on the hill meant that they did not have access to any source of water, and it is also possible that they had not carried enough food with them to the battle, which meant that the Saxons would be demoralized and tired when Arthur attacked. The Saxons would also have used all their missiles in the course of the first day, while the Britons would have been in a position to collect the missiles left on the battlefield. In spite of this, the attack was by no means easy. Geoffrey notes that the Britons lost many men when they climbed the hill, as the Saxons had the advantage of terrain on their side. It was only thanks to the superb bravery of the Briton soldiers that they managed to reach the summit in hard hand-to-hand combat. Geoffrey tells us:

> 'In this manner was a great part of that day also spent, whereupon Arthur, provoked to see the little advantage he had yet gained and that victory still

continued in suspense, drew out his Caliburn, and, calling upon the name of the blessed Virgin, rushed forward with great fury [with impetuosity, '*impetus*'] into the thickest of the enemy's ranks; of whom (such was the merit of his prayers) not one escaped alive that felt the fury of his sword; neither did he give over the fury of his assault until he had, with his Caliburn alone, killed four hundred and seventy men [*it is possible that this figure included those killed by his retinue, just like German and Russian air forces counted the kills of the wingmen in aerial combat during WWII, but one cannot exclude the possibility that Arthur really killed this many. According to Nennius, Arthur killed either 840 or 940 men with his own hand, which means that he or his source has doubled the number given by Geoffrey's source. Whatever the actual number, it is still clear that Arthur was a real killing machine, like the emperor Aurelian[9] and Natuspardo mentioned by Ammianus Marcellinus*]. The Britons, seeing this, followed their leader in great multitudes, and made slaughter on all sides; so that Colgrin, and Badulph his brother, and many thousands more, fell before them. But Cheldric, in this imminent danger of his men, betook himself to flight. The victory thus gained, the king commanded Cador, Duke of Cornwall, to pursue them, while he himself should hasten his march into Albany: from whence he had advice that the Scots and Picts were besieging Alclud, in which, as we said before Hoel lay sick. Therefore he hastened to his assistance; for he might fall into the hands of the barbarians [*this is the reason for Arthur's decision to attack the Saxons head-on; he needed to defeat them fast so that he could return on the double. The Duke of Cornwall was left in charge of the pursuit and mopping up, because he knew the terrain and was highly motivated after the Saxons had just pillaged his lands*]. In the meantime the Duke of Cornwall, who had the command of ten thousand men, would not as yet pursue the Saxons in their flight, but speedily made himself master of their ships, to hinder their getting on board, and manned them with his best soldiers, who were to beat back the pagans in case they should flee thither; after this he hastily pursued the enemy, according to Arthur's command, and allowed no quarter to those he could overtake. … Now with timorous hearts [the Saxons] fled for shelter, sometimes to the coverts of the woods, sometimes to mountains and caves to prolong a wretched life. At last, when none of these places could afford them a safe retreat, they entered the Isle of Thanet with their broken forces; but neither did they there get free from the Duke of Cornwall's pursuit, for he still continued slaughtering them, and gave them no respite until he had killed Cheldric, and taken hostages for the surrender of the rest. Having therefore settled peace here, he directed his march to Alclud, which Arthur had relieved.' (Geoffrey of Monmouth 9.4–6, tr. by Thompson and Giles, with some minor additions and changes inside square parentheses.)[10]

The account proves that the Britons attacked the Saxons head-on and did not attempt any outflanking movements. The reason for this was that Arthur wanted a quick victory and knew that the Saxons were suffering from low morale. When the battle had already lasted some time, in the course of which the Britons had only managed to gain the summit of the hill, he decided to break the deadlock through personal example, as was expected of a good commander. It was possible for battles to last such a long time because intensive periods of hand-to-hand combat would have been punctuated by periods of rest, which in this case means that the Saxons would have retreated a few steps to a distance of relative safety. Contrary to what Geoffrey says, it would not have been solely Arthur with his Caliburn that would have attacked. It is obvious that Arthur would have been accompanied by his personal retinue. Geoffrey's account doesn't state whether the final attack was conducted on horseback, but this appears very likely because the standard battle formation used by Arthur and his Britons was based on the late fourth-century Roman battle formation consisting of a line of hollow infantry squares, behind which were placed cavalry reserves (see my *Military History of Late Rome, Vols 2–4*).

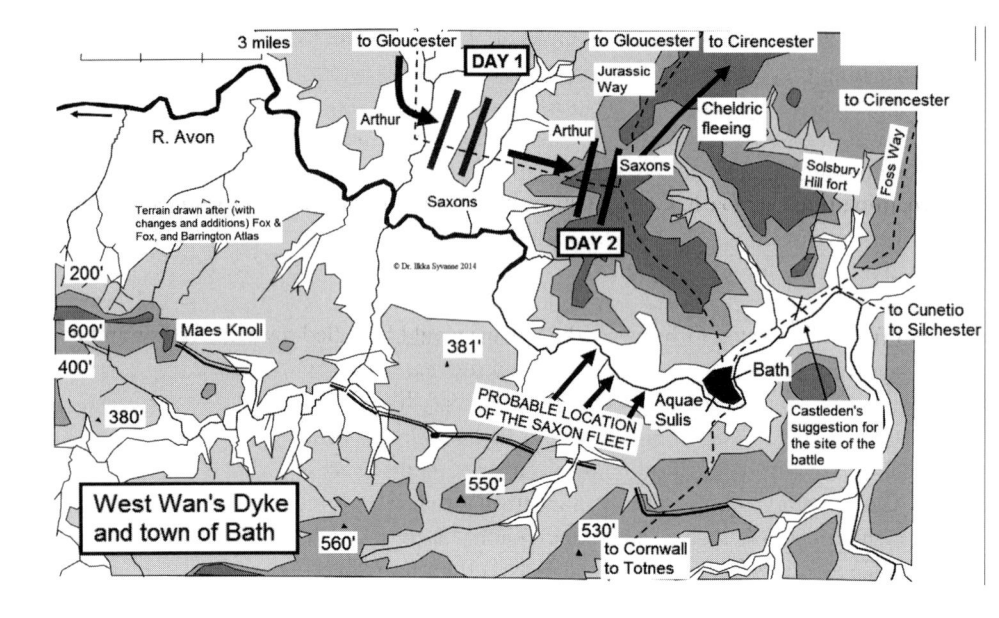

In other words, Arthur would have led forward his own personal cavalry *comitatus/bucellarii* (his 'knights') through the intervals between the infantry squares fighting against the Saxon wedges. This cavalry charge would have been aided by the fact that the Britons would have by then reached the summit of the hill. Arthur's charge proved decisive and he cut his way through the already disordered enemy formation, with the result that the rest of his army followed his example. Arthur was certainly a brave warrior king.

Arthur left the pursuit of the Saxons to Cador, the *Dux* of Cornwall, so that he could immediately return to Albany to relieve Hoel. Both men acted wisely. Instead of pursuing the fugitives immediately, Cador made certain that they could not retreat to their ships. It is not known with definite certainty whether the Saxon ships were located just west of Bath, or were still near Totnes, but the former is inherently more likely because the text states that the duke went in person to the boats. It would have been a dangerous move for him to go as far as Totnes when the Saxons were still roaming free near Bath. Consequently, it is almost certain that the Saxon ships must have been just west of Bath, so that it was possible for the duke to continue his pursuit of the Saxons almost immediately. The fact that the Saxons fled east means that Arthur cannot have marched to Bath from that direction (Cirencester or Silchester), but from Gloucester. Otherwise, the Saxons would have fled towards Arthur and not away from him. The duke clearly avoided the taking of unnecessary risks, defeating the fleeing Saxons through shadowing and guerrilla warfare. The fact that the Duke of Cornwall chose this approach when he had 10,000 men suggests that the fleeing Saxons had at least about the same number of demoralized men.

Cador conducted the pursuit so skillfully that the routed Saxons were unable to reform and ambush their pursuers. When the Saxons reached the shore opposite the Isle of Thanet, Cador attacked and cut their battle line to pieces. Cador crossed to the island and renewed the butchery. Cador stopped the slaughter only after Cheldric had been killed. The rest were allowed to surrender and were apparently allowed to settle as federates on the Isle of Thanet. However, see also chapter 14 for an alternative interpretation. After this, Cador turned around to join Arthur in Alclud, where Arthur had in the meantime brought help to Hoel.

Pacification of Scotland/Pictland in 465/466
According to Geoffrey, Arthur and Hoel defeated the Picts and Scots three times and forced them to seek refuge on the islands of lake Lomond, which Arthur and Hoel proceeded to besiege. Cador led his army to Moray, where he joined Arthur and Hoel. This account implies that the region of lake/Loch Lomond should also be considered to be part of Moray, and that Arthur and Hoel had first defeated the enemy at Alclud/Dumbarton, after which they had pursued them to the lake and in the course of their pursuit had inflicted two other defeats on them.

The other possibility is that Arthur and Hoel had defeated the enemy first at Alclud and had then invaded western Albany, so that they had defeated the Picts (and their possible Scottish allies) in Moray twice, forcing the Pictish army to retreat north, then west and then south-west along the Great Glen (the route from Inverness along Loch Ness and Loch Lochy up to Fort William), then southwards towards Alclud/Dumbarton, where their route of retreat would have been blocked by the arrival of Cador's force so that they would have been forced to seek a place of refuge on the islands of lake Lomond while waiting for reinforcements from Ireland. In light of the inclusion of Moray in the account, and the three separate battles, the latter appears the likelier, but I have included both alternatives in the maps.

116 Britain in the Age of Arthur

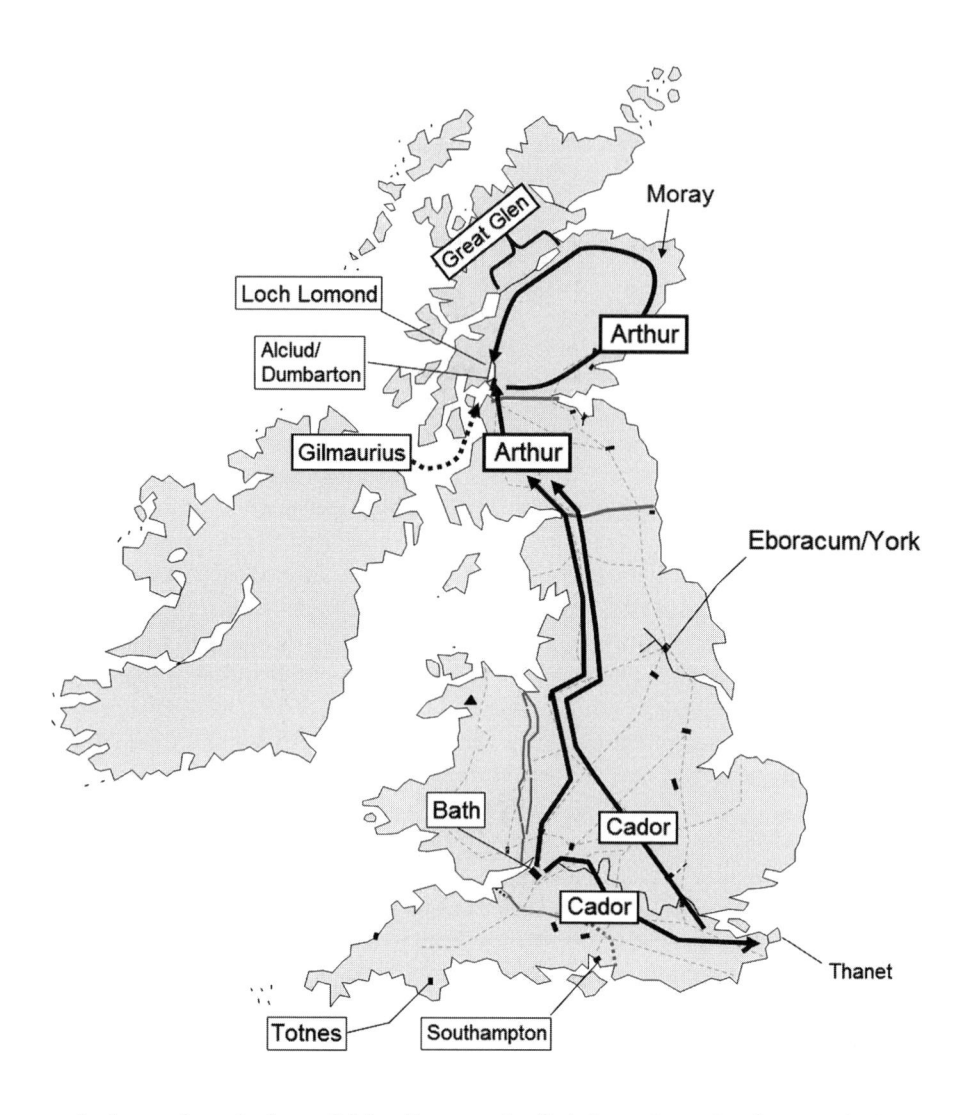

Arthur gathered a fleet of ships/boats and sailed them along the rivers to the lake, reducing the enemy to such a state of hunger that thousands died. It is probable that the boats used on the lake would have consisted mostly of smaller vessels belonging to the Briton fleet, which would have been used in support of operations in the North. The following map shows the principal features of the siege of Loch Lomond, which are based on my estimation of the relative strengths and weaknesses of each location on the lake. It is probable that the fugitives would have been located on the southern section of the lake, so there would not have been any fugitives to the north.

Aurelius/Aurelianus Ambrosius, the Arthur/Arthurus (The Bear) 464–466

I have shown on the map below the likely location of the wall during the fifth century on the basis of the extant remains of the ancient walls and on the basis of the modern road grid. It is possible that the wall had a moat, because the modern river makes a deep and sharp cut into the peninsula at about the same point where the wall is likely to have existed. The city and fortress (if it had the same density of people as a Roman marching camp) could have housed in times of crisis about 13,125 to 18,000 soldiers plus non-combatants. What is notable about this is that these numbers give Hoel about the same number of men (15,000) with which he arrived in Britain to assist Arthur. This lends additional support for the account given by Geoffrey. It is notable that the Britons had a fleet of some kind to bring supplies for Hoel and Arthur, which Arthur subsequently used during the siege of Loch Lomond.

The Dumbarton Rock
A sketch of the possible appearance of the Briton settlement of Alclud/Dumbarton at the time of Arthur. Note the ships and the wall in the distance separating the peninsula of the Dumbarton Rock from the mainland.

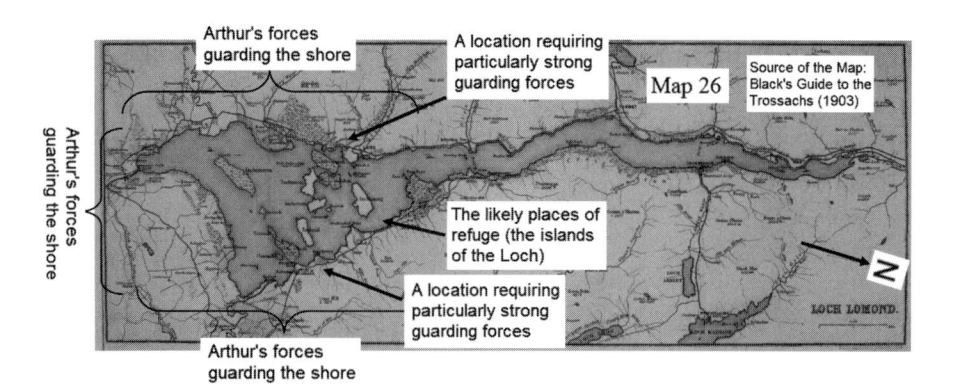

The Destruction of the Irish Relief Army in ca 465/466
It was then that Gilmarius, the King of Ireland, arrived with a fleet carrying a huge army of pagans. It is probable that most of the pagan Irish consisted of the Scots of Dal Riata, who lived on both sides of the Irish Sea. Arthur had no other alternative than to raise the siege and march against the invaders. The Irish forces were duly crushed and forced to flee back to Ireland. It is probable that the battle was fought somewhere in the vicinity of Alclud/Dumbarton.

There exists possible independent evidence to support this, if one backdates the evidence in the *Irish Annals* by about one to three years. According to the entry *anno* 468, Irish High-King Ailill Molt was defeated at the Battle of Dumae Achir in 468 (there is a possible doublet of this entry for the year ca.474). With this change in dating, the evidence fits perfectly the timetable of Arthur's campaigns. Consequently, it is possible that the *Irish Annals* may have also preserved a distorted memory of the same event, namely Ailill Molt's failed campaign against Arthur's forces near Dumbarton, which must be the town of Dumae Achir – the names of the locations certainly resemble each other. If one chooses not to backdate the evidence, then it is possible that all of the following events took place one year later. However, the fact that all of the campaigns took place before the death of Anthemius in 472 makes it more likely that the earlier dating which I have included here as the primary date is closest to the truth.

The Last Measures Taken to Pacify Albany in ca 465/466
'After this victory, he [Arthur] proceeded in his first attempt, which was to extirpate the whole race of Scots and Picts, and treated them with unparalled severity. And as he allowed quarter to none, the bishops of that miserable country, with all the inferior clergy, met together, and bearing the reliques of the saints … barefooted, came to implore the king's mercy for their people. As soon as they were admitted into his presence, they all fell down upon their knees, and humbly besought him to have pity on their distressed country.' (Geoffrey of Monmouth 9.6, J.A. Giles tr., p.184, London 1842 edition)[11]

Arthur granted them their wish. The above quote shows well how Arthur was following the standard operating procedure of the ancient Romans, which was to terrorize the enemy with unbelievably brutal treatment of the populace and to stop the use of the terror tactic only after the enemy had shown enough humility in his presence.

Chapter 8

The Reorganization of the Realm in 465/466[1]

After Arthur had completed the conquest of Britain with Albany, he marched back to York. He reached the city close to Christmas in 465/466. The city and its churches were in a pitiful state. Consequently, Arthur appointed Pyramus as new archbishop, ordered the churches to be rebuilt and to restore the city's old nobility. The latter meant the restoration of the curial class, which was now responsible for the administration, defence and taxation of the city and its surrounding areas.

As part of the reorganization of the realm, Arthur also restored Augusel to the position of king of the Scots and his brother, Urian, as king of Moray/Mureif. Loth, the son of the king of Norway, was re-established as consul of Lothian (Lodonesia) and other nearby areas. At the same time, Arthur consolidated his own position by marrying Guanhumara (Guinevere), who belonged to the nobility. She had been educated under the guidance *dux* Cador.

Christopher Snyder (p.84) usefully summarizes the evidence regarding Guinevere. She is mentioned for the first time by Geoffrey, and according to Mallory was the daughter of King Leodegrance of Cameliard, who gave her – together with the Round Table – to Arthur to seal his alliance. Of particular importance is the fact that some traditions suggest that Guinevere was Arthur's second wife, and that some Welsh traditions claim there were three separate women called Gwenhwyvar married to Arthur (Snyder, p.84). I take this to confirm my educated guess that Arthur is at the same time both Aurelius and Utherpendragon, so that Ygerna would have been Arthur's first or second wife.

The administrative hierarchy of the realm appears to have consisted of the Celtic territories (Scotland, Moray, Lothian, Venedotia, Demetia and Cornwall), which were ruled by sub-kings, and of the Roman Britons, who were ruled by duke consuls and dukes. The only problem is Cador's title. His title is *dux* until 470/471, after which it is king of Cornwall. My own educated guess is that he held both titles even before this, so that he ruled the Celtish tribesmen as their king and the more Romanized sections of the society as *dux*, but it is also possible that he received the title of king only when Arthur and the Romans had their fallout. It is also notable that all of these Celtic territories were separated from Roman Britain with walls, in the north by the Antonine and Hadrian's Walls, in the west by Wat's and Offa's Dykes, and in the south-west by Wansdyke, all of which have sections that are dated to have been in use during the fifth century. This may suggest a situation in

The Reorganization of the Realm in 465/466

which the Romano–Britons had separated themselves from the less civilized Celtic portions of the land. The map shows the likely administrative structure of Arthur's kingdom just before his foreign wars.

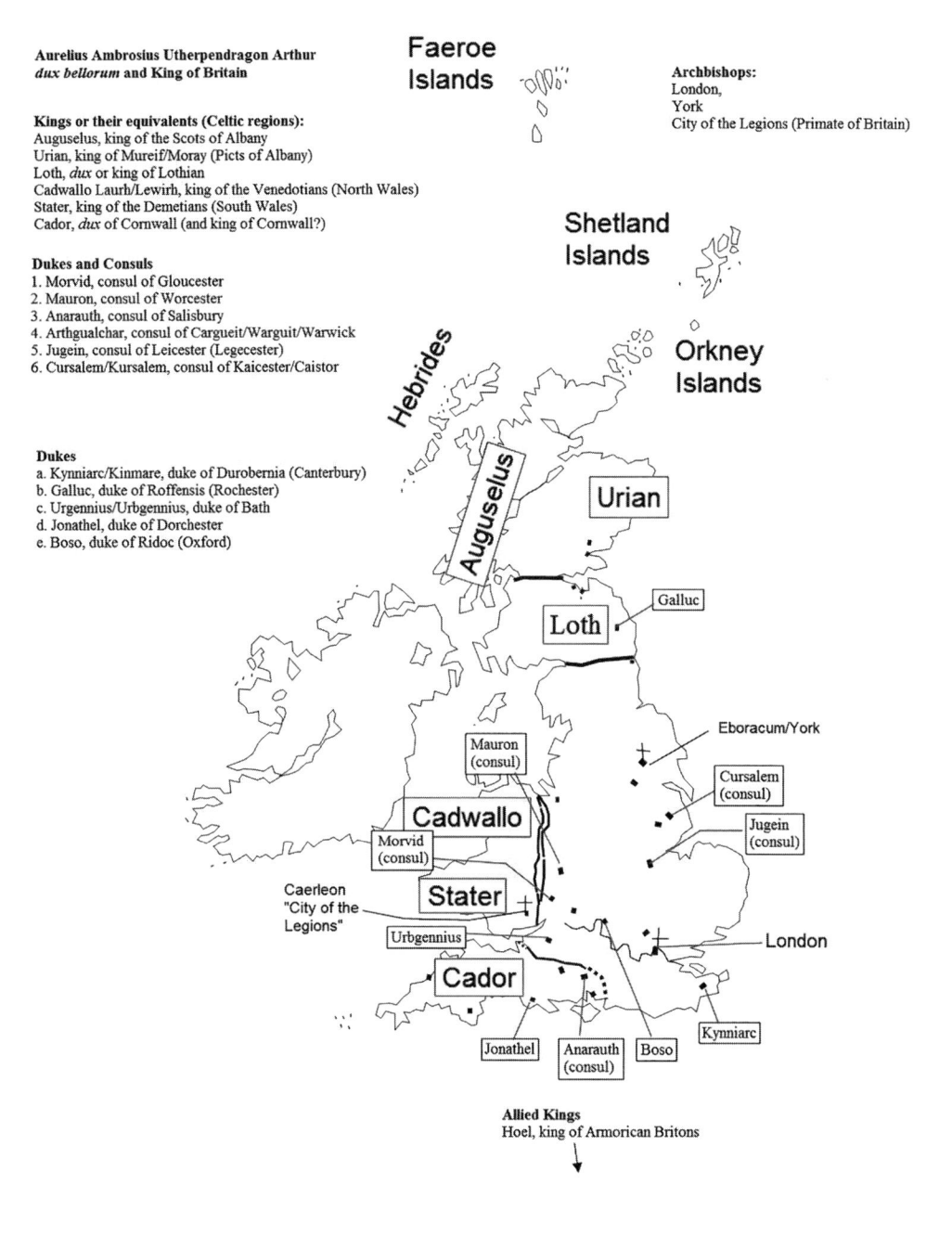

Aurelius Ambrosius Utherpendragon Arthur
dux bellorum and King of Britain

Kings or their equivalents (Celtic regions):
Auguselus, king of the Scots of Albany
Urian, king of Mureif/Moray (Picts of Albany)
Loth, *dux* or king of Lothian
Cadwallo Laurh/Lewirh, king of the Venedotians (North Wales)
Stater, king of the Demetians (South Wales)
Cador, *dux* of Cornwall (and king of Cornwall?)

Dukes and Consuls
1. Morvid, consul of Gloucester
2. Mauron, consul of Worcester
3. Anarauth, consul of Salisbury
4. Arthgualchar, consul of Cargueit/Warguit/Warwick
5. Jugein, consul of Leicester (Legecester)
6. Cursalem/Kursalem, consul of Kaicester/Caistor

Dukes
a. Kynniarc/Kinmare, duke of Durobernia (Canterbury)
b. Galluc, duke of Roffensis (Rochester)
c. Urgennius/Urbgennius, duke of Bath
d. Jonathel, duke of Dorchester
e. Boso, duke of Ridoc (Oxford)

Archbishops:
London,
York
City of the Legions (Primate of Britain)

Allied Kings
Hoel, king of Armorican Britons

Chapter 9

Ireland, the Orkneys, Iceland and Gothland/ Götaland in 466/467

Geoffrey of Monmouth (9.10) claims that Arthur's next move was to fit out a fleet with which he sailed to Ireland. This campaign can be dated roughly to the summer of 466, but it is possible that it took place in 467. One may assume that Arthur used his famous flagship *Prydwen* (Fair-face), if that was its name. The other tradition states that the *Prydwen* was Arthur's shield, which does make more sense if it had the Madonna with child Jesus on it. The Irish under their High-King Guillamurius had prior intelligence of Arthur's plans and had posted their forces in readiness to block the amphibious landing. The Irish, however, were easily routed thanks to the fact that they fought 'naked' and were poorly armed, and Guillamurius was taken prisoner. Guillamurius wisely chose to acknowledge Arthur as his lord, and his example was followed by the other kings of the island. One can find quite definite support for Arthur's campaign from the *Irish Annals* ca.466 if one assumes Domangart, son of Ness, died (*Dal Riada*) as a result of Arthur's campaign. This dating of the evidence fits perfectly the dating I have here adopted for the events of Arthur's reign, which must have taken place before Anthemius lost his ability to wage war in Gaul and was killed at Rome on 11 July 472. It is unfortunate that we do not know how long the campaign was, but in light of the evidence it was probably a short one, which allowed Arthur to continue his campaign in 'Iceland' during the same campaigning season. According to Geoffrey, Arthur subdued that island too, with the result that Doldavius, king of Gothland, and Gunfacius, king of the Orkneys, offered their submissions voluntarily. The subdual of the Orkneys would have been a necessity, because according to Nennius (38), the Saxons under Octa and Ebissa had previously occupied the islands. Arthur then wintered in some unknown place and returned to Britain, where he resided in peace for twelve years, according to Geoffrey. The twelve years are likely to be just twelve months.

This account has several problems. Iceland was only settled in the ninth century, but it is possible to explain this issue away by the fact that Geoffrey merely states that Arthur sailed there, that there were inhabitants on the island before it was permanently settled by the Norwegians in the ninth century, that there existed some other island which was called Iceland thanks to its cold climate, or that someone had the title of king of Iceland even if he resided elsewhere. Geoffrey doesn't mention any opposition, but since he mentions a king for this island, it is probable that it also had inhabitants. On the basis of this, it is possible that Geoffrey has misunderstood his source and translated the Shetland or Faeroe Islands as Iceland, but one cannot achieve complete certainty on this matter because it is possible that Iceland was actually part of some kingdom of northern Norway. Regardless, my suggestion is that Arthur sailed via the Orkneys and Shetlands to Norway.

The location of Gothland is even more problematic, because it can mean the island in the Baltic Sea or two provinces of modern Sweden. The likeliest location would be the two provinces and the adjoining areas along the western border close to Norway and Denmark. It would also be more natural to connect the voluntary submission of this area (south-west Sweden) with Arthur's campaign in Norway and Denmark mentioned in Geoffrey's next chapter, 9.11. One possible explanation for this is that the Norwegian king was allied with Arthur. The marriage of Arthur's sister with Loth, nephew of Sichelm, king of Norway, suggests that Arthur and Sichelm had formed an alliance at some point. The natural target of such an alliance would have been to wage war against the Jutes of Denmark and/or the Swedes/Goths of Gothland, who appear to have supported the Saxon invaders. This would also explain why Arthur had first sailed to 'Iceland' (probably the Shetlands) and then spent the winter in some unknown locale. What is certain is that Arthur cannot have spent the winter in Iceland, because it is extremely unlikely that the two kings would have sailed there to offer their submissions. I would suggest that the kings of the Orkneys and Shetland offered their submissions immediately after Arthur had conquered Ireland. It is possible that the king of Gothland would have offered his submission after Arthur had sailed to Norway to assist its king against the Goths/Swedes. I would suggest that it is even more likely that Geoffrey has misunderstood his source, so that the king of Gothland actually offered his submission to Arthur after Arthur had returned from the Shetlands in an effort to prevent a campaign against himself, so that he would become Arthur's ally, and the king of Gothland and Arthur would undertake a joint campaign against the king of Norway and the Jutes of Denmark. This is, in my opinion, the likeliest answer to the problems in Geoffrey's text. This would also mean that there would not have been any peaceful period of twelve years between the campaigns, as claimed by Geoffrey, but rather a period of twelve months during which Arthur made very thorough preparations for the forthcoming war against the king of Norway and the Jutes. The other possibility is that Arthur's first Gallic campaign took place during this twelve-month lull in Geoffrey's sources, so that Arthur would have campaigned in Gaul as Riothamus (High King) and then have wintered in Burgundy (the unknown locale).

It is notable that Arthur's campaigns in Ireland, Norway and Denmark also receive support from the *Mabinogion*, which mentions the presence of forces or persons from these areas in Arthur's army and court in several places. There clearly existed a tradition in Wales according to which Arthur had subdued these regions. This makes perfect sense in light of the Scandinavian operations in Britain and the corresponding need to break up this alliance of northerners with alliances of his own.

The North and Norwegian Seas formed an open avenue in which the coastal kingdoms projected their influence through their naval forces. Contrary to popular belief, naval raids did not only progress from Scandinavia and the Frisian Islands to the British Isles, but at times included naval operations from Britain to Norway and Denmark. The Late Romans also recruited some of their elite soldiers from these areas (see the appendices, with the studies of Speidel). Arthur's campaigns are probably among the earliest instances of this phenomenon, but it is likely that similar operations were undertaken even before him by the Roman fleet posted in Britain. The same phenomenon is also included in the texts of Saxo Grammaticus. For example, he claims (1.32–35) that at some point in antiquity, Tosti the Villain fled from Jutland to Britain and was then helped back by the pirate Kolli. Unfortunately, these events cannot be dated securely. It is unfortunate that we have very few references in the sources to events taking place in Scandinavia, the North Sea, Norwegian Sea and the coastal kingdoms of the Baltic Sea before the Viking age, because, for example, Finland alone has 361 known hill forts[1] and it is clear that quite a bit of fighting must have taken place in these areas.

Chapter 10

Norway and Jutland/Denmark in 468

Arthur next started to augment the size of his household by increasing the number of *famuli* (servants/attendants = the military retinue of the household = *bucellarii*, the eaters of hard-tack), which I take to refer to military preparations for the forthcoming campaign to install Loth on the Norwegian throne after his uncle the king Sichelm had died (Geoffrey 9.11). The Norwegians had instead chosen Riculf as their king. Riculf was well aware of the forthcoming invasion and fortified settlements in advance.

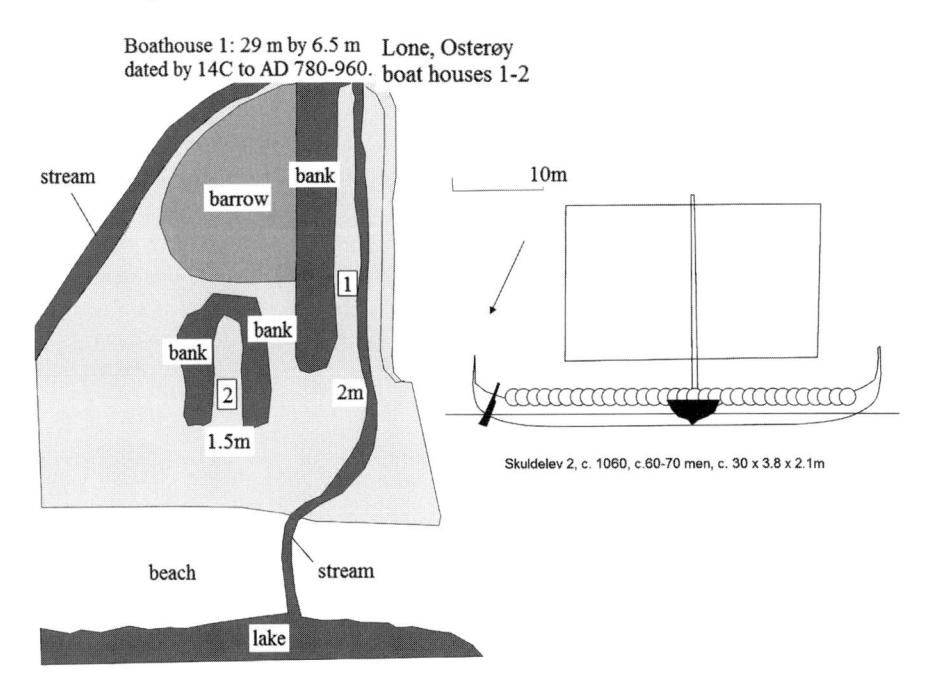

Boathouse 1: 29 m by 6.5 m dated by 14C to AD 780-960.

Lone, Osterøy boat houses 1-2

Skuldelev 2, c. 1060, c.60-70 men, c. 30 x 3.8 x 2.1m

Bjørn Myhre's analysis of Norwegian boathouses and Iron Age naval organization gives a good overall picture of the defensive arrangements of Norway at the time Arthur is supposed to have operated there (see the illustrations above; that on the left is drawn after Myhre). Boathouse 1 would have housed a slightly smaller vessel than the Skuldelev 2 shown above. According to Myhre's analysis, Norwegian defensive arrangements were based on petty tribal kingdoms which formed defensive clusters along the coastal areas and fjords. These kinglets organized the local defence so that the boathouses for the longships and the hill forts were located in the central areas of each kingdom. These calculations are based on the supposition that population levels were lower than during the Viking or High Medieval era, which means that the kings would have been forced to recruit their forces from larger areas than during the Viking era. Each king needed to collect hundreds of men to be able to man the hill forts and the true warships. Myhre's calculations are based on the attested locations of the boathouses meant for warships with average crews of about thirty-five to seventy men (the largest could have as many as 120 men), but this is based on the supposition that smaller vessels would not have been used in warfare. This is not the case, as Saxo's account proves (see Appendix 1). The Norwegians and Danes also employed smaller vessels which had twelve-man crews. This means that we should modify the above calculations so that the smaller boathouses are also included in the overall combat strength, which means that population levels were probably not as low as usually assumed. However, this does not mean that Myhre's analysis of the locations of the true war fleets was incorrect. It is clear that the true warships were clustered around the central areas of each of the kingdoms, where the bulk of the population was located. These clusters were naturally located in the coastal areas and fjords.

The division of Norway into several kingdoms meant that Arthur was probably able to exploit divisions within the realm of Riculf, and was not forced to engage the entire military might of Norway. Consequently, it comes as no surprise that Arthur was able to disembark his army on the shore unopposed, after which he advanced against Riculf. It is probable that Arthur could obtain a safe landing place from some of the kingdoms which did not recognize Riculf as their overlord. The likely location for the landing would be somewhere in south-east Norway or south-west Sweden, since the king of 'Gotland' (*Götaland* in south-west Sweden) was allied with Arthur. The other even likelier alternative is that the 'Goths' of Götaland attacked from the other side and tied up part of the Norwegian army, so that Arthur did not have to face the entire might of King Riculf.

After the landing, the Britons defeated the Norwegians with a charge, killing Riculf and his retinue. Arthur exploited his victory by pillaging and torching the towns and countryside. The campaign was continued until all Norway and 'Dacia' were subdued, and Loth installed as ruler. The Dacia in question is Dania/Jutland, which was also known by the name Dacia until at least the sixteenth century, as Olaus Magnus' maps prove. The usual interpretation for Dacia is that it meant Denmark, and Lewis Thorpe, for example, has so translated the word. Since the attack was directed against both Norway and Jutland, it is probable the king of Norway held some sort of claim to that area. It is unfortunate that Geoffrey fails to state who replaced Loth as ruler of Lodonesia and the surrounding regions. My own guess is that since Auguselus is subsequently called King of Albany instead of merely being ruler of Scots, as previously, that he became the ruler of all Albany, including Moray.

The Norwegians built their hill forts on the high hills surrounding fjords or lakes, or on an island. On occasion they also used large fortified caves, which had walls of piled stones to protect the entrance. Some of the hill forts had several walls of piled stones. The principal defence of these forts was therefore the forbidding location itself. The forts and towns were located along the waterways where most of the people lived.[1] It is these kinds of defensive structures that Arthur would have needed to subdue after he had defeated Riculf. It was not an easy task, but quite achievable for Arthur's forces, which had Roman siege engineers, because archaeological evidence proves that even the locals were able to take and burn these forts. The following illustrations (drawn after Näsman) of the refuge fortresses and towns from central and southern Sweden and southern Norway give a good indication of what types of defences these refuge hill forts possessed.

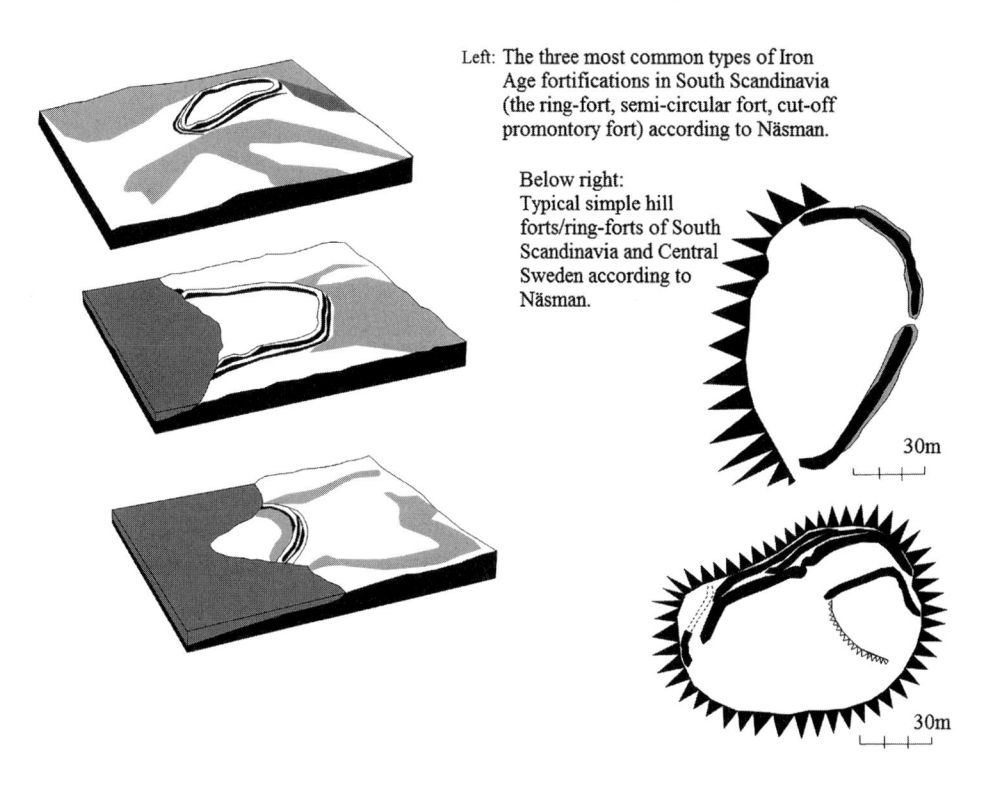

Left: The three most common types of Iron Age fortifications in South Scandinavia (the ring-fort, semi-circular fort, cut-off promontory fort) according to Näsman.

Below right: Typical simple hill forts/ring-forts of South Scandinavia and Central Sweden according to Näsman.

Anne Nørgård Jørgensen's analysis of the sea defence of Denmark provides a good overview of what types of obstacles Arthur would have faced in Jutland. Denmark, just like Norway and Sweden, was a kingdom which consisted of several tribal kingdoms, some of which recognized the high king while others did not. The fact that different sections of Jutland are divided by palisades and road-obstructions suggests that it was divided into four kingdoms. It is possible that these dykes were built at about the same time as the sea defences, as implied by Näsman (p.149). It is also possible that the island of Fyn (with the centre at Gudme) and Sjaelland (centre at Stevns) were separate kingdoms. On the basis of this, one may assume that Arthur would only have conquered the northernmost of the kingdoms of Jutland. The conquest of the northern portion of Jutland would have been facilitated by the fact that its defensive palisades faced south, and Arthur invaded from the north with ships.

The Danish defences against seaborne attackers consisted of three elements: 1) fleets; 2) coastal defences; 3) forts for the land forces. Arthur appears to have been able to avoid having to fight a sea battle, which means that he was able to reach the coast of Jutland unopposed. He faced two potential obstacles after this. Jørgensen provides a preliminary analysis of the sea defences. According to her, the Danes were already employing various types of sea defences during the Iron Age, even if most of those that have so far been dated are later. The sea defences consisted of off-shore defence works such as stakes, stones, box caissons and sunken ships that were placed in the mouths of fjords and bays. The most typical consisted of wooden stakes driven down to the bottom and floating bars of oak. She provides one good example of such a defensive system for the Haderslev Fjord. The fjord was 16km long and had two obstacles placed in its mouth at a distance of 1km from each other. Both consisted of poles driven down and floating bars of oaks, with lengths of 500m and widths of 23m and 13–15m. These obstacles were constructed in about 370, repaired in 400 and improved in 418/419. The purpose of these was not to deny access to the fjord for the invader, but to buy time for defenders to organize their defence. It is unfortunate that we do not know whether Arthur had to negotiate his

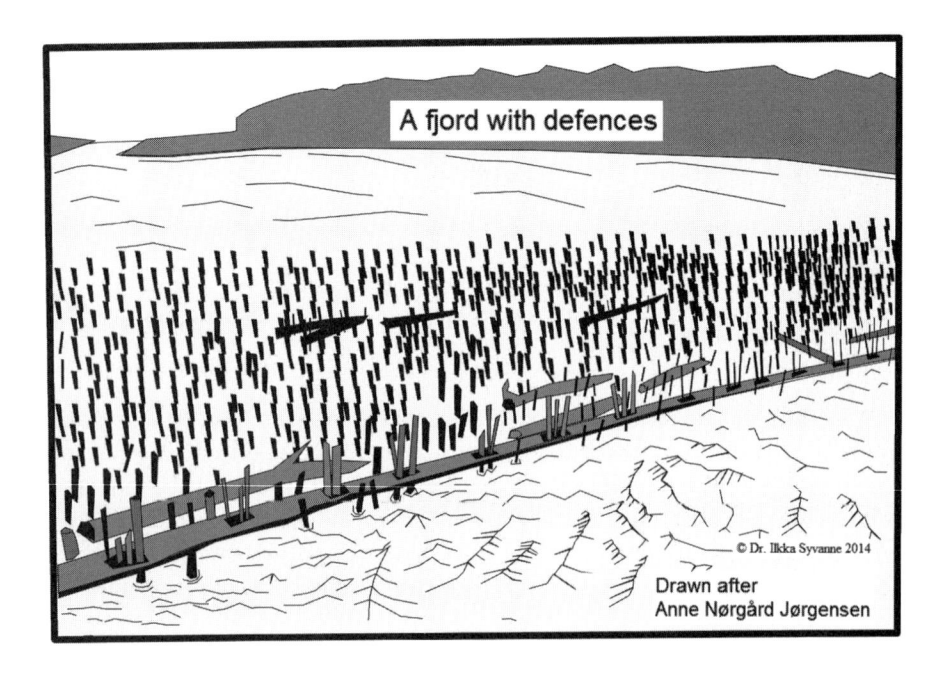

A fjord with defences

© Dr. Ilkka Syvänne 2014
Drawn after
Anne Nørgård Jørgensen

way through such defences, because archaeologists have not dated the structures found in the north, but one may make the assumption that he did have to, after which he would have faced the enemies on land.

In addition to this, the attackers would have faced the round circle forts that could have a moat and two to three earth walls with wooden palisades. These could contain more than 1,000 men and can therefore be considered to have been relatively hard to take. According to Näsman, most of the forts of Denmark were so-called refuge fortresses. It is clear that Arthur's forces were quite familiar with these types of structures, because Britain, Scotland and Ireland were full of them, and could easily negotiate the obstacles with their Roman siege equipment.

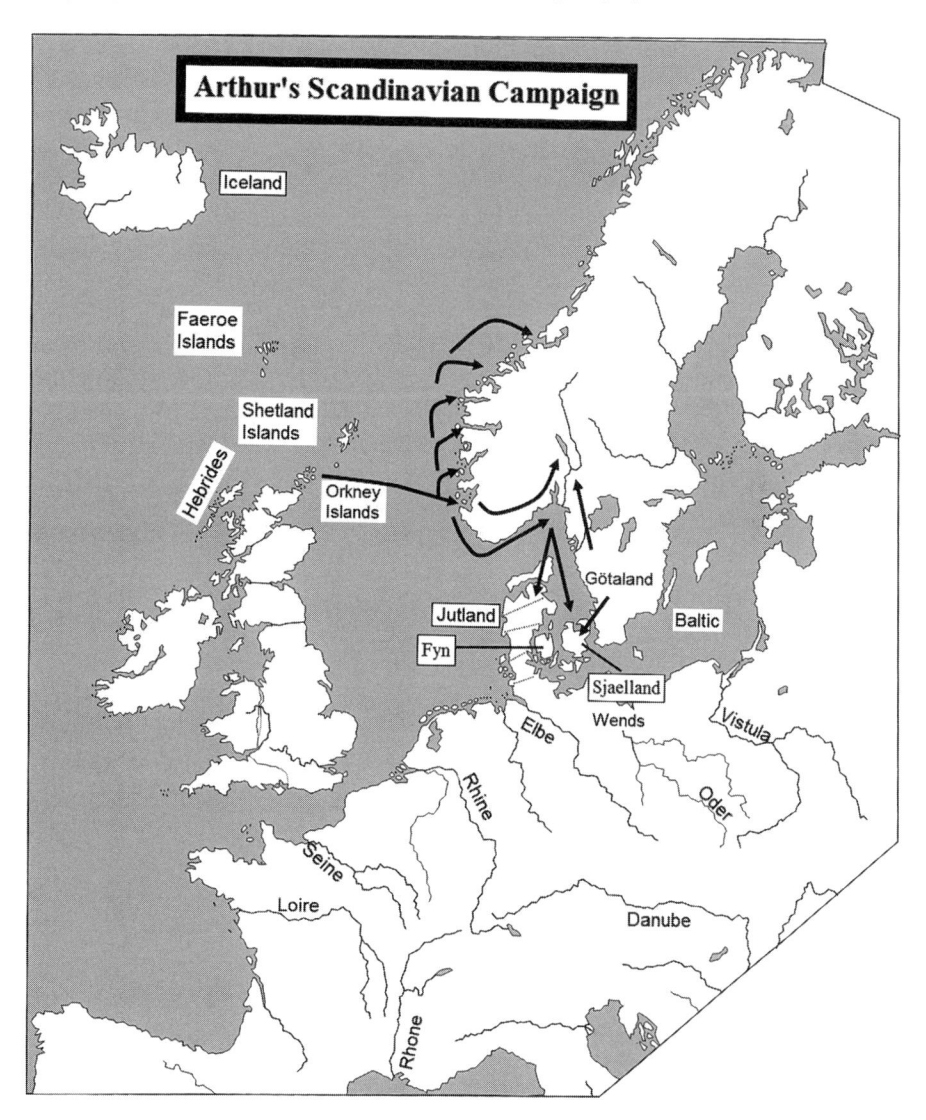

Saxo Grammaticus' books 5 and 6 include some information (or rather lack of it) that can be used to confirm the Arthurian campaign in the area. According to Saxo, one of the greatest kings of the Danes, Frothi III, ruled at the time when the Huns were powerful. He even married a Hun princess. However, the relationship then soured thanks to the infidelity of the princess. Frothi had to fight against the Huns twice. Saxo claims that after this, Frothi or his forces campaigned in Norway, Sweden, Britain and Ireland. Note that Frothi was a Dane and the invaders of Britain consisted mostly of the inhabitants of that area. It is possible to think that if Saxo's claims have any basis in truth, then the Hunnic invasions and Frothi's campaigns would all have contributed to the willingness of the Jutes, Angles and Saxons to move to Britain, away from the dangers facing them at home (see Appendix 1).

The key piece of text is actually an omission by Saxo.[2] He fails to state in Book 6 why Frothi's successor, his son, Fridlef II, was brought up in Russia. My own theory is that after the death of Frothi, Arthur campaigned in Norway and then, together with the Goths of Sweden, invaded Denmark, including the islands of Fyn and Sjaelland, forcing Frothi's successor, Alf, to accept his dominance. Fridlef had apparently already fled to Russia because he had lost a power struggle to Alf, or alternatively Arthur raised Alf on the throne, and it is probable that the daughter, Ofura, had been married to some king or nobleman. It seems quite probable that the Danish Saxo has purposefully forgotten Arthur's campaign in the area, the subjection of Jutland to the king of Norway and the subjection of Denmark to Arthur. There has to be some explanation for the sudden collapse of the Danish Empire, and the likeliest explanation is an outside invasion. The otherwise mysterious disappearance of Alf can then be explained away with the account provided by Geoffrey. Alf was Arthur's vassal, the king of Dacia Aschil/Ascilus, who was then killed at the Battle of Camlan in about 472.

Danish longboat
(source: Sophus Müller, Vor Oldtid)

Chapter 11

Campaigns in Gaul in 469/470 (Geoffrey 9.11ff.)

The Campaign of Riothamus Arthur in 469

As noted in Chapter 3, according to Geoffrey Ashe, we should equate Arthur with Riothamus (the high-king), which means that Arthur campaigned in Gaul from 469 onwards. The problem that we have is that Geoffrey of Monmouth does not mention any of the exploits mentioned in the sources that refer to the campaigns of Riothamus, and these sources fail to mention any of the material included in Geoffrey of Monmouth. My solution, which is based on the typical survival pattern of material for this period (none of the extant sources include all of the events, so the narrative has to be pieced together), is that both traditions have preserved material that complement each other, but none of these have the whole account. Furthermore, it was also very typical for period sources to cover up negative material, in its entirety or partially, so that the reputation of their heroes would not suffer from those details. However, ultimately it is impossible to say with definite certainty that any of this took place, but in my opinion the likelihood for this is far greater than the likelihood for the negative view. There is no smoke without fire! With these caveats, let us proceed with our story.

According to Geoffrey of Monmouth, Arthur's next target was Roman Gaul. The Romans were led by the tribune Frollo/Flollo, who was acting as Leo's deputy. Frollo was either a Germanic name like Rollo, the Sarmatian Froila, or alternatively a corrupted version of a Roman name (e.g. Fronto, Florianus, Florentius, Florus, Floridus), the former being the likelier. This piece of information, together with the following campaigns, allows us to date this war roughly to 469/470 or 474/475. I prefer the former date, the reasoning behind this conclusion presented in the following chapter. The details prove that the Romans had by now taken control of Armorica/Bretagne away from Arthur, which he unsurprisingly must have considered an affront, especially as he had previously formed an alliance with the Romans and had fought as their loyal ally (as Riothamus). This event is described by Jordanes (Get. 237–8) and Gregory of Tours (2.18–19, usually thought to be based on lost *Annals of Angers*). Let us then turn back the clocks to the period before the events described by Geoffrey.

According to Jordanes, the Emperor Anthemius asked the Brittones to assist him against the Visigoths who were invading Gaul. The king of the Britons, Riothamus/Riotimus (means great king = *rigo tamos*), sailed from Britain and disembarked his 12,000-man army in Bituriges (presumably somewhere close to Tours). Note that the

132   Britain in the Age of Arthur

number of men on board corresponds with the other naval expeditions conducted by the Armoricans and Britons. This campaign can be dated to 469 or 470. In other words, Riothamus sailed his ships along the Loire to a suitable landing site and then advanced to Bourges. It is probable that Riothamus' men were reinforced by the Armoricans immediately after their landing, so that the overall size of the force under him cannot have been much smaller than ca. 22,000–24,000. The aim was to unite this force with the Roman army dispatched by Anthemius. On the basis of Sidonius' letter to Riothamus (Ep. 3.9), it has been suggested that Riothamus was actually one of the kings of Armorica. This is unlikely. The likeliest alternative is that Riothamus was none other than Ambrosius/Arthur, as has been suggested by Ashe.[1] The only problem with this is that Geoffrey does not mention any defeat of Arthur/Riothamus in Gaul, but only successes. On the basis of this, it would be easy to dismiss Geoffrey's account of these successes and think that Arthur/Riothamus just suffered the one defeat, but it is even likelier that Geoffrey or his

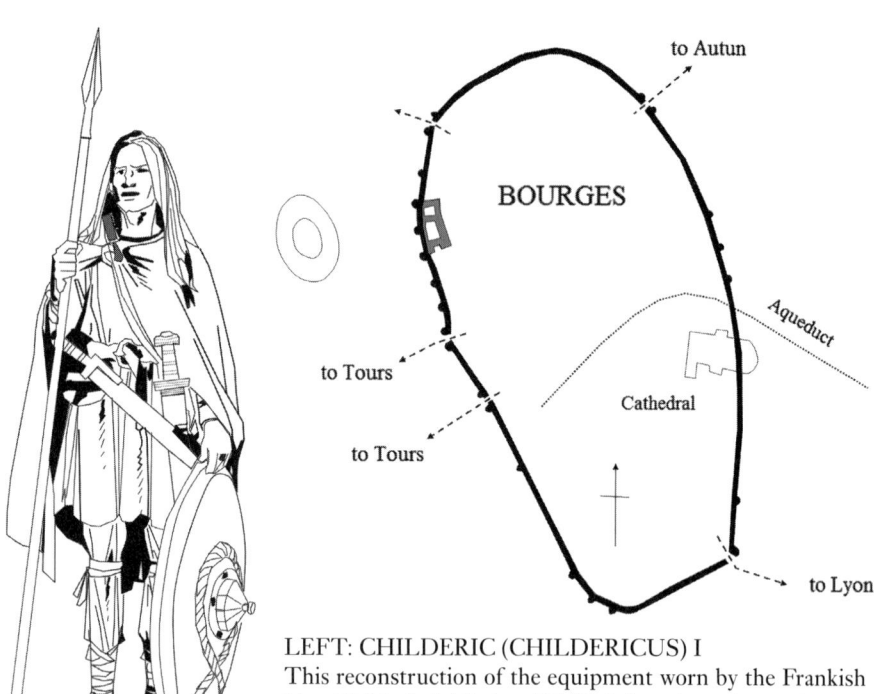

LEFT: CHILDERIC (CHILDERICUS) I
This reconstruction of the equipment worn by the Frankish king Childeric I (died c. 481/2) is based on the equipment found from his tomb. Note the lack of armour and helmet and the simultaneous use of the *scramasax* and *spatha* and the use of the pointed shield-boss. (Drawn after Lebedynsky, 2001, 98 which is based on the reconstruction of P. Pellerin; I have also included this same illustration in my earlier studies)
ABOVE: CITY OF BOURGES

source has just suppressed the initial defeat. It is also probable that the condensed account of Jordanes has not included all of the details, for it is clear that none of the sources pay any real attention to events in the north or north-east of Gaul.

The Visigoths under King Euric acted before Riothamus and the Romans could unite their forces. Riothamus was forced to evacuate Bourges after the Visigoths had inflicted a serious defeat on his army at Bourg-de-Déols/Déols. On the basis of the location of the battle, it is clear that Arthur had adopted an aggressive stance and had advanced from Bourges to meet the enemy. This was typical of him. He trusted in the invincibility of his veteran forces. The battle between Riothamus and Euric was bitterly fought, but in the end the numerical superiority of the Visigoths decided the day. Riothamus and the remnants of his army retreated to Burgundy, where their king and Roman *MVM* Gundioc offered them a place of refuge.

The Roman army, consisting of the regulars under *Comes* Paulus (presumably the *MVM*) and the Franks under their king, Childeric, arrived too late to save Riothamus.[2] This proves that Syagrius, a Roman ruler of northern Gaul, had not yet achieved the same dominance in the region as his father had before his death in 465. Paulus and Childeric attacked immediately and managed to recover the booty taken by the Visigoths. Meanwhile, the Saxons under Adovacrius/Odovacar had besieged Angers, which forced both commanders to abandon their pursuit of the Visigoths. These Saxons were clearly allied with the Visigoths against their arch-rivals, the Britons. The Roman army arrived too late once again; the Saxons had captured the city the day before the arrival of the relief army. The Romans again attacked immediately. Paulus was killed in action, but the Romans were still victorious and the city was retaken. Geoffrey's account suggests that Paulus' successor was the tribune Frollo. The Romans pursued the fleeing Saxons, while Childeric's Franks captured the islands of the Loire from the Saxons. Adovacrius/Odovacar saw no other way out, but to surrender. The Romans were ready to grant him terms because the Alamanni had in the meantime invaded Italy. Odovacar and Childeric were now both dispatched against these invaders, and the Alamanni were duly crushed (Greg. *HF* 2.18–19; Jord. *Get.* 237–8). The Romans appear to have taken full control of Armorica as a result of these events, because there was probably a power vacuum in the area. Riothamus/Arthur had lost most of his men and it is probable that the Saxons had completed the job by destroying those forces that had been left to defend Armorica/Bretagne. The opportunity was completed by the defeat of the Visigothic army. The Romans were now in a strong position to take control of Armorica and the areas just south of the Loire in Aquitania I-II, and this they did despite the fact that Riothamus had acted as their loyal ally. The Romans, however, did make one mistake, which was to let Arthur return to his kingdom, and I would suggest that this is connected with the fallout between the *Magister Peditum* Ricimer and *Augustus* Anthemius in 470, which led to the revolt of the former.

Ashe (1981, 2013) suggests that it is possible that the Romans failed to make contact with Riothamus' army thanks to the betrayal of the Praetorian Prefect of

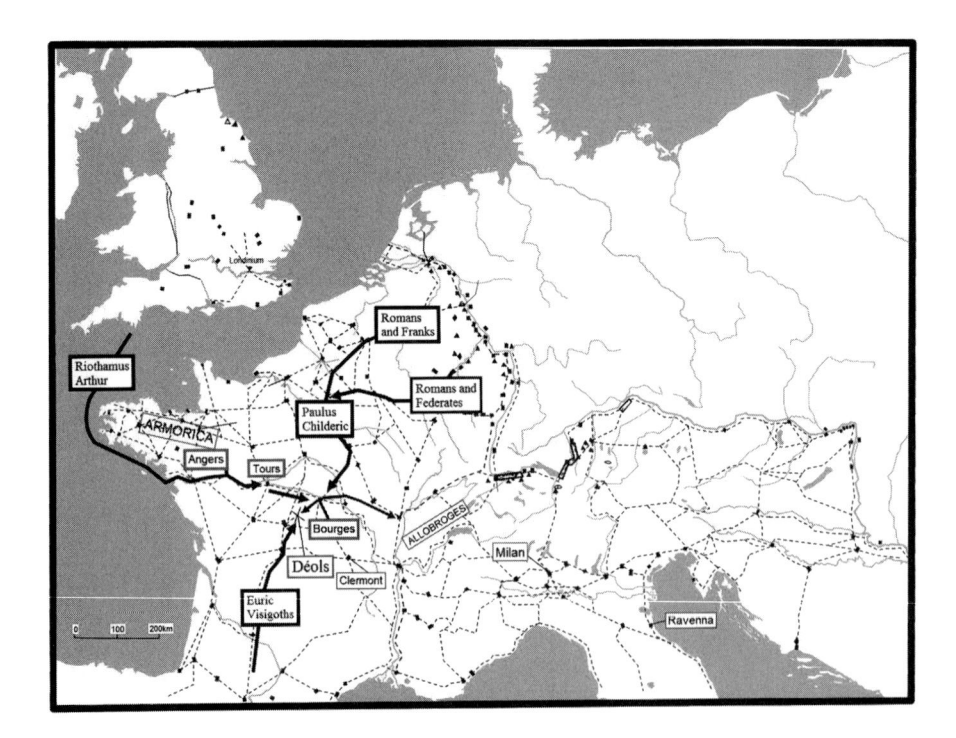

Gaul, Arvandus. According to Sidonius (Vol. 1.371–2, tr. by W.B. Anderson, with minor changes): 'Amongst other pleas which the provincials had instructed them to urge, they were bringing against him [Arvandus] an intercepted letter which Arvandus's secretary (who had been arrested) admitted to have been written at his master's dictation. It appeared to be a message addressed to the king of the Goths [Euric], dissuading him from peace with the "Greek Emperor" [Anthemius], insisting that the Britanni settled to the north of the Liger [these would be the Bretons of Armorica and/or the army of Riothamus] should be attacked, and declaring that the Gallic provinces ought according to the law of nations to be divided up with the Burgundians, and a great deal more mad stuff in the same vein, fitted to rouse a warlike king to fury and a peaceful one to shame. The opinion of the lawyers was that this letter was red-hot treason.' There are three possible ways to interpret this. The first is that Arvandus sent this letter before the arrival of Riothamus and that Euric (despite the fact that he apparently did not receive the letter in question) acted as suggested by Arvandus when Arvandus' betrayal became public. If Euric attacked Armorica before Riothamus' arrival, then this attack would have served as the cause for the alliance between Riothamus and Anthemius. The second alternative is that the arrival of Riothamus had been betrayed thanks to the activities of Arvandus, which then enabled Euric to destroy Riothamus' army as suggested by Ashe. The third alternative is that Arvandus' suggestion meant the situation immediately after the defeat of Riothamus/Arthur, when the Burgundians and Goths would have been in position to exploit the disappearance of the allied army of Riothamus/Arthur. The defeat inflicted on the Visigoths by Paulus and Childeric obviously made any such plans unrealistic, and Armorica remained in Roman hands.

This is not the only possible referral to the Britons and Arthur by Sidonius, because he also wrote a letter to none other than Riothamus in which he asked him to lend a hearing for his associate. My own educated guess is that this happened in about 471/472 when Arthur/Riothamus had already wrested back control of Armorica and the surrounding areas from the treacherous Romans.

Since we know that Riothamus obtained a place of refuge in Burgundy, it is possible that the subsequent breakup between Anthemius and Ricimer resulted from Anthemius' decision to betray Riothamus and to annex Armorica after the Visigoths had been crushed. In other words, it is possible that it was Anthemius' betrayal of Arthur that led to the revolt of Ricimer in 470, which in turn caused Ricimer to order Gundioc to help Arthur reach his homeland.

Riothamus/Arthur's response in 470
According to Geoffrey of Monmouth's account, Arthur sailed to Gaul and divided his army into several divisions, which began to devastate the land from all directions. Frollo collected all the forces under his command and advanced against Arthur. Arthur, however, had numerical superiority, thanks to the fact that he was accompanied by the youth of all the regions he had conquered. Arthur's reputation, together with a sizeable bribe, caused most of the Gallic army to desert to his side, with the result that Frollo fled from his camp to Paris with a small force. It is probable that the Gallic army that deserted to Arthur's side consisted mostly of Armoricans (and possibly also of Alans) who were ill-disposed towards the Romans. Frollo fortified Paris to withstand a siege and called auxiliary forces from neighbouring countries, which must mainly mean the Saxons, Franks and Syagrius's private army based at Soissons. Arthur, however, followed too fast and put Frollo under siege. Since Arthur was able to issue a full blockade of Paris, it is clear that he had surrounded the city on all sides. This implies that he had been able to cross the Seine and blockade the city from the opposite bank. It would have been possible for Arthur to confiscate local boats for the crossing or to have built a bridge, but I would suggest that it is inherently more likely that Arthur had ordered his fleet to be rowed upstream along the Seine to ease the crossing of the river, blockade the river and bring supplies for his own army.

When, after a month, the besieged started to be hard-pressed with hunger, Frollo challenged Arthur to a duel to decide the war. Arthur accepted the challenge. This was typical of the period. For example, Bonifatius and Aetius fought a similar duel in 432 which decided their war, just like Areobindus fought against the Persian champion in the East in 422. This was an era of heroes. Arthur and Frollo were both

Paris 500 AD

Arthur's fleet brought to aid the crossing of the Seine and to block the enemy supply lines.

to Senlis

to Rouen

Drawn after M. Rouche, p. 317.

Seine

Praetorium

Necropolis

Baptistère Cathédrale

to Meaux

Urban area

St-Etienne

500m

Thermae

Forum

to Dreux

St. Pierre
Circus

direction of Arthur's march to Paris

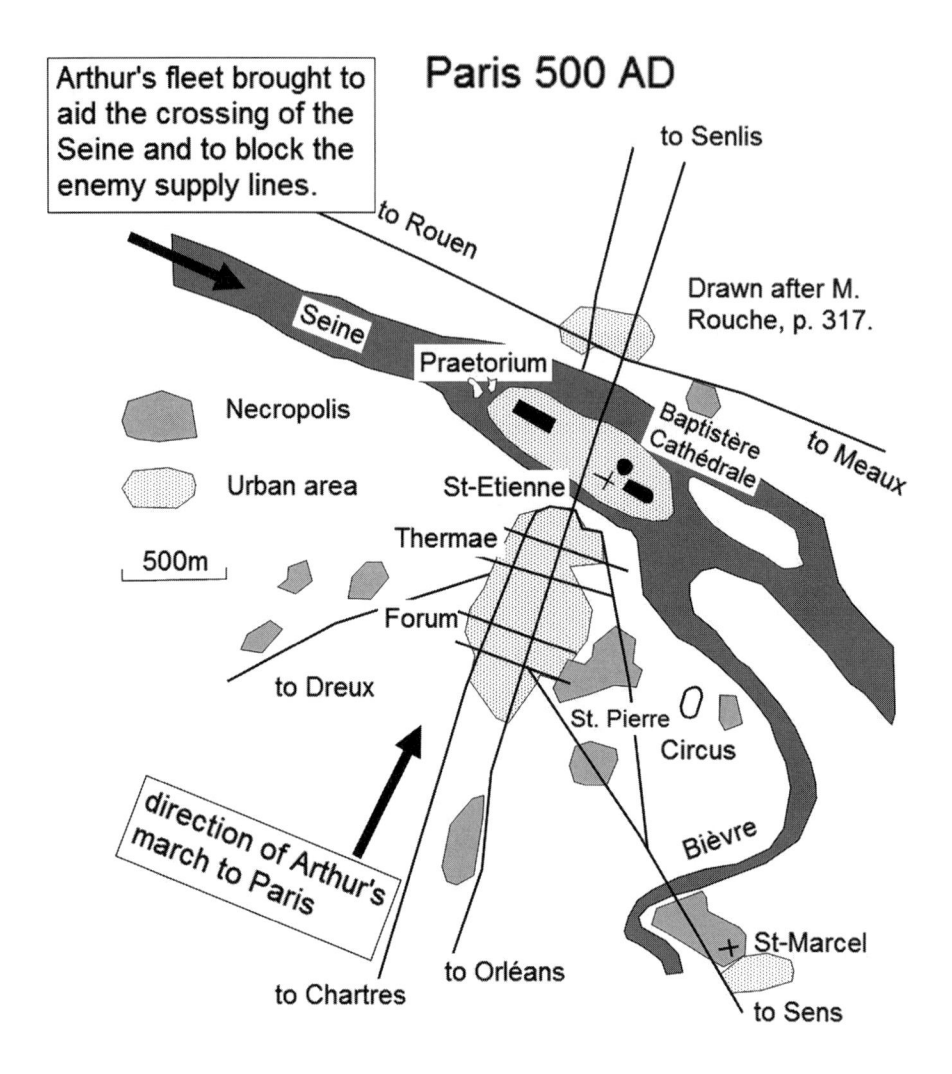

Bièvre

St-Marcel

to Chartres

to Orléans

to Sens

mounted and used lances, shields and swords. In the first encounter, Arthur avoided Frollo's lance, struck his own in his adversary's chest and unhorsed him. On the second run, Frollo stabbed Arthur's horse in the chest at the moment Arthur tried to hit him with a sword, killing his mount. In the ensuing melee, both used sword and shield. Frollo managed to hit Arthur in the forehead. His helmet saved his life, but blood still burst forth from the wound onto his chain mail armour and shield. The enraged Arthur then struck Frollo's helmet with his Caliburn/Excalibur-sword and killed him. It was apparently thanks to the superior quality of his sword that Arthur won. It is little wonder that his sword has become so famous. I would once again remind readers that these details are not necessarily invented by Geoffrey, because we know of similar details of duels fought by East Roman champions from the fifth and sixth centuries. The heroic deeds of the period's warriors were considered worthy of admiration and imitation, as a result of which they were considered worth telling and retelling. After the death of Frollo, the defenders opened up the gates and welcomed in the victor.

4th Century Boulogne (Bononia)

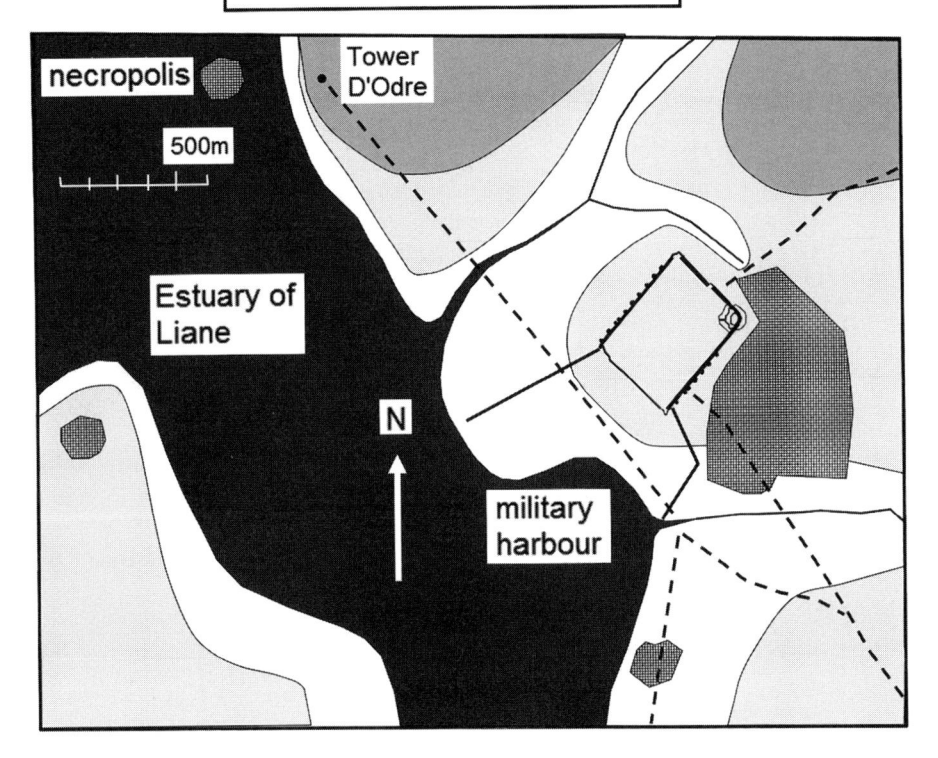

- necropolis
- Tower D'Odre
- 500m
- Estuary of Liane
- N
- military harbour

Arthur then divided his army into two divisions. One division under Hoel marched against Guitard, the commander of the Pictones (Pictavians) in Aquitania II/Poitou, while Arthur subdued the other provinces. Hoel defeated Guitard in several battles and forced him to surrender, together with his cities and forces. After this, Hoel supposedly continued his march all the way to Gascony while pillaging, but this must simply refer to fighting against the Visigoths of Aquitania. It is unlikely that Hoel could have advanced very far south from the area controlled by the Pictones. Geoffrey claims that Arthur's Gallic campaign lasted for nine years, and that in the course of it he would have conquered the entire country. The subsequent list of leaders under Arthur's rule, however, proves that while Hoel subdued Armorica and the areas (Pictones, Andecavi, Bituriges = Poitou) immediately south of the Loire – all areas that he would have controlled before the Romans got the foolish idea of capturing them – Arthur's actual conquest consisted solely of the area controlled by the Alans on both sides of the Seine and of the coastal areas controlled by the Saxons around the city of Boulogne. The implication is that these areas had been under Saxon dominance after the death of Aegidius in 465. This is confirmed by Gregory of Tours (2.18), who states that the Saxon leader Adovacrius/Odovacar had taken hostages from Angers in return for peace. This means that Syagrius, the son of Aegidius, who was based at Soissons, and other local Roman leaders, had negotiated peace treaties with the Saxons. They were now liberated by Arthur.

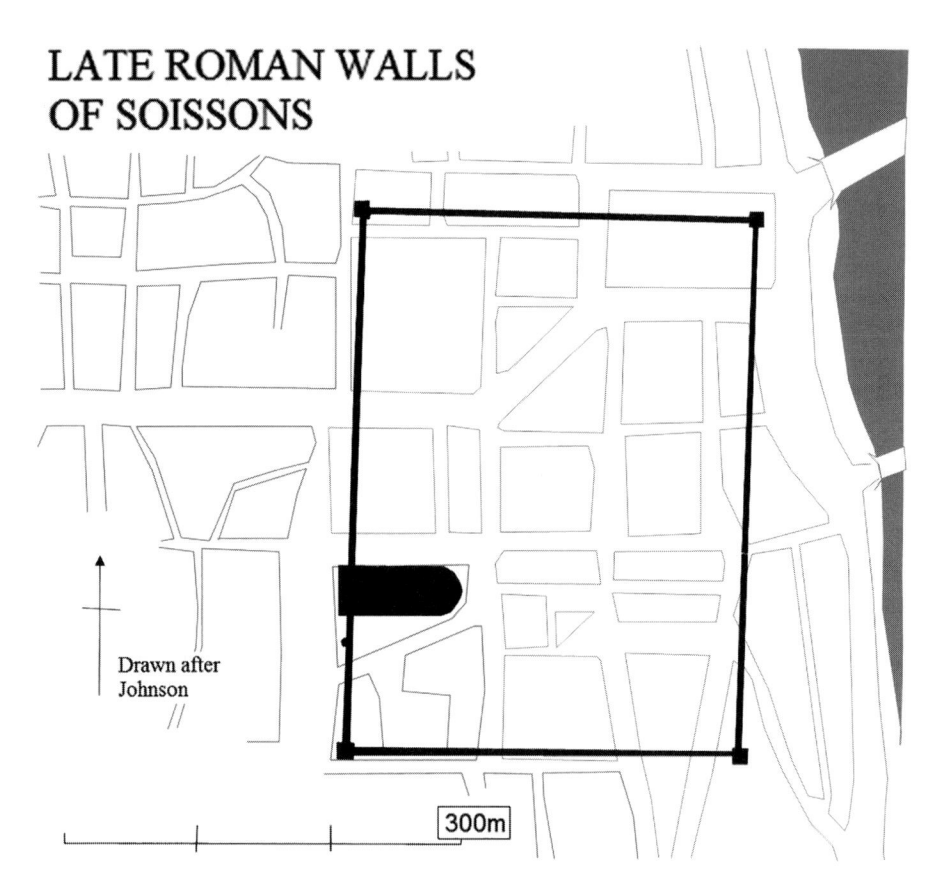

LATE ROMAN WALLS OF SOISSONS

Drawn after Johnson

300m

The local Romans were not on peaceful terms with the Salian Franks, who were led by King Childeric, because the Franks had previously killed Aegidius, who had been their king and local Roman magnate. This means that they expected help from Arthur against the Franks, but it is likely that Arthur negotiated a peace with the Franks because they are not to be found among his army or the enemy. Consequently, the nine years for the Gallic campaign must mean nine months. The incorporation of the Alans increased Arthur's cavalry component very significantly, just like the inclusion of the Gallic Saxons increased the size of his fleet.

Campaigns in Gaul in 469/470 (Geoffrey 9.11ff.) 139

After the military goals had been achieved, Arthur returned to Paris, where he summoned his court and organized the administration of the regions he had reconquered from the Romans or taken from the Saxons. The fact that Arthur's campaign was specifically directed against the Romans and Saxons in the aftermath of the peace between the Romans and Saxons achieved in 469 (Greg. *HF* 2.18) once again suggests that Geoffrey was drawing his information from some lost period source, or from a source or sources that had access to such at some point in the past. Normandy/Neustria was given to cup-bearer Bedvere and Anjou (the capital city of Angers) to Seneschal Kay. References to the presence of sons of the kings of Brittany/Bretagne, Normandy and France in the *Mabinogion* suggest that there existed a common memory of Arthur's campaigns and control over these areas. In short, there exists independent albeit very romantic evidence to support Geoffrey's version.

Chapter 12

The Crowning as High King/Augustus in 471 (Geoffrey 9.12–15)

The Crowning of the High King and Emperor

Thanks to the events outlined in the previous chapter, Arthur decided to make his break with Rome official by having himself crowned as king by the archbishops of Britain in the City of the Legions/*urbs legionis* (Caerleon)[1] at Whitsun in 471. The occasion was widely publicized and invitations to participate were sent to neighbouring kingdoms. According to Geoffrey, the city also possessed a college of 200 philosophers, who acted as astrologers for Arthur. It seems probable that this college was headed by Ambrose Merlin and resembled the other known schools of philosophy in the Late Roman world, in that its members learned not only philosophy in the modern sense but also various other sciences, mathematics, arts and engineering skills.

According to Geoffrey (9.15), at the same time as these celebrations took place, the Archbishop of Caerleon, Dubricius, and many other bishops resigned and retired. Most notably, Dubricius' successor was David, Arthur's uncle, which means that the ruler tightened his grip on the realm. Gerald of Wales (Wales 2.4) claims that all of this took place when the Pelagian heresy had once again reared its head in Wales, and that it was as a result of this that the bishops, abbots and priests assembled a great synod at Brefi, the result of which was the appointment of David as archbishop. If this is true, then Arthur used the same occasion for the purification of religion in Wales, presumably in order to tighten his grip of the church so that he could exercise greater control over the populace (and, via its services, the grip of the Crown on the people). The tightening of the grip of the Church was probably also necessary in the situation in which Arthur intended to declare himself High-King *Augustus*.

The list of participants allows one to reconstruct the administrative hierarchy of Arthur's empire. At the top, naturally, was Arthur himself with the title of king, but since he was already king of Britain and in practice also High King or King of Kings to the other kings of his realm, it is quite probable that Arthur actually assumed the title of *Augustus* (emperor) in defiance of Rome, even if this is not specifically mentioned by Geoffrey. Note that the kings of Albany, Cornwall, Demetia and Venedotia appear to have been higher in the hierarchy than the king of Moray, because these four accompanied Arthur after he had been crowned and enrobed, which implies that the king of Moray was a sub-king of the king of Albany. The odd title of *Map* may actually have been used to mean *magister peditum*, once again in defiance of Rome – in Britain, the highest-ranking person of West Rome was actually nothing more than a middle-ranking official. The audience also included the wives of the participants, but these did not wield any official power and were also secluded from the men during the festivities.

The celebrations included simulated fights on horseback, shooting with a bow and the throwing of javelins, stones and rocks, all skills needed in warfare. Note in particular the importance of archery for the Britons of this period. Geoffrey's account also includes information that can be considered to be some sort of initiation rite for warriors. He claims that the women would not give their love to any man unless he had proven himself three times in battle. This is reminiscent of the Germanic and Alan practice in which the young men had to prove their manhood by various means before they were allowed to marry and procreate. The intention was to make the men fight with greater ardour so that they could obtain what their hearts desired.

The following list shows the hierarchy of the Briton Empire.

Arthur, King of Britain, High King and *Augustus*

Britain
Kings:
Auguselus, king of Albania/Albany (Scotland)
   Urian, king of Mureif/Moray in Albany, a sub-king of Auguselus
Cadwallo Laurh/Lewirh, king of the Venedotians (North Wales)
Stater, king of the Demetians (South Wales)
Cador, king of Cornwall

Archbishops:
London
York
David of the City of Legions (Primate of Britain)

Dukes (duces) and Consuls:
Morvid, consul of Gloucester
Mauron, consul of Worcester
Anarauth, consul of Salisbury
Arthgualchar, consul of Cargueit/Warguit/Warwick
Jugein, consul of Leicester (Legecester)
Cursalem/Kursalem, consul of Kaicester/Caistor

Dukes included among the consuls but with lesser rank:
Kynniarc/Kinmare, Duke of Durobernia (Canterbury)
Galluc, Duke of Roffensis (Rochester)

Urgennius/Urbgennius, Duke of Bath
Jonathel, Duke of Dorchester
Boso, Duke of Ridoc (Oxford)

Lesser worthies:
Danaut, Map Papo
Cheneus, Map Coil
Peredur, Map Eridur
Cuiful, Map Nogoit
Regin, Map Claut
Eddelein, Map Cledauc
Kincar, Map Began
Kimmare, ?
Gorboriam, Map Goit
Clofaut, Rupmaneton
Kimbelim, Map Trunat
Cathleus, Map Catel
Kinlich, Map Neton
plus others

Client kings:
Guillamurius, king of Ireland
Malvasius, king of Iceland
Doldavius, king of Gothland (probably king of south-west Sweden)
Gunfacius, king of the Orkneys
Lot/Loth, king of Norway
Aschillius/Aschil, king of the Dacians (Denmark), (i.e. Alf, son of Frothi III?)

Armorican Gaul:
Hoel, king of the Armorican Britons with his princes
Holdin, king of the Ruteni (the Ruteni were a tribe in the south of Gaul, but in this case they are to be identified with the men of Flanders, so that Holdin's capital was located at Thèrouanne)
Leodegarius, consul of Bolonia (i.e. of Bononia/Boulogne)
Bedver/Bedevere the Butler/Cup-bearer, Duke of Normandy
Kay, Seneschal, Duke of Anjou
Borellus, Duke of Cenomania (Cenomani were an ancient Italian tribe, so it must be a mistake for Cenabum/Orleans)
Caius/Gaius the Sewer, Duke of the Andecavi (Andegavia)
Guitard, Duke of the Pictones (Pictavia, Poitou)
Guerinus Carnotensis (Gerin of Chatres) and twelve other peers/consuls

The Romantic image of Arthur. Arthur Gets Excalibur from the Lady of the Lake according to N.C. Wyeth (died 19 October 1945).

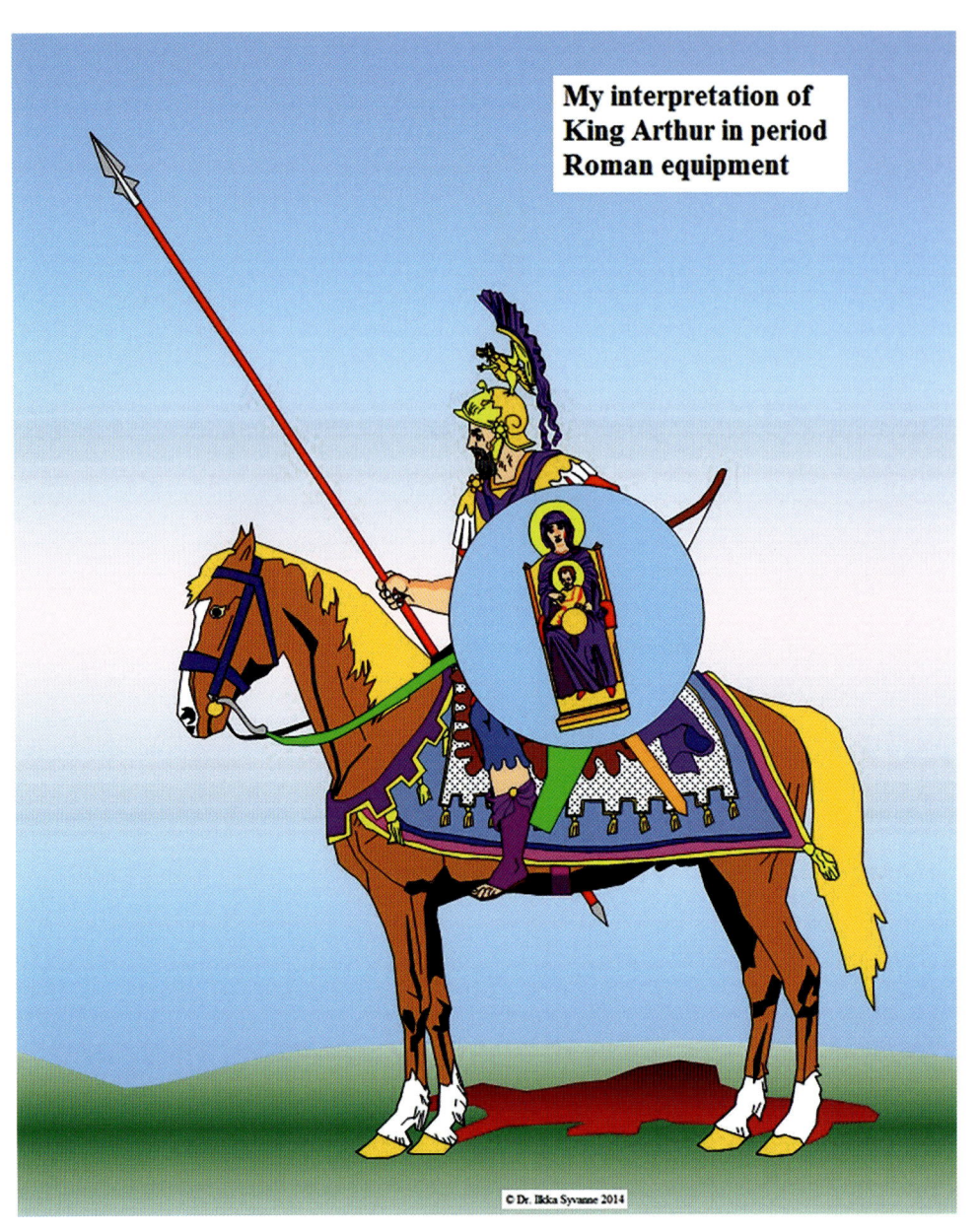

The shield emblems on the following page, the dragons of Somerset, should not be seen to be representative of period emblems. I have included those as generic emblems because we do not know what emblems were used by Arthur's cavalry forces.

King Arthur at the apex of his cavalry wedge

Top Left: A Briton legionary/heavy-armed footman equipped with a ridge helmet, scale armour (alternative would be chain mail), a large *scutum* shield (emblem is based on Cascarino's reconstruction of the *legio II* Augusta on the supposition that the Britons would have imitated the emblems of the earlier garrison forces), *hasta*-spear, and *spatha*-sword (behind the shield).

Top Centre: A Briton legionary/heavy-armed footman equipped in the standard equipment of the period. He uses leather armour; a variant of the ridge helmet, which was to form the basis of the Frankish/Merovingian helmet; round shield, *hasta*-spear, and *spatha*-sword. The emblem on the shield is based on the modern dragon of Somerset and should therefore not be considered a period emblem. It is quite possible or even probable that if the soldier used a dragon emblem in the shield that this dragon would have looked something like the draco-standard depicted here in one of the attached photos of the Finnish re-enactor Jyrki Halme.

Top Right: A foot archer equipped in the typical period equipment.

Below: A group of late Roman soldiers as depicted by the Polish re-enactor group Vicus Ultimus. The Britons would have worn similar.

Top: A Finnish re-enactor Jyrki Halme depicting a late Roman front rank fighter. (© *Jyrki Halme*)
Below: Various types of equipment worn by the late Roman and Britons as depicted by the Polish re-enactor group Vicus Ultimus. With permission of Vicus Ultimus.

Top: Late Roman soldiers and women as depicted by the Polish re-enactor group Vicus Ultimus. Geoffrey of Monmouth's text suggests that the young men soldiered to obtain wives. With permission of Vicus Ultimus.

Below Left: A Finnish re-enactor Jyrki Halme in period dress in readiness to use his knife. (© *Jyrki Halme*)

Below Right: Jyrki Halme in late Roman/Briton equipment on the frozen surface of a lake. Note the use of the muscle armour. (© *Jyrki Halme*)

A draco-banner which would have been used by the Britons and by their enemies. Note that the swastika decoration of the cloak had not yet acquired its notoriety. This has been the result of its misuse by the Nazis. (© *Jyrki Halme*)

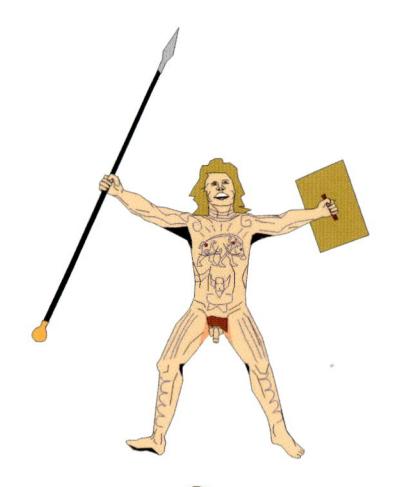

Above: Jyrki Halme depicting a late Roman soldier as he could have appeared during a leave of absence in summer. (© *Jyrki Halme*)
Top Left: Jyrki Halme depicting a late Roman soldier with a hood to protect him from the elements on the dark autumn day. (© *Jyrki Halme*)
Middle Left: Typical Pictish warrior showing his tattoos and bravery.
Bottom Left: Typical Irish warrior in his equipment.

These warriors are roughly representative of the typical Angles, Saxons, Jutes and Danes who invaded Britain and Gaul in the Fifth and Sixth Centuries. The elite warriors wore more armour and the chieftain on the bottom of the page is representative of such. Additional examples of even more heavily equipped warriors are on the following pages.

Top Left: Saxon spearman. **Top Centre:** Saxon swordsman armed with a *seax* (figure drawn after Richard Underwood). **Top Right:** Saxon foot archer armed with a wooden self-bow. The men on the left and right should be seen to be representative of the so-called young ones of their tribe who would have been led by the veteran in the middle. The more seasoned veterans would have consisted of more bulky fully bearded men. Note the use of light equipment. This, however, was not decisive in fighting. Fighting spirit and morale were the decisive factors and the Saxons were known for their pagan fury and bloodthirsty human sacrifices which frightened their less seasoned opponents senseless.

Bottom Left: An Anglo-Saxon elite warrior, chieftain or king in Britain according to Gamber and Alclud. Their reconstruction is based mainly on the Sutton Hoo treasure for which see also my photos in the plate section in *MHLR* Vol. 2.

Elite Warriors of Northern Europe (Norway, Denmark, Sweden and coastal regions of Finland)
Top Left: A Vendel helmet decoration of two footmen engaged in combat. Note the tactic of first throwing the javelin/spear followed up by the use of swords!
Top Right: A Valsgärde 7 helmet illustration of two warriors equipped with spears that have thongs to assist in throwing. In addition to this each of them wears a sword, a long chain mail armour, a shield and a helmet. Speidel has suggested that the warriors are shouting the barritus war-cry.
Below: My reconstructions of the elite warrior equipment are based on archaeological finds, extant works of art as interpreted by Gamber. It is particularly noteworthy that the elite warriors of the North were even more heavily equipped than the typical Roman soldiers.

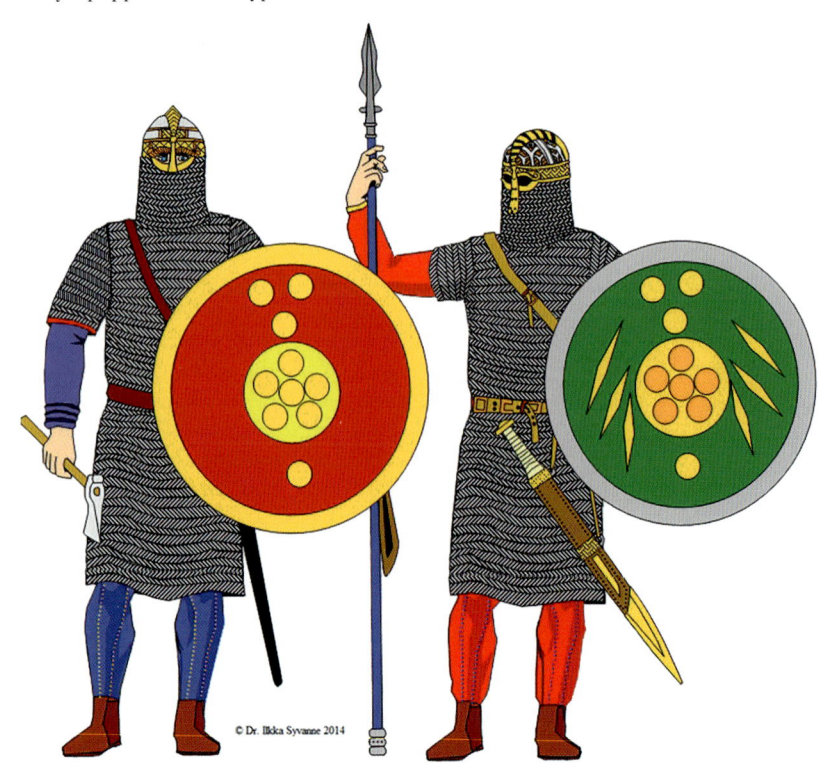

Top right and centre right: Helmet illustrations from the graves of Vendel in Sweden (ca. 600–700 AD). Both may represent Odin because both men are accompanied by two ravens.
Middle Centre: my tentative reconstruction of the helmet of the rider top right.
Bottom: my reconstruction of a North European elite warrior on horseback based on the finds at Vendel and elsewhere in North of Europe. It should be noted that the heavy cavalry was a "Swedish" specialty and it was one of the key reasons for the success they had in the area of modern Finland. The Swedes were true warriors of Odin.

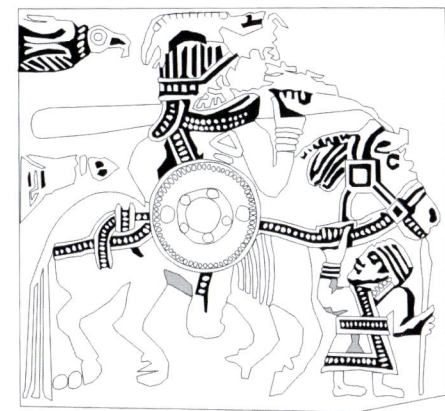

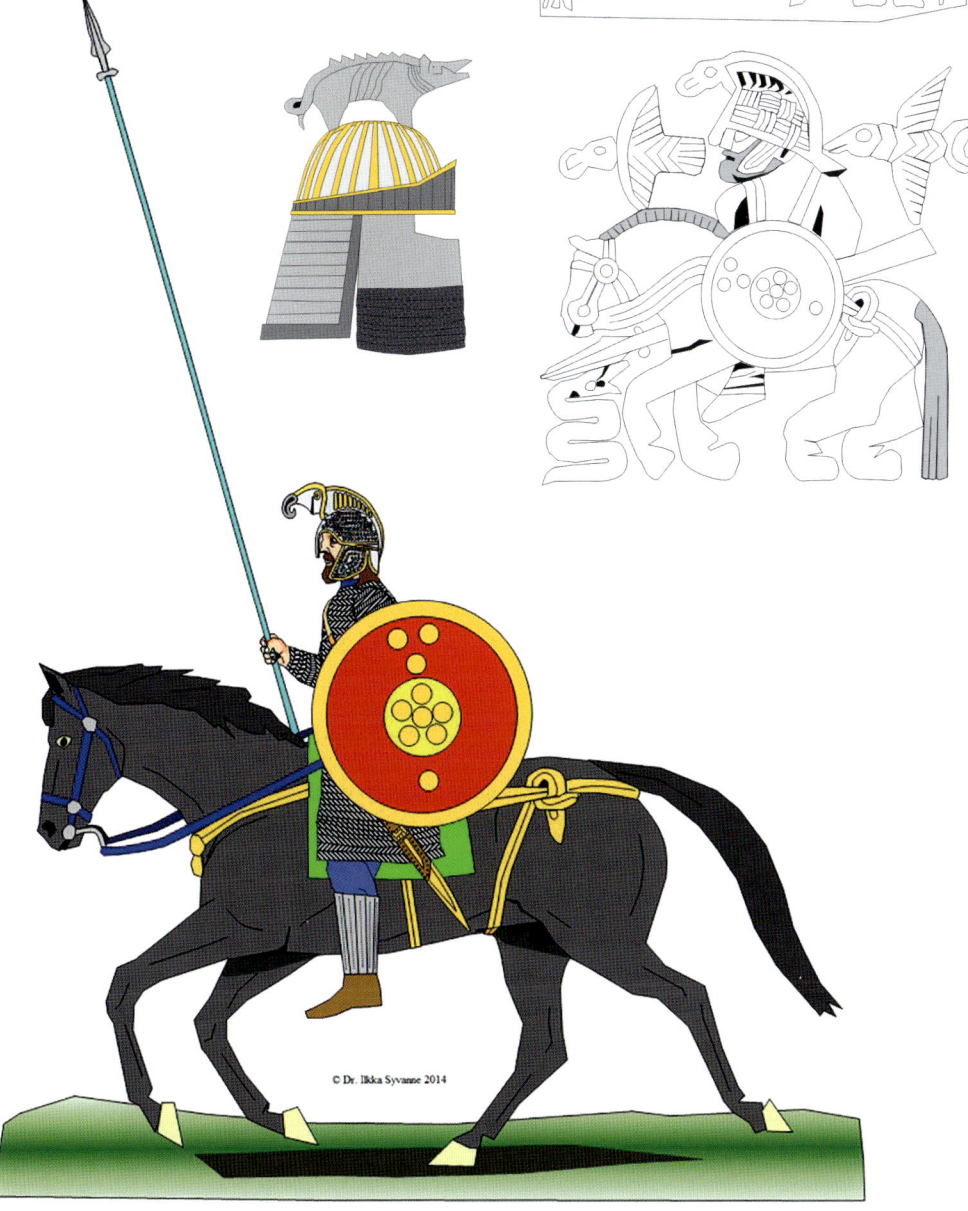

The above illustration is taken from the Valsgärde 8 helmet decoration. Note the probable use of the chain mail to protect the legs and arms. It is also possible that the neck guard consisted of segmented plates and not of chain mail as usually assumed. In this context it is relevant to note that the Vendel period grave finds have included segmented plates that have been interpreted as splinted shin guards (e.g. in Gamber). I have included one such reconstruction of rider in this book, but my own opinion is that the neck guard should be seen to include segmented plates which were possibly attached on the chain mail or alternatively the segmented plates were stitched into a leather foundation. On the basis of the extant portions of the illustration it is possible that the horseman and the horse-stabber would wear segmented plate armour, but I would still suggest that it is likelier that we should interpret the extant lines as chain mail. The "skirt" of the horse-stabber may represent Roman style leather *pteruges* or scale armour or chain mail. For further information regarding the Germanic horse-stabbers, see Speidel.

A Scandinavia elite warrior of the Vendel Period attacking

Top: This Finnish warrior on skis is meant to be roughly representative of all Nordic peoples who used skis and bows. The period archaeology does not have evidence for the use of fur cloaks and boots of this type or for the fur hat even if there exists evidence for these for later periods. However since the Finns have traditionally used the type of boots and these are particularly useful for skiing and in deep snow, I have made the educated guess that these were already used during Iron Age and Period of Great Migrations. I have made the guess that the Finns would have used fur cloaks rather than woollen cloaks because the furs were the main commercial article in these parts of the world. The other pieces of equipment are attested also in archaeology. The Biarmians, Permlanders and other Northern peoples would have used similar types of equipment. The archer has placed his mittens in the belt while he shoots arrows. I have made the educated guess that the colouring of the clothes and boots would have been such that it would have enabled the skier to hide in the snowy terrain as attested by the sources.

Below Left: Contesti-helmet used by the late Romans. With permission of Vicus Ultimus.
Below Right: Worms-helmet used by the late Romans. With permission of Vicus Ultimus.

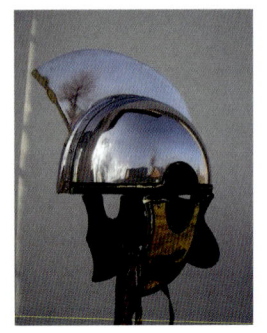

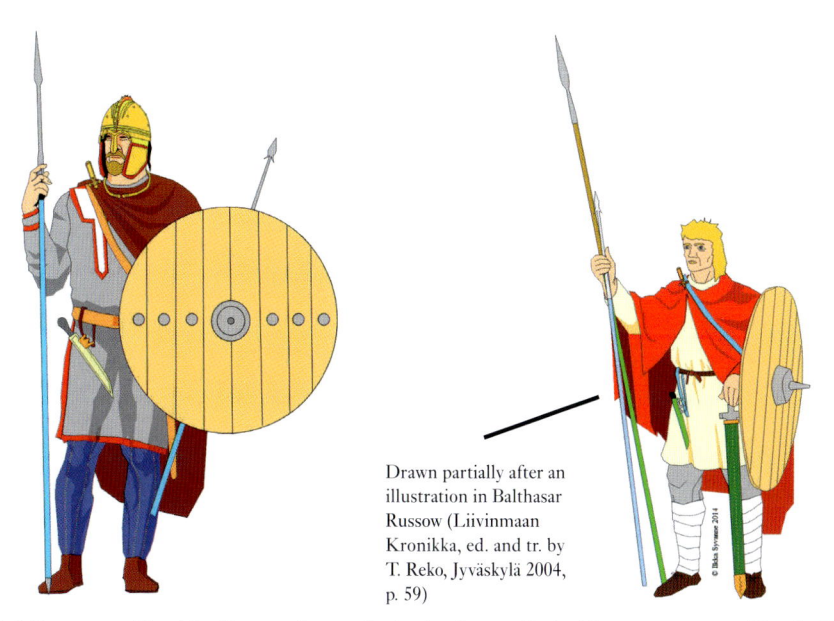

Drawn partially after an illustration in Balthasar Russow (Liivinmaan Kronikka, ed. and tr. by T. Reko, Jyväskylä 2004, p. 59)

Left: A fifth century Finnish elite warrior on the basis of grave finds. He wears a torque like the Roman soldiers rewarded for bravery. The weapons finds in graves suggest that the period Finnish warrior could use any combination of the following: a wooden shield with pointed or round boss, a scramasax/seax or double-edged sword 80-90 cm long 5 cm wide, a barbed javelin/*angon* with long shaft, a dagger, a spear with a 'rod' end to attach, a spear with a tube to attach, axe, and a knife. In addition to this some of the graves have had small numbers of arrow heads, which suggests that some of the men used wooden composite bows and/or crossbows.

Right: A typical fifth century Lithuanian warrior. The illustration is based on later archaeological finds, but the equipment can still be taken to be roughly representative of the fifth century equipment also because it is basically the same as was worn by most European peoples at that time. The quillon of the sword can be considered to be too large, but there exists examples for this type of sword from the steppe region.

Typical for all warriors of modern Finland and Baltic States is that the standard equipment of the tribesmen consisted of a spear, a barbed javelin, a shield, a knife and a sword.

Below: Traditional image of Finnish crossbowmen. However, the use of the crossbows by the Finns before the High Middle Ages is now contested. The earlier interpretation was that the Finns did use those already during the late Iron and Viking periods, but the current consensus view among Finnish historians is that they did not. In my opinion, however, the current state of evidence is inconclusive. The arrow heads that have been found could have been used in crossbow bolts and in regular arrows. Furthermore, the Picts, who originated in 'Scythia' did use crossbows.

Top: A Finnish hill-fort as it would have appeared during the so-called Viking Age. It is probable that the earlier forts would have looked similar. The hill-forts served as places of refuge during times of enemy raids, hence their other name – refuge forts. The fire signals warned of the approaching enemy so that the populace could seek shelter from behind the walls. These so-called vainovalkeat (= persecution/war fires, which presumably comes from the Russian word vojna/war) were used in Finland until early modern era to warn the populace. These forts worked relatively well thanks to the fact that the raiders lacked the means to stay in place to besiege them. The naval raiders relied on their speed to surprise the enemy settlements when they did not expect attack. The illustration (with some minor changes) is drawn after Pentti Papunen's illustration in the *Suomen Historian Pikkujättiläinen* (Porvoo 1989) and it shows the Finns in the Viking Age clothing. For additional details about Finnish Iron Age history, see e.g. Matti Huurre, *9000 Vuotta Suomen esihistoriaa* (8th imprint Keuruu, 2004) and *Suomen historia Osa 1. kivikausi, pronssikausi, rautakausi*, eds. Eero Laaksonen, Erkki Pärssinen, Kari J. Sillanpää (Espoo, 4th ed. 1989).

Below: Jyrki Halme depicting fifth century equipment used by the Romans and Britons. Note the use of metal muscle armour, wide belt, knife and torques-necklace for bravery.

Chapter 13

The War in Gaul in 471/472 (Geoffrey 9.15ff.)

The Casus Belli

According to Geoffrey of Monmouth, King Arthur's next goal was to march to Rome. He claims that the *casus belli* was the letter sent by tribune[1] and Procurator of the Republic, Lucius Hiberius/Hiberus/Tiberius,[2] in which he demanded that Arthur would have to pay tribute to the Romans, as Britain had done since the days of Julius Caesar. As tribune, Lucius was probably a member of the imperial bodyguards who had been nominated as commander of the Roman forces in the north of Gaul, while as procurator,[3] he was probably in charge of collecting rents and taxes in the north of Gaul and Britain. This combination of powers, which became increasingly typical during the Late Roman period, enabled Lucius to feed and supply the forces under him, which in its turn made it easier for him to retain control of the army placed under his command. We do not know what Lucius' other office was. It is possible that he was the *MVM per Gallias*, because the Burgundian King Gundioc and his four sons were allied with Ricimer and therefore unlikely to be Anthemius's *magister militum* at this time, but it is equally possible that he could have held honorary magistracy with the same powers.

In the same letter, Lucius supposedly also accused Arthur of having seized control of all the islands of the ocean and the province of the Allobroges (Burgundy) without Roman permission. Arthur was also ordered to appear before the Senate to be judged for his crimes. The inclusion of the Allobroges in the list may suggest that Arthur had concluded an alliance with the Burgundians and Ricimer against the legitimate ruler, Anthemius. This would have merely been an alliance in which the Burgundians and Ricimer had agreed not to interfere on behalf of either belligerent. We know that at the time Ricimer had rebelled against Anthemius and had shut himself inside Milan (he remained there for years), while the Burgundian King Gundioc (married to Ricimer's sister) or his sons stayed inside Burgundy, which means that both remained neutral, while Anthemius fought against the Visigoths and others like Arthur. It should be kept in mind, however, that when we are discussing the events of this time, there is plenty of room for alternative views. For example, the PLRE 2 states that Gundioc (Gundiocus) was the king of Burgundy from 455 until his death (in 473/474?), but Katalin Escher (p.90ff.) claims that Gundioc died between 463–469 and was succeeded by his four sons, Hilperic (the highest-ranking of the four kings), Gundobad, Godigisel and Godomar. Consequently, we do not even know the names of all parties to the conflict.

The real reason for the Roman hostility and ultimatum appears to have been Arthur's reconquest of territories from the Romans and Saxons in 470 or 471 and his declaration of independence from Rome by having himself crowned as king, and presumably also as emperor, in the City of the Legions. This piece of text is once again in agreement with the evidence so far gathered.

The Campaign Plans

Arthur convened his council consisting of kings and consuls to discuss what to do. His decision was to go to war against Rome. Hoel, king of Armorica, was to bring 10,000 men; Augusel, king of Albania/Albany, 2,000 cavalry; the Britons were to provide 60,000 fully armed foot and horsemen; the kings of the other islands (Ireland, Iceland, Gotland, the Orkneys, Norway, Dacia) were to supply 120,000 footmen; the duchies of Gaul (the Ruteni, Portunians, Estrusians, Cenomanni, Andegavians and Pictavians) another 80,000 men; and the twelve consulships were to place 1,200 men under Guerinus Carnotensis. The total number of men was supposed to be 183,200, in addition to which came an unknown number of footmen. As is clear, these figures are pure nonsense, unless considered the totals of all forces available, but still indicative that this was supposed to be a major undertaking. The figures are considerably lower in the actual narrative. The army was to be assembled at the port of Barfleur in the kalends of August. The intention was to march the army from there to the borders of the Allobroges (Burgundy), where they would then engage the Romans.

After Arthur had ordered his men and allies to put into effect the above, he dispatched the imperial envoys back to their *Augusti* (Geoffrey 9.20). Note that there were two emperors, even if Leo was considered the supreme emperor. Arthur stated that he would not pay any tribute and that he would not come to Rome to stand before a tribunal, but to act as a tribunal to those who had acted against him. This means that Arthur declared himself publicly as the sole *Augustus* of the empire.

When Lucius received Arthur's answer, he assembled his forces which, according to Geoffrey (10.1), consisted of the following: Epistrophius, king of the Greeks; Alifantinam/Ali Fatima, king of Spain; Hirtacius, king of the Parthians; Boccus, king of the Medes; Sertorius, king of Libya; Serses, king of the Itureans; Pandrasus, king of Egypt; Micipsa, king of Babylon; Polytetes, Duke of Bithynia; Teucer, Duke of Phrygia; Evander, Duke of Syria; Aethion, Duke of Boeotia; and Hippolutus, Duke of Crete. These were accompanied by other *duces* and nobles. In addition to these, there were the senators Lucius Catellus, Marius Lepidus, Caius/Gaius Metellus Cotta, Quintus Milvius Catullus, Quintus Carucius and others. The size of this force was supposedly 400,160 men, but in the actual battle the figure was much smaller, only about 80,000 men. The latter figure can be considered roughly reliable.

It is clear that the names and titles are in all probability spurious, but at the same time it is possible that these would still hide real Roman units and possibly even the names of their commanders. It is probable that the Greeks were one of the Macedonian legions; the Parthians were one of the Parthian legions; the Spaniards would have been one of the units posted there at some point in the past; the Medes would have been one of the *Comitatenses* legions of the East; the Libyans would have been a unit or units of Moors/Mauri (Berbers) and/or units of the *Dux* of Libya; the Itureans would have been the Iturean archers; the Egyptians one of the former Egyptian legions or other units from there; the Babylonians possibly one of the eastern legions; the Bithynians would have belonged to one of the praesental units of East Rome and may have included some units belonging to the *Scholae* and *Domestici*; the Phrygians would in all probability have been the Goths billeted in this area; the *Dux* of Syria would have commanded some of his own units; the *Dux* of Boeotia would have commanded forces posted to protect Thermopylae, Athens and Corinth; and the *Dux* of Crete would have commanded marines posted there. The fact that this list includes units from the Praesental Army placed in Bithynia supports the veracity of Geoffrey's list because we know that Anthemius had been commander of these forces prior to his appointment as emperor. We know this because Aspar was the commander of the forces posted in the west because his domestic Leo served there (see *MHLR* Vol. 4 with PLRE2 Aspar, Leo 6). The senators and nobles would have been accompanied by their own *bucellarii/famuli*-retinues. It is to be noted that Geoffrey's figures regarding the size of the army tally well with the information he has given if one assumes that each king was in charge of one below-strength legion and that each of the other officers were in charge of auxiliary forces. For the sake of clarity, I will call the above-mentioned units and persons by the names given by Geoffrey, but when I do so the reader should keep in mind the real meaning of the names; that each name of the king etc. hides a real Roman military unit.

This force appears to have consisted of a mix of western and eastern regulars. The presence of this army can easily be explained by the fact that Anthemius had been accompanied by a sizeable eastern army when he entered Italy in late 466 or early 467. The existence of this army in the north would also explain why the campaign under Anthemius' son, Anthemiolus, Thorisarius, Everdingus and Hermianus against the Visigoths at the same time in 471 failed miserably (see *MHLR* Vol. 4 with the PLRE2). The Romans had evidently made the mistake of dividing their field army into two. The wisest strategy would have been to deploy the Burgundians (if they still obeyed Anthemius) against Arthur and commit the entire armed strength of the Romans and other federates in Gaul against the Visigoths, and only after that against Arthur. However, as noted, this option appears not to have been a viable one in a situation in which Ricimer and Gundioc were both refusing to obey the emperor. It is possible or even probable that Lucius had been ordered to attempt to unite his army with the other Roman army, because he was clearly attempting to withdraw his army closer to the army of Anthemiolus when the presence of Arthur's force along the line of march forced him to commit his army to battle.

146   Britain in the Age of Arthur

The War Begins

When Arthur learnt that his client kings had completed their preparations and had set out towards Britain at the beginning of August, he left his nephew, Mordred, and Queen Guinevere in charge of the defence of Britain and marched with his army to Southampton. Arthur embarked his army and sailed in favourable winds to the port of Barfleur, where he awaited the arrival of the rest of his forces. It was then that Arthur learnt (Geoffrey 10.3) that a 'giant', who had arrived from Spain, had captured *Dux* Hoel's niece, Helena, and had taken refuge on Mont

MONT SAINT MICHEL TODAY

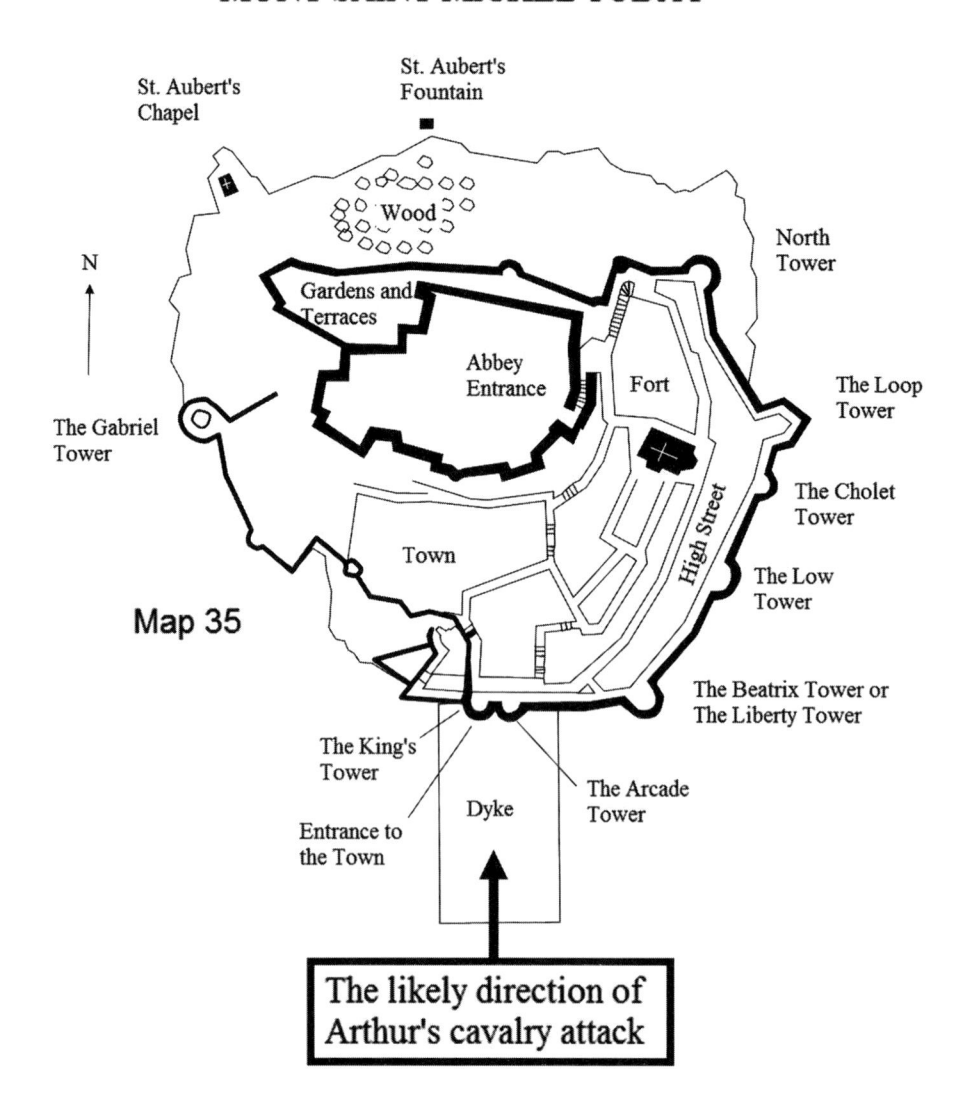

Map 35

Saint Michel. Hoel had attacked the 'giant' by sea and by land, but had achieved nothing. The ships had been sunk with huge rocks or the men killed with weapons. Those unfortunate enough to be captured were supposedly eaten by the 'giant'. It is obvious that this is a distorted memory of a fleet that had been dispatched from Spain by the Romans against the Britons. It is unfortunate that we do not know the nationality of this 'giant'. It is possible that he was a Batavian settler in Spain (the natives of modern Netherlands are among the tallest in the world), or that he was a Germanic settler (Suevi, Vandal or Goth) who acted as a federate leader, or that he was a very tall Spaniard. The sinking of the ships with rocks naturally refers to the use of some sort of stone thrower, just like it is clear that the use of weapons refers to weapons used by the military retinue of the 'giant'. It is possible that the eating of the captives suggests some sort of connection with the Germanic peoples of the north, because most of the early sagas refer to ritualistic cannibalism, even if this is shrouded as the eating of hearts of dragons or shape-changers. In sum, it seems quite probable that the 'giant of Spain' was a Scandinavian or other Germanic mercenary leader (a Herul?) in Roman service.

According to the version given by Geoffrey, Arthur decided to confront the 'giant' himself, with the assistance of Seneschal Kay and cup-bearer Bedevere, together with their squires. When the retinue approached the Mount, they observed that there was one fire on the top and another on a smaller peak. Arthur sent Bedevere to reconnoitre by boat the smaller peak, while the rest stayed on their horses. Bedevere found an old woman, who told him that the niece had killed herself when the 'giant' had attempted to rape her, with the result that the 'giant' fulfilled his sexual desires by raping the old woman every night. Bedevere promised to bring help and then returned to Arthur and gave him his report. Arthur then advanced on horseback to the taller peak, dismounted, and the men handed their horses to the squires. The tide was presumably suitable for the use of horses. When the men reached the peak, Arthur surprised the 'giant' while he was eating pigs. The 'giant' grapped his club and managed to partially deflect Arthur's sword cut, but not the following ones, as Arthur hacked at him until the brains burst from his skull. Bedevere sawed off the 'giant's' head, after which the squires took it to the camp for all to gaze at. Hoel buried his niece on the top of Mont Saint Michel and had a chapel built on the spot, which was henceforth called Helena's Tomb.

This story undoubtedly preserves a muddled account of a commando operation carried out by Arthur in person, in which he had chosen a small elite force for the attack. Bedevere then reconnoitred the Mount from the sea to find out which route of approach to take for the attack, after which it was decided that the best way to achieve the aim was to make a direct attack on horseback, presumably at low tide.

The Battle of Saussy/Siesia in September 471 (Geoffrey 10.4ff.)
When the army was finally assembled at Barfleur, presumably in mid-to-late August, Arthur began a march towards the city of Autun, where he expected to meet the emperor's army. However, when Arthur had reached the River Aube, he

learnt from scouts that the emperor's army was close by and so large that it would be difficult to defeat. Arthur pitched his camp on the riverbank so that he could easily withdraw if he wanted. The presence of the river also made it easy to find water for the men, horses and beasts of burden. The location of the roads suggest that Arthur had not yet reached the River Aube, but was rather somewhere close to Orleans, about to begin his march south towards Autun, when he then learnt that the enemy was close by and changed his line of march towards the emperor's army, which was located close to the Aube. Lucius' aim was probably to let Arthur march towards Autun and then cut off his line of retreat, or just to stop Arthur at the first opportunity. It is possible that the Romans feared that Arthur could have joined forces with the Burgundians behind the other Roman army facing the Visigoths, but the Burgundians appear to have maintained neutrality during these conflicts in order to maintain some semblance of balance of power between the different parties in Gaul. This order must have come from Ricimer, who had holed himself up in Milan. The armies then faced each other somewhere east of the Seine and the Aube.

Arthur dispatched his nephew Gawain (Walvanus, Gwaluanus), together with Boso of Oxford and Gerin (Gerinus) of Chartres, to the enemy camp with demands either to leave or fight the next day. According to Geoffrey, the young men of the court incited Gawain to provoke a battle. When the leaders met, Gawain cut off the head of Lucius's nephew, Caius Quintillianus, after which he and the other envoys mounted their horses and fled. The Romans set off in pursuit, some on foot and others by horse. All three envoys are claimed to have killed some of their pursuers, after which Gawain regrouped his horsemen and wheeled them around to face the pursuing enemy cavalry. This resulted in the death of some Roman pursuers, but there were too many of them for the Britons and they continued their flight to a pre-arranged place of ambush, where there were hidden 6,000 British horsemen in woods. When the Romans reached the site, the Britons charged as several *catervae*[4] (probably wedge-shaped irregular arrays) behind their round shields (*clipeis*) and levelled spears. The Romans fled; some fell from their horses as a result of spear strikes, were captured or killed, but the rest were rescued by the senator Petreius, who had with him 10,000 Roman horsemen. Petreius forced the Britons to flee back to the woods from which they had attacked. The arrival of reinforcements under Hyderus, the son of Nu, balanced the situation so that the Britons were able to reform their lines in the woods. Hyderus' force may have been the cavalry reserve of the Britons, or he may have been posted in the rear as a second ambush force[5] which left its position to assist their comrades when it became apparent that they needed help.

After this, the battle became a typical prolonged cavalry clash, in which the different units and sections of the line advanced and retreated as instructed by their officers. When Boso realized that Petreius directed the attacks, retreats and use of reserves with great skill, and that the Britons were losing, he resorted to a desperate ploy. Boso assembled a chosen group of Britons and charged through the enemy formation in a wedge (*cuneus*)⁶ array straight at the enemy leader, whom he grasped by the neck and threw to the ground. Boso was clearly at the apex of his cavalry wedge, just as Petreius appears to have been at the apex of his own. The Romans appear to have used two cavalry lines, both of which consisted of wedge-shaped units. The Romans rushed to the rescue of their commander, while Boso's dense *caterva* of Britons (i.e. a wedge, despite the use of the *caterva*) protected him long enough for him to take Petreius back to the British lines. The Britons are claimed to have been better fighters with a spear, sword and missile/javelin (*quis hasta, quis gladio, quis telo*). It is possible to interpret '*telo*' as either an arrow/missile or javelin (the usual interpretation), and it is unfortunate that the narrative does not provide enough details to make a decision in this case. The leaderless Romans were then easily routed, the pursuing Britons unhorsing, killing or capturing those who were too slow in flight.

According to Geoffrey, the reason for Boso's desperate act had been that the three Briton leaders had started the battle without Arthur's permission, and it would have been too shameful to return to Arthur after having suffered a defeat. It is possible that this was a later invention to hide Arthur's duplicity, like his despicable treatement of Gorlois and Ygerna, but in this case it is quite possible that the young British leaders had acted without Arthur's permission.

The young British leaders returned to their camp full of pride and handed over Petreius Cocta and the rest of the captives to Arthur, who congratulated the men and promised greater rewards in the future if they fought as bravely. Arthur decided to send the prisoners to Paris on the following day, which suggests the probability that Paris served as his logistical base of operations. It would have been easy to ship supplies along the Seine to Paris, and from there in whichever direction Arthur wished. Arthur ordered *Dux* Cador, Bedevere the cup-bearer, Borellus of Cenomania (Orleans) and Richerius (a *dux* or *map*?), together with their retinues (*famuli*), to escort the captives until they would not have to fear a Roman rescue attempt.

According to Geoffrey (10.5), the Romans soon found out what the Britons intended to do, which suggests that they had a spy or spies inside Arthur's camp. It is probable that the previous ambush by Gawain's men had succeeded precisely because Arthur had not ordered it. At Lucius' command, the Romans chose 15,000 horsemen, who advanced behind the Britons during the night to a spot where they expected them to pass. The commanders were senators Vulteius Catellus and Quintus Carucius, together with Evander, king of Syria, and Sertorius, king of Libya. According to the *Notitia Dignitatum* (*ND*), the *Dux Syriae* had ten units of *equites* (ca. 512 horsemen each), two legions (ca. 3,000 men each), two *alae* (each ca. 512 horsemen) and four infantry cohorts (each ca. 480 footmen). It is clear that the *Dux* cannot have taken all of these troops with him. My educated guess is that the *Dux* would have had a detachment of about 3,000 men with him. The extant versions of the *ND* do not include any units for the *Dux Libyarum*, because the relevant part is missing, but one may estimate that he would have had approximately the same number of men as the *Dux Syriae*.

The Britons set out from their camp at dawn, little expecting that the Romans had bypassed them to lay an ambush. Consequently, when the Roman cavalry launched its ambush, the Britons were utterly surprised. The fact that the Romans did not deploy their cavalry as orderly *turmae*, but in irregular array, suggests two things: 1) the terrain where the troops were hidden was such that it made it difficult for the cavalry to deploy in an orderly manner; 2) the Roman combat doctrine recommended the use of an irregular formation (called *droungos* in the *Strategikon*) when speed was of essence, as it was when launching an ambush. The speed of the Roman cavalry charge left too little time for the Britons to organize their defence, and the Romans broke their line with ease. The scattered Britons re-formed as best they could. Richerius and Bedevere formed a circle (*agmen*) around the prisoners, while Cador and Borellus attempted to put their *agmina* (divisions) into order for a counter-attack. This proved impossible and the Roman cavalry inflicted huge losses on the Britons, who would have lost their prisoners if they had not suddenly and unexpectedly received help.

According to Geoffrey, Guitard, the Duke of the Poitevins (*Guitardus/Gwitardus, dux Pictavensium*), had learnt of the ambush and arrived on the scene in the nick of time with 3,000 horsemen. Geoffrey fails to state how Guitard had learnt of the ambush, which means that we can only speculate. The two likeliest ways are: 1) Guitard's guards intercepted the traitor who had previously told of the Briton convoy to the Romans when he was attempting to re-enter the Briton camp, and when he was then interrogated he spilled out the details; 2) Guitard had some agents/spies inside the Roman camp who managed to convey their message only after the Briton convoy had already left the camp. The arrival of these reinforcements tilted the balance in favour of the Britons, who now forced the irregularly arrayed Romans to flee with all speed. The battle, however, had been a huge disaster for the Britons, because before the arrival of the reinforcements they had lost Borellus when Evander (*Euandros*) had thrust his *lancea* through Borellus' throat, and four other brave noble leaders (Hyrelgas of Periron/Hireglas de Perirut, Maurice/Mauricius Cador of Cahors/Cadorcanensem, Aliduc of Tintagel and Her/Er, son of Hider/Hyder) had also been killed. The Britons pressed their pursuit relentlessly until they had killed Vulteius Catellus and Evander.

Not unnaturally, Lucius Hiberius took the news of the latest defeat harshly. He appears to have pondered his options, which were: 1) to attempt to ambush Arthur by making a feint withdrawal; 2) to fight a full-scale pitched battle with Arthur; 3) to retreat inside Autun to await for the Emperor Anthemius/Leo's relief army. Lucius opted to attempt to ambush Arthur by retreating to Langres. His aim was to surprise Arthur if he followed (see Lucius' speech at Geoffrey, 10.8). As to why Lucius opted to march towards Langres instead of marching straight to Autun to wait for the arrival of Emperor Leo's reinforcements, the obvious answer would be

The War in Gaul in 471/472 (Geoffrey 9.15ff.)   151

that Lucius feared to cross the Aube in the presence of Arthur's army and therefore marched along the Aube to Langres.

When Lucius noted that Arthur did not follow I would suggest that he decided to march to Autun to wait for the arrival of Leo's army, led by Anthemiolus (Anthemius' son), which had been dispatched to support Anthemius just like the army under Lucius.

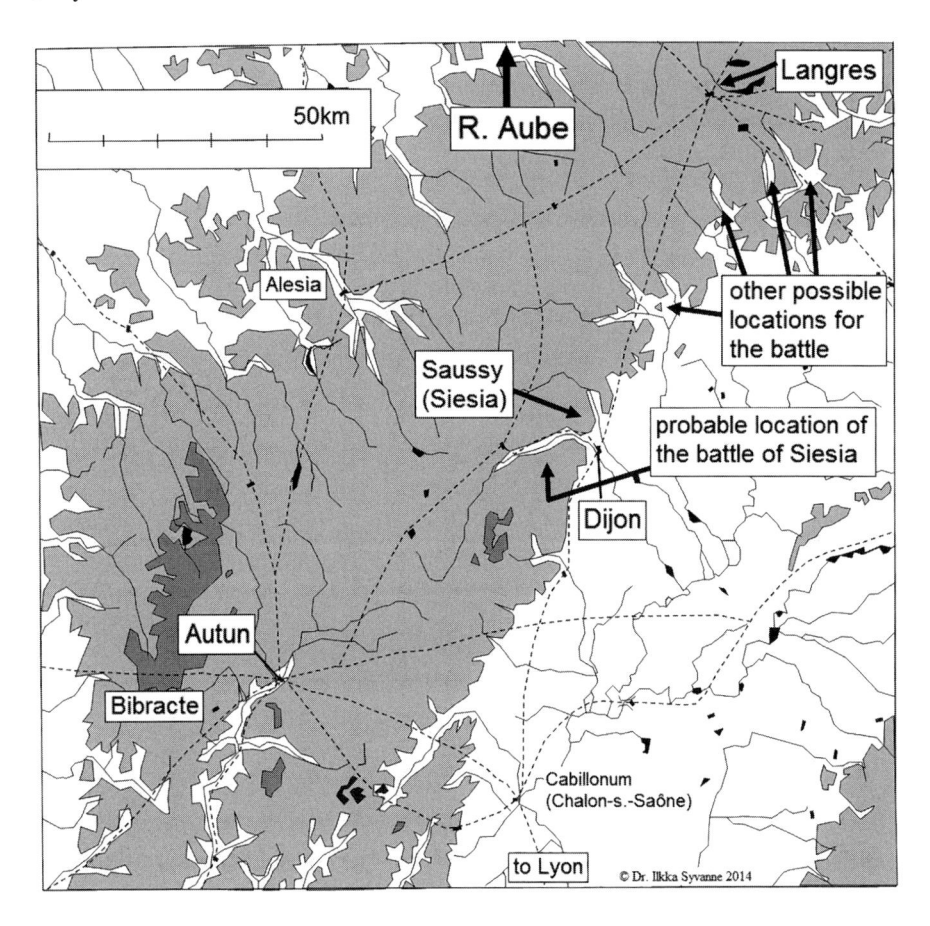

When the scouts reported that Lucius had withdrawn to Langres, Arthur decided to cut off his route to Autun. Consequently, Arthur bypassed Langres with a night march so that he left it on his left flank and advanced to a valley called Siesia. The location is not known, but the usual guess is that it must be the small town of Saussy (the name resembles Siesia) near the city of Dijon. This is where Arthur deployed his army in readiness to intercept the enemy. The subsequent battle, however, cannot have taken place at Saussy, which is located on a hill, but in the adjacent valley. I have shown the likeliest locale and other possible locations for the battle in the map on the previous page. The reason why I have located the battle is that the valley there is close to Saussy[7] and it intercepts the two main roads from Langres to Autun.

According to Geoffrey, Arthur placed one legion under Morvid, the Consul of Gloucester. His orders were to stay in the reserve and attack the enemy from behind. The rest of the forces were divided into seven *catervae* (divisions). Contrary to what Thorpe (p.247, n.2) states, Geoffrey's arithmetic is not faulty. Geoffrey counts only those who were Britons (eight divisions) and does not include the two divisions commanded by the foreign rulers (the Scandinavians and one of the French divisions) in this figure. Each of these divisions consisted of 5,555 fully armed men, and each of these contained cavalry and infantry. The infantry *catervae* were deployed according to the British custom as hollow squares, with right and left wings. The cavalry was given orders to attack the enemy's flank obliquely with closed ranks at the very same moment as the footmen engaged them. It is unfortunate that Geoffrey fails to specify how the Scandinavians (Norwegians and Danes) were deployed, because their kings had been instructed to bring only footmen with them. However, I have here made the educated guess that the Scandinavians would also have been deployed as a hollow infantry oblong/square and that they could receive cavalry reinforcements from the rest of the army as shown by the narrative so that they could perform the same functions as the rest. The sources prove that the Germanic peoples knew the defensive hollow square array and circle array, so that they possessed the readiness to adopt the Briton/Roman way of fighting when required, even if it is probable that they were not quite as good at it.

Arthur's battle array consisted of two lines of four divisions and one reserve division under him, and of the above-mentioned legion of ambushers under Morvid. The right wing of the first division was commanded by Auguselus, king of Albany, and the left wing of the first *caterva*/division by Cador, Duke of Cornwall. I take this to imply that each commanded the cavalry reserves posted behind on the flanks. The second division was commanded by Gerin of Chartres and Boso of Oxford. The third division was commanded by Aschil, king of the Danes, and Loth, king of the Norwegians. The fourth was commanded by Hoel, king of the Bretons, and Gawain, Arthur's nephew. Loth and Gawain were probably placed in neighbouring divisions because they were father and son. Behind these were another four divisions. The first of these was commanded by Kay the Seneschal and Bedevere the cup-bearer (these appear to have been placed on the left wing because they were fighting in support of the Scandinavians). The second was commanded by Holdin, the *Dux* of the Ruteni, and by Guitard, *Dux* of the Poitevins. The third was placed under Jugein of Leicester, Jonathel of Dorchester and Cursalem of Caistor, and the fourth under Urbgennius of Bath. I agree with Thorpe (p.248, n.1) that Geoffrey has obviously made a mistake here, so we should transfer Cursalem to the fourth division. Behind all stood Arthur with his elite legion of 6,666 men and his personal standard, the Golden Dragon. This force served as the last rallying point of the army.

The War in Gaul in 471/472 (Geoffrey 9.15ff.)   153

The following reconstruction of the battle array is based on three sources of information: 1) the narrative of Geoffrey; 2) the width of the valley, which was approximately 3–3.5km; 3) the organization and tactics of the Roman forces during the fifth century. My estimation of the length of the battle line is based on the assumption that each 5,555-man (plus supernumeraries) legion would consist of about 5,000 footmen and 500 horsemen, with 4,800 footmen arrayed as one oblong and the extra men left behind in the marching camp. Since the width of the level portion of the battlefield/valley was approximately 3–3.5km, it is probable that the front and rear halves of the square would have been longer, so that both would have had 1,800 men and the flanks 600 men. The front would have had a width of ca. 330m (front depth of six men, with four heavies and two light; rear depth of four heavies and two light; plus intervals). The frontage of the flanks would have been ca. 110m long, with one interval. If the Britons adopted the *testudo*/tortoise array for extra protection, as is possible, then the corresponding frontage would have been about 165x55m. However, I would suggest that the initial array was the standard close array, in which the files occupied on average 80–100cm of space. The width of the infantry oblongs in formation, without any intervals, would therefore have been about 1,320m or 660m. This means that each infantry oblong was separated from the other with an interval of about 336m or 468m, if an equal amount of space was left on both flanks of the array.

Considering that the size given for the legion corresponds with the figures of Vegetius and Modestus, it is possible that the cavalry contingent of each consisted of approximately 736 horsemen, plus the supernumeraries, but in light of the overall strength of the legion the traditional contingents of either 512 horsemen or 608/640 horsemen plus the supernumeraries are actually more likely. If the cavalry was deployed as sixty-four-man wedges for greater mobility and penetrative impact, as is likely, then: 1) the 512-horsemen detachment would have consisted of four wedges on the left and four on the right (each four-wedge group would have occupied a width of about 120m); 2) the 608/640-man detachment would have consisted of either nine wedges and one thirty-two-man oblong, or of ten wedges (with five wedges on each side, each group would have occupied about 150m in width); 3) the 736-horsemen contingent would have consisted of eleven wedges and one thirty-two-man oblong. It should be noted that the commanders could have their own personal bodyguards who are not included in these figures. My reconstruction is based on the assumption that the Briton system followed the traditional 512-horsemen standard, so there would have been four cavalry wedges on each flank of the hollow infantry oblong and each legion would have occupied 570m in width. This means that the Briton array (with intervals, at most ca. 2,500m) did not cover the entire width of the valley, which was roughly 3–3.5km wide. This was the reason for the use of the hollow oblong arrays. If the enemy managed to outflank the Britons, they could not defeat the infantry because the footmen were deployed as hollow oblongs; and if the enemy outflanked the first line of oblongs, it faced the prospect of being attacked in the rear by the next line of oblongs and cavalry. This was a very efficient way to deploy the army.

It is probable that Arthur's own reserve would have resembled the Late Roman legion described by John Lydus, for which there also exists evidence for the fifth century (see Syvänne, *MHLR* vols.3–4), so that its infantry component would have been about 4,800 men and its cavalry contingent about 1,600. The infantry would have been deployed in the same way as above, but since the cavalry contingent was larger, it would have occupied a wider space, so there would have been thirteen wedges on both sides of the oblong if the cavalry detachment consisted of 1,664 horsemen. The thirteen cavalry wedges would have occupied an area of 390m, which means that Arthur's *caterva/legio* (infantry oblong plus the two cavalry wings) would have occupied an area 1,110m wide. In other words, despite its small size, Arthur's reserve covered about half of the width of the entire array.

According to Geoffrey, Lucius found out about the trap Arthur had laid out for him, which means that his scouts operated effectively and/or that he had spies inside Arthur's camp, just as he had had previously. Lucius called a meeting of his *duces*, and declared his intention not to avoid battle but to attack Arthur in the valley. The nearby *castrum* of Dijon would not have offered him and his army a place of refuge – it was too small (see map below) – and he would not have wanted to march to Burgundy because it was allied with Ricimer. He could have attempted to withdraw to Langres, but his soldiers would have interpreted this as a sign of cowardice. Therefore, it can be said that Lucius adopted the only sensible course open to him, which was to engage the enemy. To have done otherwise would have

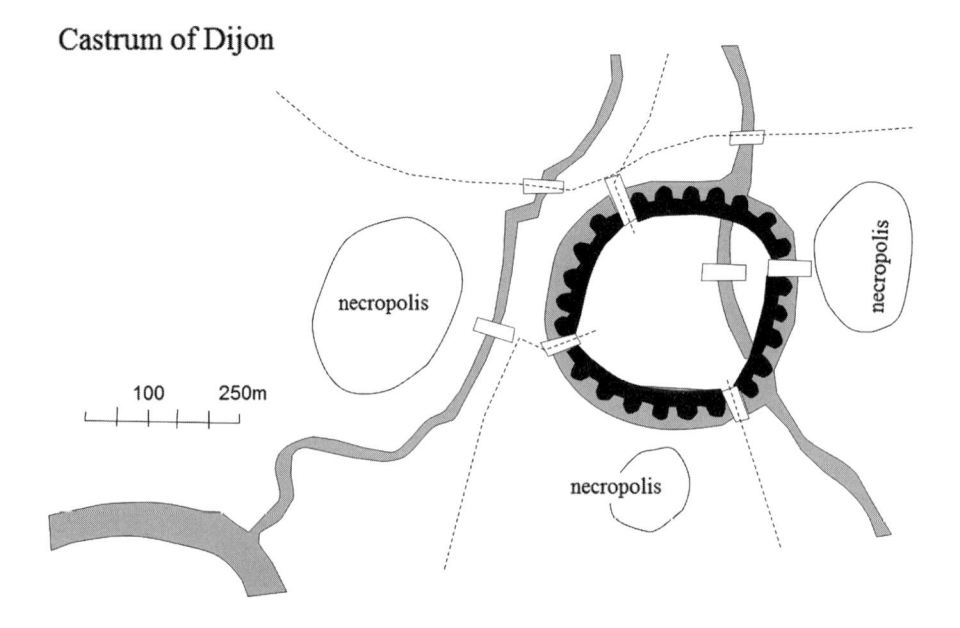

Castrum of Dijon

The War in Gaul in 471/472 (Geoffrey 9.15ff.)   155

endangered the morale of the army, which had already suffered as a result of the previous defeats and retreat from the River Aube. Arthur had played his cards really well and had forced his foe to fight a decisive battle in a place chosen by him.

Geoffrey claims that it was only after Lucius had learnt of the ambush that he led his men out of Langres to fight against Arthur. If this is true, then it is probable that the Roman march from Langres to the battle site took two days, because Siesia/Saussy is over 50km from Langres. Lucius deployed his army in twelve wedge-shaped divisions, all of them infantry. All of the units were deployed in the Roman manner as wedges, so that each division (*legio/agmen*) under its *ductor* (leader = *dux*) consisted of 6,666 men.[8] These were deployed in three lines of four divisions. This means that Lucius dismounted his cavalry for the battle. There are two likely reasons for this decision: 1) the battle was to be fought in a valley and Lucius thought that this terrain suited infantry better than cavalry (but this proved to be a mistake); 2) the previous disastrous battles against the Britons had been fought by cavalry and it is probable that Lucius wanted to make certain that the cavalry, which undoubtedly suffered from poor morale, did not flee in the middle of the battle, by forcing them to dismount.

My educated guess is that each of the Roman infantry wedges consisted of 6,440 footmen (ca. 4,800 foot and 1,640 horse) or 6,666 infantry as stated by Geoffrey. In the former case, the recruits were left in camp, and in the latter these were included in order to widen the frontage. I have also made the educated guess that the Romans would have adopted a compromise solution regarding the depth and width of the array, so that the men would have been deployed twelve deep (eight heavies and four light) to widen the frontage against the Briton cavalry while also retaining the 'punching power' of the wedge with eight heavy-armed men. The frontage of the 6,440-man wedge would have been about 537m, while the 6,666-man wedge would have had a width of ca. 556m. If the Romans tightened the array for extra protection as tortoise, then the corresponding frontages would have been ca. 269m and 278m. There was no need for this, as the Romans were fully-equipped, but it is possible that some units would have adopted this array in the middle of battle for the extra protection it offered.

Note, however, that the tortoise/*foulkon* used against cavalry did not require the shortening of the frontage, but only the kneeling of the front rank in regular close order. The use of the infantry wedge was quite justifiable as it enabled the Romans to pit their best men against one point of the enemy infantry oblong, while the rejoined wings of the wedge enabled it to withstand the attacks of the Briton cavalry with formations that were like hollow wedge when the sides of two wedges faced cavalry between them.

The first Roman line of four divisions consisted of the following. The first *agmen* (= *legio*) was commanded by Lucius Catellus (senator and commander of the left wing?) and Ali Fatima ('the King of Spain' – the name is clearly spurious). The commanders of the second *agmen* were Hirtacius ('the King of the Parthians') and

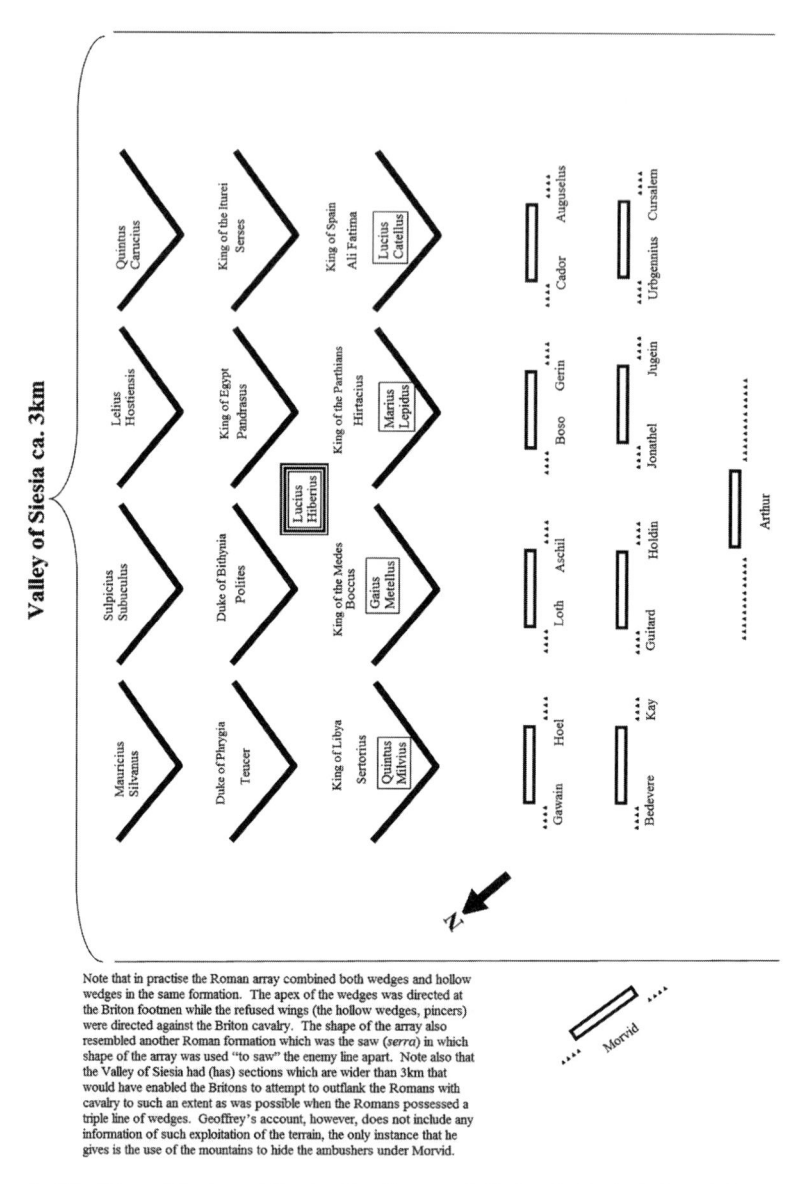

Note that in practise the Roman array combined both wedges and hollow wedges in the same formation. The apex of the wedges was directed at the Briton footmen while the refused wings (the hollow wedges, pincers) were directed against the Briton cavalry. The shape of the array also resembled another Roman formation which was the saw (*serra*) in which shape of the array was used "to saw" the enemy line apart. Note also that the Valley of Siesia had (has) sections which are wider than 3km that would have enabled the Britons to attempt to outflank the Romans with cavalry to such an extent as was possible when the Romans possessed a triple line of wedges. Geoffrey's account, however, does not include any information of such exploitation of the terrain, the only instance that he gives is the use of the mountains to hide the ambushers under Morvid.

Stage 1: The King of Spain and Lucius Catellus attack Cador the Duke/King of Cornwall and Auguselus the King of Albany.

Stage 2: Boso and Gerin come to the rescue and break through the enemy wedge. Urbgennius and Cursalem die when they and their cavalry attempt to do the same on the other flank. I have made the educated guess that the Briton difficulties on their right flank also meant the rout of the front division commanded by Auguselus and Cador.

Stage 3: Boso and Gerin exploited their success by charging the wedge of Hirtacius, the King of the Parthians, and Marius Lepidus from the flank and possibly also from behind at the same moment as it attempts to attack the flank commanded by Aschil, the King of the Danes. The greater width of the Roman wedge enabled it to engage two Briton oblongs simultaneously.

The War in Gaul in 471/472 (Geoffrey 9.15ff.) 157

the senator Marius Lepidus (commander of the centre-left?). The third legion was commanded by Boccus ('the King of the Medes') and the senator Gaius Metellus (commander of the centre-right?). The fourth division was led by Sertorius ('the King of Libya') and the senator Quintus Milvius (commander of the right wing?). The second line consisted of the following: the commander of the first *agmen* was Serses/Sexes ('the King of the Iturei/Iturians'); the second *agmen* was led by Pandrasus ('the King of Egypt'); Polites (the *Dux* of Bithynia) led the third; and Teucer/Teucrus (the *Dux* of Phrygia) commanded the fourth.

The third and last line consisted of: the first *agmen*, commanded by the senator Quintus Carucius; the second, led by Lelius Hostiensis; the third, supervised by Sulpicius Subuculus; and the fourth, led by Mauricius Silvanus. The overall commander, Lucius, did not assume command of any particular unit, but moved with his battle standard of the Golden Eagle wherever was needed. The orders of battle are given on the accompanying diagram.

The fact that each of the Roman divisions in the front line was commanded by a duo may suggest that, unlike claimed by Geoffrey, these would still have consisted of both infantry and cavalry detachments, in the same manner as the Britons, but since Geoffrey is adamant about the use of only infantry, I have reconstructed events accordingly. Furthermore, it is likelier that the senators were actually commanders of sections of the line (as I have added inside brackets above and in the order of battle), so that each commanded all three legions in a row. This corresponds with the Greco-Roman practice.

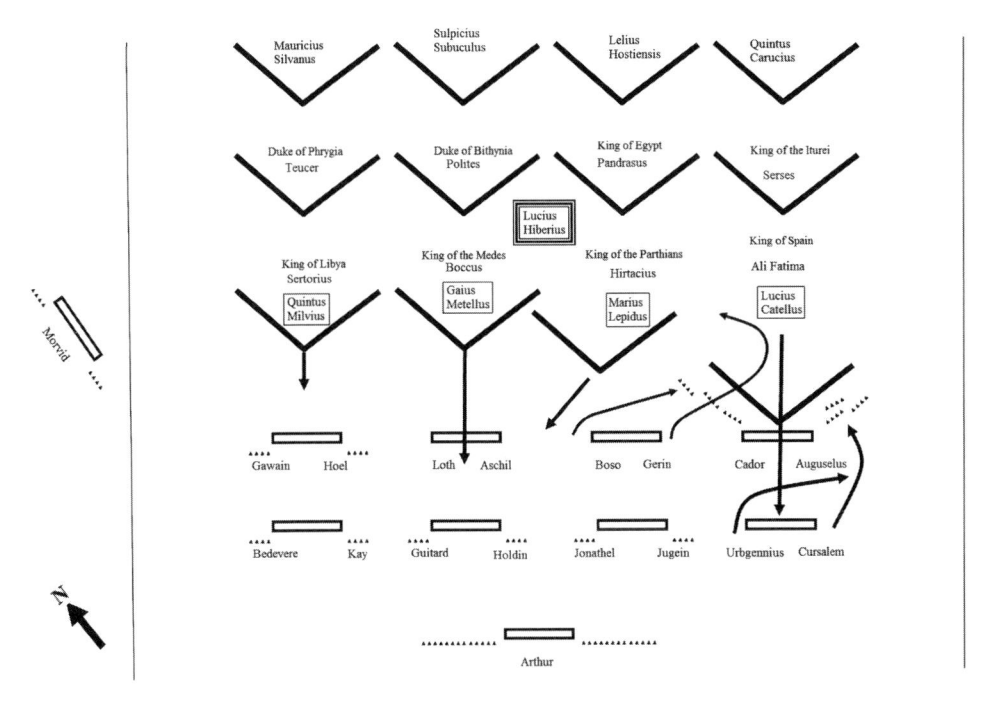

When the armies stood opposite each other with javelins raised (*erectis steterunt telis*), the trumpets sounded the *classicum* to signal the beginning of the battle. The battle started on the British right. The *agmen* commanded by the king of Spain and Lucius Catellus (note that I consider this one to be commander of the left wing) charged at the *caterva* of the king of Albany and Duke of Cornwall, but they could not break up the tight Briton array. When the Romans pressed the attack and apparently achieved a breakthrough, because the list of killed commanders include Cursalem and Urbgennius, the *caterva* commanded by Gerin and Boso came to the

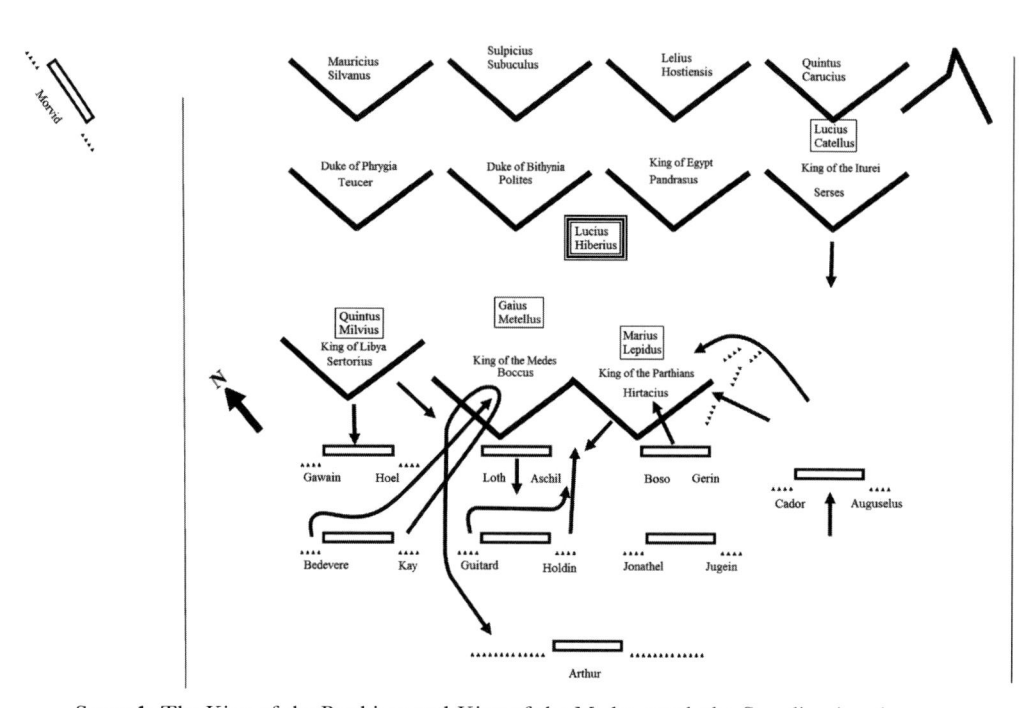

Stage 1: The King of the Parthians and King of the Medes attack the Scandinavians because they do not possess cavalry to support them. Bedevere and Kay bring their cavalry to the left flank while Guitard and Holdin bring their cavalry to protect the right flank. In the meanwhile, Gawain and Hoel defend themselves successfully against the division attacking them and kill Quintus Milvius.

Stage 2: Boso and Gerin crush the division of the King of the Parthians and kill Marius Lepidus. In the meanwhile (my educated guess) Cador and Auguselus take command of the reserve division and regroup the survivors of their own division with them and then lead the men forward to fill up the hole in the frontline.

Stage 3: The Scandinavians are forced to retreat and Loth is killed. Bedevere penetrated the enemy array and is killed by Boccus while Holdin is killed by some other Roman. Kay is surrounded by the Medes and is mortally wounded, but managed to fight his way through only to be crushed by the division of Sertorius. In spite of this, Kay and some others managed to flee back to Arthur.

rescue. It is not known whether the Britons also lost the infantry oblong alongside their commanders Cursalem and Urbgennius, because it is possible that they could have just charged forward with their cavalry to help the front line. Despite the use of the word *caterva* for the men of Gerin and Boso, in this case Geoffrey's next line makes certain that Gerin and Boso attacked the Romans only with cavalry, stating that the Britons broke through the bravely fighting Romans with a cavalry charge (*cursu equorum impetum*), and then advanced against the king of the Parthians, who was attacking Aschil, king of the Danes. It is possible or even probable that Loth was killed in this encounter, because there is another king of Norway present at Camlam. However, the tactic described is entirely in keeping with the standard British tactics to deploy cavalry against the attacking enemy wings. The Britons' counter-attack was successful, because the list of killed Roman commanders includes Ali Fatima and Marius Lepidus.

It was at this moment that the sides came into contact along their entire front line. Geoffrey's account of subsequent events is disjointed by his concentration on the heroics of Bedevere, Kay and Hyrelgas (Bedevere's nephew). However, the list of killed commanders given after this allows one to reconstruct the events that led to the situation in which these three performed their heroic fighting. Those who died on the Roman side were Ali Fatima, the king of Spain, Micipsa the Babylonian (of the Parthian division?) and the senators Quintus Milvius and Marius Lepidus. On the Briton side, Holdin, the Duke of the Ruteni (second line), Leodegarius of Boulogne (part of Holdin's division), Cursalem of Caistor (second line), Guallauc of Salisbury (Cador's division of Cornwall in the first line) and Urbgennius of Bath (second line) all fell. Gawain and Hoel defended their section of the line successfully – the list of dead enemy commanders includes Quintus Milvius. The list of killed Britons also means that the Romans concentrated their attack against the Scandinavians, who lacked horsemen, with the result that all nearby cavalry forces (except those under Gawain and Hoel) rushed forward to save them. These included Bedevere, Kay, Guitard and Holdin. Bedevere came face-to-face with Boccus, but the latter ran his *lancea* through Bedevere and he fell to the ground. Kay attempted to exact revenge, but was surrounded by the 'Medes' and received a mortal wound. In spite of this, he managed to lead his men through the enemy encirclement. Unfortunately, he led his horsemen straight at the *agmen* led by the king of Libya, Sertorius, whose forces routed the Britons. Despite this, the mortally wounded Kay and a few of his followers, with Bedevere's corpse, managed to retreat to the Golden Dragon and Arthur. The details given here suggest that the Romans used one of the standard tactics against cavalry, which was to open the array to let the enemy through and then engage them with a separate force (which could be a reserve unit or a section or sections of the phalanx detached from it temporarily for this purpose).

Bedevere's nephew, Hyrelgas, thought it his duty to exact revenge. He collected 300 of his followers and charged through the enemy lines straight to the spot where he saw the standard of Boccus, the king of the Medes, and killed him. It is possible that Hyrelgas used a larger variant of the cavalry wedge which had 384 horsemen, familiar to us from Late Roman and Byzantine contexts, but Geoffrey does not state this.

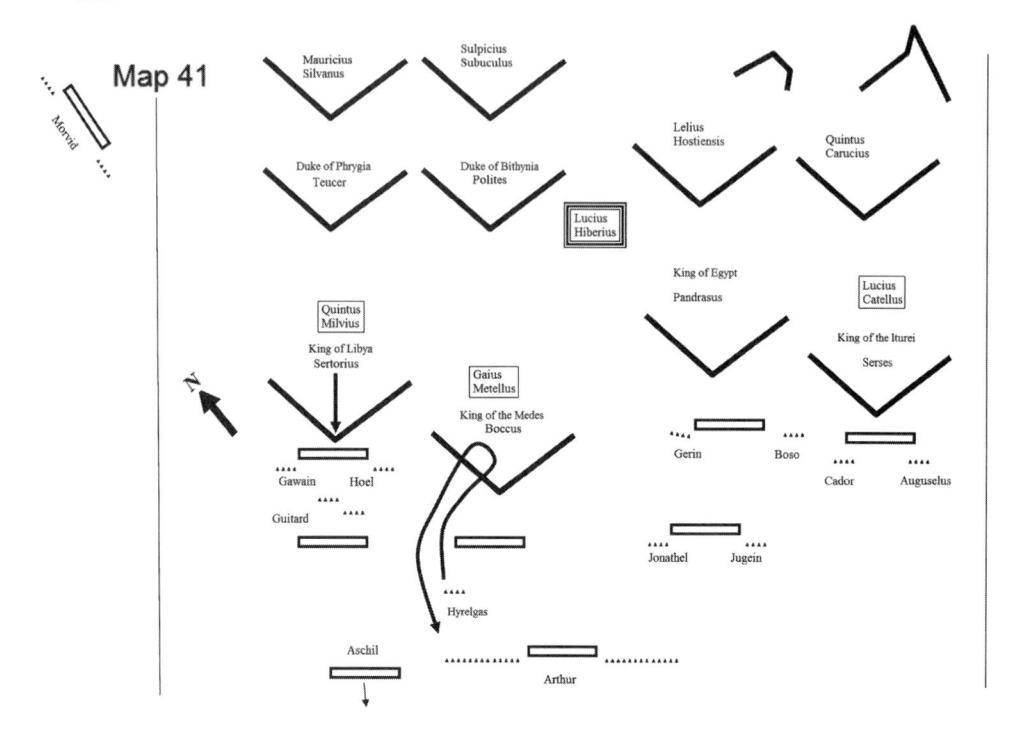

Map 41

[Battle map showing positions of forces: Morvid, Mauricius Silvanus, Sulpicius Subuculus, Duke of Phrygia Teucer, Duke of Bithynia Polites, Lelius Hostiensis, Quintus Carucius, Lucius Hiberius, Quintus Milvius, King of Libya Sertorius, Gaius Metellus, King of the Medes Boccus, King of Egypt Pandrasus, Lucius Catellus, King of the Iturei Serses, Gawain, Hoel, Guitard, Gerin, Boso, Cador, Auguselus, Jonathel, Jugein, Hyrelgas, Aschil, Arthur]

Hyrelgas carried Boccus' body back to his own lines and then exhorted his fellow countrymen into a fury so that they would charge at the enemy in waves until they were defeated, with the result that the Britons attacked all along the line. Geoffrey claims that the horsemen who had been commanded by Holdin, Leodegarius, Cursalem, Guallauc and Urbgennius regrouped when they reached the battle line of the Armorican Britons led by Hoel and Gawain. This is likely to contain a mistake, which is the inclusion of the horsemen of Cursalem and Urbgennius among them. If any of these survived, they would have regrouped with Auguselus, Cador, Boso and Gerin. However, the rest of the surviving horsemen would have indeed regrouped behind the division commanded by Hoel and Gawain, and would then have charged at the enemy at the same time as the men encouraged by Hyrelgas. Geoffrey fails to state what happened on the British right flank, but one can make the educated guess that the surviving Britons under Auguselus, Cador, Boso, Gerin, Jonathel and Jugein defended themselves successfully against the Romans (Pandrasus, Serses) opposing them.

The War in Gaul in 471/472 (Geoffrey 9.15ff.)   161

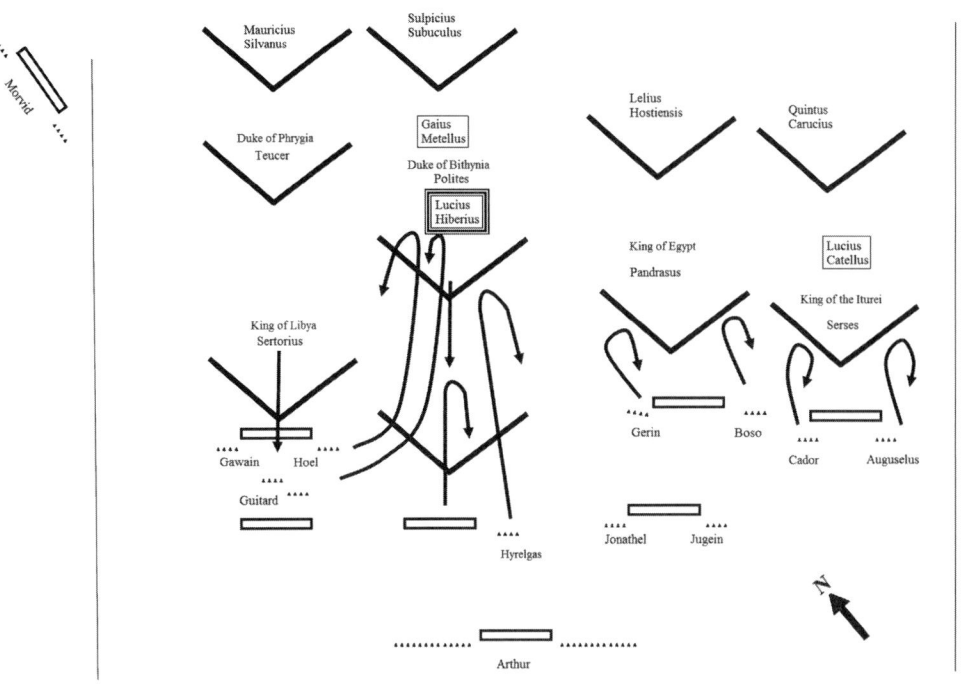

Stage 1: The Briton cavalry regroup behind the *caterva* of Gawain and Hoel, and then attack with them against the leaderless division to their right at the same time as Guitard's oblong and Hyrelgas attack them frontally. It is probable that the Romans and Britons fought each other to a standstill on the Briton right because Geoffrey has no information about the events on that wing.
Stage 2: The Briton counter attack is successful. The division formerly commanded by Boccus is scattered.
Stage 3: Lucius launches a counter attack with the Imperial Bodyguards (Polites) and Sertorius. It is a success and the Britons are forced to retreat all the way up to the reserves under Arthur.

Consequently, the Britons launched a general attack on their left flank which was directed against the division previously commanded by the king of the Medes. The attack met with success and the leaderless Roman division was crushed, but it was then that Lucius launched a counter-attack with the emperor's bodyguards, which appear to have consisted of the division led by the 'Duke of Bithynia'. The use of the Duke of Bithynia in the context of Imperial Bodyguards once again supports the basic veracity of Geoffrey's account. The unknown original author clearly knew that the praesental forces were housed in Bithynia during peacetime. The Imperial Bodyguards battered the Britons badly. When Hoel and Gawain reached the Imperial Bodyguards, they and their men were cut off by the Romans, but the two brave knights attacked first in one direction and then in another, and did not give up. Gawain attempted to kill Lucius, and when the men saw each other Lucius did not decline the challenge. Lucius was in the prime of his life and did not fear his enemy. The two men fought, but in the end it was Gawain and Hoel who retreated to their line because the Roman counter-attack had been such a success. The subsequent details prove that Lucius's bodyguards also included mounted *bucellarii*, and it is possible that some of the men belonging to the Imperial Bodyguards may also have been mounted, so it was the combination of infantry and cavalry that surprised and crushed the Britons.

The list of killed Briton commanders shows that when the cavalry under Gawain and Hoel had attacked the leaderless *agmen* formerly commanded by Boccus, the Roman division under Sertorius attacked the infantry oblong of Gawain and Hoel, which now lacked cavalry support. Chinmarchocus, the Duke of Tréguier (located in Brittany and therefore probably under Hoel), was killed, along with 2,000 men. Three other commanders killed were Riddomarcus, Bloctonius and Iaginvius of Bodloan (located in Maine, France). This proves that the Romans wiped out the entire foot division (the rest would have fled in panic), and Geoffrey states that it was as a result of the Roman counter-attack led by Lucius that the Romans came face-to-face with Arthur. This suggests that the Romans had also defeated the infantry oblong formerly commanded by Holdin and Guitard, which also lacked cavalry support, and may even have included the infantry division formerly commanded by Kay and Bedevere if it joined the flight of the others.

Arthur drew his *Caliburnus*-sword ('*Caliburno, gladio optimo*') from its scabbard and shouted words of encouragement to his own men, and insults at the enemy, then led his men forward. The use of the sword instead of the spear signalled to the men that this was a fight to the death, and Arthur delivered death to the enemy. The enemy were either trampled, cut into pieces or had their horses killed with a single blow, which shows that Lucius' bodyguard consisted of *bucellarii* who were mounted. According to Geoffrey, the enemy ran like sheep before a lion, their armour offering no protection against the Caliburn. He says Arthur cut off the heads of Sertorius and Polites and sent them to hell. Arthur's example encouraged the rest of the Britons to join the attack; they all attacked as one man, both infantry and cavalry. It is probable that these Britons included those who had previously fled, but had been re-formed behind Arthur's reserve. The Romans fought back furiously under their brave commander Lucius, and the fight became evenly matched, but then Morvid, whose division was higher up in the hills, launched his ambush and attacked the Romans in the rear. The Romans panicked and thousands of them were killed in the rout that ensued, including Lucius, whose killer remained unknown. The fact that the killer of Lucius is not one of the heroes lends further credence to the account given, suggesting that the account is indeed based on real events, even if it is impossible to know how accurate the extant version is.

The Britons pursued the fugitives as fast as they could. Most of the Romans simply surrendered. Those who could fled to nearby forests, towns, forts or cities. Once Arthur was certain that the enemy would not be able to regroup, he ordered

The War in Gaul in 471/472 (Geoffrey 9.15ff.) 163

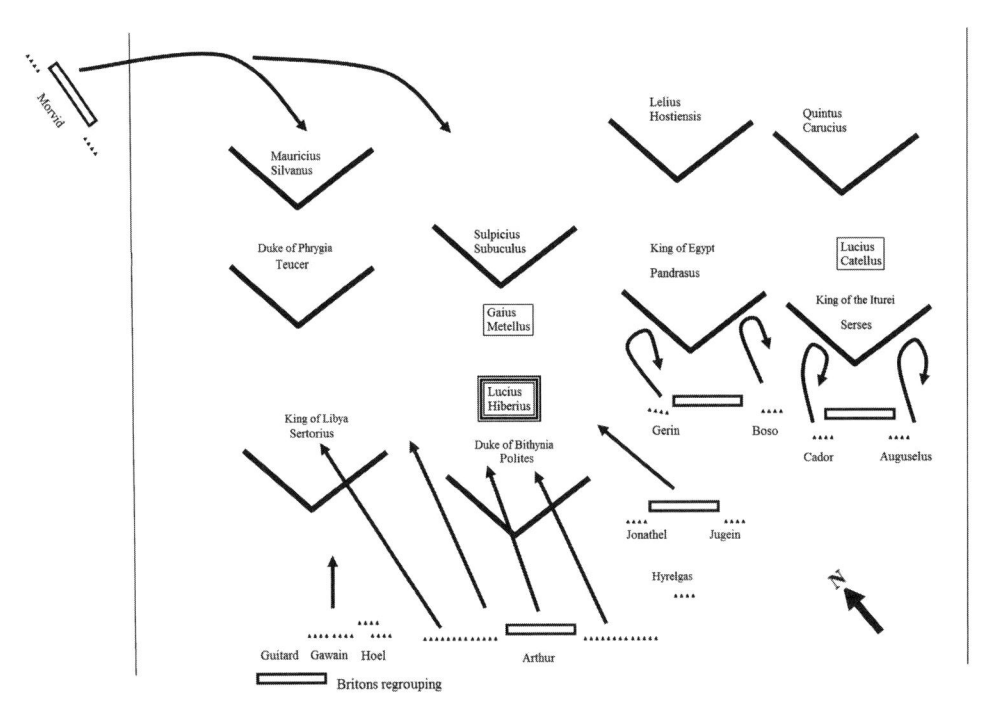

[Battle diagram showing troop positions with labels: Morvid, Mauricius Silvanus, Duke of Phrygia Teucer, Sulpicius Subuculus, Lelius Hostiensis, King of Egypt Pandrasus, Quintus Carucius, Lucius Catellus, Gaius Metellus, Lucius Hiberius, King of the Iturei Serses, King of Libya Sertorius, Duke of Bithynia Polites, Gerin, Boso, Cador, Auguselus, Jonathel, Jugein, Hyrelgas, Guitard, Gawain, Hoel, Arthur, Britons regrouping]

Stage 1: Arthur leads his cavalry and infantry forward and counter attacks. He defeated in succession both enemy divisions facing him.
Stage 2: Arthur's example encourages the rest of the Briton army to join the counter attack, but the brave resistance of Lucius and Romans balance the situation.
Stage 3: The stalemate is broken by the sudden attack of Morvid who launched his ambush against the Roman rear with the result that the Romans panic and are routed.

the dead Briton leaders sent back to their homes for burial, while the rest, including the Romans, were apparently buried on the spot by the locals, who were ordered to perform this onerous duty. Lucius's corpse was sent to the Senate to send a message to the Romans. Notably, Geoffrey is not the only source to mention Arthur's victory over the 'Greek army' of Leo. The *Mabinogion* (pp.138, 190) mentions Arthur's conquest of 'Greece' and the presence of Greeks in his army, which can be interpreted as a confused memory of Arthur's actual victory over the army of Anthemius and Leo.

The Aftermath of the Battle of Siesia
According to Geoffrey, Arthur subdued the cities of the Allobroges in the same district in the course of the following winter, with the intention of continuing his march to Rome the following summer. The inclusion of the Allobroges in this case is a mistake, because these areas did not belong to the Burgundians occupying the

former areas of the Allobroges. The cities subdued by Arthur were just north of Burgundy and, thanks to their potential threat to his lines of communications, needed to be subdued before Arthur could continue his march to Rome.

Geoffrey's information is in agreement with that provided by the other sources, which state that in 472 the Burgundians marched under Gundobad to Italy to support Ricimer against Anthemius. Geoffrey's account allows us to add the name of Arthur to the list of forces marching to support Ricimer. It is quite possible that the intention was to raise Arthur to the throne, that Arthur intended to do that as a rival claimant or that he acted as an ally of Ricimer. However, this was not to be, because Arthur's nephew, Mordred, had rebelled and lived adulterously with Queen Quinevere. Arthur had no other alternative than to return to Britain.

It should be noted that the revolt of Mordred and the disappearance of Loth from the sources after the Battle of Siesia may be connected somehow. The sources fail to state what Loth did when the Romans attacked Aschil. Did he flee or did he betray the Britons? If he did betray the Britons, why would Gawain still have remained loyal? Was he executed after the news of the revolt of Mordred was brought to Gaul, or were his heroics in combat simply hidden after his son, Mordred, betrayed his king? The likeliest answer is that Loth was killed in combat, which caused Gawain to perform the heroic deeds he did. It is also probable that the news of the death of his father released Mordred from the psychological restraints that Loth had imposed on him, even from a distance, if Geoffrey is correct in stating that Mordred was his (adopted?) son. It is even possible that Mordred may have accused Arthur of the death of his father to convince himself that it was OK to revolt – and as a member of the imperial family, Mordred must also have felt that he had the right to usurp power. However, as noted, it is inherently more likely that Mordred was actually the son of Budicius and Anna. Consequently, even if the traditional story of lust would have been the principal reason for the revolt, and it is probable that it was, there could still have been other reasons as well. The dating of the second Saxon raid to Ireland by the *Irish Annals* to 471 also suggests that Mordred had already formed an alliance with them in that year, and that he had started to plan the overthrow of Arthur even earlier.

It is probable that Sidonius' famous letter to Riothamus (Sidonius 3.9) was sent during the winter of 471/472, when Riothamus Arthur was besieging Autun and other nearby cities. We know that the letter was sent after Sidonius became Bishop of Clermont in 470, and since the city of Clermont is not far it is likely that it was sent in late 471 or early 472. Riothamus Arthur was also close by in about 469 when he was a fugitive in Burgundy, but this date is out of the question because Sidonius was not yet Bishop of Clermont. However, it is probable that it was then that the two men became so well acquainted that Sidonius felt able to ask for his assistance in a question in which a humble person had complaints regarding the behaviour of the armed Britons.

The city maps below show what were presumably the largest cities (Langres, Cabillonum/Chalon-sur-Saône and Autun) that Arthur subdued in the region.[9]

These maps also show why it was possible to feed such large armies in the theatre of operations. The cities in the area possessed sizeable populations, which in turn had made it necessary for the Romans and Gauls to organize adequate supply of provisions for them, alongside enough storage space to keep these supplies. It was easy enough for the authorities to tap these reasources for other uses when they did not care what happened to the civilians. The result of this, naturally, was famine, which is recorded as happening in Gaul in ca. 472–473, especially in Burgundy (Gregory of Tours 2.24). This is no surprise in light of the events that took place.

The defences of Langres after 1842

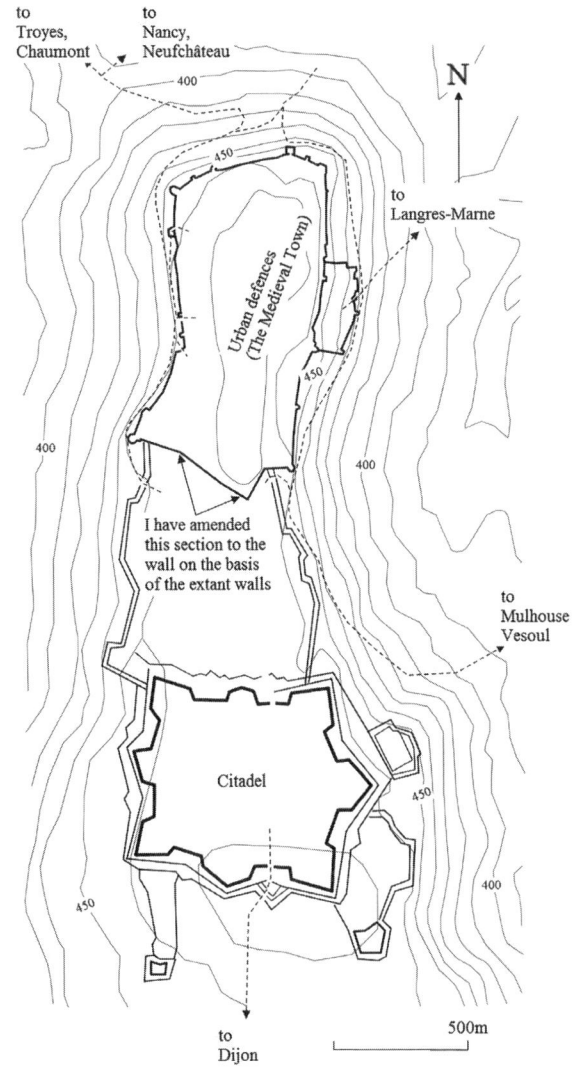

The city of Langres had and has two peaks so that the medieval town and the citadel are situated on higher ground than the area between them. In light of this it is uncertain whether the entire top of the hill was fortified during the Roman period, but since the standard defensive solution in ancient cities was always to have a citadel to serve as last place of refuge this seems probable. It is also probable that the ancient citadel encompassed the entire top of the hill so that it may have been even larger in extent than its modern counterpart, but with the difference that it is improbable that the ancient fortress would have had any outlying forts or bastions despite the fact that the pointed towers were becoming increasingly fashionable in the course of the fifth century (see Syvänne, *MHLR* vols 3–5). The modern citadel was meant to house a garrison of 3,000 infantry and one may make the guess that it could have housed a similar number of men (garrison or paramilitary urban militia). If the city encompassed the entire top then it had a population of about 75,000 to 94,000 inhabitants, which would have provided an ample supply of militia forces to man the walls in times of crises. Even in the case that the city encompassed only the medieval area, the city would still have had a population of about 50,000 to 63,000 inhabitants and an ample supply of militiamen.

AUTUN

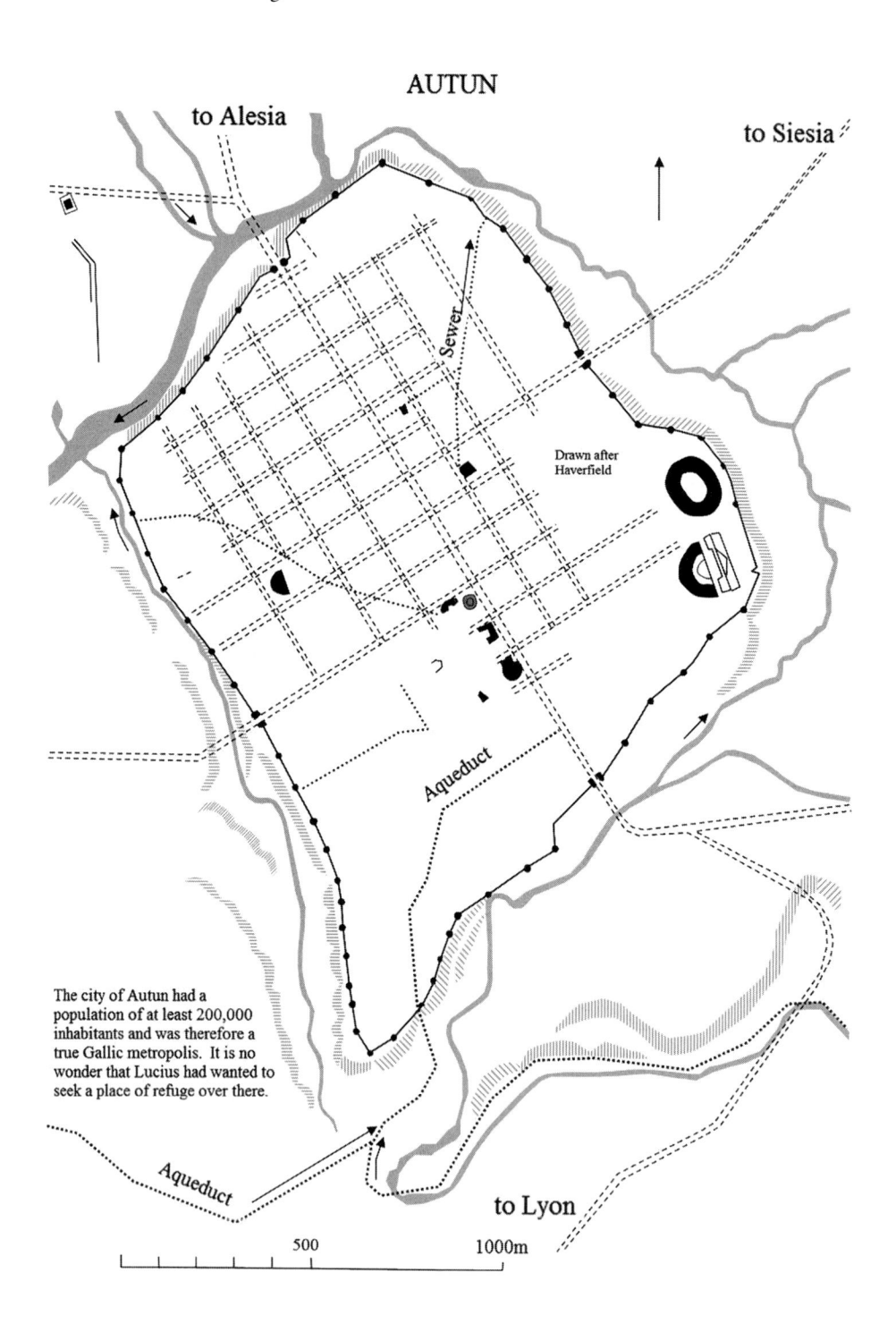

to Alesia

to Siesia

Drawn after Haverfield

Sewer

Aqueduct

Aqueduct

to Lyon

The city of Autun had a population of at least 200,000 inhabitants and was therefore a true Gallic metropolis. It is no wonder that Lucius had wanted to seek a place of refuge over there.

500   1000m

The War in Gaul in 471/472 (Geoffrey 9.15ff.)   167

The departure of Arthur's forces to Armorica and Britain created a power vacuum in northern France (*Armorica, Lugdunensis II, Belgica I, Belgica II, Sequania*) which the forces of King Syagrius moved in to fill. He became the king of the Romans in his capital, Soissons. Syagrius was free to do so because the Gallo-Roman resistance (especially the siege of Clermond, that lasted from 471 until 474) and the threat of a Roman counter-attack in the south kept the Visigoths preoccupied, at the same time as the Burgundians faced the prospect of having to fight against the Alamanni, Visigoths and East Romans.[10]

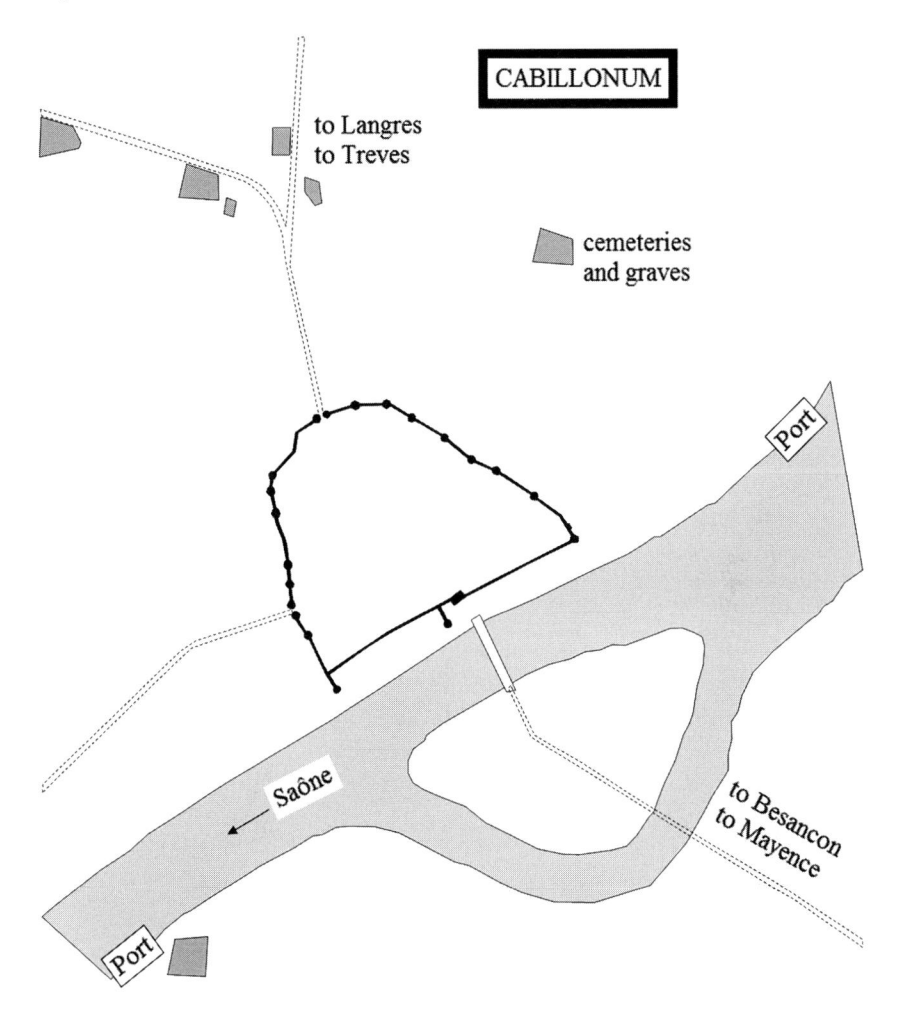

As noted, the destruction of Anthemius' armies by Arthur at Siesia and by the Visigoths (who destroyed Anthemiolus' army) somewhere east of the Rhône in 471 changed the balance of power in Italy. Ricimer, together with his 6,000-man retinue, had been forced to hide inside the walls of Milan ever since he had revolted against Anthemius in 470. Now the destruction of Anthemius' two field armies enabled Ricimer to reassert his position in 472 with the help of his nephew, Gundobad, who was one of the Burgundian princes. Ricimer advanced to Rome and put Anthemius under siege. Ricimer nominated Gundobad as *MVM Praes.* and Olybrius as his puppet emperor. After a two-month siege, Anthemius was finally captured and killed by Gundobad. Soon after this, both Ricimer (19 Aug. 472) and Olybrius (2 Nov. 472) died, Gundobad assuming the role of kingmaker. He nominated Glycerius as the next emperor on 3 March 473, but this was not accepted by the Gallo-Romans or the East Romans. This series of events led to the collapse of West Rome a few years later. One can say that the final straw that broke the camel's back had been the destruction of the last West Roman field armies outside Italy by King Arthur and King Euric. The decisive element in this was that these armies had consisted of the regular units of both East and West, which meant that the vast majority of the remaining field forces in Italy now consisted of the federates. Eastern nominee Nepos brought additional forces from the East on ships to Ravenna in 474. In order to conserve his forces, Nepos handed over (or in some cases accepted the situation on the ground) power to the Visigoths of Euric Spain, and Gaul from the Pyrenees up to the Loire and Rhone. In spite of his concessions to the barbarians, Nepos' forces were still too few to offer resistance against the barbarian warriors of Orestes, and Nepos was forced to sail back to Salona in 475. Orestes nominated his son, Augustulus, as emperor on 31 October 475, but was himself crushed by the barbarians (mainly Heruls, Sciri and Torcilingi/Turcilingi) of Odovacar/Odoacer in 476, who duly nominated himself as king of Italy. This effectively ended Roman rule in the West, and it can be said with some confidence that Arthur's role in the fall of Rome was not insignificant. The Visigothic King Euric resumed the offensive in 476/477, capturing Arles from the Burgundians and Marseilles from the Romans. At the same time, the Burgundians secured for themselves those parts of Roman Gaul which bordered the areas controlled by Syagrius or the Alamanni. Syagrius' kingdom was now the only island of Roman presence left in Gaul, and it was crushed by Clovis, the king of the Franks, in 486/487, thus ending the last Roman presence in Gaul.

Chapter 14

The Revolt of Mordred and Arthur's Last Campaign in 472[1]

'… he had news brought to him that his nephew Mordred, to whose care he had entrusted Britain, had by tyrannical and treasonable practices set the crown upon his own head; and that the queen Guanhumara [Guinevere], in violation of her first marriage had wickedly married him … On the matter now to be treated of, most noble consul, Geoffrey of Monmouth shall be silent; but will nevertheless, though in mean style, briefly relate what he found in the British book above mentioned, and heard from that most learned historian, Walter, archdeacon of Oxford, concerning the wars which this renowned king [Arthur], upon his return to Britain after his victory, waged against his nephew.' (Geoffrey, tr. by Giles, pp.189–90)

The above quote has often been used as evidence of Geoffrey's use of an ancient British source, and I do the same because there are no really good reasons to suspect that Geoffrey has in his treatise preserved the gist of the real exploits of Arthur, even if in muddled form. It is a great pity that we do not know how Walter had learnt what he knew, and what bits of the story were taken from the 'little book' and what from Walter.

Preparations in the spring of 472
Mordred had used the intervening period well. He had already made a deal with the Saxon warlord Chelric, or Cheldric(?), presumably in 471, because there exists an entry in the *Irish Annals* which states that the Saxons pillaged Ireland for the second time in that year. It is more than likely that these raiders would have consisted of the Saxon mercenaries who had arrived to serve Mordred. In return for Chelric's support and warriors, Mordred had promised the territory formerly held by Hengist and Horsa in Kent and the territory between the River Humber and Scotland/Albany. Armed with these promises, Chelric sailed to Germany to recruit and conscript as many men as possible. Chelric managed to assemble a force of pagans which required 800 ships to transport back to Britain. On the basis of the subsequent location of Mordred's army, these men were apparently landed at Richborough, which lay close to the Isle of Thanet, that had been promised to the Saxons.

It is possible that the name Chelric (according to Thorpe, this is the correct reading) hides beneath it that of Cheldric. Some of the manuscripts (e.g. *CH, DE*) do call the leader by the name Cheldric, not Chelric. If this is correct, then it is probable that Cador had not killed Cheldric on the Isle of Thanet, as claimed by Geoffrey, but had concluded a treaty with him so that the Saxons were allowed to settle there. It is too much of a coincidence that the name of Mordred's Saxon commander resembles that of the previous Saxon commander, the enemy of Arthur, even if one cannot rule out the possibility that there were several Cheldrics or Chelrics.

In addition to the Saxons, Mordred had formed an alliance with all those Britons who opposed Arthur, and with the Scots, Irish and Picts who had similarly been worsted by Arthur and had a grudge against him. These Britons probably included those who opposed a war against the legitimate government of Rome. The size of Mordred's army was about 80,000 men, some of whom were pagans and others Christians.

As noted above, when Arthur learnt of the revolt, he cancelled his campaign against Leo (i.e. Anthemius) in Italy and started to make preparations for his return to Britain. It is probable that the army that turned back to Britain was at full strength because it is highly likely that Arthur would have used the winter to recruit new conscripts and mercenaries for his Italian campaign.

According to Geoffrey, Arthur's first order was to dispatch the leader of the Bretons, Hoel, with the Army of Gaul to restore peace in Armorica. It is unfortunate that Geoffrey fails to tell who the invaders were. It is possible that they were Saxons attempting to retake what they had previously lost on behalf of Mordred (especially if Mordred was Hoel's full brother, as I have speculated), but in my opinion the likeliest candidate is actually Euric and his Visigoths. The reason for this conclusion is that the Visigoths did not conduct any major operations against the Romans or Burgundians when the Burgundian army had marched to Italy to support Ricimer against Emperor Anthemius in 472. They did nothing to exploit their victory over the Roman army commanded by Anthemiolus in 471; it was actually in the interest of the Visigoths that Ricimer regain power, because Ricimer's mother was a Gothic princess. Consequently, they turned their attention towards Arthur's Armorica/ Bretagne/Brittany, which was also vulnerable, thanks to the revolt of Mordred. As can be seen, once again the events described by Geoffrey do fit the circumstances of the period.

The landing at Richborough/Rutupiae in the early summer
On the basis of the location of the landing, it is easy to guess that Arthur assembled his forces at Boulogne. He had at his command his British army and fleet, which was reinforced by the kings of the islands (Norway, Denmark, 'Iceland' and the Orkneys). Arthur put to sea at the first opportunity, with the object of landing at Richborough/Rutupiae/Rutupis. Despite possessing over 800 ships, Mordred did

not attempt to engage Arthur's fleet at sea, because Mordred's ships (longships and curraghs) could not meet the Romano-Briton war galleys on equal terms – it is more than likely that Arthur had taken his war fleet with him when he had sailed to Gaul, which means that Mordred would not have had more than a couple of true warships left to use. The subsequent account makes it clear that Mordred had anchored his fleet at Southampton, possibly in an effort to block that harbour from the Britons or simply because he wanted to place his fleet in some safe location out of Arthur's reach.

Geoffrey's account of the landing (Geoffrey, tr. by Giles, pp. 190–91) is very sparse in details but allows the making of some educated guesses when it is combined with the geography:

> 'His [Mordred's] whole army, taking pagans and Christians together, amounted to eighty thousand men; with the help of whom he met Arthur just after his landing at the port of Rutupi [Richborough], and joining battle with him, made a very great slaughter of his men. For the same day fell Augusel [Auguselus], king of Albania [*Albany, Scotland; he was the uncle of Mordred because Loth was his brother, just like Arthur was Mordred's uncle because Mordred's mother Anna was Arthur's sister*], and Walgan [*Gwaluanus, Gawain; note that the brothers Mordred and Gawain fought fiercely against each other at this battle*], the king's nephew, with innumerable others. Augusel was succeeded in his kingdom by Eventus [Huivenius, Ywain], his brother Urian's son, who afterwards performed many famous exploits in those wars. After they had at last with much difficulty, got ashore, they paid back the slaughter, and put Mordred and his army to flight. For by long practice in war, they had learned an excellent way of ordering their forces; which was so managed, that while their foot were employed either in an assault or upon the defensive, the horse would come in at full speed obliquely, break through the enemy's ranks, and so force them to flee. [*This implies that the Britons landed their forces in the same order as they usually fought their battles on land, namely that the infantry disembarked from the ships first and attempted to form themselves into hollow squares, and when they had reached the shore the cavalry would then disembark from the second line of ships to support them.*] Nevertheless, this perjured usurper got his forces together again, and the night following entered Winchester. [*This summarises the events of several days, in the course of which Mordred regrouped his scattered forces.*] As soon as queen Guanhumara [Guinevere] heard this, she immediately, despairing of success, fled from York to the City of Legions [Caerleon], where she resolved to lead a chaste life among the nuns in the church of Julius the Martyr, and entered herself one of their order.'

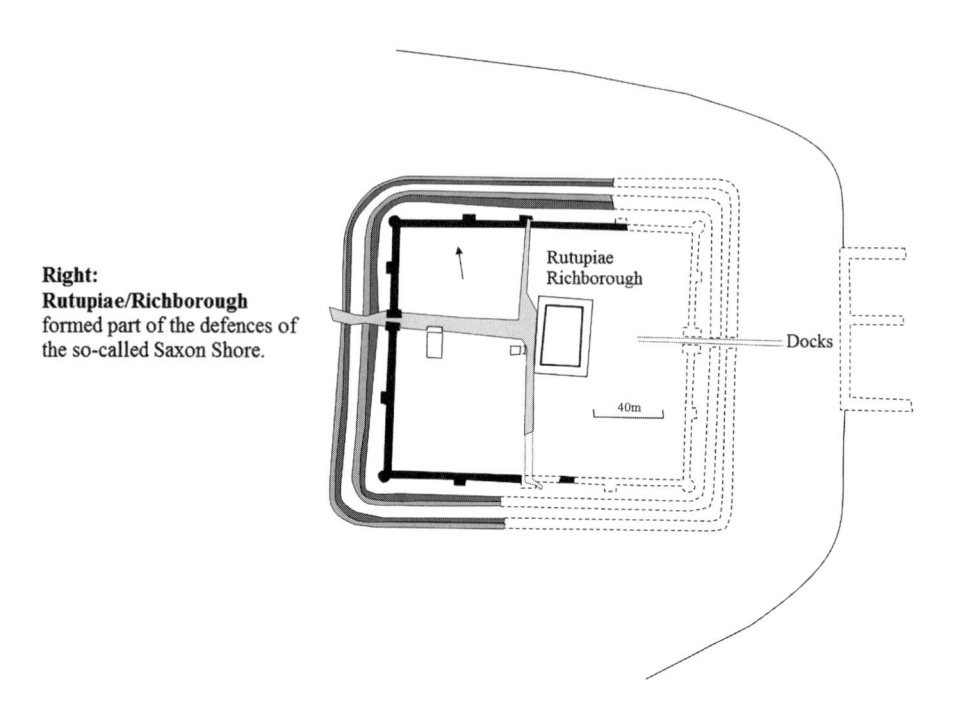

Right:
Rutupiae/Richborough
formed part of the defences of
the so-called Saxon Shore.

On the basis of the above, it seems probable that the first wave to land consisted of at least the men of Auguselus and Gawain, but may also have included others. It is probable that Gawain and Auguselus were placed at the forefront of the attack because: 1) as close relatives of Mordred, these two men had most to prove; 2) Arthur wanted them to prove their loyalty; 3) Mordred had taken away from both men their possessions and had handed those over to others, which made both men eager to exact revenge on their disloyal relative. This was a family feud on many levels. The attack of the first wave was fierce, and so was the resistance. Hundreds of Britons fell beside their leaders, but when the Britons finally managed to gain a foothold on land, they were able to form themselves up in their standard combat formation and force the enemy to retreat and then flee in disorder. It was not the tactical brilliance of Arthur that won the day for the Britons, but the long military experience and perseverance of the fighting men, their reluctance to give up – a trait that the inhabitants of Britain have proven again and again in combat over the centuries.

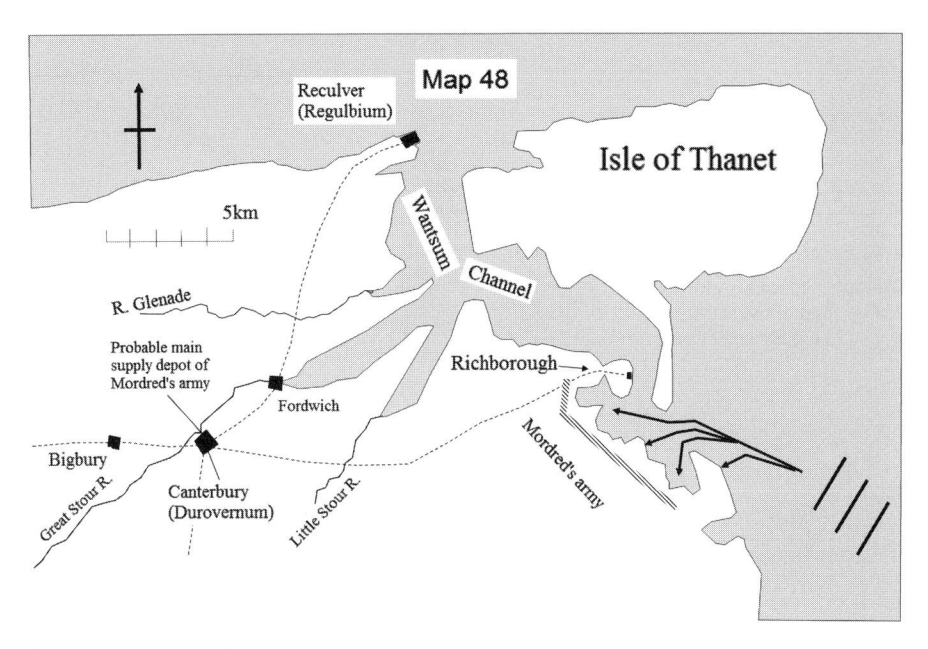

The Revolt of Mordred and Arthur's Last Campaign in 472   173

Map 48: Arthur's landing area showing Reculver (Regulbium), Isle of Thanet, Wantsum Channel, Richborough, Fordwich, Canterbury (Durovernum), Bigbury, R. Glenade, Great Stour R., Little Stour R., and the probable main supply depot of Mordred's army. Scale 5km.

Arthur's Landing at Richborough
– The above map shows the ancient waterline which was much higher than it is today.
– Arthur's amphibious landing appears to have been done on the mainland and not on the Isle of Thanet because Mordred was subsequently able to flee and because Richborough is located on the mainland. The probable reason for the abandonment of the Isle of Thanet by the Saxons is that it would have been impossible to defend when Arthur had naval superiority. It was thanks to this that the Britons could direct their landing straight at Richborough without first having to take the Isle.
– If we assume that the first wave of ships (consisting of two groups of ships: 1) infantry transports; 2) horse transports) brought to the shore 11,110 men (Auguselus and Gawain) and that each of the regular transport ships (100 ships) could carry about 100 men while the horse transports (32 to 42 ships) following them could carry about 25 to 32 horses and riders each, then the length of the first wave would have been about 2,500 meters. It is probable that the first attack wave would have headed straight at the chosen landing beach. Since the width of the straits between the Isle of Thanet and mainland closest to Richborough is less than 2 km, it is clear that the first wave had to be rowed in three lines/waves, or as a column, or as columns into the Wantsun Channel where it would then have spread out/deployed so that the ships could be landed in the order of battle. Since we know that the first wave would have occupied in battle formation not more than about 1 km in width after the landing, it is clear that the ships would have landed their men and horses in turns rather than simultaneously. This would have taken a while to do. Consequently, it is no wonder that the first wave suffered horrendous casualties even when the landing was probably protected by the ballistae of the war galleys. It is unfortunate that we do not know the location of the forces under Auguselus and Gawain in the final battle array as this would have enabled one to make further conjectures regarding the order of attack.
– It is unfortunate that we do not know whether the following waves of ships were directed to the same spot as Auguselus and Gawain or elsewhere, but as far as can be deduced from Geoffrey's account, it seems probable that all forces were landed on the same spot south of the fort of Richborough so that the Briton army assumed its typical order of battle under the protective cover of the first two hollow squares/oblongs. The other less likely alternatives are: 1) the rest of the fleet disembarked the men further south unopposed; 2) the rest of the fleet sailed around the Isle of Thanet and landed north of Richborough. Since it is apparent that Mordred's 80,000 strong army could have been used to cover the entire width of the beach south of Richborough up to the promontory, it is probable that the Britons would have landed the rest of their army along the entire length of the beach up to the promontory and would then have defeated the enemy through sheer doggedness resulting from their years of experience.

The Battle of Winchester in Early Summer 472

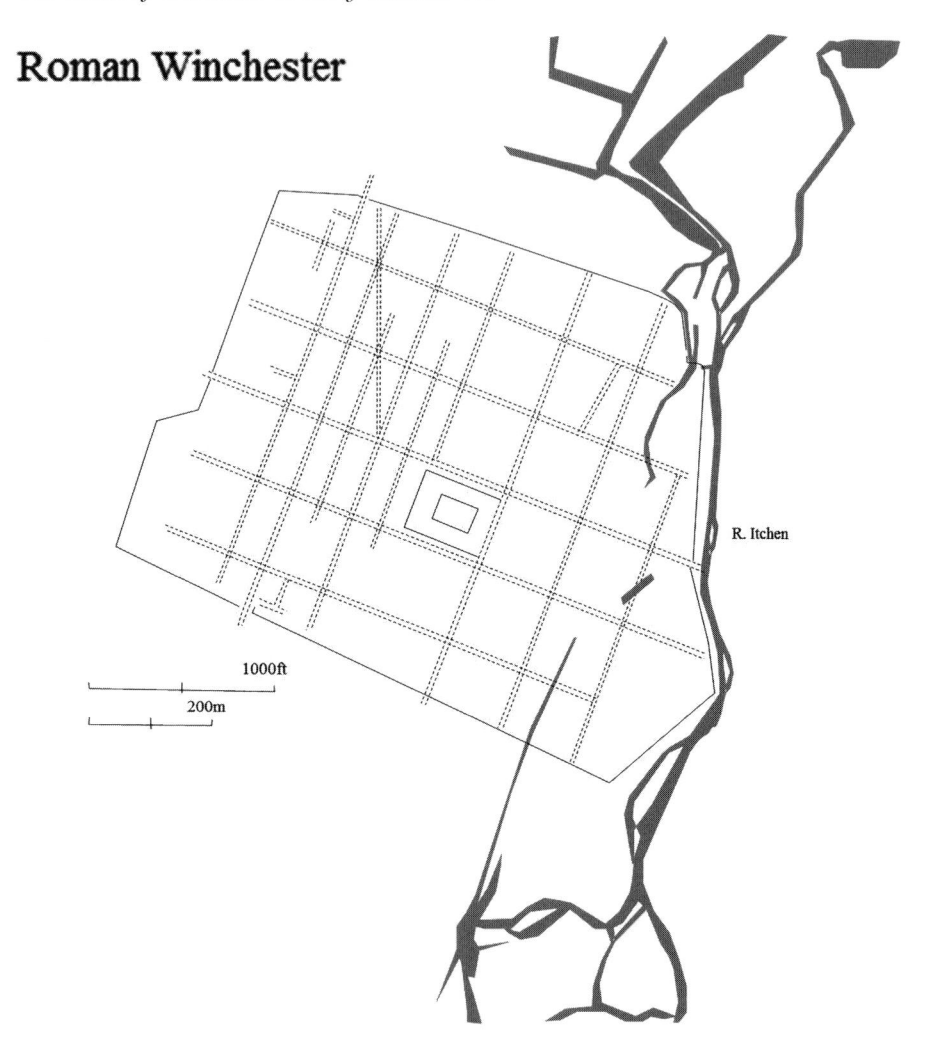

Roman Winchester

Arthur spent the following three days in burying the hundreds of dead soldiers from the battle, and then marched to Winchester to besiege his ungrateful nephew. Mordred, with his mostly foreign army, decided that it was not to his advantage to become besieged, and marched out of the city to meet Arthur on the field. Geoffrey does not provide any details of the battle arrays adopted by the armies, but one may make the educated guess that it would have resembled the ones both sides used in the following battles. Therefore, it is probable that Mordred placed his barbarians in the first line and Britons in the reserve, and that the length of the battle line would have been roughly 4.2km if the barbarians used the wedge arrays.[2] Arthur in his turn would have used the standard Briton array he had used in all of his battles.

Once again there were no brilliant tactical manoeuvres on either side, but a doggedly fought frontal battle in which both armies suffered terrible losses, which ended the same way as previously. Mordred's forces suffered a greater number of casualties, and were therefore forced to retreat and then flee from the battlefield.

Probable location of the battle of Winchester

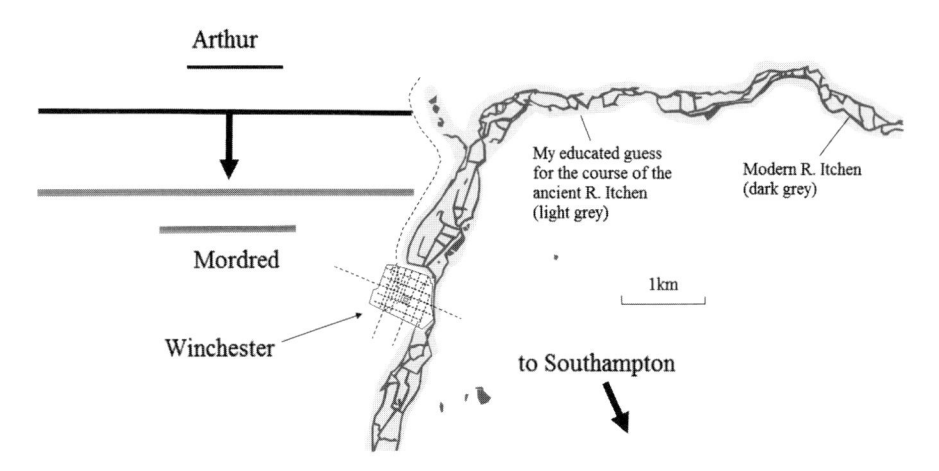

Arthur

Mordred

Winchester

My educated guess for the course of the ancient R. Itchen (light grey)

Modern R. Itchen (dark grey)

1 km

to Southampton

We are told that Mordred fled as fast as his ship could carry him to Cornwall. In other words, Mordred and his army fled to the coast, where it boarded the ships anchored there. The likeliest location for the boarding of the ships is naturally Southampton, because it was the closest major port south of Winchester. The *DE* manuscript of Geoffrey even states that Mordred fled to *Portus Hamonis* (Southampton) and from there to Cornubium (Cornwall). It is very improbable that Mordred would have boarded a ship located on the river beside Winchester, as a longship or river boat could not have been rowed fast enough for it to be an effective means of escape for him or his army in the presence of enemy cavalry, unless of course the army was marched on the opposite side of the river from the enemy. On the basis of this and the *DE* manuscript, it is very probable that Mordred had placed his fleet of 800 Saxon ships at anchor at Southampton, which enabled him to embark most of his men and save the remnants of his army. Otherwise it would be difficult to conceive how Mordred could have evacuated his army by sea. By now, Mordred's losses were about 20,000 men (according to Thorpe's edition of Geoffrey 11.2).

The Battle of Camblam/Camelford in June/July 472
Mordred reorganized his army in Cornwall and chose to wait for the arrival of Arthur by the River Camblam (flumem Kambri, River Camel) at a location which is today called Camelford. The loyalty of Cornwall to Mordred can easily be understood, because Arthur had previously murdered its lord and had not protected it effectively

against the Saxons. In addition to this, Arthur's war against the emperor of Rome must have upset at least the most loyal Romano-Britons. Mordred was prepared to either win or die. Arthur did not hesistate, but quickly followed so as not to give his enemy another chance of flight.

Mordred had 60,000 men left (Thorpe's edition), which he arrayed in two lines. His first line consisted of 40,000 men (*CH* manuscript), which he arrayed as six *turmae*-divisions, each of which had 6,666 men. Each of the divisions was commanded by a single *dux* appointed by Mordred for this purpose. The remaining 20,000 men were organized in the second line as one *turma* under his own command. Geoffrey does not state what formations were used, but one may make the educated guess that the front line would have consisted mostly of the barbarians and therefore of infantry, and since the wedge was one of the standard defences against enemy cavalry it is likely that this array was used by all front line divisions. Consequently, if the divisions were deployed as wedges with depth of twelve ranks (eight heavy infantry and four light), then the frontage of each division was about 555.5m and the length of the entire front line was 3,333m without intervals, or with intervals 3,633m (with 60m intervals between divisions, as recommended in the *Strategikon*). If the front line consisted mostly of the barbarian allies, then it is probable that the second line consisted of Mordred's Britons. The likeliest battle formation for these would have been the hollow square/oblong with cavalry wings, and I have here made the assumption that this was their array. I have also made the assumption that Mordred's personal division would have had at least 2,000 horsemen. The hollow infantry oblong would have had a frontage of about 1,300m and each of the cavalry wings a frontage of 210m, making a total of 1,720m.

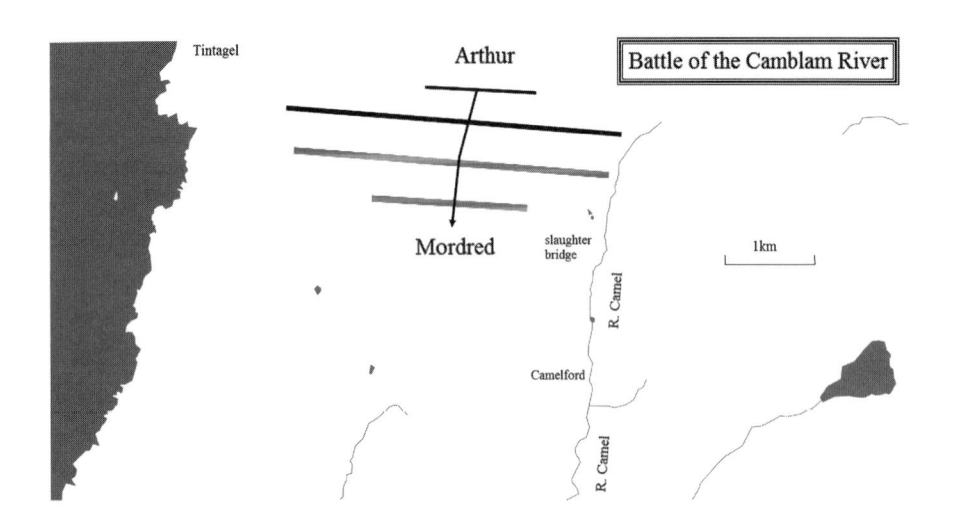

Arthur divided his army into nine *agmina* of infantry, each of which was drawn up as a square, with right and left cavalry wings. If these were still at full strength after earlier casualties had been replaced by recruits, then the total strength of the front line was approximately 50,000 men, but it is probable that there were not enough recruits for this – it is unlikely that there would have been time to collect them. Each of the full-strength front line divisions would have occupied a frontage of 570m (the infantry oblong ca. 330m, and each cavalry wing 120m), so that the maximum length of the front line would have been 5,610m. However, as noted, it is clear that Arthur's forces had suffered casualties and it is also probable that he would have wanted to adopt a deeper infantry formation for the sake of security, so it is likely that the Briton line was actually no longer than that of the enemy. Most importantly, the space between the River Camel and the sea was not wide enough for a battle line longer than ca. 4.5km. As usual, Arthur placed behind the front line the reserve of 6,666 men under his personal command. This force would have had a frontage of about 1,110m (330m for the infantry oblong, and each of the cavalry wings 390m). Arthur encouraged his men with a speech in which he disparaged the enemy as an inexperienced bunch of barbarians which his veteran troops would defeat with ease. The battle, however, proved otherwise, for it was once again hard-fought. The Saxons, Germans, Irish and Picts fought with a dogged determination brought about by their desperate situation, as did the rebel Britons under their equally desperate leader.

Most of the day passed in mutual slaughter in which both armies fought hand-to-hand, but then Arthur led his reserves forward against Mordred's division. His men hacked their way through the enemy array and killed the usurper, together with thousands of his followers. The death of Mordred did not bring an end to the battle, the rest of his army gathering together – possibly at what is today known as Slaughter Bridge – and being attacked by the Britons. The barbarians knew that they could expect no mercy and fought with desperation. Many leaders fell on both sides. Mordred's forces lost several Saxon (Chelric, Elaf, Egbrict and Bruning) and Irish (Gillapatric, Gillasel and Gillarvus) *duces*, together with many leaders of the Scots and Picts. Arthur's forces lost Odbrict, king of Norway (note that he had succeeded Loth to this post); Aschil, king of Denmark (Alf?); Cador Limenich; Cassivellanus; plus thousands of men. Most importantly, however, Arthur received a mortal wound and was taken off battlefield. He handed over the crown of Britain to his cousin, Constantine, the son of Cador, Duke of Cornwall, and ordered himself to be carried to the Isle of Avalon for treatment. Thanks to Arthur's mortal wound, the Britons failed to press their attack and allowed the enemy to regroup for a counter-attack. In the later legendary versions of the tale, the Battle of Camblam was further elaborated into a story in which Mordred and Arthur fought against each other, Mordred inflicting a mortal wound on Arthur before the latter killed him. This is, in my opinion, a later 'flashy' addition to the (probably) quite accurate story given by Geoffrey. Geoffrey merely states that Mordred was killed (presumably by some unknown soldier) when Arthur's reserve attacked, while Arthur was struck down after this by some unknown enemy.

The *Annales Cambriae* (AD 539) confirm that both Mordred (Medraut) and Arthur died in the same battle, even if it dates the battle quite differently, but it should be noted that the dating of the material in this source is contested because it does not use the AD dating (see Snyder, pp.72–73). Geoffrey's dating is no better, because he dates the Battle of Camblam to 542. It is unlikely that he would have made this mistake unless he was using an old Welsh source, because anyone familiar with the Roman sources would have known that there was no Roman emperor with the name Leo at that time and West Rome had already fallen.

According to Geoffrey, the Saxons united under the sons of Mordred and attempted to overthrow Constantine, and when this failed they fought a series of battles and then fled. This implies that the Saxons regrouped under the sons of Mordred and then counter-attacked the Britons beside the River Camel, and when this failed they retreated, in the course of which they suffered additional losses before being defeated completely. The remnants of Mordred's army followed the two brothers, one of whom took control of Winchester and the other the city of London. As noted above, the identity of the sons of Mordred is uncertain. It is possible that they were actually only followers of Mordred, but what is more likely is that Geoffrey has not dated the remarriage of Anna accurately or has not understood that Mordred was the son of Budicius and Anna.

Arthur's legacy had a long reach, as can be witnessed from Gerald of Wales' account. The fact that Arthur disappeared after the Battle of Camblam led the people to think that he had not died, but would some day return to rule them. It is quite possible that this was done on purpose so that the Britons would not loose their morale after the death of their leader, and when Constantine was then victorious, the pretence was kept up by not revealing what had happened. The hiding of the death of the king and the creation of a mythical ending was a device that could easily have been created by Merlin, for example, in order to maintain better control over the superstitious people; Geoffrey of Monmouth's *Vita Merlini* claims that it was Merlin who took Arthur to the Island of Apples so that Morgan could heal him.

When Gerald of Wales wrote in the late twelfth century, the Britons were still expecting Arthur to return and overthrow the Normans so that they would once again rule Britain. The Welshmen believed that Arthur had been taken to the Island of Avalon by the sorceress Morgan (Arthur's cousin) to be cured (according to Gerald of Wales), or by Merlin to the Island of Avalon/Island of Apples to be healed by Morgan (Geoffrey of Monmouth, *Vita Merlini*). In order to remove this solace for the Britons, the King Henry II ordered the corpse of Arthur dug up from Glastonbury. The monks did as asked and duly found the corpse of Arthur and his second wife, Guinevere. Obviously, it is very likely that we are dealing here with a Medieval political forgery, despite the fact that Glastonbury apparently bore the name of the Island of Avalon or Island of Apples. It should be noted, however, that this is not absolutely conclusive. It is still possible that Arthur had indeed been buried at Glastonbury, even if the finding of his corpse appears too good to be true from the Norman point of view.[3]

Chapter 15

Arthur's Immediate Successors[1]

Constantine V, 472–477

Constantine did not give up his pursuit of the enemy, managing to crush each of them separately, his first target being the Saxons, who were forced to submit. After that he captured Winchester and London, killing one of the brothers in front of the altar in the church of St Amphibalus in Winchester and the other beside the altar of the monastery of friars in London. According to Gildas' version,[2] the two brothers and their followers were killed with sword and javelin in the presence of their mother in two ambushes at the altars. On at least one of these occasions, Constantine had dressed as an abbot, in which attire he surprised his enemies when they arrived before the altar. Gildas also claims that Constantine was a sodomite and sinner who had divorced his wife and lived in useless adultery for many years. According to Geoffrey's version, Constantine suffered a just punishment for his deeds four years after having killed the sons, being struck down by the vengeance of God. Geoffrey's *Vita Merlini* explains that Conan (Conanus) rebelled against Constantine, waged war on him, ravaged the land and killed him.

Despite the harsh moralizing words of these two churchmen, it is clear that Constantine had ruled well. He had crushed the revolt and united Britons under him. It is unclear whether he still controlled Albany and the Orkneys and Shetland, but it is probable that he did. What is certain, however, is that he lost control of Armorica, Gaul, Ireland, Norway and Denmark.

Aurelius Conanus, 477–480

Constantine was succeeded by his nephew Aurelius Conanus, but he achieved this only by attacking his uncle, who was the legitimate successor. Conanus threw his uncle into prison and killed his two sons. The fact that Conanus was able to fight a civil war without losing control of Britain proves that the realm was still secure thanks to the great efforts of Aurelius Ambrosius Arthur and Constantine V. According to Gildas, Conanus was a vicious murderer, fornicator and adulterer like his predecessor, and died after having ruled for only three years.

According to Geoffrey's *Vita Merlini*, after Merlin had taken Arthur to the Island of Apples (Island of Avalon) to be cured by Morgan, Merlin assumed his position as king of South Wales. Then, after many years had passed under many kings, a major war broke out between several chieftains and many cities were destroyed. In these conditions, Merlin and his three brothers joined ranks with Peredur, king of the

North Welsh, and Rhydderch, king of the Cumbrians, against the king of Scotland, Gwenddolen. The Britons were victorious, but the three brothers of Merlin died in combat. As a result of this, Merlin was griefstruck and retreated into the woods. Merlin's sister, who was married to Rhydderch, eventually managed to ambush and capture Merlin, and bring him back among the people. According to the *Vita*, this happened when Conan was still ruling without any plan. This dating is slightly at odds with the above-mentioned many years passing after the death of Arthur, but not irreconcilable. It is possible to take Geoffrey's referral to the years and rulers figuratively. Merlin exposed Rhydderch as an adulterer and Rhydderch died very soon after this. One may presume that the death was not accidental but brought about by Merlin's skills, even if this is not stated in the *Vita*. After the death of Rhydderech, Merlin withdrew back to the woods. Maeldinus and Taliesin became his pupils and his sister, Ganieda (the widow), joined them.

According to Gerald of Wales, Geoffrey of Monmouth has confused two separate Merlins with each other: Merlin Ambrosius, who was a contemporary of Vortigern, and Merlin Silvester (Celidonius), a contemporary of Arthur and the one who retreated into the woods.[3] It is difficult to know whether Gerald is correct, but there is no compelling evidence to back up his claim. There is nothing improbable in the existence of a single Merlin who would have lived from the reign of Vortigern at least up to the reign of Conan, and as can be seen from the narrative, I have treated the information accordingly.

Vortiporius/Vortipore, ca 480–490?
Vortiporius/Vortipore, the king of the Demetians, succeeded Conanus on the throne. According to Gildas, Vortiporius was an elderly man (was he the imprisoned uncle of Conanus?) who was a son of a good king. Vortiporius, however, became famous for divorcing his wife so that he could marry his daughter. It is therefore not surprising that the Saxons revolted and brought help from Germany. Despite being a depraved individual, Vortiporius was still a good soldier and defeated the Saxons decisively in a single battle to regain control of the entire kingdom. According to Geoffrey, Vortiporius governed his subjects frugally and peacefully after this incident. This is confirmed by Constantius of Lyon in his *Life of St Germanus* (*Vita* 27). According to Constantius, the orthodox Christian faith was intact at the time he wrote his treatise. Modern editors of the text suggest a date of about 480 or slightly after for his *Vita*.

Cuneglasse, ca 490–495?
Geoffrey claims that Vortiporius was succeeded by Malgo, but this appears to be a mistake because Gildas names Cuneglasse immediately after Vortiporius. According to Gildas, Cuneglasse was yet another sinner in the mold of the previous ones. He had thrown out his wife and had taken his wife's sister as his wife, despite the fact that she was a nun.

Malgo/Maglocune the Dragon of the Island, King of Kings, ca 495–508?
Cuneglasse's successor on the throne was Malgo/Maglocune, who was a handsome man and a brave warrior. However, he was also a rampant homosexual and was therefore condemned by both Gildas and Geoffrey, despite his great achievements, which do not pale in comparison with those of Arthur. According to Gildas, Malgo gained his throne in a civil war fought against his uncle the king. Was he Cuneglasse? After this, he killed many tyrants and annexed their kingdoms. According to Geoffrey, he conquered the six neighbouring 'Islands of the Ocean': Ireland, Iceland, Gotland, the Orkneys, Norway and Denmark. It is clear that he was one of the great warrior kings of Britain, and that his memory was suppressed solely for the reason that he was a homosexual – it was because of this that Arthur became the once and future king for the Welshmen, even if his career had ended so abruptly through treachery. The Christians considered a heterosexual person to be far more suitable as a hero. It is also probable that it was because of this that the unsavoury character traits of Aurelius Arthur were hidden beneath the name Utherpendragon. Malgo's successor on the throne was Keredic, and it was under him that the achievements of Arthur and his successors started to unravel, but that story will be told in another book.

Chapter 16

Arthur the Once and Future King

There exists plenty of evidence to suggest that there existed an Arthur, whose career has been preserved in a mutilated form by Geoffrey of Monmouth. It is too much of a coincidence that the events described by Geoffrey fit like a glove the known circumstances and events of the time. On top of that, his account is corroborated by the evidence provided by Jordanes, Gregory of Tours and Sidonius regarding the exploits of Riothamus, the High-King of Britain, as has been pointed out by Geoffrey Ashe. The fact that they have preserved only glimpses of his career is not conclusive, because none of them have provided us with a complete and detailed overview of the events that took place in Gaul after ca 463. Therefore, the silence regarding his other exploits does not prove that Geoffrey's account is false.

My reconstruction of Arthur's reign has also made evident that the Arthur preserved by Geoffrey Monmouth is a later fabrication. It is very probable that Geoffrey, or the little book that he used as a source, purposefully divided one person – Aurelius/Aurelianus Ambrosianus Utherpendragon Arthur – into three different people so that the reputation of the last, Arthur, could be used as a national hero for the Welsh and Bretons. This was possible only by separating Utherpendragon, the despicable womanizer, and Arthur, so that the latter could be described as a cleancut hero who was betrayed by his wife. The process of falsification, however, was not complete, because Geoffrey or his source failed to streamline the text, and it is thanks to this that the text betrays these changes. It is not a coincidence that Anna is sometimes called the sister of Arthur and at others the sister of Aurelius Ambrosius – she was both, because Arthur and Aurelius are one and the same person! It is also because of this that Gawain, the son of Anna and Loth, is sometimes called Arthur's cousin and at others his nephew.

Aurelius Ambrosius' reign marked a real watershed in British history, which is proven by his later legendary fame. Ashe has quite correctly described him as a British version of the Roman *restitutor orbis*, the honorary title of the Emperor Aurelian – the fact that Anthemius asked for his help proves that Aurelius had indeed achieved a restoration of Roman rule in Britain. His untimely death prevented him becoming *restitutor orbis* – he did not become the saviour of the Roman Empire, but rather the opposite. His exploits ensured the fall of the West Roman Empire. Arthur and Euric destroyed the last two field armies of Anthemius, which had been dispatched to assist him by the Eastern Emperor Leo. After this, the Romans were entirely reliant on their federate forces, and it was this that sealed their fate. Odovacar finally put an end to the West Roman Empire in 476.

Regardless of the fall of Rome, which was the unintended outcome of the policies of Arthur, his career can still be called a great success. He had managed to stem the barbarian onslaught and then defeat them decisively, after which he had even forged a short-lived empire encompassing Britain, Ireland, Norway, southern Sweden, Denmark,[1] Armorica and other parts of north-west Gaul. His death meant that the empire was short-lived, but his successes ensured the survival of Romano-British culture for another fifty years. It was not his fault that his successors indulged in civil discord and failed to stem the Saxon onslaught.

Arthur was not a great innovator in the fields of administration or military matters, but he was clearly quite adept at using his Roman heritage. Arthur ruled his realm by using a combination of methods he had inherited from the Romans and Britons. It was based on three pillars: 1) the personal retinue of the high king; 2) the members of the British Council, who were required to contribute their forces when required; 3) the Catholic Church.

Arthur kept in being the administrative system the Romano-Britons had formed after 410. This was based on administrative areas centred on cities, each of which was ruled by a council and/or king/*dux*, who in their turn were members of the British Council. The kings and *duces* were either local tribal chieftains or local magnates with military means, who had become *de facto* rulers of their own territories in the absence of official Roman rule. The Church formed the only functioning organization that survived the absence of the official Roman administrative system, and it is not surprising that Arthur sought to revive its organization wherever the enemy had destroyed it. The members of the Church enabled Arthur to retain control of the population and army. The Church upheld the morale of the population and army and controlled their own respective areas. In addition to this, it could be expected to provide information regarding the mood of the populace and its rulers.

Arthur's armed forces consisted of the military retinues of the nobility, foreign federate mercenaries, foreign tributary allies, remnants of Roman military units and local paramilitary forces. His greatest achievement was to forge this heterogenous group into one united force able to defeat the foreign invaders threatening Britain. The most amazing aspect of this achievement is Arthur's ability to train his army to fight in the Late Roman manner so that all the different units fought as one cohesive entitity.

In sum, I hope that I have been able to prove that there exists an alternative way to interpret the evidence, which suggests a relatively high probability for the existence of King Arthur. It also appears quite likely that Geoffrey of Monmouth's history is based on very real events, even if in its current form it contains clear misunderstandings and falsifications. It is unfortunately impossible to say how accurate this version is, but at least my interpretation of the evidence should give food for thought regarding the historicity of Arthur and his likely role in the fall of West Rome. Please note, however, that my reconstruction of the career of Arthur has been based on varying degrees of probability. We simply do not possess enough evidence for this period of history to state anything with absolute confidence.

Appendix I

The Reign of Frothi III the Magnificent

Background

Modern treatment of the early information in Saxo Grammaticus is a case in point concerning my criticism of the ultra-conservative approach to the narrative sources as practiced by some Classicists and Medievalists. The various modern interpretations of the evidence have usefully been collected together by Davidson and Fisher in their Saxo Grammaticus Vol. 2. Almost all modern historians dealing with Saxo have sought to discredit the information he provides, with far-fetched claims that Saxo has either copied some ancient source or the Bible to piece together a false story, or postulated into the past the events of his own day. This approach is wrong on so many levels that it is impossible to detail all of them in this appendix.[1]

Firstly, Saxo includes material that is supported by several of the extant sagas, even if there are also variant versions of the same events, which proves that he did not invent his characters and events. The claim that he would have used these various sagas as his sources is preposterous, as his version includes significant differences. Secondly, it is simply idiotic to claim that Saxo would have used ancient Roman sources as sources of inspiration to narrate invented events and battles. It is quite incomprehensible to claim that Saxo would use Zosimus' description of the Romans' naval defeat of the Greuthungi Goths on the Danube in 386 as his source for the floating corpses and wooden shields after a naval battle between Danes and Rutenians, and even if this description had inspired him, it does not follow from this that the naval battle between the Danes and Rutenians was invented. Anyone with even a modicum of intelligence understands that after a naval battle the site at which it had been fought would have been congested by floating corpses and shields, among other matter. Thirdly, it is very odd to claim that if there was a naval battle in the eastern Baltic in the twelfth or thirteenth century, that there cannot also have been such in the fifth century. Should we really believe that Saxo merely invented these wars for the fifth century? The locations of the nations and seas were the same, and it is quite well attested through archaeology that the peoples of the Baltic Sea employed ships and had fortified places well before the birth of Christ. It is clear that the peoples of these coastal areas were constantly engaged in trading, piracy and fighting throughout their history. Fourthly, if there are similarities between the account of Saxo dealing with Frothi's war against the Huns on the one hand, and the accounts of *Hervavar Saga* and the saga of the *Battle of the Goths and Huns* on the other, this does not mean that there would not have been a war between Frothi's Danes and the Huns. It is quite possible that the saga storytellers would have confused the two separate wars, while Saxo in his turn would have had access to better sources than these or had known that these were quite separate events. The historical reality actually requires that something like that which is described by Saxo would have happened. It is otherwise very difficult to explain why the Huns would have failed to subdue the Danes, while they included the Ripuarian Franks among their subjects. The reason must be that the Huns were unable to challenge the Danes on the Baltic Sea, thanks to the naval superiority of the latter. The Huns could only threaten Jutland, but not the islands, as long as the Danes controlled the seas.[2]

I am not denying here that Saxo's account still poses some very serious questions, as it has clearly been compiled from multiple sources and Saxo has sometimes misplaced different pieces of evidence to the wrong place in the narrative. However, what I am trying to prove is that we should analyze the information provided by Saxo rather than attempt to claim that he has invented his narrative by compiling a fictive account from multiple sources, which is the ultra-conservative Classicist way of interpreting the evidence.

Therefore, contrary to what most modern historians would let us believe, Saxo Grammaticus' book 5 (the main source of this narrative) provides us with a good overview of the events that took place during the reign of Frothi III. We should probably identify Saxo's Frothi III either with Snorri's Dan the Magnificent or Frothi the Magnificent/Peaceful, or even conclude that these are actually one and the same person. Saxo's account also allows us to pinpoint his reign to the first half of the fifth century, because it was before 454 that the Huns ruled most of Europe up to the Rhine. It was at the beginning of this period that Frothi married a Hun princess called Hanunda. The marriage was undoubtedly political. It was wise to marry into the Hunnic royal house when its armies had reached Central Europe. Note that I give all inhabitants of modern Denmark the name Danes, just like I do with other areas of the north, for the sake of convenience, even though all of these areas consisted of several tribes and kingdoms.

Early Reign
According to Saxo, the young Frothi and his retinue were initially foolish young men who did not know how to behave. Gøtar, king of Norway, decided to exploit the situation, but was persuaded by Erik to test the mettle of the enemy first. It should be noted that Gøtar was not the only king of Norway, but rather the high king with very limited powers or even just one of the kings. Gøtar dispatched Rafn to harass the Danes, but Rafn and his forces were annihilated by Oddi's fleet thanks to the 'sorcery' employed by Oddi. According to Saxo, Oddi clouded the enemy's eyesight

so that they believed that the Danish swords emitted beams and flashes like fire. Only six ships managed to escape. A more sensible explanation of this is that Oddi deployed his ships with the sun behind them. The survivors, however, brought back the message that Frothi's subjects wanted to get rid of him.

Gøtar eventually dispatched Erik with three ships to investigate. Erik in his turn sent two Danish-speaking spies into the enemy camp, who reported back that Oddi intended to surprise Erik with a night attack and had loaded his ships full of stones for throwing. Erik had fewer ships, but this information enabled him to formulate a plan. He rowed a small boat silently to the enemy fleet and, unnoticed, drilled holes near the ships' waterline. The night must have been dark and there must have been other noise, such as rain and wind, for this to be possible. When Oddi then launched his ships, the vessels sunk slowly until they were swallowed by the sea. It was then that Erik attacked with his three ships. Oddi and his fleet of seven ships sank with all hands. Erik had now killed the entire force posted to guard Sjaelland, so he was able to sail unhindered to the island of Laesø, where he halted. He dispatched two vessels loaded with booty back to Norway, and then sailed to Sjaelland. The men were dispatched to collect food. They felled a herd of oxen, but this did not go unnoticed. The owners sailed after the robbers, but Erik managed to escape punishment by sinking the carcasses below his ships when the owners boarded his vessel.

Erik continued his journey to Frothi's court, where he caused dissent among the enemy by accusing Queen Hanunda of adultery, which was true, and creating other havoc through his intellect and ready tongue. This is what would today be called 'hybrid warfare'. Erik's ultimate goal, however, was to betray his own motherland and become the leading member of Frothi's retinue. Erik incited the king to anger with various ploys, and then fled, together with Gunvara, the sister of the king, back to his ship. Before this he tampered with the ships of the royal fleet so that they would sink if they put out to the sea. The enraged king and his retinue followed, only for their ships to suddenly sink, with the fully armoured king forced to swim to safety. It was then that Erik returned and captured the king. He was able to gain the king's trust when he promised to set him free if the king would make Erik his retainer. This pact was sealed with the marriage of Gunvara to Erik. Note that the name Gunvara bears some resemblance to Guinevere, which makes it possible that Guinevere was actually a Dane – we should remember that the Anglo-Saxon invaders consisted of Danes (Jutes, Angles and Saxons), which makes it possible that the later British authors have purposefully hidden a possible alliance between King Arthur and one section of the Anglo-Saxon invaders. At the same time as this happened, Frothi divorced his unfaithful queen, who was then married to Roller, Erik's brother.

Excepting the use of sorcery[3] etc., there is nothing in this tale that would be particularly unreliable or unbelievable. Plots of much greater complexity are known from the Roman world and believed by most modern historians, which begs the question why many historians have chosen to disbelieve these stories. Historians should take into account the special nature of the Nordic sources, just as they do with the Greek and Romans sources. The narrative structure of Saxo Grammaticus (just like the narrative structure of the sagas) undoubtedly resembles that used in modern fiction, but it still hides very real events, just like the invented speeches put into the mouths of Roman leaders. We historians, Classicists and Medievalists, should start to pay greater attention to the Nordic storytelling and use it as sources that can help us truly portray events of the past. It is high time to give back Scandinavians and the peoples of the Baltic Sea their history, which has been forbidden by generations of historians unable to discern fact from fiction.

Erik and Roller returned to Norway to fetch their father's buried treasure. King Gøtar learnt of their arrival and formed a plan to kill Erik. He acted as if he wanted to appoint Erik as his successor by marrying him to his daughter, while he, as a recent widower, would marry Erik's wife, Gunvara. Erik pretended to go along with the plan so that he could flee without having to fight. The presence of Erik's forces nearby, under Roller, suggests that he intended to assassinate the king. The king also planned to kill Erik during the marriage celebrations. Erik and Gunvara, however, managed to kill the assassins when they entered their chamber. Roller then sounded a trumpet and the brothers' forces rushed inside the palace. The king fled to his ship and Erik's followers looted the palace and then sailed away with Gøtar's daughter, Alvild/Alvila, and his treasure. When the king learnt of their flight, he collected the few forces he had available and pursued them. They were hit by a storm and forced to seek a place of refuge in the harbour of Ømi/Aumum (near Stavanger). Frothi duly married Gøtar's daughter so that his offspring would become legitimate rulers of Norway.

Baptism of Fire: The Birth of a Warrior King
News then arrived of an invasion by the Slavs (Wends) and Frothi ordered Erik to proceed against them with eight ships while he mustered a large fleet. This suggests three things. Firstly, the Slavs had not yet invaded in strength (they had sent some raiders), but were expected to do so shortly. Someone had clearly observed the mustering of the Slavic fleet. Secondly, it is probable that the Slavic invasion had been instigated by the Huns, who would by then have heard of the treatment of Hanunda, which required a retaliatory expedition. Thirdly, Erik's mission consisted of two elements, to delay the enemy enough to enable Frothi to assemble his fleet, and conduct a reconnaissance in force.

En route, Erik came across a force of seven enemy ships. On the spur of the moment, he formulated a plan, hiding seven of his ships in a narrow winding inlet and camouflaging them with tree branches. He then advanced with one ship towards the 'pirates', and feigned flight. The Slavs foolishly followed into the narrow inlet. The Slavs realised their mistake too late when they observed to their horror that the 'woods' started to sail alongside them. The Vikings jumped on to the decks, while

Erik directed his own ship on to the beach, from where he used a ballista to shoot stones at his pursuers. I purposefully use the word 'Viking' here, even if the word only came into use later, because the Scandinavians were really Vikings well before the so-called Viking Age. Note the use of the Roman-style ballista on board, but which was now employed from the shore, possibly because it was not attached to Erik's ship or was easier to use from land. Most of the Slavs were killed, with forty being captured. Since Saxo claims that these too were killed through starving and torture, one can make the educated guess that the prisoners were first tortured for information and then sacrificed to the gods.

The advance of the Slavs to the Elbe is usually dated to the late fifth or early sixth century, but in my opinion we should actually date its first phase to the early fifth century on the basis of Saxo's information. It is unlikely to be a coincidence that the migration of so many Germanic tribes westwards from 395 onwards (with the main migrations taking place in 405, 406 and 408) coincides with the events described by Saxo. It is very probable that the Slavs served as loyal followers of the Huns during these conquests, because they certainly inhabited territories held by the Huns. Consequently, I would suggest that the Slavs migrated to the west as allies of the Huns in the first decades of the fifth century, at the same time as these areas were evacuated by the fleeing Germans.

In the meantime, Frothi had collected a large fleet, consisting not only of Danes but also of their neighbours, which suggests that all those in the region, with the exception of Gøtar, recognized the potential danger posed by the Slavs if they were allowed to cooperate with the Huns. It is very difficult to see any other reason for the sudden readiness of the many hostile Scandinavian kingdoms to cooperate but the prospect of some very serious threat, the only likely candidate for this being the Huns. This was the correct reaction on the part of Frothi and his neighbours to the threat facing them. It was wiser to make a pre-emptive strike against the closest Slavs, whose fleet could pose a serious threat to all of Scandinavia if it was used to transport the Huns to the islands of Denmark, and to Norway and Sweden. It is curious that Saxo states that even the smallest vessels of Frothi had twelve rowers. This must mean that even smaller ships were occasionally used as vessels of war. It is noteworthy that Saxo's information also finds support from rock carvings in Sweden, which have fleets consisting of small boats and larger longships (see Appendix 2). On the basis of Saxo's text, one should therefore understand that Frothi's fleet had many different sized ships, which probably implies that most of the ships had crews of about twenty-six to thirty-five men, while the largest vessels had crews of about fifty to seventy, or even up to about 120.

The Slavic peoples from the borders of Denmark (the Wends) up to Lithuania and Belorussia specialized in the use of round circle forts, which could have two to three earth walls with a 'kettle' structure in the middle, that could occasionally have room for more than 1,000 men. The smallest forts, however, had room for only about 100 men. The shape of the fort could also be square or angular if the lay of the land demanded this. Whenever possible, the Slavs sought to place their forts in places that were surrounded by water or swamps. The earth walls were protected by wooden palisades.[4] These were the defences that Frothi and his followers had to encounter when they landed on the enemy shore.

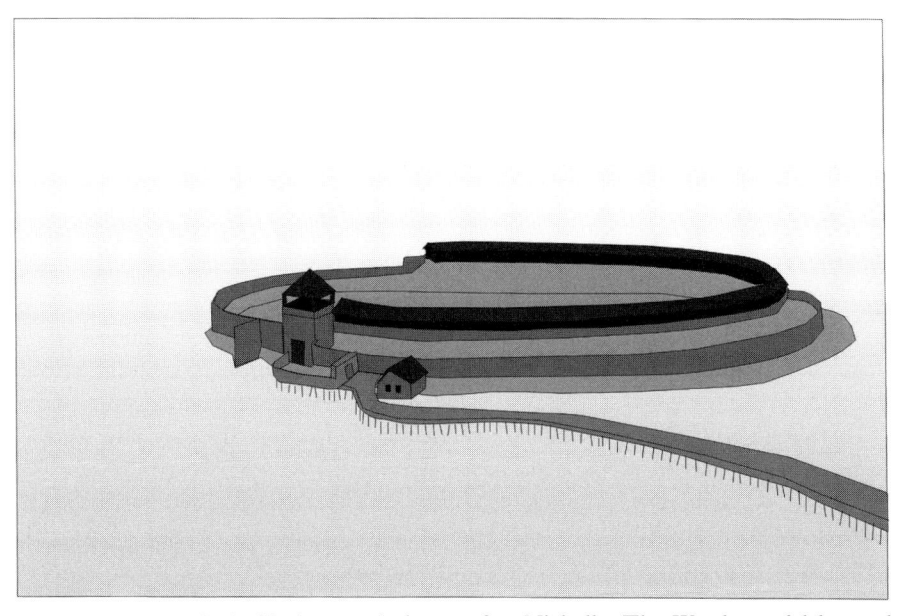

Fort of the Wends (a Slavic group) drawn after Nicholle. The Wends used lakes and swamps to enhance their defences.

During the sea voyage to 'Slavia', the fleet encountered Slavic vessels that had run aground and were attempting to free themselves. Erik engaged and destroyed these. I would suggest that the reason for this was that the Slavic pirates had tried to beach themselves so that the crews could flee, but because their ships were too large, they ran aground before they could reach the beach, while the smaller and lighter Viking vessels were even able to operate in shallow waters. Saxo claims that it was only then that Erik gave Frothi the advice to divide his army into two divisions, comprising a land army of cavalry and the fleet carrying the infantry. The cavalry was to advance from Jutland, while the fleet transported the rest of the troops on the ships. I would suggest that Saxo has misplaced this piece of advice. It is far more likely that it had been the plan all along, because it would have been very difficult to change the campaign plan while the fleet was already advancing towards the enemy. On top of that, the land army was supposedly so large that hills had to be flattened, marshes made passable, and lakes and gorges filled to build roads. If the cavalry army was exceptionally large, then it is difficult to see how such feats could have been achieved without major preparations at the same time as the fleet was assembled. The Slavia in question was clearly very near Denmark for this operation to be possible.

It would be all too easy to dismiss this on the grounds that the Vikings were not known for their cavalry. However, we have plenty of evidence for the existence of cavalry in Denmark, Sweden and even for Finland for this era. Archaeology has produced plenty of equipment that resembles closely the cavalry equipment worn by the East Roman and Persian armies, and narrative sagas, histories and art works also include direct references to cavalry. I have included some illustrations here to demonstrate this. For the Swedish warriors of Vendel, see the illustrations in the Plates section and Engström.[5]

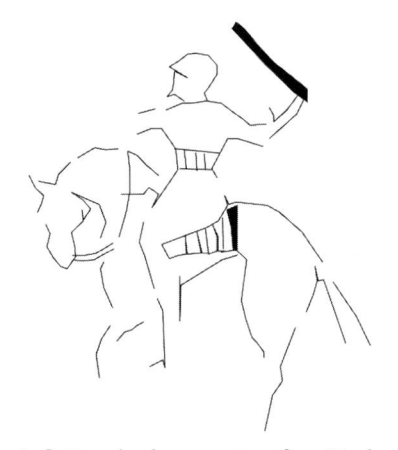

Left: Drawing in a runestone from Uppland with a rider that resembles Roman illustrations (drawn after a photo in Montelius).

Right: My line drawing of a gold medallion from Uppland in Montelius.

The Slavic king Strumik took fright at the prospect of having to fight this force, and dispatched envoys to ask for a truce. Frothi refused: the opportunity was too good to pass. The enemy had not yet completed its mobilization, so Frothi ordered an immediate attack. Strumik and his retinue were killed in a hard but sharp fight, with the rest of his forces surrendering. Frothi then played a ruse, announcing through a herald that all Slavs who were skilled pirates or magicians were to step forward so that they could be rewarded.[6] When more than half of the Slavs stepped forward, Frothi ordered the remaining Slavs to kill them if they wanted to live. This they did. Saxo doesn't state what happened next, but one may imagine that those Slavs who survived became outcasts among their own tribe, with the result that the Slavs of the area were divided and not united against the Danes.

Following this great victory, Frothi legislated how the division of spoils of war was to be conducted in the future. There was clearly a need for this. In addition, he legislated that women were free to choose their spouse and many other laws that dealt with important matters of state – he was clearly an enlightened ruler. Militarily, the most important of these were his legislation against treason and the very curious instruction to reward those who advanced before the standard-bearer in combat so that a slave would become a freedman, a peasant a nobleman, and a nobleman a jarl. This last mentioned is the exact opposite of what Roman military instructions detailed, even if the Roman armies also had similar heroes who, through their personal example, made the entire line go forward. Roman combat doctrine was clearly meant to instil obedience and order, while the Danish combat doctrine favoured the bold and the brave, the berserks of Odin (see Appendix 3).

Meanwhile, Gøtar had used the intervening time to assemble his forces for a war of revenge. Frothi, well aware of this, launched a pre-emptive strike with a large fleet. When Frothi's fleet reached the island of Rennesøy near Stavanger, Gøtar dispatched envoys to sue for peace, but to no avail. Gøtar then led his fleet against the Danes, but was killed in action. Frothi rewarded Roller by making him king of Gøtar's kingdom, which consisted of seven provinces. Erik also gave his province to his brother.

The War against the Huns ca 416–419
Saxo claims that the next three years were peaceful, and that it was during this period that the king of the Huns learnt of the treatment of his daughter, with the result that he prepared an expedition against the Danes. As said earlier, it would seem more likely that the three years mentioned should be considered to have included the campaigns against the Slavs and Gøtar. It is very unlikely that news of the treatment of Hanunda would have travelled that long, as stated previously. The Hun leader ordered Olimar, the 'king of the East/Ruthenia/Rutenia', to prepare his fleet for a war against the Danes.[7] The Hun plan was to use the Rutenian fleet and Hunnic land forces to subjugate the Northerner. The Huns and the Rutenians spent two years in making their preparations. The elimination of the Wendic threat close to Denmark paid off handsomely; the Huns were unable to use their fleet and were forced to rely on the Rutenians, whose fleet would have to sail from the eastern Baltic to Denmark. We do not know whether the Rutenians only had control of the rivers leading from Lake Ladoga to Kiev or whether they also controlled the Baltic coasts. In either case, it was possible for the Rutenians to sail their fleet against the Danes.

As usual, Frothi wanted to strike first before the enemy was able to assemble all of its forces. He dispatched Erik to spy upon the enemy. Meanwhile, Frothi collected a vast fleet and army, consisting not only of Danes, but also Norwegians and Slavs (Wends). According to Saxo, Erik came face-to-face with Olimar somewhere near Russia (Ruscia) and after a short discussion rode to inspect the Hunnic army. The 'Russia' in question can mean Novgorod or Kievan Russia of Saxo's own day. Whatever the meaning, it is still probable that Olimar was somewhere near the south-eastern Baltic coast in the area running from modern Poland up to the River

Neva. The word 'neva' comes from the Finnish, in which the meaning is a treeless swamp, such as St Petersburg was until the time Peter I (the Great) built his great city around the river. The king of the Huns realised that Frothi had dispatched Erik to spy upon him, but since he was confident that the size of his army would frighten Erik and the Danes, he allowed Erik to leave unmolested. According to Saxo, the Huns had fifteen *vexilla*, each of which had 100 *signa*, behind which stood another twenty *signa*; behind this throng stood an equal number of standards. These forces were led by two Hun kings, of whom one was the senior. It is very difficult to see that the *signa* could have been given to any force smaller than twenty to sixty men, which means that the army was indeed a very significant concentration of forces.

According to Saxo (5.130), Erik reported that the Rutenians had six kings, each of whom commanded a fleet of 5,000 longships (to be amended to 5,000 sailors and sixteen ships), and that each of the ships had 300 rowers. The fleet therefore consisted of about 30,000 rowers/sailors. Each *millenarium* (millenary) consisted of four wings (*alae*), each wing had 300 men (i.e. one ship) and the whole *millenarium* 1,200 men (four ships). This means that the ships were very large by the standards of the day, suggesting that the primary purpose was to transport the Huns with their horses to Sjaelland. It would also have been impossible to use such ships along rivers, which means that the fleet was built close to the shores of the Baltic. The numerical evidence has once again been seen to prove that Saxo has invented the details, but as said previously, it is quite probable that the Roman influence was felt far and wide, and that many peoples followed roughly the same principles. It is very probable that the ships in question were copied from the Romans because of their great size. In fact, there exists concrete evidence for the copying of Roman ships by the Huns for this particular era. See the discussion later.

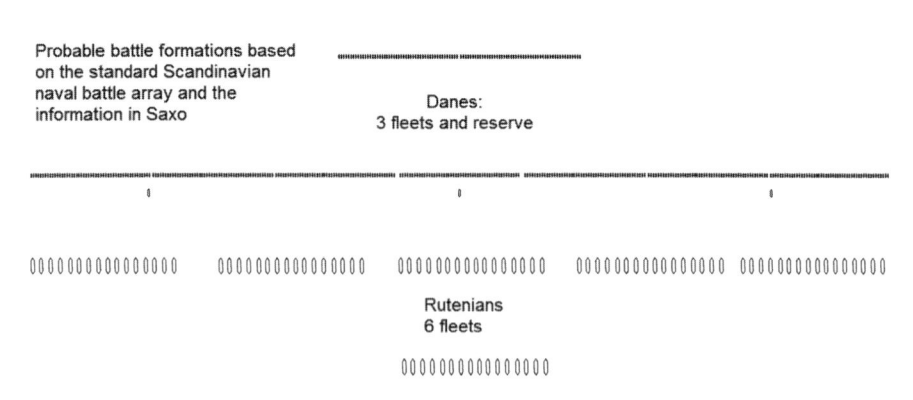

Probable battle formations based on the standard Scandinavian naval battle array and the information in Saxo

Danes: 3 fleets and reserve

Rutenians 6 fleets

Erik advised Frothi to collect his fleet and attack all 'islands' between Denmark and the east. The Danes subdued all the islands (such as Öland and Åland, and ports along the Baltic?) and then advanced against the Rutenians. En route, the Danes encountered some Rutenian ships, and when Frothi was unwilling to engage so

The Reign of Frothi III the Magnificent   193

small an enemy force, Erik interfered and advised action. The Rutenians were sunk. After this, the Danes attacked the main fleet. The huge ships of the Rutenian fleet were too slow for manoeuvring, and their king chose to wait for the Danes to open the attack. The Danes then defeated the Rutenians, mainly because the Rutenian ships, with their sizeable crews, were simply too cumbersome. The Danes must have had a minimum of 450 longships, so they could send four to five ships against each enemy behemoth. I have given here the likely battle arrays of the fleets, which is based on the information we know of Danish naval arrays (see Introduction and Appendix 2) and Saxo's text. It was quite easy for the more manoeuvrable Danish longships to avoid frontal encounters with the enemy, and to advance from the direction of their own choice. The Rutenian fleet could not retreat close to the shore thanks to the great size of their ships, and was forced to fight on the open sea, where the Danes could outmanoeuvre them. The Rutenians and their kings were killed. The Rutenians would have been rather inexperienced in the use of such massive ships, which would also have worked against them in the encounter. Only two kings, Olimar and Dag, together with their followers, survived the butchery, but were apparently taken prisoner.

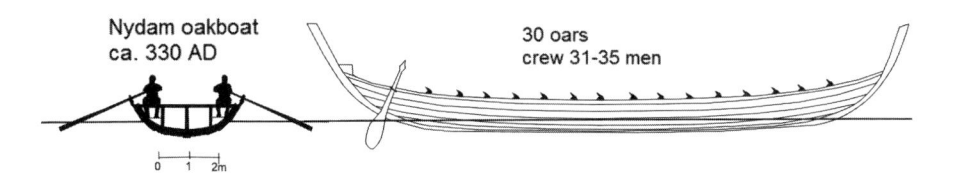

Nydam oakboat ca. 330 AD

30 oars
crew 31-35 men

The Danish force was too small to engage the Huns, and Frothi retreated back to Denmark. The campaign against the Rutenians, however, had served its purpose. The Huns no longer had a fleet with which they could threaten Fyn and Sjaelland. Erik's sound advice was to defeat the Huns through the use of scorched earth tactics: the sinking of the Rutenian ships ensured that the Huns would have to live off the land. The resulting devastation of Jutland is also confirmed by the archaeological record. According to Jørgensen (p.205), during the period 380/400–425/430, a series of attacks took place in eastern Jutland and western Funen, traces of which can be detected in Nydam, Illerup and Kragehull. Thanks to the strategy adopted by Erik, the Huns were forced to advance through trackless wastes and swamps (presumably mainly the Wendic lands and Jutland, with some other areas devastated by Danish pirates). It did not take long for the hungry Huns to consume their pack animals, after which they were forced to eat their horses, asses, dogs and anything else remotely edible. The Hunnic army started to dissolve as entire units deserted and fled.[8] The highest-ranking deserter was Ugger/Uggerus, the seer of the Hunnic king.[9] He provided the Danes with detailed information of the enemy and its strategy. It is quite possible that Hun deserters like Ugger became such Hun mercenaries as are mentioned in the context of British events, even if those Huns cannot be the same Huns mentioned here. It is also important to understand that Saxo has misplaced the order of the events, so that the collapse of the Hunnish invasion should be placed only after the arrival of forces that Frothi had sent to forage in foreign countries.

According to Saxo, it was then that Hithin, one of the kings of Norway, arrived with 150 ships. Hithin chose twelve of those and advanced towards the Danes with a shield on his mast to signify that he had come in peace. Hithin had brought his army to help Frothin against the Huns. The figure of 150 ships means that Hithin had brought with him at least 4,500 men (thirty men per ship). This piece of text should be placed before the collapse of the Hunnish invasion. The fact that Hithin subsequently married Hild, who was a daughter of Høgin, a *regulus* in Jutland (a minor king, the true kings being called *rex* in Saxo), suggests that Frothi and Hithin had both assembled their forces there against the Huns, and that most of the guerrilla war against the Huns took place along the entire length of the peninsula, possibly with the help of ships. It would have been this marriage between Hithin and Hild that subsequently gave Loth his claim to the northernmost region of Jutland that Arthur then fulfilled. This makes it quite obvious that the Scandinavians also took the Hun threat very seriously, just like the Western European peoples did in 451. Everyone, even those who were usually enemies, felt compelled to unite their forces against the common threat, the horrible Huns.

The guerrilla war in Jutland was not only costly to the Huns. Frothi had been forced to assemble so large a force of natives and foreigners that he was close to being ruined. He did not have enough money to feed this force through the following winter season. At first Frothi tried to solve the problem by dividing his forces into townships while collecting extraordinary taxes for their support, but even this proved insufficient, which is not at all surprising considering the devastation caused by the Huns. There was a very real danger that the foreign contingents would start to pillage their hosts. Consequently, Frothi sent a fleet under Revil and Mevil to the Elbe to prevent the Huns from crossing, and presumably also to find subsistence for the men of the fleet through foraging and pillaging. As noted by Davidson and Fisher (Vol. 2, p.85), 'Raefill' and 'Maevill' were among the famous sea-kings in Snorri's Prose Edda. There must have been a good reason for this. It is very probable that Revil and Mevil were dispatched to the Elbe to cut off the supply lines of the Hun army operating in Jutland. The operation appears to have been a success.

In addition to this, Frothi dispatched Roller to Norway, Olimar to Sweden and King Ønef together with the pirate chieftain Glomer to the Orkneys. Their missions were to obtain supplies. This must have happened in the late winter, because Hithin and Høgin joined the expedition. Thirty kings and friends (*reges et amici*) remained with Frothi. According to Saxo, when the Huns learnt of the dispersal of forces, they collected a fresh force. Høgin also betrothed his daughter to Hithin. When the winter season was over, Hithin and Høgin decided to conduct a piratical raid in the

Orkneys, presumably because they were also fast running out of supplies, but there is another possibility which is that the Huns were actually threatening to overcome Høgin's forces in Jutland, despite the presence of Hithin's forces. One may imagine that in such a situation Høgin would have evacuated part of his forces and their families to the islands while the rest of his forces would have joined the piratical raid to the Orkneys.[10]

The collectors of supplies returned in the following autumn. This means that the Huns had been allowed to roam in Jutland almost without opposition. Note once again that this is confirmed by the archaeological record. The only opposition that the Huns would have faced would have consisted of the defence of some fortified locales and harassment by the Danish cavalry and fleet. For the type of defences the Huns would have faced, see Arthur's campaign against Norway and Denmark. It was not easy to overcome these because the Huns had not yet learnt how to capture fortifications with such ruthless efficiency as they demonstrated in the 440s. They must have learnt these skills from some Roman prisoners and turncoats in the 430s (see my *Military History of Late Rome Vols 3–4*). All of the forces dispatched by Frothi met with success. It was after the arrival of the foraging/pillaging fleets/parties that the Hunnish invasion collapsed completely. Roller had killed Arthor, king of Søndmøre and Nordmøre in Norway, and had forced these provinces to pay tribute. The tribute would obviously have been used to pay for the upkeep of the army and navy fighting against the Huns. For once I agree with Davidson and Fisher (Vol. 2, p.85) in that this Arturus/Arthor had nothing to do with the King Arthur of Britain. However, I would suggest a possibility that Britain's King Arthur could have received his nickname/honorary title Arthur because of his connection with Norway.

According to Saxo, Olimar had achieved similar successes in the areas belonging to the Swedes. He had defeated Thorias the Tall, the king of Jämtland and Hälsingland. In addition to this, he had defeated two other equally powerful leaders not mentioned, and also the Estonians, Kurlanders, Ölanders and other islands along the Swedish coast. He had sailed with thirty-five ships and now returned with seventy. In order to achieve such a success, at least some of the thirty-five ships must have consisted of the very large craft that the Rutenians had built and Frothi captured. If true, the aim of the attack against Estonia (Estland) and Kurland must have been to prevent the flow of supplies from there to the Huns in Jutland and/or to create a diversion. However, I would suggest that there is a possibility that Saxo has misplaced the sequence of events, as he has done in many places, and has confused two separate campaigns against the Swedes and Huns that were thirty years apart from each other. Olimar's campaign to Jämtland and Hälsingland could easily have taken place only after or simultaneously with Erik's campaign in Sweden, or Olimar's campaign in Estonia and Kurland could have been preparatory actions for a larger campaign along the Russian rivers up to the region of what was later Kiev after 453. In other words, it is possible that these would not have taken place when the Huns were pillaging Jutland, but obviously one cannot entirely exclude the possibility that Olimar would indeed have conducted a diversionary campaign in the East. However, it is difficult to connect such a campaign with operations against the kingdoms of Sweden. It is here that analytical tools (the military probability, general probability and geographical realities) come into play. It is inherently more likely that Olimar's and Frothi's campaigns took place in such a geographical and political sequence that would have enabled the use of military forces in a logical manner.

Ønef, Glomer, Hithin and Høgin had also been successful in the Orkneys, returning with ninety captured ships. Saxo claims that these campaigns added twenty kingdoms to the thirty Danish kingdoms already ruled by Frothi, which meant that his armies now possessed enough supplies to continue the campaign with the additional forces provided by the new subjects.

It was then that Frothi was supposedly ready to launch his campaign against the Huns. He joined combat with them in Russia so that the 'three principal rivers' (possibly the Volga, Dnieper and Don, or Volkhov, Lovat and Dnieper)[11] were filled with enemy corpses. Saxo claims that corpses covered a distance of a three-days' horse ride on land. The fighting supposedly lasted for seven days, after which King Hun (which was claimed to be his name) fell and his brother, with the same name, capitulated when he saw the front line fleeing, which meant the surrender of 170 kings of the Huns and their subjects. On the surface it would seem possible that Saxo has confused the poem *The Battle of the Goths and Huns* with the war Frothi fought against the Huns in Jutland, but I would suggest that there are good reasons to believe that Frothi actually fought in Russia, but only after the death of Attila in 453.

Frothi rewarded his followers amply. Olimar was made king of Holmgard[12] (Novgorod). This would not be the Novgorod later founded by the Vikings, but the older settlement next to it. Ønef was appointed king of Kønugard (Kiev). Once again, this would not be the Kiev of the Rus but its Slavic predecessor. The 'Hun' was given Saxony, while Revil received the Orkneys. Dimar was rewarded with the provinces of the Hälsings, the Jarnbers, Jämts and both Lapps. Dag was given command of Estonia/Estland. It is very probable that Saxo has misplaced the campaign in Russia and the subsequent division of the spoils by about thirty years, so that the campaign in Sweden described below took place before these events. Frothi's kingdom now extended from Russia to the Rhine.

When the Danes advanced into Estonia and Russia, they would have faced not only the field forces of their enemies, but other obstacles, the most important of which were the huge distances involved and the hill forts of the local peoples.

Iron Age Forts in 'Estonia' and 'Latvia'
If Frothi's fleet operated in the eastern Baltic and the Gulf of Finland, and then along the rivers up to Kiev, as claimed by Saxo, then it is possible that his forces may

have faced the forces fielded by the Latvians and Estonians. However, since Saxo doesn't specifically state this, then one may presume that Frothi bypassed these or was given permission by the local peoples to use their harbours during his voyage. I have included this information only to demonstrate what kind of obstacles Frothi faced if he was forced to row through hostile waters and anchor his ships close to such forts. As elsewhere in the north, most of the Latvian and Estonian fortresses were placed along the waterways. Typical Latvian fortresses were 100–160ft high, with flat tops. Estonian fortresses tended to be 20–40ft high, with a single wall and sizeable courtyard which had a well in the middle. The inhabitants of the island of Saaremaa placed their forts either in the middle of a swamp or surrounded them with moats. The round or oval walls were constructed of stones and sod. Even though the islanders only occasionally built their forts on hills, they always made certain that the yard between the walls was higher than the surrounding area, and that each of these had a well. Most had two gates, which could have extra defences on both sides. All of the walls had breastworks with a wooden or stone palisade. Estonian fortresses had living quarters inside and could provide shelter for thousands of men and animals. Such fortresses were called land or hill castles (linnamäki, linnanmäki, linnapää, loss mägi, linna mägi). These appear to have served as shelters for the entire population of a single 'county'.[13] If Frothi had to face such fortresses and garrisons, he would have had a very hard time in dealing with them. It is well-known that strong Estonian forces in their fortresses were able to defeat entire armies of Vikings.

Iron Age Forts in 'Russia' and 'Ukraine'
Forts in northern Russia were often so-called round circle forts that had walls of earth topped with wooden palisades and ditches, if the locale lacked suitable hills and stony terrain. The forts, located close to areas where historians and archaeologists have attested the presence of Finnish-speaking peoples, are usually placed close to waterways. The forts in the areas south and east of modern Estonia and Latvia, up to Lake Ladoga, Moscow, Kursk, Kharkov and Kiev, were also placed on hills bordering rivers and/or lakes, or on low-lying meadows with water around them. The Late Roman era saw a great increase in the number of forts in these areas, just as it did in Scandinavia, which can be connected with the arrival of the Huns and the resulting migrations of peoples. Additional migrations followed after the downfall of the Hun Empire.[14]

Some archaeologists suggest that the Huns advanced as far north as Lithuania and Smolensk, having proven that some locations in these areas were destroyed in the fifth century. Nomadic arrows have also been found at these locations. This is contested by Kazanski (p.51), on the grounds that the Russian, Belorussian and Lithuanian forests would have been sufficient to protect these areas against nomads. He has suggested that the invaders would have rather been Slavs, who had also adopted the use of nomadic arrows. I would suggest a compromise. In my opinion, it is very probable that the Huns advanced this far north, as these areas are likely to have been part of the Greuthungi Empire of Hermanaric,[15] but I would suggest that the Huns did this together with their Slavic subjects, just like the sixth-century Avars used their *Sklavenoi* against the East Romans. The real beneficiaries of this were the Slavs, who remained there even after the Huns had been overthrown.

A fortified settlement of the Touchemlya culture.
Note the different approach to the use of fortification between the Scandinavians and Finns on the one hand, and the Finns of Touchelmlya culture on the other hand. The former preferred the use of refuge forts while the latter preferred to fortify their settlements. The key difference was probably that the main threats to the former were the pirates that used routes that could be effectively guarded while the latter faced a far more complex form of threat because the enemy could approach from any direction. Drawn after (with some minor changes) Tretyakov/Chmidt's illustration (1958) in Michel Kazanski's *Les Slaves. Les origines Ier – VIIe siècle après J. –C.* (Paris 1999).

The forts in this area naturally followed the lay of the land, so their shape could be triangular, round, semi-circle or oval. The fortresses of the Finnish and Baltic peoples in the north-west of modern Russia consisted mainly of refuge fortresses, with several villages building one in a central location, but some fortified towns are also known. The reason why so many Finnish-speaking tribes were left on the Russian side of the border is that the Slavic groups conquered and assimilated most of them. It has been suggested that the Russians in the Moscow region and the north of Russia actually consist of mixed groups of Slavs and Finns. The truth is obviously more complicated, as the Russian population – like the other peoples of Europe – descends from a large mix of different tribes.

The people of the Touchemlya civilization used small forts ranging from 0.4–8 hectares, but most encompassed just 1–2ha. An example of this type of fortress is given above. The Touchemlya civilization was destroyed in the seventh century, but some of their forts had been burned to the ground during the fifth century. It is not known who the fifth-century invaders were, but possible candidates range from the Huns to the Finns, Swedes and Danes.[16] My suggestion is that the invaders were the Huns, and possibly also the Danes of Frothi. The circle forts near modern Kiev were placed on mounds and had two to three earth walls for protection.[17]

Saxo claims that it was after this Russian campaign that Frothi continued his legislative programme. He legislated that the vassal kings were to pay the soldiers in their retinue three silver talents (according to Davidson and Fisher, this meant 3lb) during the winter, a common soldier and mercenary two talents, and one talent for soldiers who had just retired from service. Saxo criticized this law in the strongest terms because it rewarded the rank rather than the bravery of the soldier. Notably, Frothi also made the rape of a virgin punishable. The Scandinavians were just as strict in their moral code as the Christian sources claim that the Visigothic, Suevic and Vandalic conquerors of Gaul, Spain and North Africa were when they arrived in those regions during the fifth century. As regards their sexual behaviour, during this era the Germanic peoples appear to have treated their female captives with greater respect than did the Romans (see my *Military History of Late Rome Vols. 3–4* and ASMEA presentations 2014–2015). This certainly was not the case, however, with the later Vikings.

Meanwhile, the relationship between Hithin and Høgin had deteriorated because some slanderers claimed that Hithin had slept with Høgin's daughter before the marriage. Saxo here returns to the story that he had interrupted with the misplaced Russian campaign. Høgin believed the story, gathered his fleet and attacked Hithin when the latter was collecting taxes from the Slavs. Høgin was defeated and fled to Jutland. When Frothi learnt of the quarrel, he ordered the men to solve it with a duel. Høgin badly wounded Hithin, but did not kill him. However, seven years later they met again and killed each other. This was a bad loss for Frothi. The fact that neither Høgin nor Hithin play any role in the Russian campaign and the distribution of the spoils proves that their quarrel and death took place before the Russian campaign.

Conquests in the North
At the same time ('*Eodem tempore*'), there arose a quarrel between the Swedish High-King Alrik and the king of Götaland, Gestiblind. Gestiblind asked Frothi to assist him. Frothi promised help and dispatched Erik and Skalk of Scania. Erik advised Gestiblind to first attack Alrik's son, Gunthiof, who was the king of Värmland and Solör. When Gunthiof was killed, Alrik was eager to exact vengeance. Alrik first attempted to persuade Erik to abandon the campaign, but to no avail. Then he attempted to challenge Gestiblind to a duel, but Gestiblind refused because he was too old. It was then agreed that the war would be resolved by a duel between Erik and Alrik. Erik was badly wounded, but Alrik was killed. In reward for his great service, Frothi appointed Erik as king of Sweden, Värmland and the Islands of the Sun (Söleyjar, i.e. Solör in modern Norway). It is possible, or even probable, that the campaign of Olimar

against the Swedish islands (presumably Öland and Gotland), and then in Jämtland and Hälsingland, took place at about the same time as Erik campaigned against Alrik. Geography and military probability suggest this but obviously there is no certainty regarding this.

Iron Age Forts in 'Sweden'[18]
Most of the forts of southern Scandinavia had earth walls with a wooden palisade, but most of the Fenno-Scandia had piled up dry-walls of stone. The Swedish forts resembled the Norwegian ones, with most located on hills. Most of the forts and towns were placed along waterways, where most of the people lived. Some of the Swedish forts had two to three walls of piled stones. Inside these forts, archaeologists have found piles of throwing stones located next to the walls, which suggests that the people prepared for sieges by collecting stones in advance. The same phenomenon can also be seen in Finnish hill forts. As the narrative has shown, this was not restricted to forts: Nordic peoples collected similar throwing stones for their boats and ships when they planned to engage in combat. According to Näsman, there is dearth of evidence for the ring-forts in southern Scandinavia (Denmark and parts of Sweden on the plains of Västergötaland, Östergötaland, south Halland and Skåne) as earth walls in this region appear to have been destroyed over time. He has noted, however, that in those regions which have stone walls, historians and archaeologists have found dense clusters of them in north Halland, Bohuslän, north Småland and east Östergötland, on Öland and Gotland (these islands are quite flat) and in the Svea region around Lake Mälaren. This suggests that these areas had sizeable populations, but it is still probable that lowlands with a poor supply of stones to build walls would also have been inhabited, because it was in those areas that one would find the best agricultural land.

The structure of the Swedish forts was also restricted by nature, so that for example the forts of Öland were placed on level terrain. These were often round or oval in shape, with circumferences of 124–127m, or according to Näsman 38–44m and 160–210m, and had walls of granite or limestone. Öland appears to have possessed the most sophisticated walls in the region, thanks to the availability of limestone, with dry-stone walls of un-hewn limestone blocks and filling. Such walls could be 4–6m thick and 4–6m high, with crenellated tops. The forts of Öland were inhabited and served as refuge forts for the surrounding population. Öland had a population of about 9,000, with 1,500 households, 800 farms and 1,800 warriors. Some of the forts of the Mälaren region had a special feature: they had manors inside them, so these forts were permanently inhabited.[19] In my opinion, this same phenomenon can be witnessed in the Pohjanmaa region of Finland.

The following two illustrations ,one drawn after Oscar Montelius (1906) and another after Anne-Sofie Gräslund, give a good indication of what types of forts and towns (in this case Birka) the invaders faced. Birka is later (it developed in the so-called Viking Age) but is undoubtedly still representative of the largest commercial settlements in the area.

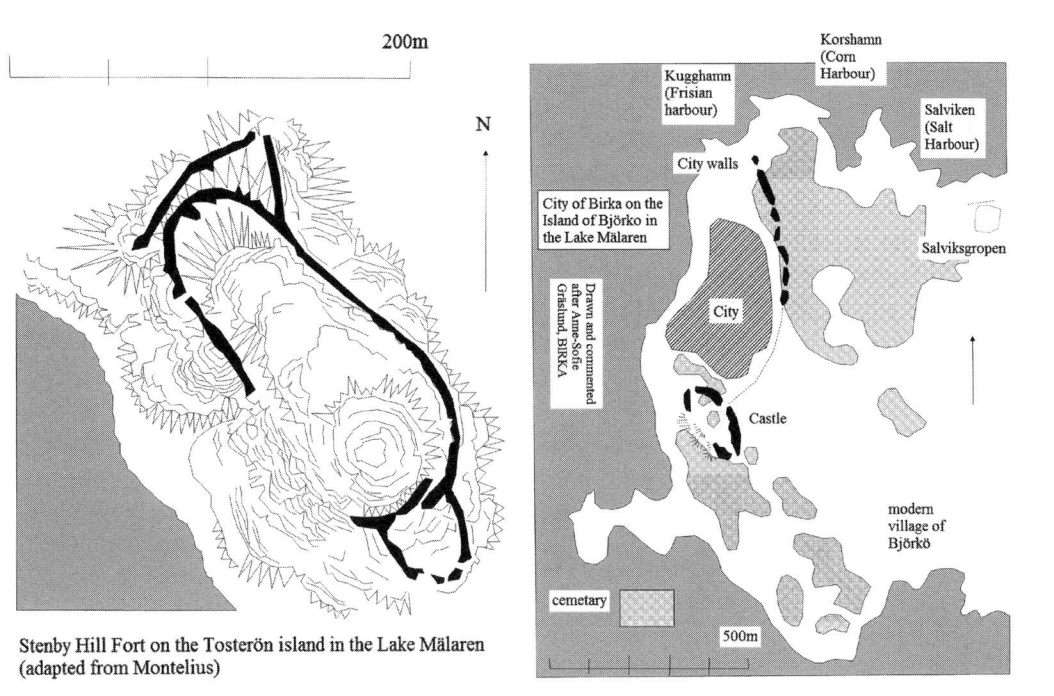

Stenby Hill Fort on the Tosterön island in the Lake Mälaren
(adapted from Montelius)

LEFT: The Stenby hillfort, which is located on the Tosterön Island in the Lake Mälaren is a good example of Swedish hillforts during this era.
RIGHT: Birka is called the oldest city of Sweden. It is usually thought that the city was founded in about 800 by the king of Adelsö (the location of the king's Mansion/Castle) to serve as a centre of local and international trade. It had three harbours/ports: Port for western vessels; port for the transporting of corn; a laguna located at Salviksgropen, which may have been originally called Saluviken (Market Bay). Modern knowledge of the city is based on the digs conducted by Hjalmar Stolpe in 1871–1895. The 12 hectare area of black earth shows where the city was located. The walls were built after about 923. In my opinion, it is very probable that similar market places/cities already exitsted before the year 800. The sources refer to such and it is practically certain that there were also such cities, because the area was certainly inhabited and relatively populous. The Birka is a good example of how such market places/cities would have looked like.

It should be noted that the people of northern Sweden consisted of Finnish speakers (there are such even today) and that the border between the Swedes and Finns lay further south in antiquity. The reason why such large numbers of Finnish speakers were left in Sweden was that when the Russians conquered Finland in 1808/1809, they failed to conquer northern Sweden. The ethnic composition was and is always more complicated than the political map. It is very probable that the male warriors of northern Sweden were Germanic in origin and had just become Finnish through their language.

According to Saxo, soon after the victory over the Swedes, Frothi gave Erik the right to collect annual tribute from Hälsingland, both Lapplands, Finnmark and Estland/Estonia. I would suggest that the rights to tax Lapplands, Finnmark and Estonia were given to Erik only after Olimar and Angrim had conquered northern Sweden, and Olimar had conquered Estland/Estonia, the latter of which must have taken place after 453. The conquest of the rest of Sweden and Norway was the natural continuation of the conquests so far taken by Frothi and Erik. The conquest of Estland/Estonia had more to do with the planned Russian campaign.

The next stage in Frothi's Scandinavian campaign was to secure the southern sector of the border region between modern Norway and Sweden. Erik was ordered to attack Hedmark and Vik from the west while Frothi, with his fleet, attacked from the south. The Norwegians despaired and fled to Halogaland. Frothi ordered Erik to proceed there by land, while he would sail there. When Frothi reached the borders of Halogaland, he disembarked his troops on the shore without any opposition (no fighting is mentioned). The armies engaged each other and separated at nightfall after having suffered terribly. Erik and his army arrived next morning and the armies fought once more. Casualties on both sides were again high. Saxo claims that out of the 3,000 ships of Frothi, only 170 returned home. A more realistic estimate would perhaps be that out of the 300 ships only 170 returned. Norwegian casualties were even worse, with four-fifths of the population of Halogaland killed.[20]

The heavy casualties seem to have convinced Frothi to pause his military campaigns, for Saxo claims that Frothi next established peace throughout his domains and spent seven years in complete peace, during which he fathered a son, Alf, and daughter, Ofura. During that time, a Swedish champion called Arngrim came to Denmark and asked for the daughter's hand in marriage. Arngrim had become overly bold because he had just killed Skalk of Scania in a duel after the latter robbed a ship from him, but this did not convince Frothi of his worth. Consequently, Arngrim sought help from Erik, who advised him to prove his worth through combat by subduing Thengil, king of Finnmark, and Egther, king of Biarmaland. Saxo's dates are incorrect. It is clear that Ofura must have been close to marrying age, which means that there was a longer period between the Norwegian campaign and Arngrim's campaigns. Arngrim eagerly accepted Erik's advice and advanced against the Finns. Saxo describes the Finns as the northernmost of the peoples who pursued a nomadic existence. The Finns excelled in the use of skis, javelins, bows and magic. It would be easy to think that Saxo would equate the Finns with the Lapps, but this is not the case. Even though the majority of the Finns of this period were farmers, there still existed a class of hunter whom agriculturalists pejoratively called Lapps. The real Lapps are an ethnically different group. These hunters gathered furs and collected tribute in the form of furs from the Lapps for markets abroad; it is these Finns that Saxo meant in this case.

When Arngrim attacked the Finns of Finnmark, he encountered serious difficulties, which were claimed to have resulted from the use of magic. When the

Finns scattered in flight, they are claimed to have thrown behind them three stones which looked like three mountains, and Arngrim stopped the pursuit due to these obstacles. A more prosaic description would be that the Finns retreated past three mountains and Arngrim did not follow because he feared an ambush. Arngrim's forces engaged the enemy again the following day, but then the Finns created an illusion of snow that looked like a river and they were once again able to flee. A likelier explanation would be that the Finns retreated behind a river. On the third day, the armies met again, but this time the Finns were unable to flee, which resulted in their surrender after their battle line faltered. The Finns were ordered to pay him one sledge filled with animal pelts per ten persons every three years. After this, Arngrim moved against the Biarmalanders, which means that he probably marched through northern Norway or northern Finland. He defeated Egther, 'the *dux* of *Biarmie*', in a duel and imposed tribute on them of one skin per person.

It is unfortunate that we do not know what the power structure of these lands looked like during this period. What is known is that the Finns of Pohjanmaa in modern Finland had forts with houses that resembled closely the forts of Gotland in Sweden. These forts were completely unlike the hill forts in the south of Finland, which consisted mainly of refuge forts. My own view is that it is also probable that the houses resembled the halls/mansions of the Mälaren region in Sweden, but this requires further study by archaeologists on both sides of the gulf. This suggest a strong connection between Sweden and the Pohjanmaa region for this period, and also that Pohjanmaa was subjected to Swedish control. Saxo's account can be used to suggest this, because Arngrim did not have to fight against the inhabitants of Pohjanmaa and Lappland when he advanced against Biarmaland, but this is not conclusive, because Arngrim could have advanced to Biarmaland through northern Norway. The presence of scattered forts that faced north may suggest that the Lapps were under Swedish control, while Pohjanmaa was not, but once again this is not conclusive, because it is possible that these forts were just meant to control the movements of the Lapps for taxation purposes or to protect the local inhabitants against them. It is also not also not known what the relationship was between Pohjanmaa and the south of Finland. Did the Swedes also rule south of Finland at this time? Or were these areas hostile towards each other? If the latter was the case, did any campaigns take place? I have included below a short excursus on the fortifications in this area, together with some illustrations of what types of obstacles the invaders of these regions would have faced if they were forced to fight against local tribes.

Iron Age Forts in Finland
Finnish forts consisted of hill forts (refuge forts) and fortified towns, which were located in the south of Finland and in Carelia (Karjala); and of the so-called churches/castles of Pohjanmaa.[21] Typical hill forts were built on hills 15–40m high with circumferences of 80–160m. These were usually located by the sea, a lake or

river, or in a swamp/low-lying meadow. The hills were usually approachable only from one direction, which was protected by a single wall of stones that had been placed on top of each other without any connecting substance. The forts naturally followed the lay of the land and were therefore irregular in shape. The only attested town with walls is Tiurinlinna at Räisälä in the territory lost to the Soviet Union in 1944, but one may suspect that other towns would also have existed with similar protections, the traces of which have been lost when they grew into modern towns and cities. Some of the counties had particularly large concentrations of forts, which presumably reflects the importance of the location. These include the counties of Saltvik and Finström in Ahvenanmaa (Åland), the city of Hämeenlinna, Tuulos and the bays of Lake Ladoga (Laatokka) in the territories lost to the Soviet Union in 1944.

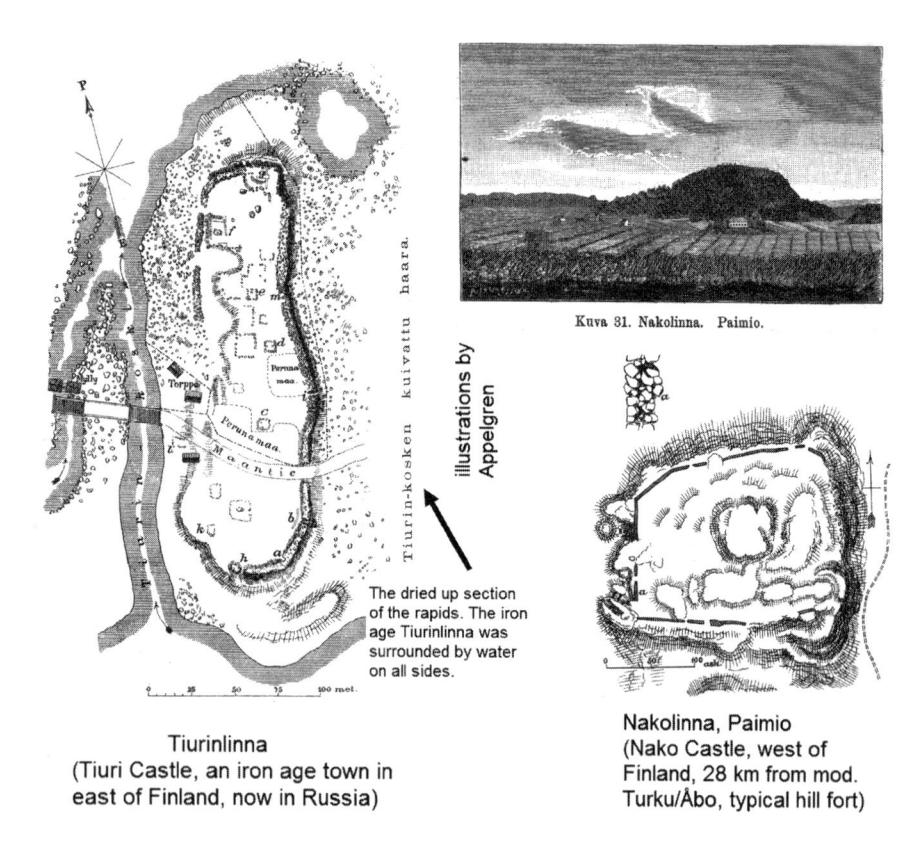

Kuva 31. Nakolinna. Paimio.

illustrations by Appelgren

The dried up section of the rapids. The iron age Tiurinlinna was surrounded by water on all sides.

Tiurinlinna
(Tiuri Castle, an iron age town in east of Finland, now in Russia)

Nakolinna, Paimio
(Nako Castle, west of Finland, 28 km from mod. Turku/Åbo, typical hill fort)

During this era, the Swedes apparently did not have to face the types of forts present in the south of Finland and Carelia/Karjala, but only those in Pohjanmaa. The forts of Pohjanmaa were a special case, as their structures differed considerably from those elsewhere. Part of the reason was that the terrain was more flat in these areas, but this is not the only explanation. The forts of Pohjanmaa appear to have been influenced by the Swedes of Gotland/Götaland, as both have houses/halls at the highest position of the fort. These houses resembled those that have been found everywhere in the northern areas where the 'Vikings' roved. The highest concentration of these are in the Raahe and Oulu regions. This, in my opinion, suggests that the central area of one of the kingdoms of Finland was located in this area. Three other forts are attested in the north, and one may speculate that these were outposts of this kingdom. These forts were probably meant to contol the Lapps and serve as bases for their taxation. Appelgren dates these to ca 450–700, which corresponds roughly with the time Frothi's Swedish supporters supposedly operated in the north of Sweden and Finland, and in Bjarmaland.

Frothi's Campaign in Britain and Ireland
When Arngrim returned in glory to Sweden, Erik escorted him to Frothi and recommended the man to Frothi. Frothi was convinced and Arngrim got his wife. She bore him twelve sons, who were later killed at the Island of Samsø. Note that twelve oarsmen per boat were typical for a raiding vessel of this period. The seas, however, were still infested with pirates (Picts and others?) from the British Isles. Frothi decided to put a stop to this and assembled a fleet with 'myriads' of ships consisting of Danes and their clients. The 'myriads' of ships should be interpreted as myriads of men, as in the case of the Rutenian fleet,[22] so that the maximum number on board would not have surpassed the figure of about 30,000–35,000 men which can be attested for the Viking period. In order to ship this number of men, Frothi would also have required more ships than the later Vikings, because the fifth-century longboats were not as big as the later ships, unless Frothi had ordered his subjects to build more of the larger vessels, for which there is no evidence. Instead of this, Saxo clearly points out the small size of period vessels by stressing that the smallest vessels of Frothi had crews of twelve men.

The 'ruler of Britain' knew that he could not oppose this force, so offered to pay tribute. At the same time he offered a banquet to 1,200 Danish nobles to celebrate the treaty, but only with the idea of killing of his guests. Frothi and his advisors suspected treachery. The British ruler sought to allay their fears by increasing the number of guests to 2,400 men. Now Frothi accepted the invitation, but still secretly dispatched scouts to scour the nearby woods for a possible ambush. They found a British encampment inside the woods, which enabled Frothi to set up a counter-ambush against them. Frothi and his retinue of 2,400 men entered the banquet lightly-armed and started to empty the wine tankards as proper Danes. The British locked the Danes inside the hall and set the building on fire. This indicates that Frothi had not come to the banquet with all 2,400 men, but only with his immediate retinue. The figure of 2,400 men must mean the number of men who disembarked on the shore. The Danes inside reacted by battering the walls and managed to fight their way out. It was then that Frothi ordered the trumpet to be sounded and his men burst forth from their hiding places. The British were butchered. After this, Frothi sailed to Ireland.

Who was the king of Britain and who were these Britons? It is very improbable that they would have been Vortigern and his followers, because he lacked the naval resources for piratical raids in Danish waters, but it was not impossible. However, the inhabitants of the Orkneys and Scotland did possess the resources for such operations, and we should remember that Frothi's fleet had previously conducted a major raid against the Orkneys. Its inhabitants would certainly have wanted to pay back in kind. It is quite probable that the Britons in question were Saxons and/or Picts. The best proof for the presence of Saxons as allies of the Picts is that they conducted a joint campaign in Wales in 429 (the occasion of Germanus's Alleluia Victory) and that the first recorded Saxon raid in Ireland took place in 434 (ca.434). The devastation caused by the Huns during their campaign in Jutland in about 418/419 would surely have contributed to the willingness of the inhabitants to seek new homes. It is particularly noteworthy that the first migrants consisted of the tribes of Jutland and not of the inhabitants of the islands or of Norway. Since Frothi's next target of attack was Ireland, it is possible that the Irish Scots, Picts and Saxons had all cooperated in their naval expeditions against Frothi's domains in Norway and Denmark, but it is equally possible that all of these had conducted their piratical raids independently of each other. Frothi would have another good reason for his campaign against the Saxons, Angles and Jutes because he would have considered these tribes as his own subjects who had deserted him. In my opinion, it is quite possible, even if this is ultimately unprovable, that this was the fleet dispatched by the Romans to Britain in about 429/430.

The Irish had been warned of Frothi's approach, and spread iron caltrops in the likely landing places. According to Saxo, the Irish were lightly equipped warriors who shaved the back of their head. Their style of fighting was highly mobile, and they had been trained to throw their javelins at their pursuers. Saxo fails to tell us how Frothi landed his forces, but says that he was not fooled by the feigned flight of the Irish and advanced with caution. The war was decided when Irish *dux* Kervillus/Kervil was killed in battle. His brother surrendered and accepted client status.

The likeliest date for this campaign would be 429/430, when Germanus campaigned.

The illustrations below show Vendel age warriors from Scandinavia (see also the Plates section).

After these successes, Frothi returned in glory and is claimed to have spent thirty years in peace until he was killed ingloriously by a woman and her children who had 'shape-changed' and become a sea-cow and her calves. Obviously there is something amiss with this story. Firstly, it is probable that the thirty years is merely a guess by Saxo or that it was the period between the two Hunnish wars, which is quite possible, because this amount of time appears to have passed between the defensive

It is probable that we should interpret this helmet to represent a walrus (lived along the coast of modern Norway at the time) rather than an elephant. However, if the helmet was really meant to represent elephant, it still gives us a good idea how the Northerners would have constructed a helmet to represent a walrus.

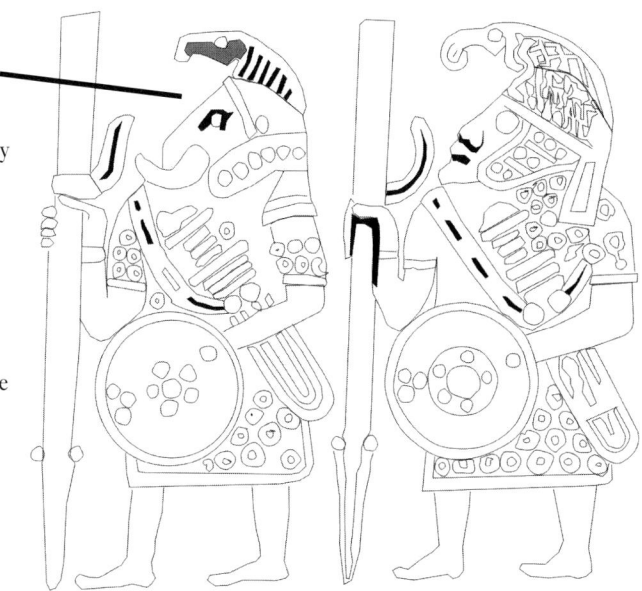

war and offensive wars. Secondly, no sane person believes in shape-changing, which means that Frothi was accidentally killed by cows (walruses are less likely than real cattle) or by an angry woman and her children who had 'shape-changed' in the same manner as berserkers did. The berserker shape-change meant only the adoption of furs and/or fur/leather coats so that the person resembled the chosen animal. The above illustration from Vendel shows one warrior dressed possibly as a walrus, even if the tusks point upwards like an elephant's – the saga sources could have called such a warrior a walrus. In either case, the death was an inglorious one for the great warrior king, and undoubtedly a source of great shame for his bodyguards. Thirdly, it is clear that Saxo's account has misplaced Frothi's campaign in Russia against the Huns, which can have happened only after the death of Attila and the collapse of the Hun Empire.

The Reign of Frothi III the Magnificent Reconstructed
On the basis of the above account and Arthur's campaigns in the area, it is easy to pinpoint Frothi's reign to ca 406–460, but we can achieve even greater accuracy by including evidence from other sources.

Firstly, the Theodosian Code (CTh 9.40.24, dated 24 September 419) proves that some barbarians had been taught how to build ships by Roman boatwrights in the city of Chersonesus in the Crimea in about 417/418 (tr. by Pharr, p.258): 'The same Augustuses to Monaxius, Praetorian Prefect. Those persons who have betrayed to the barbarians the art of building ships, that was hitherto unknown to them, shall be freed from imminent punishment and imprisonment because of the petition of the Most Revered Asclepiades, Bishop of the City of Chersonesus, but We decree that capital punishment shall be inflicted both upon these men and upon any others if they should perpetrate anything similar in the future.' This same piece of legislation has also been noted by Maenchen-Helfen (p.95), who notes that the only candidates as pirates in Crimean waters were the Huns and Goths, but that the former were the likelier perpetrators.[23]

In the context of this appendix, this legislation suggests two things. Firstly, since we know that the legislation was issued in 419, it is probable that the event had taken place before this. Secondly, the culprits would not have been pardoned if their actions had resulted in any serious piratical activity against Roman interests in the Black Sea, which means that the ships were probably used elsewhere, the likeliest location being the Baltic Sea region. We are now in a position to reconstruct the likely course of events preceding this.

We know that it was the westward advance of the Huns that launched the major migrations of tribes against Roman frontiers in 403–405, 406 and again in 408. This means that the Huns were at that time advancing towards the Rhine. The Huns are attested to be near the Rhine for the first time in about 430, when Burgundian rebels attacked the camp of the Hunnish ruler Ottar/Octar,[24] but it is very probable that they had already reached the river well before this, immediately in the footsteps of the fleeing Germanic tribes, in about 409/410. The Huns maintained control of the middle and upper Rhine at least until 451, when they included among their clients the Ripuarian Franks and Thuringians.[25] It would have been in the aftermath of the Hunnish advance to the Rhine region that Frothi would have concluded his marriage with the daughter of the Hunnish king. It is possible that at this time the Huns were ruled by two to four separate kings, just as they were later. We know that the brothers Ottar and Ruga were joint rulers in about 430, and that they had two other brothers. Since Ottar was operating in the middle to upper Rhine and Ruga was in Pannonia, it seems quite probable that the other brothers were operating in the northern regions and Steppes at the same time. It is unfortunate that we do not know the names of these Hun rulers for the 410s. The only name that we know of comes from fragment 19 of Olympiodorus, who mentions Charaton as high-king of the Huns. It is not known who the others were.

The *Saga of the Volsungs* (24, 29ff.) refers to the use of similar marriage contracts between the Huns and their neighbours. According to the *Saga*, Attila's sister, Bekkhild (bench-battle), was married to Heimir (who lived in the land of the Franks, i.e. north or east of the Rhine), and his other sister, Brynhild (coat of mail-battle), to Gunnar (probably the Burgundian King Gundaharius), who lived south of the Rhine. It is by no means impossible that the story of these marriages is based on real events.

The breakup between Frothi and the Huns resulting from the infidelity of Hanunda and subsequent divorce would have taken place in about 414/415. It was followed by the stealing of Gøtar's daughter and Frothi's marriage to her to obtain the right to Gøtar's throne, and by the pre-emptive strike against the Wends in neighbouring Denmark. It is actually possible that the breakup between Frothi and the Huns had resulted from the arrival of the Wends in the region, which had led to the inescapable conclusion that the Wends and Huns posed a threat to the Danes, so had to be dealt with through war.

It was probably in about 415/416 that the Huns learnt of what had happened. They knew that the principal strength of the Nordic nations and tribes lay in their naval forces, which meant that they needed a fleet of their own. The plan was to use two separate forces – a fleet provided by the Slavs and a land army, the core of which consisted of the Huns. The land forces were presumably intended to be used against the Danes of Jutland (Jylland), while the fleet was to offer support by protecting them from Frothi's fleet, defeating the Danish fleet if possible, carrying supplies and then transporting the land army from Jutland to Fyn and Sjaelland. The key to the success of this operation was the Slavic fleet assembled in the lands of the Wends. Frothi and Erik realised this and destroyed the two Slavic fleets (Wends, Rutenians) with pre-emptive strikes, as well as the Hunnic land army through a scorched earth strategy.

Since the ships of their clients were inferior to those used by the Danes, the Huns needed another source for their ships, which was East Rome. They also needed ships that could transport their horses – hence the use of the large ships with 300 rowers mentioned by Saxo. These ships would have been built by the Rutenians in about 416/417, with the Danes launching their pre-emptive strike against them in about 417/418. Since the threat posed by the Huns was so severe, Frothi managed to assemble a huge army and fleet against them, just as Aetius later did. The Huns would have launched their land campaign against Jutland in the same year. The Danes knew that they could not oppose the Huns on land, so resorted to scorched earth tactics and guerrilla warfare. This war lasted for two campaign seasons and ended in the defeat of the Huns during the second season in about 418/419. The Danes and their allies survived because they spread out their forces into townships and sent part of their forces to pillage foreign lands.

What is notable about the assembly of forces under Attila opposite Gaul in 451 is that it did not include any tribes north of the Ripuarian Franks. This suggests that Saxo's account must have had some basis in truth, which has been denied by those historians who follow the very biased and racist attitude towards the Nordic and Germanic sources, resulting from the bias of the ultra-conservative branch of the Classicist school of historiography. The Scandinavians had successfully defeated the Huns through their use of the navy and a scorched earth policy on land. Frothi and Erik thus deserve to be added to the list of the great captains of the Middle Ages.

Saxo's referral to Viking raids in 'Hunland' are by no means unique in the sources. The following examples prove that there were other similar stories of contact between the Scandinavians and other Germans with the Huns. For example, the *Saga of the Volsungs* (1, 8, 11–13) refers to Viking raids and the occupation of 'Hunland' that can be dated roughly to the third, fourth and fifth centuries. The Hunland in question must be the 'Land of the Swedes' in the east, referred to both in the *Yngliga Saga* and *Edda*, and Estland/Kurland of Saxo, because these areas clearly had very close contacts with Denmark and Sweden. It is possible that the naval attack of Alf, the son of King Hjalprek of Denmark, together with King Lyngvi against King Sigmund of Hunland should be connected with Frothi's war against the Rutenians, even if the reasons and details are at disagreement. Lyngvi's campaign against Sigmund and Eylimi had been caused by the marriage of Eylimi's daughter to Sigmund rather than to Lyngvi. In the course of this campaign, Alf captured the famous Sigurd/Siegfried the Dragon-Slayer, who later served as a mercenary leader of cavalry under the Burgundian kings. If the Rutenians of Saxo were descendants of the Swedes (see for example Aesir and Odin, Appendix 3), it is easy to understand why these men would have been placed in charge of building the ships and why the relationship between the Scandinavians and Estonians/Kurlanders was so close.

Sigurd/Siegfried the Dragon-Slayer was famous as the killer of a dragon and for the killing of the brothers Fafnir and Regin (Shilbung and Nibelung in the *Nibelungenlied*). When one carefully reads the *Saga of the Volsungs* and the *Nibelungenlied*, it becomes obvious that the dragon was actually a very rich Danish king whose name was Fafnir. Sigurd had apparently been paid to kill Fafnir by his brother, Regin, but instead of performing his mission, Sigurd had killed Regin as well and had looted Fafnir's treasure (the Nibelung's treasure). This murder and pillage made Sigurd and his mercenary band outlaws, and they had to flee to the land of the Franks, which must correspond with the region of Xanten in the *Nibelungenlied*. The *Nibelungenlied* places Siegfried's home there, but it is clear that the *Saga* is correct in stating that it was the area ruled by Heimir. Sigurd continued his journey from there to the Burgundians, who then employed his mercenary band. The Burgundians could be pleased with their decision to employ Sigurd. He was famous for his handling of sword and shield, spear and javelin throwing, bending of the bow, horsemanship and foresight as military leader – in other words, Sigurd and his horsemen fought like the Huns. It is possible that their horses were also armoured, because the *Saga* (34) claims that the horses of the Danes, Langobards, Franks and Saxons were armoured in about 450. Unfortunately for Gundaharius, he foolishly had Sigurd assassinated as a result of the plotting of the wives and because of his greed for the gold of Sigurd. In about 437, the entire royal family was butchered by the Huns in Roman service and the gold taken to the East. The exploits of all these persons passed into legend.

The *Saga of the Volsungs* (31) also claims that the sons of Gjuki (Gibica), Gunnar (Gundaharius, Gunther), Hogni (Gernot?) and Guttorm (possibly Gislaharius, Gisleher) had killed a king of the Danes and the brother of King Budli (Attila's father). One possible way to use this piece of information would be to connect it with what we know of the Burgundians during the first half of the fifth century. We know that the Burgundians were divided into Roman federate forces protecting Worms, Metz and Alzey region (also known from the *Nibelungenlied* 1ff.) and those who had remained on the other side of the Rhine controlled by the Huns. This can be interpreted to mean that some of the sons of Gibica had served as mercenaries of the Huns during their invasion of Jutland in about 418/419, in the course of which they had killed one of the kings of that region,[26] after which they had revolted against the Huns and killed Hun King Uptaros/Octar in about 428–430 (Socrates, *Hist. Eccl.*). I will discuss these matters at greater length in another study.

I will now return to the account of Saxo. He also mentioned the conflict between Hithin and Høgin at a time when Hithin was collecting taxes from the Slavs, presumably very soon after the war (ca 420?) against the Huns. This quarrel ended in the death of both seven years later. It was during those days that the Swedish war arose. On the basis of this, it is very difficult to pinpoint the exact year. It is possible that Saxo meant 420/421, 427/8 or some time between. My own educated guess is that it was in about 421 that Frothi dispatched Erik, together with Olimar, to subject Sweden under his rule. Soon after this, possibly in about 422/423, would have followed the joint campaign of Erik and Frothi against Hedmark, Vik and Halogaland.

Saxo claims that this was followed by a seven-year peace, which would take us to 429/430. It was presumably during those years, rather than later, that Arngrim conquered Finnmark and Biarmaland for Frothi. On the basis of Saxo's dates, Frothi's campaign to Britain and Ireland would have coincided with the Alleluia Victory of Germanus, which is actually quite possible. The sources, however, fail to state any connection between Frothi's campaign and Germanus' presence in Britain. In spite of this, it is possible that these two events were connected, because the discrepancies in the sources suggest strongly that Germanus' campaigns have not been covered in all of their detail. It is therefore feasible that the Britons and Germanus had contacted Frothi and asked for his help against the Saxons, who were after all supposed to be his subjects. What is almost certain is that Frothi's operation was not directed against the Britons themselves, who lacked adequate naval might at the time, but against the Saxons and Picts in the north and the Irish in Ireland, and these were the enemies the Britons were facing at the time – hence the possibility that Frothi could have acted as a Roman ally.

As we have seen, according to Saxo, Frothi spent the next thirty years in peace until he was killed ingloriously. This would take us to 459/460. However, as stated above, I would suggest that Olimar's conquest of Estonia and Frothi's campaign against the Huns in Russia took place before this. The likeliest time period for any campaign along the Russian rivers would be after the death of Attila in 453. It is possible that Frothi was one of the Germanic kings who joined the grand alliance against the Huns in that year, tying up Hunnic resources in the north while the great coalition of tribes crushed the Huns at the Battle of Nedao River in about 454, or that he acted opportunistically after the collapse of the Hun Empire and invaded 'Greater Sweden' through the river network, inflicting a crushing loss on one of the surviving sons of Attila, who had retreated to the neighbourhood of Kiev in the aftermath of the defeat. Both alternatives are possible.

According to the *Saga of the Volsungs* (29), Attila's sister, Brynhild, had once fought a campaign against the king of the Gardariki. The *Saga* doesn't provide us with any concrete information according to which one could pinpoint this event, but some tentative conclusions can be made. The Gardariki means the Vaeringjar, Vaerings or Varangians – in other words, the Scandinavian/Northmen traders in the East or the Varangian Guard of the East Roman emperor.[27] While the *Saga* always specifies the Danes, it is clear that the Gardariki cannot be the Danes. This leaves open the possibility that Brynhild would have fought against one of the guard units of the East Roman emperor, perhaps in 422, or had fought against the raiders under Olimar in about 419, or against the Danes when they were in Greater Sweden.

It seems probable that very soon after the death of Frothi, in about 460, his kingdom started to unravel, because we find no mention of his son, Alf, and daughter, Ofura, and then we learn that another of his sons, Fridlef II, was brought up in Russia. This probably means that Alf had won the power struggle among the siblings, with Fridlef forced to flee to Russia. On the basis of Geoffrey's account of Arthur's campaigns in Norway, Sweden and Denmark, it appears probable that Ofura had been married into one of the Norwegian kingdoms, so Loth had some sort of legal claim to part of Denmark, which Arthur then secured for him. It is unfortunate that Saxo does not describe the role of Fridlef's elder brother, Halfdan, in these events. It is during this chaotic period in Danish history that King Arthur appeared on the scene.

It is possible to connect the above account with Snorri's *Saga of the Ynglings* (25ff.), because Snorri mentions that Aun was the king of Sweden during the lifetime of Dan the Magnificent, his son, Frothi the Magnificent/Peaceful, and then his sons, Halfdan and Frithleif (Fridlef). Just like Saxo, who left out humiliating parts of Danish history, Snorri has left out of his story the most shameful part of Swedish history, describing only the events that followed the death of Frothi the Magnificent. However, on the basis of *The Saga of King Hrolf Kraki*, and Saxo and Geoffrey of Monmouth, the sequence of Danish rulers after Frothi III appears to have been: Alf (Aschil, Aschilus, died in ca 472), Fridlef II, Frothi IV, Halfdan (Half-Dane, son of Frothi IV), Frothi V (the younger brother and killer of Halfdan), Helgi (son of Halfdan and king of Denmark; his younger brother, Hroar, became the king of Northumberland through marriage) and Helgi's son, Hrolf. This Hrolf had a famous champion called either Bodvar Barki or Beowulf. As is well-known, Beowulf performed many a memorable deed, but I will leave analysis of his heroics and of the history of Denmark and Scandinavia to be dealt with at a later date.

As the above account should have made abundantly clear, it is worthwhile also to analyze the sources that have been dismissed as worthless. On the basis of this analysis, we should be able to add plenty of details to the annals of the peoples of the North that are otherwise missing, and should also add the name of Frothi the Magnificent to the annals of the greatest captains of all time. This analysis also explains why it was that the Huns failed to conquer the areas north of the Franks and what happened to the eastern portions of Attila's empire after his death.

Appendix II

Swedish Rock Carvings and Naval Tactics

These rock carvings from Sweden date either from the Bronze or Early Iron Age. The date is contested. I have included these here because both illustrations demonstrate that the Swedes and other peoples of the Baltic Sea were engaged in constant naval warfare from the Bronze Age onwards. Each of the illustrations also clearly tells a tale. These have already been interpreted in previous studies,[1] but I have still chosen to point out some important details in the illustrations in order to prove that the Scandinavians did indeed engage in large-scale military operations of which we have very little knowledge.

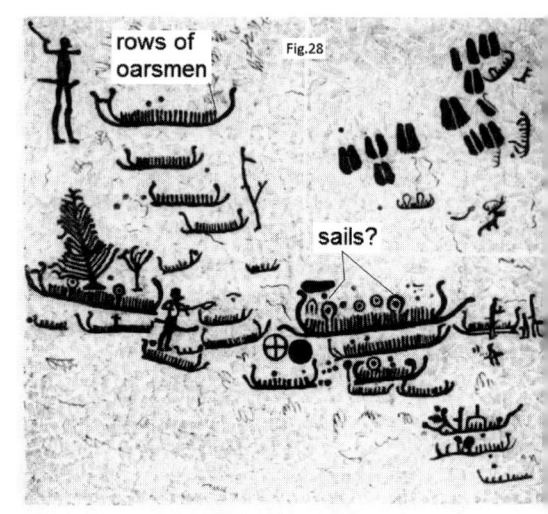

FIG. 88.—Rock-carving in Lökeberg in Bohuslän.

The illustrations are taken from Montelius (1888, 1906); the comments are mine. On the basis of a comparison of different illustrations, the lines above the ships have been proven to represent oars or paddles. This means that we can estimate the size of the ship from the number of oarsmen. The largest of these have twenty-four, twenty-six, twenty-seven and twenty-nine rows of oarsmen, which means that the minimum crew for the large ships varied from fifty-one to sixty-one men. The smallest vessels appear to have had crews of ten to twelve oarsmen. These crew sizes are comparable with the information provided by Saxo regarding those employed by Frothi III in the fifth century.

Swedish Rock Carvings and Naval Tactics 215

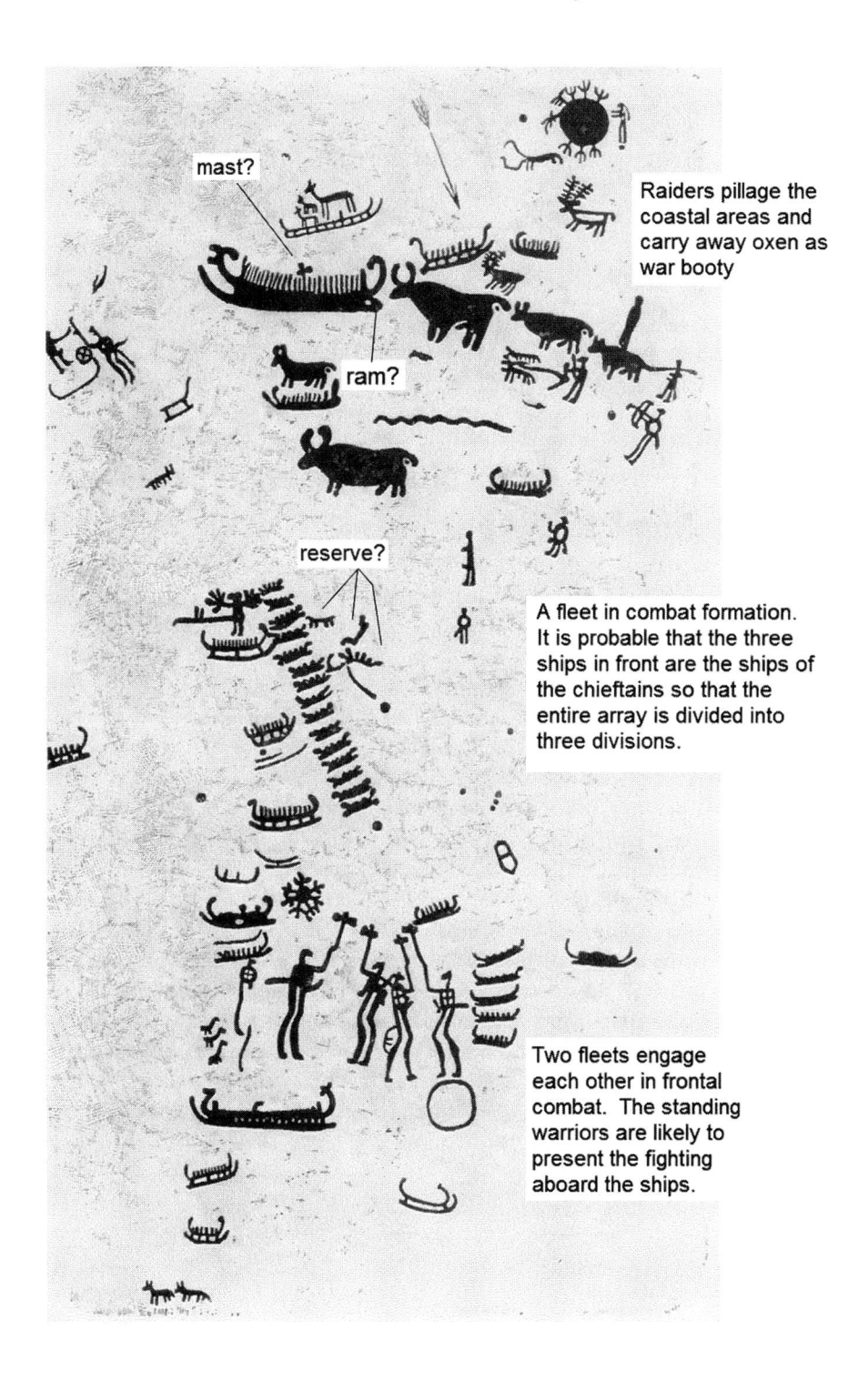

mast?

ram?

reserve?

Raiders pillage the coastal areas and carry away oxen as war booty

A fleet in combat formation. It is probable that the three ships in front are the ships of the chieftains so that the entire array is divided into three divisions.

Two fleets engage each other in frontal combat. The standing warriors are likely to present the fighting aboard the ships.

Appendix III

Odin the Man

There is a consensus among modern historians that we should dismiss the evidence presented by Snorri (*Yngliga Saga*, *Prose Edda*) and Saxo Grammaticus, and to think that Odin was only a Nordic god and nothing else. In this case it is Saxo and Snorri who actually represent the 'sober' picture of history, while it is the so-called 'sober' ultra-conservative historians who should be considered to be hallucinating. I do understand their logic behind this argument, which is that the Nordic leaders would have wanted to invent illustrious ancestors for themselves, therefore none of the sources should be thought of as accurate, or that the Christian Snorri and Saxo purposefully associated the Nordic gods with human beings, but this is done only by dismissing the actual evidence with one's own subjective romantic view of the past. It also dismisses the other pieces of evidence which I present here. Therefore, it comes as no great surprise that it was an outsider, Thor Heyerdahl, who first sought to prove the veracity of the *Yngliga Saga*'s claim that Odin was a very real person who managed to convince the Scandinavians that he was a god. Thor Heyerdahl's interpretation was that the Aesir of Odin lived close to the River Don near the Black Sea at the time the Romans were advancing into this area in about 60 BC. It is not even remotely surprising that leading Norwegian academics reacted with hostility and launched an immediate and vehement attack against Heyerdahl's theory. These academics have become so entrenched in their own theories that it is impossible for them to think outside the box. It requires an outsider. The general attitude of these academics is actually quite surprising, because the two leading authorities of Odin, Snorri and Saxo Grammaticus, both refer to him as a mortal who managed to convince the people of Europe that he was a god, but then again this rigidity of thinking is the typical attitude for the vast majority of Classicists and Medievalists in Scandinavia, Finland and the rest of Western Europe. Have they forgotten that the pagan emperors of Rome also claimed to become gods when they died, and that Odin is certainly not the only mortal man to have claimed to be a living god?

Regardless of these comments regarding the reaction to Heyerdahl's theory, my own view is that Heyerdahl did indeed make a mistake in identifying the time period, and probably also the place of origin, but he was certainly right to challenge the established view that Odin is to be identified with the Germanic god Wodan. It should be the job of historians to challenge the consensus when there is reason to do so, and not to perpetuate old misunderstandings only because their position in academia requires that. There is something inherently wrong in the Western university systems for this to have happened. This does not preclude the probability that when Odin assumed godly status, his supposed powers would not have overtaken the powers previously supposedly held by Wodan,[1] just as Snorri states, but it does mean that we should not overlook the evidence presented by the two early and eminent Scandinavian historians – is it really methodologically sound to dismiss their evidence on the basis of a general belief, when even the *Anglo-Saxon Chronicle* (a.449), Bede (*Ecclesiastical History* 1.15), Nennius (31) and Edda (10) support their claim, as can be seen in the claim that Hengist was a descendant of Wodan, in other words a descendant of Odin?

I will begin my account of Odin with two quotes from Saxo Grammaticus' *History of the Danes* (Book 1 and Book 6, tr. by Elton) to demonstrate his views regarding this. However, I do not include here an analysis of Saxo's version of Odin's life, because he has scattered the evidence throughout his *History* in such a manner that it requires a full study for the historian to be able to separate the different time periods and events from each other. My own account (after the quotes) is entirely based on the 'sober' account of Snorri (*Yngliga Saga* and *Edda*), but I would still urge that someone would take up the task of analyzing the various scattered pieces of evidence for the historical Odin in Saxo, Edda and other sources, by looking at the different strata of evidence for their reliability and probability against other extant sources. There is more to be said about the mortal man Odin than I have been able to do in an appendix. If nobody does that in the near future, I will certainly do it myself at the first possible opportunity.

Book 1: 'At this time there was one Odin, who was credited over all Europe with the honour, which was false, of godhead, but used more continually to sojourn at Uppsala … The kings of the North, desiring more zealously to worship this deity, embounded his likeness in a golden image …'

Book 6: 'For there were of old certain men versed in sorcery, Thor, namely, and Odin, and many others, who were cunning in contriving marvellous sleights; and they, winning the minds of the simple, began to claim the rank of gods. For, in particular, they ensnared Norway, Sweden and Denmark in the vainest credulity, and by prompting these lands to worship them, infected them with their imposture. The effects of their deceit spread so far, that all other men adored a sort of divine power in them, and thinking them either gods or in league with gods, offered solemn prayers to these inventors of sorceries … Hence it has come that the holy days … are called among us by the names of these men … For the days, called among our countrymen Thors-day or Odins-day, the ancients termed severally the holy day of Jove or of Mercury. … Thor was Odin's son.'[2]

According to the *Yngliga Saga* (2ff.), the Aesir lived in the area east of the Don (Tana Fork, corrupted from Vana?; Vana/Vanha, by the way, means 'old' in Finnish languages), with its capital being Asgarth. Their ruler was called Odin. This area was called Svitjoth (land of the Swedes). Odin was a great warrior king and magician/sorcerer. Asgarth served as a place of sacrifices, and had twelve priests called *diar* (gods) who also acted as judges. Note the number twelve and the twelve councillors in the context of Arthurian events and the twelve Christian Apostles. The twelve priest councillors of Odin may reflect Celtic traditions. The *diar*, like many other words in the sagas, were originally Celtic. Many historians have noted the resemblance of Odin the god with the Celtic god Lugus, who was also a god of intellect, magician, poet, carried a spear and was accompanied by ravens. This suggests a possible connection with the Celts (i.e. with people who spoke Celtic languages; the Celts were and are an ethnically diverse group) who lived north of the Black Sea, or at least a very strong Celtic cultural influence. These would not have been the only Celts in those regions, as for example the case of the Bastarnae proves. It is possible that a significant portion of the male population of Odin's kingdom, or at least its upper classes, had originally travelled from Scandinavia (Sweden?) to this area, at the same time as the coastal areas of modern Finland had been occupied by Germanic warrior groups. Considering the location of the kingdom and vocabulary, it is also possible that there may have been some form of Finnish influence present in the realm of Odin.

However, in the *Edda* (3ff.), Snorri mistakenly places the Aesir in Turkey (Asia Minor) and Asgarth at Troy. This mistake has obviously resulted from his classical education. Snorri has undoubtedly seen somewhere in his sources the claim that the Aesir came from the land of the Turks, which he mistakenly placed in Asia Minor (where they were after the Battle of Manzikert in 1071), without realising that it actually meant the Steppes east of the River Don, where the original land of the Turks was located. This raises one very interesting prospect, which is that Odin's kingdom would have formed the western half of some steppe kingdom in the area, so he would have acted as the equivalent of the Wise King of the West in Xiognu/Hun terminology and would have had under him twelve leaders of 10,000 horsemen, as did the Wise King of the East. We should not forget that, according to the legend, Odin's horse, Sleipnir, had eight legs, which can be seen to refer to the steppe practice of using two horses (in Greek theory a separate class of cavalry with the name *amfippoi*)[3] simultaneously to increase the mobility of the horseman. In light of this, it is not surprising that Odin/Woden's descendants, Hengist (Stallion) and Horsa (Horse or Mare), were named after horses, or that the Swedes employed knightly cavalry during the Baltic Crusades. This could also explain the origin of the female name Nanna in Scandinavia. Its origins could be in the Central Asian Goddess Nana. In short, it is quite possible or even probable that Odin acted as a ruler of the eastern half of some steppe kingdom which followed Xiognu practices, and that his people, the Aesir, consisted of a mixed population of Celts, Germans, Sarmatians, Scythians, Slavs, Finns and others.

Top Left: Odin and his horse Sleipnir as represented in Viking art.
Top Right: Odin, his horse Sleipnir, and two ravens as represented in the Vendel Period (6th-7th centuries) art. Of particular note is the fact that the earlier works of art give a more realistic picture of Odin and his horse and the later ones do not. This suggests an ever growing disconnection between reality and myth as time passed. For the Vikings Odin and his retinue were no longer mythical men who became gods, but were real gods.

At some point, Odin left his two brothers in charge of Asgarth and travelled, together with the *diar* and many other people, to Garthariki (Russia), and from there to Saxland (Saxony, north-western Germany). This was a mass migration of people, including young and old, women and men (*Edda* 10). This happened at a time when the Roman generals were conquering Europe (*Yngliga Saga* 5). There are two likely dates for this migration. The first is the Marcomannic War of 167–180, and the other is in the 260s. These two periods saw a massive movement of peoples against the Roman frontiers, which must have been caused by similar mass movement behind them. The likeliest causes in both cases would be climate change, a pandemic, wars or over-population. Whatever the date, it is probable that Odin's movement to the west would have left a power vacuum in the area east of the Don, which in turn invited new settlers there.

The first alternative would mean that Odin's migration along the Baltic coast to Denmark caused the Marcomannic Wars, which in turn would have caused the Goths and Heruls to move to the areas vacated by Odin, but in my opinion this date is too early to be considered.

The second alternative is that Odin began his westward trek in the 260s, which then caused the Goths and Heruls to migrate en masse against the Roman borders in 267–271. This alternative is the likeliest on the basis of the three generations separating Hengist from Odin, but even then this assumes that all of the men sired their successors late in life. The problem with this dating is the reference to the conquests of Roman generals, but in light of the above this is still the most likely alternative. It would have been easy for Snorri to sum up events of a longer period into a single sentence. It is in light of this that we should see the Pictish traditions (Bede 1.1), according to which their original home was in Scythia. It is noteworthy that the arrival of the Picts in the British Isles coincides roughly with these events. This in turn would mean that when Odin began his trek, he either moved to the areas recently vacated by the Picts or forced them onwards, or that the Picts accompanied him. However, it is also possible that the original migration of the Pictish warriors, their young-ones, took place during the reign of Septimius Severus (see Syvänne, *Caracalla*) and that those who were left behind followed them roughly at this time so that they became the dominant power in "Scotland".

To sum up, the dating of the trek to the 260s has the following advantages:

1) This date tallies with the massive migration of the Goths and Heruls against the Roman frontiers in 267–271. Contrary to popular belief, the massive numbers (320,000 warriors) given by the sources are entirely believable in light of the fact that this involved the mass migration of several tribes in their entirety, and that the Romans faced very real difficulties in dealing with the invasion.[4]
2) This would also tally with the likely date for the appearance of the second Hun Empire in Central Asia, which must have existed at some point before the fourth and fifth centuries, when the separate Hun tribes of the Chionatai, Hephthalites, Kidarite Huns and Huns made their appearance in Eurasia. It is uncertain whether these tribes or other Central Asian nomads pushed Odin westward, or they moved into the power vacuum created by his migration.[5]
3) It would also match with the Irish tradition, which suggests that High King Cormac mac Art (ca. 227–266), the creator of the Fianna, conquered Alba (Albany, Caledonia, Scotland) and most of Ireland (*Annals of the Four Masters*: ca.226–266, conquest of Alba in ca.240), which would therefore have taken place before the arrival of the Picts. The Irish in their turn would have exploited the destruction caused by Septimius Severus and Caracalla, and invaded Albany, but they would have lost their hold on Albany when the remaining Picts from the east reinforced them in the late 260s or 270s.
4) The date and subsequent progress of Odin's march to Saxony and Denmark would also correspond with what we know of the movements of other peoples (Vandals, Burgundians, Alamanni, Semnones, Longiones and Franks) against the western frontiers of Rome in the late 270s. According to these sources, the above-mentioned Germanic peoples invaded Gaul en masse in ca 274–276, with Probus forced to conduct a campaign against them in about 277. It is also quite likely that the arrival of Odin in Denmark led to the beginning of Saxon raids.[6]

ASC a. 449	ASC a. 547	Nennius 31	Bede (Ecc. 1.15)	Edda (Prol. 10)
	Geat	Geta,		
	Godwulf	Folegauld,		
	Finn	Finn,		
	Frithuwulf	Fredulf,		
	Frithowald	Frealof,		
Woden (i.e. Odin)	Woden (Odin)	Vuoden(i.e. Woden/Odin),	Woden (Odin)	Odin (Woden)
Wecta	Beldeg	Guechta,	Vecta	Veggdegg
Witta	Brond	Guitca,		
Wihtgils	Benoc	Cuitglis,	Victgilsus	Vitrgils
Hengist and Horsa	Aloc	Hengist and Horsa	Hengist and Horsa	Vitta Hengist
	Angenwit			
	Ingwi	(Nennius calls Geta a false		
	Esa	pagan god, which is naturally		
	Eoppa	a mistake, but it is possible		
	Ida (reigned	that he has preserved the names		
	AD 547 ff.)	of the ancestors of Odin)		

5) Most importantly, the date tallies with the ancestry given by all sources to Hengist and Horsa, leaders of the Angles, Saxons, Jutes and Frisians who arrived in Britain in the early fifth century to act as mercenaries/federates of Vortigern and the Britons. Notably, Odin was also an ancestor of Ida, the king of Northumbria.

According to Snorri, when Odin reached Saxony, he stayed there for a long time, in the course of which he conquered the surrounding land. It is quite possible that it was then that the Saxons started to raid Roman territories. He appointed his son, Veggdegg, as ruler of East Saxony. Veggdegg's son was Vitrgils, and his sons were Vitta, father of Hengest, and Sigar, father of Svedbegg/Svipdag. The above diagram summarizes the family tree of Hengist and Horsa, and shows that the evidence regarding their ancestry tallies with each other and with the dating given. Odin's second son, Beldegg/Baldr, was appointed as king of Westphalia. Baldr's son was Brand, his son Friodigar/Frodi, his son Freovin, his son Wigg and his son Gewis/Gavir. The descendants of Odin's third son, Freovin (his son was Rerir), became the ruling house of France, and from it descended the Volsungs. This is not quite as improbable as it seems to many researchers. The ruling houses of different tribes were in the habit of concluding marriages, so it is entirely plausible that the Salian Franks were ruled by descendants of Odin.

After this, Odin decided to continue his march further north and left his sons in charge of the lands he had just conquered. The first objective was Reidgotaland/Jutland. He then dispatched his son, Skjold (his son was Fridlef), over the sea. He conquered the Island of Othinsey (Odin's Island, Odense, mod. Fyn). Following this, Odin or his followers conquered Sjaelland, Skjold was appointed ruler of Denmark and his descendants became the family of Skioldungs, or alternatively Skjold became king of Sjaelland with a capital located at Hleithrar (Leire), and from there ruled the rest of Denmark. Odin continued his march to Sweden. Its king, Gylfi, surrendered without a fight and offered the newcomer whatever land

ODIN'S ODYSSEY

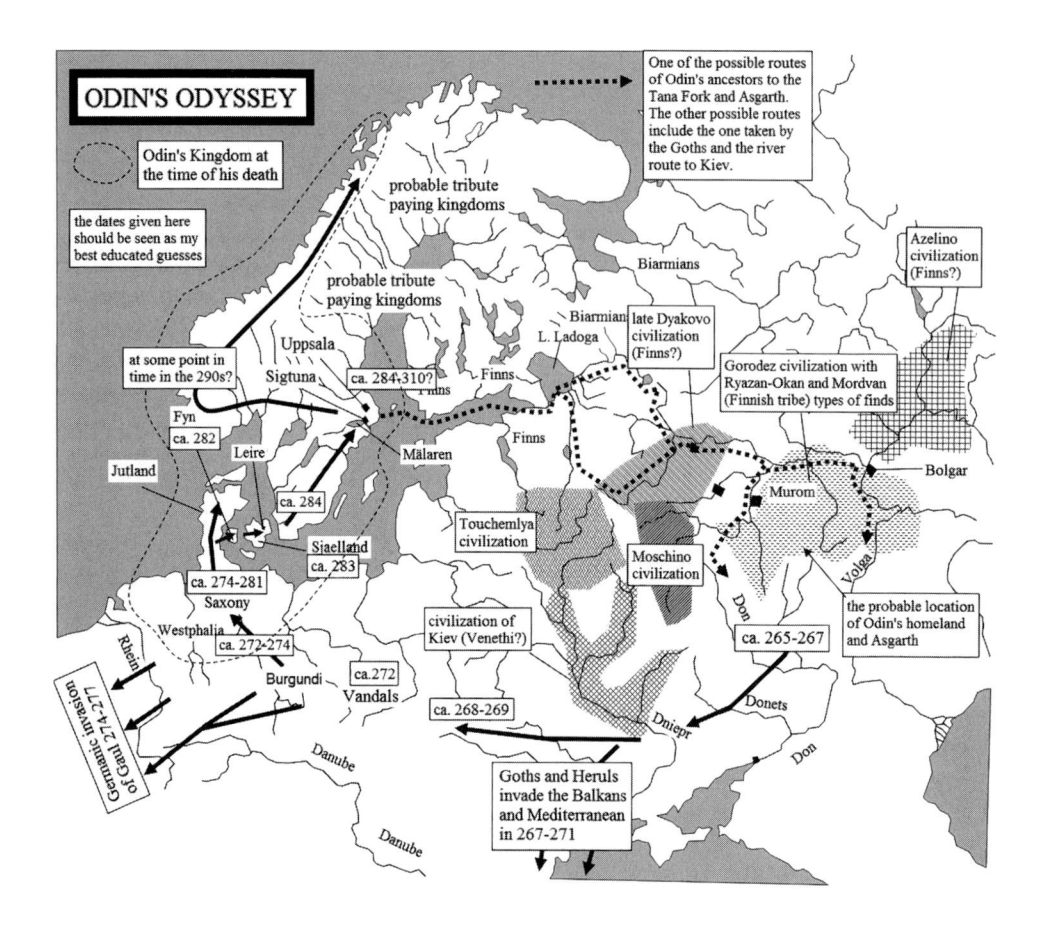

[Map showing Odin's odyssey across Europe, with Odin's Kingdom at the time of his death, probable tribute paying kingdoms, and routes marked with approximate dates. Key locations and dates include:]

- Odin's Kingdom at the time of his death
- The dates given here should be seen as my best educated guesses
- One of the possible routes of Odin's ancestors to the Tana Fork and Asgarth. The other possible routes include the one taken by the Goths and the river route to Kiev.
- probable tribute paying kingdoms
- Biarmians
- Azelino civilization (Finns?)
- at some point in time in the 290s?
- Uppsala
- Sigtuna ca. 284, 310?
- Biarmian L. Ladoga
- late Dyakovo civilization (Finns?)
- Gorodez civilization with Ryazan-Okan and Mordvan (Finnish tribe) types of finds
- Fyn ca. 282
- Leire
- Mälaren
- Finns
- Bolgar
- Jutland
- ca. 284
- Murom
- Sjaelland ca. 283
- Touchemlya civilization
- Moschino civilization
- the probable location of Odin's homeland and Asgarth
- ca. 274-281 Saxony
- Westphalia ca. 272-274
- civilization of Kiev (Venethi?)
- ca. 265-267
- Germanic invasion of Gaul 274-277
- Burgundi ca. 272
- Vandals
- ca. 268-269
- Goths and Heruls invade the Balkans and Mediterranean in 267-271
- Danube, Dniepr, Don, Donets, Volga

he chose. Odin settled at Sigtunir in the Mälaren district of Sweden, close to or at modern Sigtuna. His followers were settled in the surrounding districts. It is possible that Odin's journey to Sweden resembled that of some of the Heruls back to Sweden which is described by the sixth-century author Procopius.

According to Snorri, Odin continued his campaign to the north facing the sea and his son, Saeming (do the Sami/Saami get their name from him?), became the king of Norway, with the kings and nobles of Norway descending from him. Saxo includes an account which details the adulterous behaviour of Odin's wife, Frigg, with another man, as a result of which Odin decided to leave Sweden for a while. Could the Norwegian campaign be the result of this? Odin had children by other women, but it was certainly not acceptable for his wife to have affairs. Odin returned when the queen died. In the meantime, however, another man had assumed the godly position of Odin in the Mälaren region, but when Odin returned this man fled to Denmark, where he was killed. According to Snorri, Odin had kept his son, Yngvi, beside him, and it was from him that the royal family of Sweden, the Ynglings, descended.

The *Saga of Ynglings* claims that Odin was able to scare his enemies with the use of unarmoured berserks. We know that practically all Indo-European people had their own versions of berserker rage and/or fighting naked, but could it be that the berserker rage of the Scandinavian Viking warriors originated in the Celtic traditions brought there by Odin? What is certain is that Odin and his followers and descendants were duly worshipped as gods, just like Augustus was, and that he became to be associated with Woden. The inclusion of magic and sorcery should not blind us to the fact that some real events lay behind these stories. These men and women were not gods, but real people who acted as priest rulers and gods to their followers, just as the *Yngliga Saga* describes them.

Top: Art works found at Torslunda (source: Maailman historia). Top right: This illustration shows berserker warriors. The man on the left is Odin guiding the "wolfman". The man on the right dons a wolf skin and acts as a "shape changer" wolfman.

Unarmoured germanic warriors and Berserks

The stories of the *Yngliga Saga* and *Edda* should be interpreted as sources of real historical events, just like the stories of the *Bible* (the *New Testament* included) or Classical narrative histories. The fact that the locals started to worship these men as gods doesn't make the stories any more unbelievable. Odin was eventually burned on a pyre, like any mortal ruler in the North. He was certainly flesh and blood, even if he managed to convince his superstitious followers that if they died in battle they could join him in Valhalla. It was Frey, the grandson of Odin, who created a temple for Odin at Uppsala and ordered that all tribute to himself and Odin were to be sent there.

The following illustrations of the tombs of Odin, Frej and Thor in Uppsala show that we should pay a lot more attention to what the sources state. These were actual men and not some mythical gods from the past. The tombs in question are now dated to the sixth century, but there are earlier ones in the area too.

The name of Odin should be added to the list of great captains of all ages. His greatest gift was to convince his followers that he was a living god. It was thanks to

Fig.34

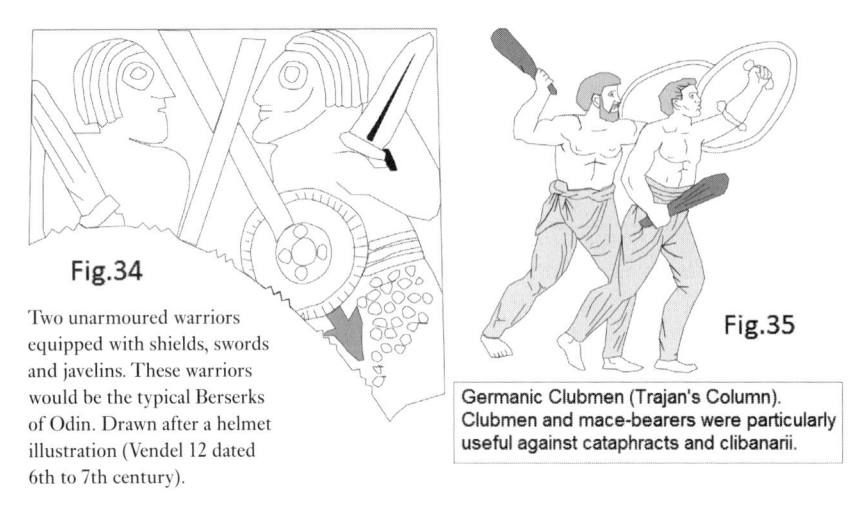

Two unarmoured warriors equipped with shields, swords and javelins. These warriors would be the typical Berserks of Odin. Drawn after a helmet illustration (Vendel 12 dated 6th to 7th century).

Fig.35

Germanic Clubmen (Trajan's Column). Clubmen and mace-bearers were particularly useful against cataphracts and clibanarii.

Left: Odin's Berserks
According to *Yngliga Saga* 6, Odin's men fought without coats of mail and behaved like mad dogs or wolves, and bit their shields in their berserker rage. The reconstructions on the left are based on the Vendel works of art and on the descriptions in the sagas. For further information regarding the berserks in Indo-European culture and among the Scandinavians, see: Michael P. Speidel, *Ancient Germanic Warriors* (London 2004); Vincent Samson, *Les Berserkir* (Paris 2011).

this that his warriors fought like madmen to gain a seat in Valhalla. It is not known whether Odin's followers also used hallucinogenic mushrooms or other foods, together with ale or mead, to help them to get into the right state of mind, like the later Vikings, or hashish, like the later Medieval Muslim 'Assassins'. There have

Odin the Man 225

View of the tombs of Odin, Frej, and Thor in Uppsala ca. 1874

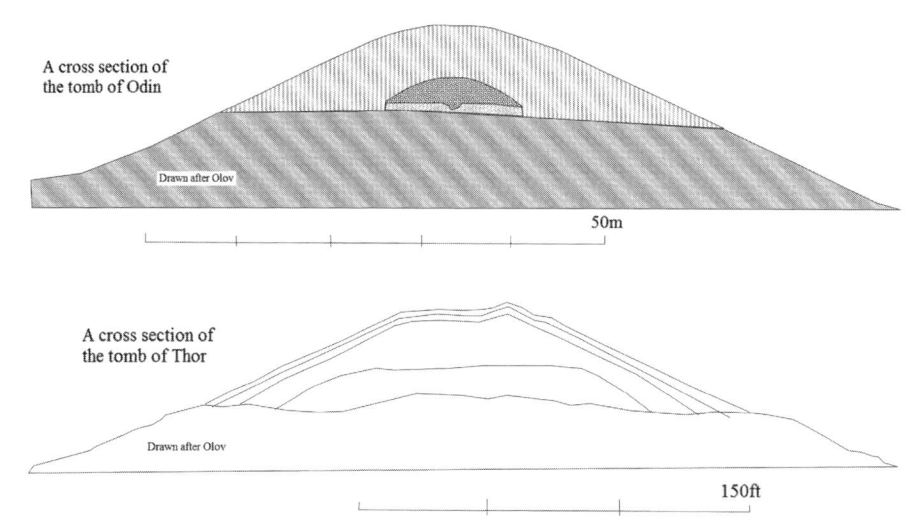

Odin's Tomb   Frej's Tomb   Thor's Tomb

A cross section of the tomb of Odin

Drawn after Olov

50m

A cross section of the tomb of Thor

Drawn after Olov

150ft

always been people who are ready to follow the prophecies of charismatic leaders, and some of these have been lifted to the status of gods. That is no mean feat. It requires great communication skills and a plentiful supply of superstitious people, the latter of which are always available. It is no wonder that the word Odin meant, in Old Norse, mad, furious, violent, wit, intelligence and poetry. It is probable that Odin's name came to signify these things, rather than that he took the name because of its significance. It should be noted that higher education does not vaccinate a person against superstitions, as testified by the great numbers of believers in New Age theories and the somewhat smaller numbers of occultists in universities. So Odin was a man of flesh and blood, not a god, even if he was certainly among the greatest warriors of all ages.

Odin's great successes as a military leader have had far-reaching and very unwelcome consequences in modern times. As a result of nineteenth-century romanticism and the rise of German nationalism, Odin/Woden and Valhalla became symbols of the new united Germany. It was thanks to this that most of the

Viking era work of art depicting Odin with his eight legged Sleipnir horse. Below a Viking ship. Photograph by author, Historiska Museet, Stockholm.

high-ranking members of the National Socialist Party of Nazi Germany saw the mysticism of these symbols as part of their national identity. One can therefore say with some justification that Odin contributed indirectly to the rise of the Nazis in Germany, which in turn resulted in the Holocaust and death of millions of innocent people. It should be stressed that Odin was not responsible for the misuse of his identity, even if his inheritance was certainly martial and bloody in content. The Nazis just stole the image of Odin for their own use, just like they stole the swastika and the Roman salute.[7] The association between Odin/Woden/Valhalla and far-right groups has persisted up to our own day, and it is high time to demonstrate to members of such extreme groups[8] that their beliefs are based on mistakes perpetuated by historians who have failed to rely on what the sources actually state.

In addition to the use of the berserks as holy warriors, it is probable that Odin also invented the rhomboid *svinfylking*/boar's head array, as stated by Saxo, one form of scissors array against it and possibly also the use of reserves in naval combat (see Introduction).[9] The scissors counter-tactic and the use of the reserves were obviously invented and reinvented separately by many peoples and cultures at different times, but it is entirely possible that it would have been Odin who brought these inventions to Scandinavia or reintroduced them. Since we know that Odin lived east of the Don, he would have been in contact with the Parthians and Armenians, who employed the rhomboid cavalry formations.[10] It would not have been too difficult for Odin to copy the same idea for his infantry formations. Saxo (7. 248ff.) claims that it was Odin who advised different individuals how to organize the wedge and organize a naval battle formation with a reserve, and also advised how to organize the scissors formation against the wedge. It has been far more typical to claim that the *svinfylking* cannot have been invented by the Norse or Odin, but would have been copied from the Roman fourth- or fifth-century *caput porcinum* formation, as Mark Harrison does (pp.96–97) in an otherwise good study of the Viking Hersir. I believe it was the other way around, that the Romans would have copied this array from the Germans. Why else would the Romans have suddenly started to give the *cuneus* a Germanic name? Even more importantly, the rhomboid *svinfylking/caput porci/caput porcinum* formation does not resemble the traditional Greco-Roman phalangial wedge (*cuneus/embolon/embolos*). Vegetius' reference (3.17–18) to the use of reserves in the forming of the *caput porcinum* suggests that its shape may have been the otherwise unattested infantry rhombus, in which the reserves formed the rear.

Yngliga Saga 7 associated Odin also with a ship called *Skítblathnir*, with which he sailed over the seas during his conquests. The *Saga* also claims that it could be folded like a cloth. I would suggest that it is probable that there indeed existed a special ship which Odin used, just like other heroes of the sagas used their own special ships. I would also suggest that it is very probable that the folding of the ship refers to a real feature of the ship, namely that it could be taken apart and reassembled, like those Roman vessels that their armies carried on carts and wagons for use whenever they faced water obstacles. This 'miraculous' ability would have caused the legend of folding like a cloth.

It is to be noted that the fourth successor of Odin, Sveigthir (*Yngliga Saga* 12), reputedly wanted to find the god Home and Odin the Old (Odin the Vana?). He travelled to the land of the Turks (i.e. the Steppes east of the Don) and Svithjoth the Great (the land of the Swedes east of the Don). He there met many kinsmen, as one would expect. It is perhaps not a coincidence that the Nordic Heruls migrated close to this area. One may assume that the Goths, Heruls and Odin's people had all migrated to this area, possibly at the same time, or that the former followed in the footsteps of the latter when news of their successes travelled back north. A place called Vanaland (Vana Land, i.e. Old Land?) was also located somewhere in the east, where the king married a woman called Vana (Old), with whom he begat a son called Vanlandi (Old-Landic?). The close contacts between the peoples of this area are also apparent from the fact that Vanlandi (*Yngliga Saga* 13) was subsequently invited to spend a winter in Finnland with Snaer (Snow) the Old (note the possible connection with Vana and Vanaland) for the purpose of marrying Snaer's daughter, Drifa (Snowdrift). Drifa gave birth to a son, Visbur, but Vanlandi returned to Uppsala and did not go back, with the result that the *Saga* claims that a Finnish sorceress caused Vanlandi to wish to return to Finnland, causing him to die in sleep when Vanlandi's followers prevented this. A more likely explanation is that the 'Finns' poisoned Vanlandi. He died in his bed when suffering from spasms. He was succeeded by Visbur, the son of Drifa. It is very probable that the ruling classes of the Finnish tribes were somehow related to the other ruling classes of the Baltic region. There exists considerable probability that Finland was ruled by a Germanic group (note the DNA of the males) that had close contacts with the Swedes of the Mälaren region, and that this group became 'Finlandized' through their mother language. It is therefore quite possible that Finland, and most of modern Russia and Ukraine, at this time already belonged to Greater Sweden – and we should not forget that the Goths were also originally from Sweden. Sweden was indeed the womb of nations at that time, and Odin was just one of the men whose ancestors had come from there and who then returned.

The probable Finnish connection in the context of Sveigthir's travel to Tana Fork (god Home), land of Odin the Old, together with his son's exploits, suggests the possibility that the ancestors of Odin's folk had travelled there through Lake Ladoga (Laatokka), and from there through the river network to the region between the Don and Volga. It is in fact highly likely that the so-called Gorodez civilization is the homeland of Odin, and that one of its ritual centres (possible locations include Murom and Bolgar) was the capital, Asgarth. Similarly, it is very likely that one of the neighbouring civilizations, the late Dyakovo or Moschino civilizations, was the so-called Vanaland. The late Dyakovo civilization is the likelier, because Sveigthir married Vana when he was returning to Uppsala.

Appendix IV

Saint Patrick and the 'Spiritual' Conquest of Ireland[1]

Saint Patrick (Patricius) was a native of Britain. His father, Calpurnius (Cualfarnus), was a decurion and deacon of the village of Bannaventa/ Banavem Taberniae (Bannavem Thaburinde), otherwise called Ventre (Venta?),[2] while his mother's name was Concessa. His grandfather, Potitus, was a presbyter, which means that he belonged to a Christian family. In short, St Patrick belonged to the landed gentry of Roman Britain.

However, at the tender age of 16, he, together with thousands of others, was captured by Irish ('Scottish') pirates. According to St Patrick, it was thanks to this that he lacked proper training in Latin and other necessary skills such as literacy in the same language, but he was able to rectify this in older age. This means that St Patrick's native language was Celtic and that the local aristocracy was only partially Romanized, despite St Patrick's claims to the contrary. Therefore, it is possible that he descended from the Dessi, who emigrated from Ireland to South Wales in the third century, or from other Irish who settled in Somerset, Devon and Cornwall.

St Patrick spent the following six years as a goat herder of a chieftain called Miliucc in Ulidia (north-east Ireland). The young Patrick sought solace from Christianity, and it was this that kept him sane during his period in slavery. A dream then prompted Patrick to flee. After having travelled for about 200 Roman miles (ca 298km), he found a port and a foreign ship about to leave. It is unfortunate that we do not know the nationality of the sailors – all that we know is that the men were heathen and that the cargo consisted of dogs (probably Irish wolfhounds, as stated by Bury). The shipmaster refused to take Patrick on board, but then one of the crew told him to join them. Patrick, in his *Confessio*, claims that he refused to be intimate with the men ('to suck their breasts'), but the circumstances suggest the opposite was true. The sailors appear to have taken Patrick on board to act as their sex slave. Patrick's own *Confessio* suggests the same if one reads between the lines. He states that at one point during this trip he dreamed that a Satan fell upon him like a stone, so that he was unable to move his limbs, but then the rays of the rising sun awoke him and the heaviness was removed when he shouted Helias/Elias (which resembles the sun-god Helios). St Patrick calls this a nightmare, which he would remember as long as he lived. A more prosaic interpretation would be that one of the sailors raped Patrick and then left him in peace after the sun rose.

The ship reached land after three days. As noted by Bury, the location can only be Gaul. After this, the crew is claimed to have wandered in a desert for twenty-eight days, which I take to mean that they re-embarked on their ship and lost their course, rather than losing their way in Gaul. St Patrick regained his freedom after sixty days of captivity, after which he returned to Britain.[3] Tirechan's account of this stage in St Patrick's life is different, but I find Muirchú's version more reliable. His parents had in the meanwhile died, but his relatives welcomed St Patrick like a son. The whole account of St Patrick's captivity is shrouded in mystery, probably because he did not want to dwell on its details. Captivity had changed him, and St Patrick now wanted to deepen his understanding of Christian doctrine through study. Consequently, he left his relatives to travel to Rome, but stopped at Auxerre when he met its charismatic bishop, St Germanus, who became St Patrick's spiritual teacher, patron and mentor.

St Patrick spent the following years with St Germanus. Consequently, it is very likely that St Patrick accompanied St Germanus and Lupus to Britain in about 429/430, when they crushed the Pelagian heresy there and famously defeated the Saxon and Pictish invaders near Mold in North Wales. It is therefore very probable that St Patrick was thoroughly schooled in the same arts as St Germanus, who used a combination of religious trickery (fake miracles) and military action to convince his followers and enemies of an intended outcome.

In 430 (this is likelier) or 431, in response to the situation in Britain and Ireland, Pope Celestinus dispatched Palladius to Ireland to be its bishop. It is very difficult to see how Palladius could have accomplished his mission of converting pagan warlords without the threat of military force. Palladius was presumably a member of the Gallic Palladii noble family, which produced several high-ranking and important figures at this time, and some of the forces accompanying him undoubtedly consisted of his private military retinue. It is very probable that the appointment of Palladius was done as a result of St Germanus' advice. It is also highly likely that Palladius had accompanied St Germanus to Britain in 429/430, because Palladius is known to have fought against the Pelagian heresy in Britain (Bury).

Palladius and his entourage, which included Augustine and Benedict (and a significant number of soldiers not mentioned by the sources), sailed to Ireland in about 430. His mission was to ensure the orthodoxy of the Irish Christians, spread the Faith and secure allies for Rome. Palladius seems to have landed in Leinster (according to Bury), which was apparently usually allied with the Britons thanks to their tribal connections with the Irish settlers of Wales and Cornwall. On the basis of subsequent events, it is almost certain that the Leinstermen and their king were Christians and that they acted as allies of Rome against the pagans of Irish High King Loegaire/Loigaire. Palladius was unwilling to linger in the wilderness that was Ireland, starting his return voyage the next year. According to Muirchú and Nennius, Palladius crossed the sea and died in British territory in the land of the Picts. It is possible that Bury is correct in suggesting that since Palladius had sailed

Saint Patrick and the 'Spiritual' Conquest of Ireland   231

to the lands of the Picts, it is likely that Palladius died in Ulidia, but in light of the extant evidence it is still safest to think that Palladius would have continued his journey from Ulidia to Britain. Ulidia had a population of Picts and was the second place visited by St Patrick in the footsteps of his predecessor.

According to Muirchú's account, St Patrick wished to convert the Irish, as a result of which St Germanus dispatched him to Ireland. This probably happened in 431 (Bede) rather than 432 (*Irish Annals*), as usually suggested. Since St Germanus refused to consecrate St Patrick as a bishop, he ordered the priest Segitius to accompany him to Ireland, where they were to join Palladius. When news of the death of Palladius reached St Patrick, he and his companions made a detour to see bishop Amathorex, who duly appointed him as Bishop of Ireland. After this, St Patrick and his companions boarded a ship to Britain and sailed from there to Ireland. Since Amathorex was the predecessor of St Germanus, it has usually been thought that this is a mistake (e.g. by Bury), and that it was St Germanus who appointed St Patrick as bishop. However, this is contradicted by St Patrick's own *Confessio* (29–32), which makes it quite clear that St Germanus refused to consecrate him as bishop. He had very good reasons for this: he knew that St Patrick was primarily motivated by revenge. It is also possible that past events, as well as lack of a proper education, affected St Germanus' decision. It is probable that the appointment of a priest to act as a companion was meant to rectify this lack of education. On the other hand, it is equally possible that Segitius was meant to act as a military advisor for St Patrick. It is quite likely that St Germanus would have schooled St Patrick in the military arts, but this would not have been a substitute for real-life military experience. We do not know what Segitius' background was, which makes it possible that he may have served in the military before becoming a priest, just like St Germanus, which would have made him an ideal companion for St Patrick in a campaign involving the use of military force.

In order to achieve his goal of converting Ireland, St Patrick certainly carried with him gold and silver to bribe key people, together with religious relics to convince the unbelievers of the supremacy of the Christian faith, as stated by Bury. Circumstantial evidence (mainly the reference to the killing of enemies) proves that St Patrick's companions included not only priests but also soldiers of some kind. It is probable that these soldiers consisted primarily of members of the military entourages/retinues (*bucellarii*) of Palladius, St Germanus and St Patrick himself. Tirechan (20/2.3, 29/2.13) notes the presence of Romans, Franks and non-Romans in the staff. This makes it practically certain that this was a Roman operation to pacify Ireland with a Crusade. The sources also make it certain that St Patrick's companions consisted of so many men that it was necessary to transport them in several ships. Consequently, St Patrick was well prepared for the task ahead.

232   Britain in the Age of Arthur

The Landing at Leinster to Secure an Alliance
St Patrick landed at the mouth of the River Dee (Vartry) in the country of the Coolenni close to the later town of Wicklow in Leinster. The location was well chosen, as Leinster possessed a significant Christian population and its king was an ally of the Romans against High King Loigaire. As noted by Bury, it is probable that it was then that St Patrick negotiated with the local king and formulated his plan to sail to the kingdom of Ulidia.

Alliance with Ulidia against Miliucc of Dal Riata
The circumstances suggest that St Patrick's goal was to secure the alliance formerly concluded by Palladius with the Pictish King Dichu of Ulidia. The aim was to threaten the high king simultaneously from the south and north. In addition to this, St Patrick had a personal motive to travel to the north, which was to exact revenge against his former master, Miliucc. The sources claim that St Patrick aimed to convert his former master, but the details provided by the sources make it certain that St Patrick's real goal was to punish him (Muirchú 11, tr. by White, p.80):

'So he sought thence the north country – to wit, and earthly and a heavenly – to that heathen man Miliucc, in whose house he had once lived in captivity, that he might deliver from captivity him whom he had formerly served as captive.'

Consequently, the ships were turned northwards. His first objective was one of the islands belonging to the Isles of the Children of Cor, a place which ever after would be known as Inis Patrick. After this, St Patrick sailed along the coast of Meath, past the mouth of the River Boyne to the coast of Conaille Muirthemni. From there he continued his journey until he reached the sea-portal/strait of Lake Strangford. The boat was rowed to the southern shore of the bay at the mouth of the Slan/Slain stream.[4]

The landing of St Patrick and his retinue was observed by a swineherd of King Dichu. The swineherd assumed that the men were thieves and robbers, which proves beyond any reasonable doubt that St Patrick's companions were armed. The man fled from the scene and told Dichu that pirates had landed. According to Muirchú (11, tr. by White, pp.80–81): 'the Swineherd [porcinarius] brought him [Dichu] upon them without their being aware of it. Now he had purposed in his heart to slay them; but when he beheld the countenance of St Patrick, the Lord turned his thought to good. And Patrick preached the faith to him; and there he believed in Patrick before any one else did; and the Saint rested with him not many days. But wishing to go with all speed to visit the aforesaid Miliucc, and bring him his ransom, and thus convert him to the faith of Christ, he left his ship in charge of Dichu, and began a land journey into the country of the Cruidneni and he reached Mount Mis.'

It is unfortunate that the account leaves out the number of followers accompanying St Patrick, but on the basis of the success he had he must have had significant numbers of armed followers with him. If he used a Roman ship, as is

Saint Patrick and the 'Spiritual' Conquest of Ireland   233

The first movements of St. Patrick

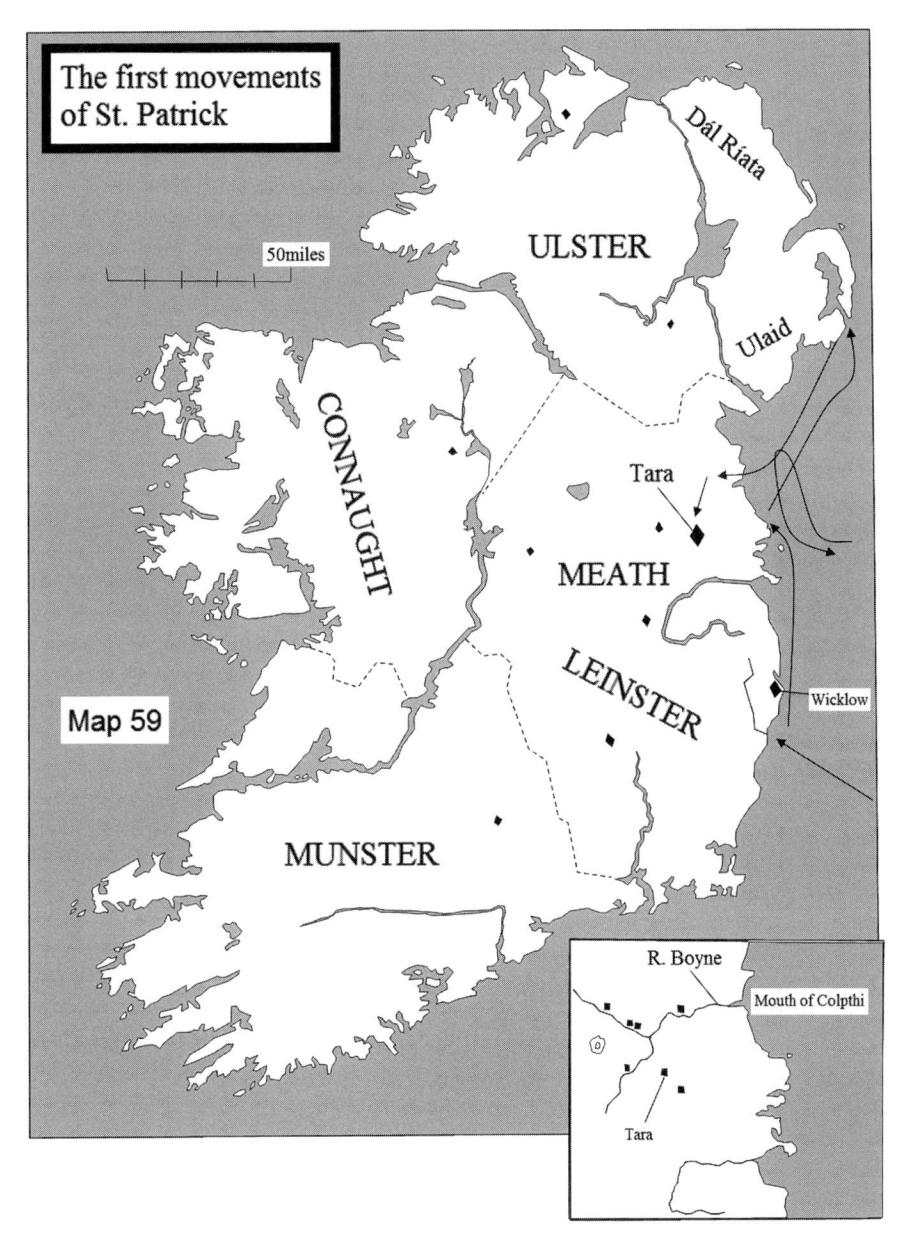

Map 59

likely because he arrived from Britain, he could have had between seventy and 100 followers in a single ship, but since it is probable that St Patrick's officers had their own ships, and that local Irish allies also contributed men to the mission, it is very likely that the actual numbers would have been considerably greater, perhaps in the neighbourhood of at least 300–500 men. It is more than likely that Dichu was

234   Britain in the Age of Arthur

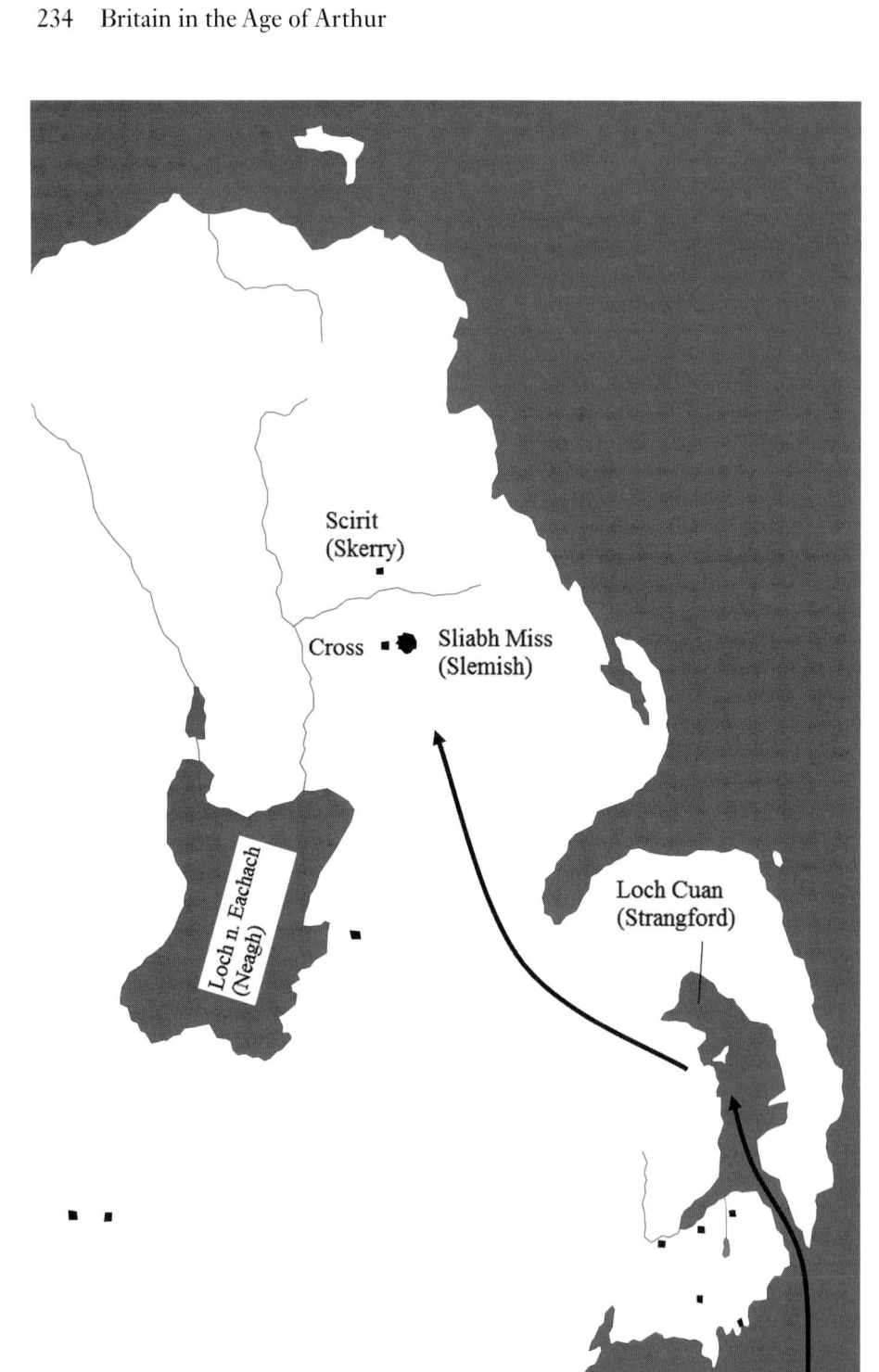

Saint Patrick and the 'Spiritual' Conquest of Ireland 235

already allied with the Romans, and that it was thanks to this that he did not attack Patrick and his retinue – the other alternative being that St Patrick had so large a following that Dichu chose to submit rather than attempt to attack by ambush with too few men.

Muirchú (12, tr. by White, pp.81–82, with my comments in parentheses) continues: 'Now when Miliucc heard that his slave was coming to see him, to the end that he should, at the close of his life, adopt, as it were by force [*i.e. St. Patrick possessed the means to force Miliucc to follow his will, which should be interpreted that St Patrick had a military retinue to back up his words, consisting of his own retinue and forces provided by Dichu and the king of Leinster. St Patrick would have needed enough men to defeat at least 700 warriors, which was the average military strength of a typical Irish king*], a religion which he disliked, … lest he should be in subjection to a slave, and that he … should lord it over him, he committed himself to the flames, at the instigation of the devil and of his own accord. [*According to Bury, p.122, Gosact, the son of Miliucc, was ordained as a priest of the church of Cell Raithin in Granard by St Patrick, which to me suggests the possibility that St Patrick may have captured Gosact first and then forced his father to commit suicide. This would have been a sound military tactic, and certainly not the only underhand ploy used by St Patrick to further the cause of the Catholic Church in Ireland.*] Having collected around him every article in his property, he was burnt up in the house in which he had lived as king. Now St Patrick was standing in the aforesaid place on the southern side of Mount Mis [*St Patrick had occupied the highest strategic locale and had thereby gained an advantageous position for his forces*], where, coming with such gracious purpose [!], … he beheld the burning of the king … and said, God knoweth; – none of his sons shall sit as king upon the throne of his kingdom from generation to generation; moreover his seed shall be in servitude evermore. [*This should not be seen as a prediction, but as a political move by St Patrick, who clearly took captive the entire family of Miliucc and later ordained his son, Gosact, as a priest and thereby made him a slave of Christ. If Gosact was the only descendant to survive Milucc, this meant that Miliucc's bloodline also ended with Gosact – a horrible revenge indeed.*] Having said this, he prayed and armed himself with the sign of the cross; and quickly bent his steps to the country of the Ulaid, by the same way that he had come, and arrived again at the Plain of Inis, to Dichu; and there he stayed many days; and went around the whole countryside, and chose clergymen …; and there the faith began to grow.'

While it is clear that the principal reason for the destruction of Miliucc was personal, it probably also had a positive political and military outcome. The revenge proved that St Patrick was more powerful than his former master, and proved that he possessed the military means to exact revenge against anyone who dared oppose him and his religion. It is also probable that this raid deep into Dal Riata (and Airgialla/Airthir?) secured the domains of Dichu from raids from that quarter, but it is important to note that Dal Riata of the Scots was not conquered for Christ at this time and that St Patrick's operations were directed to securing the territory of Dichu and its alliance against High King Loegaire. After this, St Patrick was ready to make his move against the high king of Ireland, whose territories were now placed between a hammer (Leinster) and anvil (Dichu). St Patrick's – or his advisors' – plan was not based on conventional warfare but on the use of a surgical strike against the very heart of the enemy kingdom. Before this, he still had one important thing to do, which was the securing of Dichu's territory for the Church. With this in mind, St Patrick travelled around the countryside and chose priests for each district and village to spread the word of God.

The Paschal Human Sacrifice for God (Muirchú 14ff.) in 432 or 433
St Patrick's next object was to strike at the very heart of Irish pagan worship and earthly power. The pagan kings, satraps, *duces*, *principes* and *optimates* of the people, together with the magi, enchanters and augurs, assembled every year at the town of Temoria/Tara to celebrate a heathen feast in the presence of High King Loegaire during the Christian/Jewish Paschal/Passover. During that night, the high king would light a fire before anyone else – it was forbidden to kindle a fire before this. St Patrick's plan was to exploit this. According to Muirchú, St Patrick sailed in one ship to the harbour of the mouth of the Colpdi/Colphti, left the ship there, and then marched on foot to the great plain of the chief kingdom of Ireland, where the greatest and holiest heathen celebration was to take place. St Patrick and his retinue reached The Graves of the Men of Fecc/Fiacc in the evening. Subsequent events make it clear that St Patrick's companions cannot have consisted only of men who could have been carried on one ship, but must have included significant numbers of followers carried by several ships. The Irish graves were quite unlike our modern ones. These graves were really fortresses consisting of moats, ditches and dirt walls that were dug up by large numbers of slaves at the behest of their lords, in this case by the slaves of Feccol Ferchertni, one of the nine great prophets of Breg. St Patrick's forces were undoubtedly outnumbered by the military forces of the various kings and nobles, and as infantry were also in need of a safe location for battle.

St Patrick lit a fire, which shone bright in the dead of night for all in the plain to see. When this was observed from Tara, the king asked for advice. The magicians stated that unless the fire was immediately extinguished, it would shine forever. Loigaire yoked nine chariots and took two magicians to serve as advisors. It is unlikely that the nine chariots would have represented the entire armed strength accompanying the king when he faced a revolt, so we should consider them to represent nine leaders of men and their servants, in addition to which there would have been footmen accompanying their leaders. When the men reached the graves, the leaders dismounted and sat just outside the enclosure, ordering those inside to demonstrate their obedience and worship the king. According to Muirchú, St Patrick came to the chariots singing a verse of the Psalmist, but only one of the Irish rose to meet him. This man was Ercc, the son of Daig; St Patrick blessed him and he became a Christian. This must represent the desertion of one of the Irish leaders and his men to the Christians, and must also have been prearranged to demoralize the Irish leadership.

This desertion caused the Irish leadership to begin to parley with one another, until finally one of the magicians called Lochru started to shout insults. Muirchú claims that St Patrick gave the magician a stern look and asked God to kill him; the blasphemer was lifted into the air and then fell head-first on a rock so that his skull broke into pieces. The heathen Irish, astonished, panicked. A more prosaic version of events would be that one of St Patrick's followers grasped the magician and hit his head on the rock.

This enraged the king and his people (Muirchú 18), and he ordered his men to apprehend St Patrick. The heathens rushed at St Patrick, but according to Muirchú, he rose up and said with a clear voice (tr. by White, p.87): 'Let God arise, and let his enemies be scattered: let them also that hate him flee before him.' Muirchú adds (tr. by White, p.87, with my comments inside parentheses): 'And straightaway darkness came down [probably means that Patrick's men shot a volley of arrows from the parapet], and a certain commotion arose [the men engaged each other in hand-to-hand combat with spears and swords], and ungodly men fought among themselves [Loegaire's followers fought against the deserters serving under Ercc], one rising up against another, and there was a great earthquake, "and He bound the axles of their chariots, and drove them with violence", and they rushed in headlong flight – both chariots and horses – over the level ground of the great plain, till at last only a few of them escaped half alive to the mountain of Monduirn; and, at the curse of Patrick, seven times seven men were laid low [the figure of forty-nine dead is likely to be an underestimation] by this stroke in the presence of the king and his elders, until there remained only himself and his wife and two others of his companions; and they were sore afraid. So the queen approached Patrick … And the king, compelled by fear, came and knelt before the Saint, and feigned worship Him whom he did not wish to worship. [Contrary to common opinion among researchers, there is no reason to suspect that the king converted now out of fear to save his life; he did not remain a Christian, but apostated, as we shall see.]'

The details in Muirchú make it quite obvious that St Patrick was leading a force of warriors which he had placed in an easily defended location, from which they were able to surprise and defeat the Irish warriors with a single charge. The desertion of Ercc sealed the fate of the Irish army, and must have been prearranged. According to Muirchú, after he had been released, the king made one last attempt to kill St Patrick. He asked St Patrick to come to him, but St Patrick was not fooled. He took eight men and a boy, and went to the king. When this attempt failed, the king returned to Tara; St Patrick followed him the following morning.

The Massacre at Tara and the surrender of the Irish Leadership in 432 or 433
The king and the other kings, princes and magicians were all gathered in Loigaire/Loegaire's house. According to Muirchú, St Patrick entered the house with only five men, but it is unlikely that this would have been the entire armed strength accompanying him to the town. It is more than likely that he deployed the rest of his men outside the palace of Loegaire as a safety measure. Dubtach-accu-Lugir, who was accompanied by a young poet called Fiacc, the later bishop, rose up to honour St Patrick and became the next Christian king to desert Loegaire.

In this context, Muirchú describes a contest of magical tricks performed by St Patrick and magician Lucetmael, which ended in the victory of the former. It is possible that some such tricks were performed, but it is not worthwhile describing them here because none of them had any supernatural qualities, despite claims to the contrary by Muirchú. If St Patrick performed any such tricks, it is clear that they belong to the same category (skilled manipulation of the senses and use of scientific methods to create illusions) as those used by modern magicians. The result was the death of Loegaire's magician, which enraged the king. According to Muirchú 20 (tr. by White, p.91, with my comments inside parentheses): '… he [Loegaire] almost rushed upon him [St Patrick], minding to slay him: but God hindered him. For at the prayer of Patrick and at his cry, the wrath of God [St Patrick's retinue, soldiers and allies] fell upon the ungodly people, and many of them perished [this means that Patrick ordered his forces to launch a massacre of the townspeople and men present at the hall]. And St Patrick said to the king, Unless thou believest now, thou shalt die speedily, because the wrath of God [St Patrick's retinue] will fall upon thy head. And the king feared exceedingly, "and his heart was moved", and his whole city with him.'

This describes a massacre of the people by St Patrick's soldiers at the city of Tara to force the king and his people to convert immediately. The attack was a great success thanks to the desertions and casualties inflicted on the previous day. St Patrick had secured Ireland for the Romans and Christ with a single, well-planned campaign. According to Muirchú, the saint set out to baptize the king and many others besides him, and is claimed to have predicted that even if the king's reign was prolonged, none of his descendants would rule after him. However, according to Tirechan (12–15/1.12–15), Loegaire was allowed to remain pagan, in return for which he agreed to support St Patrick's converting efforts – the first objective of which was the conversion of the west of Ireland. I would suggest that Muirchú is here likely to present the more accurate version regarding the events of the initial conquest of Ireland by force. It is probable that Loegaire was indeed forced to convert at this stage, because the above account does indeed describe a violent conquest of Tara and its populace, and that Loegaire was only later – after his revolt – allowed to remain a pagan, so long as he did not attempt to prevent the conversion of the rest of the populace.

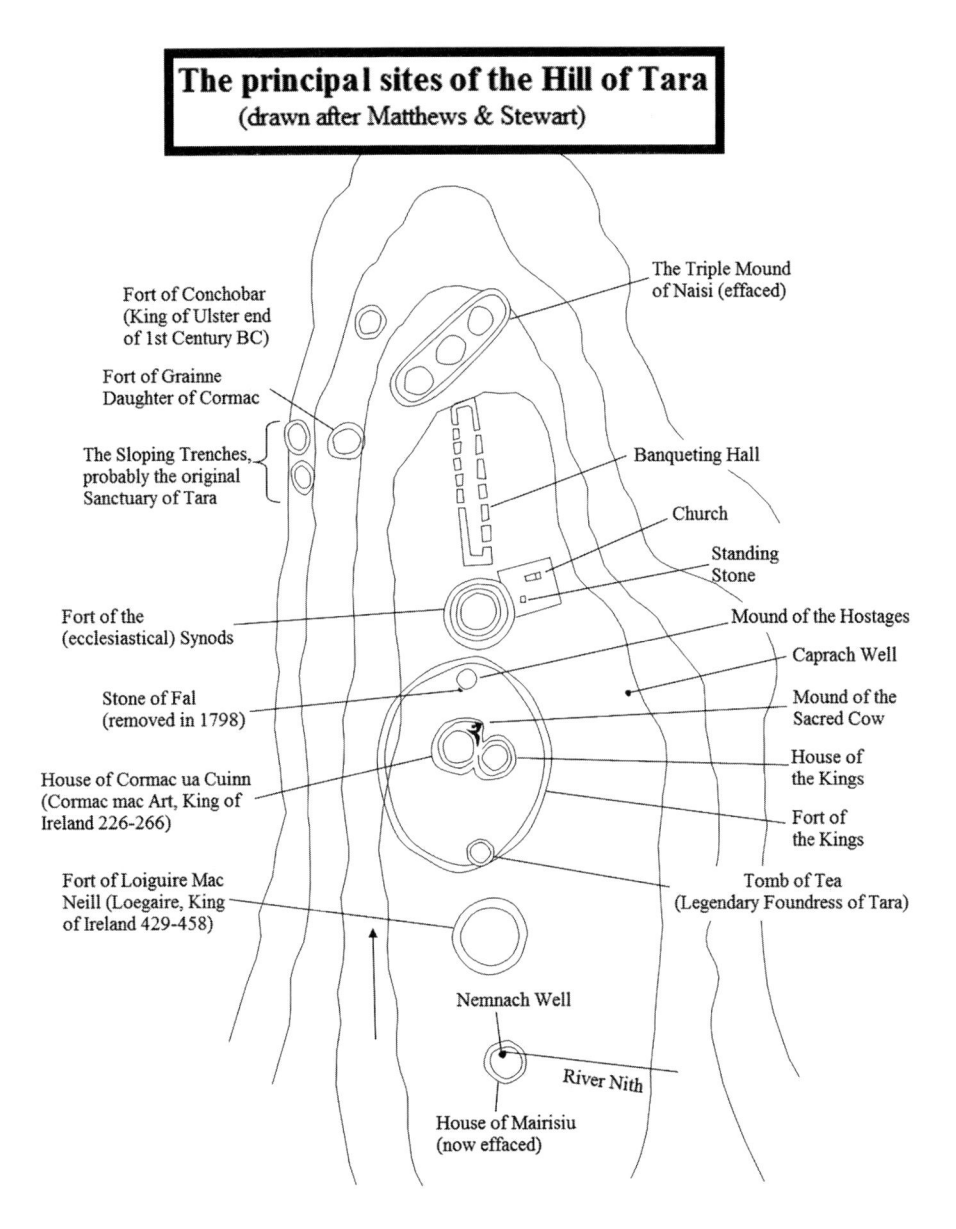

The principal sites of the Hill of Tara
(drawn after Matthews & Stewart)

- Fort of Conchobar (King of Ulster end of 1st Century BC)
- Fort of Grainne Daughter of Cormac
- The Sloping Trenches, probably the original Sanctuary of Tara
- The Triple Mound of Naisi (effaced)
- Banqueting Hall
- Church
- Standing Stone
- Fort of the (ecclesiastical) Synods
- Mound of the Hostages
- Caprach Well
- Stone of Fal (removed in 1798)
- Mound of the Sacred Cow
- House of Cormac ua Cuinn (Cormac mac Art, King of Ireland 226-266)
- House of the Kings
- Fort of the Kings
- Fort of Loiguire Mac Neill (Loegaire, King of Ireland 429-458)
- Tomb of Tea (Legendary Foundress of Tara)
- Nemnach Well
- River Nith
- House of Mairisiu (now effaced)

After the Tara incident, Muirchú gives a long and confused list of St Patrick's travels around Ireland to convert the people. Tirechan includes a similarly long list of travels and miracles performed. What is notable is that both say that St Patrick faced resistance when he sought to obtain converts and land for his churches. I believe that we should interpret most of the miracles that convinced the people to convert or hand over land, either to have resulted from the use of force, threat of violence, or fake miracles performed by the master trickster and conjuror and his staff. It is clear that it would have been impossible to force the 'wicked' ruler of Ulaid, Macc Cuil moccu Greccae, into exile to the Isle of Man (Muirchú 1.23) without the use of military force. The men of Ulaid were fierce Picts and not easy to subdue without the presence of a sizeable army to back up St Patrick's orders. The petty nature of St Patrick is also in evidence. Whenever someone showed any signs of disrespect, he punished the culprit and his family harshly. He also turned brother against brother, so that the one who obtained his support became the ruler of the area (see Muirchú 1.25ff.; Tirechan 32/2.14, 36/2.18). There is no reason to believe in any of the miracle versions (results of curses) in these cases, as usually claimed by Muirchú and Tirechan, but to suppose the use of force and/or poisons or magical tricks. One of the main results of this first phase of conversion under St Patrick was the founding of the city of Armagh in ca 444 (*Irish Annals*).

When one combines the version preserved in the *Irish Annals* with the accounts of Tirechan and Muirchú, it becomes obvious that even if St Patrick's mission was initially successful, it ran into trouble by the late 440s, when ever larger numbers of Irishmen had grown tired of St Patrick's mission and Loegaire joined them. Tirechan (18/2.1) states this quite clearly when he says that the deserters, arch-robbers and warlords of Ireland hated St Patrick's supremacy. The principal reasons would obviously have been the resistance of the druids and pagans, and the resentment felt against the forceful abduction of land for the churches and monasteries, but there is another possible, overlooked reason for the hostility. According to Tirechan (5/1.5; 43/2.25; 46/2.28), St Patrick chose and took small boys away from their families to groom them into priests and bishops. In one instance (5/1.5), Tirechan notes that the 'Saint' took a liking to a boy called Benignus, who liked to sleep with St Patrick. St Patrick took this boy away from his parents and groomed him to become his successor in the church of Armagh. Tirechan notes that when Patrick once again tried to take away the son of Mace Dregin, the father became distressed at the thought that the son would accompany St Patrick, but when St Patrick stated that the son would be entrusted to Bron (St Patrick's 'beloved' in Tirechan 46.5/2.28.5) and Olcan, the father apparently became less distressed. It is obvious that the intention of the biographers was to present these events in an innocent way and not imply anything sexual, but this does not mean that the Irish would not then have entertained any doubts (hence the distress of Mace) or that we should not have our own doubts about his behaviour. It does not really matter whether St Patrick was a paedophile gay who loved small boys (we just do not know this), but he might have seemed as such to all those who saw him surrounded by small boys, some of whom also slept with him?[5] What is certain is that there must have been at least two reasons for St Patrick's decision to take these boys away from their parents: 1) they could be used as hostages; 2) thanks to their youth, they could also be fully indoctrinated in the Christian faith. It is up to every reader to decide for themselves whether he also had other motives.

Saint Patrick and the 'Spiritual' Conquest of Ireland 241

According to the *Irish Annals*, the Irish celebrated the Christian Easter on 24 April 451 (Celtic Easter was 1 April). According to the same source (ca.452–454), this was followed by a war between the Leinstermen and Loegaire and the celebration of the Feast of Tara by Loegaire in 454. I would suggest that the celebration of the Christian Easter in 451 was an affront that caused the revolt of the Irish and Loegaire, and that it took place at Tara, which would have been the straw that broke the back of the camel. The slaughter of the Leinstermen by the Britons in 452 removed the last obstacle to the revolt, and Loegaire routed the Leinstermen (these were probably now federates of the Britons) again in ca.453, after which he celebrated the Feast of Tara (*Feis Temro*) at Tara in 454. It is probable that this is the revolt mentioned by Tirechan (18/2.1) against St Patrick's supremacy. St Patrick could do very little in the circumstances. It is probable that we should connect the baptism of Monesan, the daughter of some unknown king (Muirchú 1.27), and her immediate death, and the ambush of Loegaire's daughters, Ethne and Fedelm, at the well of Clébach by St Patrick and a 'holy assembly of bishops', and their baptism and immediate death, with these events (Tirechan 26/2.9). It is very likely that these actions represent the targeting of the families of the kings in revolt, in a situation in which St Patrick was unable to face Loegaire's forces in the open – why else would the daughters have died immediately after their baptism? It is probable that this type of guerrilla warfare brought the desired result. The reason for this conclusion is Tirechan's claim that St Patrick allowed Loegaire to remain a pagan in return for his protection when he converted the west of Ireland. This sort of agreement would have been out of place after the pillage of Tara, and does not fit the description of the event given by Muirchú. However, in a situation in which St Patrick lacked adequate forces to compel Loegaire, while the latter lacked the resources to crush the militant Christians, it does fit the picture. Consequently, it is probable that St Patrick managed to stabilize the situation between 454 and 457. It is unlikely that this would have happened in 458 or later, because the Leinstermen defeated and captured Loegaire in 458 (*Irish Annals*), and even more so if St Patrick died in 457, as suggested by one of the dates given by the *Annals*. The Leinstermen set Loegaire free in return for swearing on oath by the sun and wind that he would release them from cattle-tribute. On the basis of Geoffrey of Monmouth's account, Loegaire appears to have turned against the Britons and Leinstermen, so that he broke his oath, and died in Wales in 462 or 463. This would have happened after the death of St Patrick, either in 457 or 461.

In sum, we should see St Patrick's actions in Ireland as representing Roman and Briton interests there. It should also be recognized that St Patrick used both peaceful and military means to obtain his objectives – he was certainly not a 'saintly man' as we would understand today. Despite the many setbacks he suffered in the 450s, he was ultimately successful, as his later false reputation so well attests.

Bibliography

Original sources available on the web:
Gildas, Gregory of Tours HF, Jordanes *Get.*, Nennius *HB*, Saxon Chronicle, Bede (Ecclesiastical History of England and Chronicle), Geoffrey of Monmouth, Gerald of Wales, St Patrick, Muirchú, Irish Annals, Annals of the Four Masters, Annals of Clonmacnoise, Annals of Ulster, Saxo Grammaticus, Snorri Sturluson, Tirechán. Most of the other sources (chronicles, annals, poems etc.) not mentioned in this list can also be accessed from the web. Good places to start seeking are the list of sources in Wikipedia together with Google Books and Internet Archive.

Secondary Sources and Translations of the Primary Sources:
Aitchison, Nick (2003), *The Picts and the Scots at War*. Stroud.
Alcock, Leslie (1971/1989), *Arthur's Britain*. London.
Appelgren Hjalmar (1891), *Suomen Muinaislinnat*. Helsinki (still the most comprehensive collection of evidence for the ancient Finnish hill forts because some of the remains have been lost since).
Ashe, G. (1981), 'A Certain Very Ancient Book'. Traces of an Arthurian Source in Geoffrey of Monmouth's *History,* in *Speculum* 56.2, pp.301–23.
—— (1985/2013), *The Discovery of King Arthur*. Stroud.
Bachrach, Bernard (1973), *A History of the Alans in the West*. Minneapolis.
Blanchet, Adrien (1906), 'Villes de la Gaule romaine aux 1er et IVe siècles de notre ère', *Comptes rendus des séances de l'Academie des Inscriptions et Belles-Lettres*, 50e année, N.3, pp.192–96.
Burne, A.H. (1950/1951/2002), *The Battlefields of England*. London.
Bury, J.B. (1905), *The Life of St. Patrick and His Place in History*. London.
—— (1902), 'Tirechán's Memoir of St. Patrick', *English Historical Review* 17.66, pp.235–67, with Supplementary Notes p.700–04.
Casey, Piter John (1993), 'The End of Fort Garrisons on Hadrian's Wall', in Vallet and Kazanski, pp.259–67.
Castleden, R. (2000), *King Arthur. The truth behind the legend*. London.
Crumlin-Pedersen, Ole (1997), 'Large and small warships of the North', *MA*, pp.184–94.
Dickinson, W. Howship (1900), *King Arthur in Cornwall*. London, New York, Bombay.
Edda (1907), *The Elder Edda of Saemund Sigfusson*, tr. by B. Thorpe, and *the Younger Edda of Snorre Sturleson*, tr. by I.A. Blackwell. London, Stockholm, Copenhagen, Berlin, New York.
Elton, Oliver (1894), *The First Nine Books of the Danish History of Saxo Grammaticus*. London.
English Heritage Website, a very useful source of reference.
Engström, Johan (1997), 'The Vendel Chieftains. A study of military tactics', *MA*, pp.248–55.
Escher, Katalin (2006), *Les Burgondes Ier-VIe siècles apr. J. –C.* Paris.

Fox, Aileen and Cyril (1958), 'Wansdyke Reconsidered', *Archaeological Review*, pp.1–48.
Franklin, Simon, and Shepard, Jonathan (1996), *The Emergence of Rus 750–1200*. Harlow.
Geoffrey of Monmouth, *The History of the Kings of Britain*, tr. and intr. by Lewis Thorpe. London (1966).
Gerald of Wales, *The Journey Through Wales/The Description of Wales*, tr. and intr. By Lewis Thorpe. London (1978). Includes selections of *De principis instructione* (1.20) and *Speculum ecclesiae* (1.8–10) dealing with the discovery of the so-called grave of Arthur and Guinevere at Glastonbury.
Grässlund, Anne-Sofie (1980), *Birka IV*. Stockholm.
Green, Alice Stopford (1925), *History of the Irish State to 1014*. London.
Hallsall, G. (2013), *Worlds of Arthur. Facts & Fictions of the Dark Ages*. Oxford.
(2003), *Warfare and Society in the Barbarian West, 450–900*. London and New York.
Härke, Heinrich (1997), 'Early Anglo-Saxon military organization: an archaeological perspective', *MA*, pp.93–101.
Harrison, Mark (1993/2002), *Anglo-Saxon Thegn AD 449–1066*. Oxford.
—— (2006), 'The Viking Hersir', *The Vikings*, pp.82–141. Oxford.
Haverfield, F. (1913), *Ancient Town-Planning*. Oxford.
Haywood, John (1991/2006), *Dark Age Naval Power. Frankish & Anglo-Saxon Seafaring Activity*, 2nd ed. Frigarth.
Hoare, F.R. (1954), *The Western Fathers*. London and New York.
Huurre, Matti (2004), *9000 vuotta Suomen esihistoriaa (9,000 years of Finnish pre-history)*. Helsinki.
The Irish Annals = I have combined all Irish Annals under one heading so that it contains the following: *Annals of the Kingdom by the Four Masters from the Earliest Period to the Year 1616*, tr. by J. O'Donovan, Vol.1, 2nd ed. Dublin (1856); *Annals of Ulster*, tr. by W.M. Hennessy, Vol.1, Dublin (1887); *Annals of Clonmacnoise,* Mageoghagan; *The Chronicle of Ireland*, 2 Vols, tr. by T.M. Charles-Edwards, Liverpool (2006). Johnson, Stephen (1973), 'A Group of Late Roman City Walls in Gallia Belgica', *Britannia* 4, pp.210–23.
Jones, A.H.M. (1964/1992), *The Later Roman Empire 284–602*. Baltimore.
Jones, M.E. (1986), 'The Historicity of the Alleluja Victory', *Albion* 18.3, pp.363–73.
Jones, W. Lewis (1914), *King Arthur in History and Legend*. Cambridge.
Joyce, P.W. (1920), *A Social History of Ancient Ireland*, 2 vols. Dublin.
Jørgensen, Anne Nørgård (1997), 'Sea defence in Denmark AD 200–1300', *MA*, pp.200–209.
Kazanski, Michel (1999), *Les Slaves. Les origines Ie – VIIe siècle après J.-C*. Paris.
Konstam, Angus, ill. Peter Dennis (2008), *British Forts in the Age of Arthur*. Oxford.
Kouznetzov, V., and Lebedynsky, I. (2005), *Les Alains*. Paris.
Lebedynsky, I. (2011), *La campagne d'Attila en Gaule*. Clermont-Ferrand.
MA = *Military Aspects of Scandinavian Society in a European Perspective AD 1–1300* (1997), eds A.N. Jørgensen and B.L. Clausen. Copenhagen.
The Mabinogion, tr. by Jeffrey Gantz. Harmondsworth (1976). For ease of presentation, I have referred in the footnotes to the page numbers of this translation rather than attempted to refer to each different story separately.
Matthews, J., and Stewart, B. (1988), *Celtic Battle Heroes*. Poole.
Matthews, William (1974), "Where was Siesia-Sessoyne", *Speculum 49.4*, 680–686.
Montelius, Oscar (1888), *The Civilization of Sweden in Heathen Times*, tr. by F.H. Woods. London and New York.
—— (1906), *Kulturgeschichte Schwedens*. Leipzig.
Morris, John (1973/2004), *The Age of Arthur*. London.

Mortimer, Paul (2011), *Woden's Warriors*. Ely, Cambs.
Muirchú (www.confessio.ie.), tr. by L. Bieler with Latin text, *Royal Irish Academy* (2011).
Myhre, Bjørn (1997), 'Boathouses and naval organization', *MA*, pp.169–83.
Näsman, Ulf (1997), 'Strategies and tactics in Migration Period defence', *MA*, pp.146–55.
Nibelungenlied, tr. by A.T. Hatto. London (1965/1969/1988).
Olausson, Michael (1997), 'Fortified manors in the Migration Period in the eastern part of central Sweden – a discussion of politics, warfare and architecture', *MA*, pp.157–68.
St Patrick, www.confessio.ie.; White (1920).
Pollington, Stephen (2nd ed., 2006), *The English Warrior from Earliest Times till 1066*. Ely, Cambs.
The Saga of King Hrolf Kraki, tr. by Jesse L. Byock. London (1998).
The Saga of the Volsungs, tr. by Jesse L. Byock. London (1990/2013).
Saxo Grammaticus, *The History of the Danes*, 2 vols, tr. Peter Fisher, ed. Hilda Ellis Davidson, comm. Fisher and Davidson. Cambridge (1979); See also Elton.
Snorri, Sturluson, *Heimskringla. History of the Kings of Norway*, tr. by L.M. Hollander. Austin (1964/2009).
—— *Edda*, tr. and ed. By Anthony Faulkes. London (1987/1995).
Snyder, C. (2000), *Exploring the World of King Arthur*. London.
Sturluson, see Snorri.
Syvänne, Ilkka (forthcoming), *Military History of Late Rome*, Vols.1–6. For detailed background information of the tactical formations described in this book, see my articles on the *academia.edu* website, *Slingshot* and *Desperta Ferro*.
—— (2004), *The Age of Hippotoxotai*. Tampere (2016) research paper "Holy War and a Place in Paradise? Development of East Roman Holy Ear from the 4th until the 11th Century", ASMEA Conference. (PowerPoint version available at academia.edu).
Thorpe, see Geoffrey.
Tirechán (www.confessio.ie), tr. by L. Bieler with Latin text. *Royal Irish Academy* (2011).
Underwood, Richard (1999/2001), *Anglo-Saxon Weapons & Warfare*. Stroud.
Yngliga Saga, see Snorri.
Vallet, F., and Kazanski, M., eds (1993), *L'armée romaine et les barbares du IIIe au VIIe siècle*. Condé-sur-Noireau.
Wagner, Paul (2002), *Pictish Warrior AD 297–841*. Oxford.
Welch, Martin G. (1997), 'The archaeological evidence for federate settlement in Britain within the fifth century', in Vallet and Kazanski, pp.269–78.
White, J.D. (1920), *St. Patrick. His Writings and Life*. London and New York (also includes also Muirchú's Life).
Wood, I. (1987), 'The Fall of the Western Empire and the End of Roman Britain', *Britannia* 18, pp.251–62.

Notes

Chapter 1
1. A case in point is the translation of the term peltasts on the basis of its original meaning in ancient Greece. For this, see my preface on the academia.edu website for my *Desperta Ferro* article dealing with Alexios Komnenos' war against the Normans. The meaning of the term changed from light-armed javelin thrower to a spearman of Iphicrates, and it finally came to mean light-armed horseman under Alexios. In addition to this, there exists the meaning of medium infantry in military treatises and specialist units of the Hellenistic era. In short, it is very dangerous to attempt to understand the meaning of the term on the basis of its original meaning without taking into account the contents, just as it would be foolish to think that American cavalry units would still use horses.
2. In this case, however, the typical Classicist has the preconceived idea borrowed from previous research that Late Roman society and barbarian societies were incapable of putting into the field large numbers of men, despite the fact that the same Classicists are quite aware that there existed cities with tens or hundreds of thousands of men in the Roman Empire. As regards the barbarian numbers, it is obvious that they could not have taken so many large fortified cities, as they did in 406–410 in Gaul, Spain and Italy, if they had armies of only 5,000–10,000 men, as sometimes suggested. The original source of this faulty approach appears to be Delbrück, and his approach has already been heavily criticized by Bernard Bachrach, Haywood (1991, p.83) and by myself in 2004 (*The Age of Hippotoxotai*), and in many other studies since.
3. It should also be stressed that some sex scandals are being covered up so that politicians and civil servants who have been implicated for example in paedophile activities simply leave their office so that a large-scale political scandal can be avoided. In some cases this is probably wise, but the little moralist within me still thinks that they should be punished properly – or considerably more harshly than the current legal system allows.
4. Note that this is the modern view. At the time, Plato's actions were not quite as unacceptable as today, and the so-called 'age of consent' was also quite a bit lower then. At the same time, it should be noted that this behaviour was also not as universally accepted in antiquity as the politically correct view would suggest. It was because of Hadrian's quite public behaviour that Antoninus Pius made pederastry illegal. Similar examples abound, if one just wants to seek them.
5. I will return to criticism of the methodology employed by ultra-conservative historians and Classicists in general in future articles and studies. I will in particular include criticism of the politically correct approach to history (this is like putting a Marxist-Leninist straightjacket on research), which limits the scope of research and the possible avenues of argument. The use of fashionable theories is also to be frowned upon, because it affects directly the way in which the sources are analyzed. It should also be noted that the bias in favour of sources written in Latin or Greek among historians of the ancient and Medieval periods often results from the fact that the historians in

question understand these languages, but not the Middle Eastern or other languages. Such historians may still use the translations, but since they do not undertand the original text, they tend to dismiss the information so they would not have to face the potential difficulty of having to rely on the accuracy of translation. This is the wrong thing to do. One should not dismiss evidence on this basis. One should either rely on the translation or learn the language. The list of ranting regarding the historian's tools of the trade will be improved upon in forthcoming books and articles.

6. I agree with Halsall and other overly sceptical historians only on one point, which is that the evidence is indeed inherently uncertain and that one cannot know with absolute and definite certainty anything that took place in Britain and Gaul during the so-called Dark Ages, thanks to the poor survival of evidence. This also means that all evidence concerning Arthur is suspect, but I still think that the case for his existence is stronger than the case that he did not exist. There is no smoke without fire! In other words, when Halsall considers all sources that mention Arthur suspect on the grounds that they mention him, the opposite could also be argued – namely that all sources that fail to mention Arthur are suspect on the grounds that they fail to mention him. Halsall and so many others fail to understand this other side of the coin. It would not be the first time in history that someone has suppressed unwelcome details if the Anglo-Saxons failed to mention their greatest opponent at a time when the Welsh saw this man as a sort of Messiah.

Chapter 2

1. In truth Constantine III; see the narrative.
2. *Aspidoforoi* = *skoutatoi* = *scutati* = *scutum*-shield-bearers (large round or oblong shields).
3. Syvänne, *MHLR* vols 1–3.
4. Syvänne, *MHLR* vols 2–3; *De rebus bellicis* 19; Ammianus 27.10.6; Pacatus 35.3.
5. For the Late Roman equipment, see *MHLR* vols. 1–4, with further references therein.
6. This chapter is based on my *MHLR* vols. 1–4, and on Aitchison and Wagner.
7. Alcock (p.327ff.) notes on the basis of the archaeological finds that the Irish did not employ the longer *spatha*, the type of weapon favoured by the Germanic peoples.
8. This chapter is based on my *The Age of Hippotoxotai* and the *MHLR* vols. 1–4. I have also found the studies of Alcock, Härke, Pollington, Gamber, Harrison and Underwood very useful, even if I disagree with them on the tactics and structure of the wedge. For those interested to learn more of the Saxons, I recommend all of these as further reading. Pollington is particularly useful for its description of the English warrior and his cultural background, and for his analysis of the weaponry (esp. pp.101–81, but additional info can be found throughout the treatise). In addition, I would recommend Paul Mortimer's *Woden's Warriors* as a very useful synthesis of the Scandinavian background of the Saxons. It also contains the best set of photographs of the equipment worn by the Scandinavians, Saxons and other Germanic peoples of the north.
9. For a discussion of the weaponry based on archaeological finds, see Pollington, Alcock (p.327ff.), Harrison, Gamber, Underwood, and Mortimer.
10. Härke, p.93ff. esp. p.99.
11. The length of the spears in the Nydam bog in Pollington, p.131.
12. *Globus* (globe) was a separate detachment of footmen or horsemen operating independently. My reconstruction (2004) of the *svinfylking* is closest to that of Davidson and Fisher (2.120–123), but many other reconstructions have also been suggested (see e.g. Underwood).

13. This same tactic was also found useful in cavalry warfare in thirteenth-century Spain, as the use of the so-called *punta* (point) formation proves. In this case, the Spaniards placed three horsemen in front, twelve in the second rank and twenty in the third, after which followed the entire throng.
14. Despite the use of *turma/turmae* and *ala/alae*, these units did not consist of horsemen.
15. The usual conclusion would be that Saxo must have used Vegetius as his source and that his information would therefore be entirely unreliable. My conclusion is the exact opposite. Why should we dismiss all extant evidence on the basis of this? This should rather be seen as proof of what I have already stated on the basis of numerous sources. The Germans had copied part of their tactical repertoire from the Romans, and vice-versa. The fact that Vegetius' treatise was so popular in the post-Roman West should be evidence enough! On top of that, we should not forget that Vegetius actually does not describe any similar rhomboidical wedge in any detail, even if it is possible to think that Vegetius' wedge with the inclusion of the reserves could be similar, but in light of the extant evidence it would rather suggest that the Romans copied the Germans. On the other hand it is possible that the Romans invented or copied the rhomboidical wedge as a result of the Marcomannic Wars. See the discussion in Syvänne (*Caracalla*) and in Appendix 3.
16. See also Vol. 1 of *Military History of Late Rome*, together with *Caracalla: A Military Life* and the forthcoming study of the age of the soldier emperors.
17. See Syvänne, *Military History of Late Rome*, Vols. 3–5.
18. The various theories regarding the author and his sources have usefully been included in the introduction of Thorpe's translation.
19. The mistakes in the dating start in the preface. Note, for example, the dating and lengths of the reigns for Jovianus, Valentianus, Grannus, Horsa, Hengist, Gurtheirno and alter Valentianus on page xl. The fact that the dates in the Annales are not reliable has, for example, caused Alcock to re-date several events.
20. I date this to an even earlier period, namely to the reigns of Caracalla, Heliogabalus and Alexander Severus. See my *Caracalla. A Military Life*.
21. Casey.
22. See also Welch, who uses archaeology to date the federate settlements in Britain to the first half of the fifth century. My own view is that there had been federate forces in Britain ever since the third century, which makes it very difficult to use certain pieces of equipment to prove the arrival of the Saxons.
23. It is also possible that Nennius or his source has confused the usurper Maximus (409–411) and Maximus (383–388) with each other, so that the rule of Vortigern would have started in about 451, but this does not tally with St Germanus' stay on the island.
24. Based on the evidence presented by Morris (p.62ff.). For the missions of Palladius and St Patrick, see Appendix 4.
25. Note e.g. Olympiodorus fr. P.27 (Blockley, ed.).
26. This list of ancestors would seem to make it possible that Hengist and Horsa could have been descendants of Odin if each of the men had begot their sons late in life. See Appendix 3.

Chapter 3

1. As regards this and the following chapters, you can find additional evidence from a different perspective in my *MHLR* vols3–5, which stick closer to the traditional interpretation, but if you want an alternative but different and still plausible

reconstruction of the events taking place in the Gallic Prefecture between 406 and 418, I recommend Matthews' excellent study of the western aristocracy (1975/1990, pp.306–28, with scattered references to the same era thereafter). It should always be kept in mind that the evidence for the period is so poor that it allows several different interpretations.
2. Drinkwater (1998), p.272 (partially after Seeck).
3. This and the following chapters are covered more fully in *MHLR* Vol. 3.
4. According to Geoffrey, Maximianus married Conan's cousin. However, it is actually quite possible that Conan's cousin was married to Constantine III. This would make Arthur related to Constantine III. However, it is still likelier that the sources have just muddled the evidence through misunderstandings when they have interpreted different texts back and forth.
5. See my biography of Caracalla, also by Pen & Sword.
6. See *MLHR* Vol. 3.
7. I do not want to make any political statements with this. I am only stating the facts, regardless of how disgusting those seem to me and the modern audience, which certainly includes most of the descendants of these settlers. I find racism in all its forms extremely sickening. As I have repeatedly stated, political correctness in the analysis of the past (and present) will only lead to a false image of reality, and if one does not recognize the problem (or problems) caused by this, one cannot solve it either – this also means various forms of racism, which cannot be solved unless the situation is assessed with open minds.
8. Geoffrey 5.15.
9. See *MHLR* Vol. 3.
10. See Syvänne, *Caracalla: A Military Life*.
11. Once again, see *MHLR* Vol. 3, this time with the PLRE.
12. It is probable that Geoffrey has actually confused the nicknames of Conan, just as he appears to have done with Arthur.
13. This is a judgment call on my part. In this case I have opted to follow the majority opinion (all of which are probably based on Gildas), even if this approach is not always correct, as I stated in the introduction. However, my judgment call is not based on the majority opinion, but on the fact that the dating of other pieces of evidence fit better the majority opinion in this case.
14. For a fuller analysis of the dates of St Germanus' trip, see Vols. 3–4 of my *Military History of Late Rome*.
15. Despite the official version of St Germanus' life, this does not meant that St Germanus would have become celibate in practice. The period sources are full of stories of lusty bishops (according to these stories, falsely accused) and it would have been quite easy for St Germanus as a bishop to organize meetings with his former wife.
16. Only a gullible person buys these stories, but unfortunately there is always a plentiful supply of those, even among the academics.
17. Based on the evidence presented by Morris (p.62ff.). See also the Appendix.
18. Ashe (2013, pp.47–48).
19. I follow here Charles-Edwards' hypothesis that there existed one original *Irish Annals*, no longer extant, that was later used as a source by the various existing *Irish Annals*. Charles-Edwards has conveniently collected these various annals together as one reconstructed *Irish Annals* (the title of his book, however, is *The Chronicle of Ireland*).

The same information can also be found in *the Annals of the Four Masters* and *Annals of Ulster*. I have grouped all of these sources together as one reference, *The Irish Annals*.
20. Notably, there was a British bishop also involved in Finland (the first Bishop of Finland) who was killed by a local pagan farmer on a frozen lake with an axe when he had spent a night in his house (had he or members of his retinue raped the wife, or just 'taxed' the house?). Whatever the bishop did, it angered the farmer when he returned home. The farmer, who was called Lalli, skied after the bishop, and when he caught up with the retinue, he used his axe to good effect. It should be noted that a very significant portion of modern Finnish historians (in my opinion the ultraconservatives) consider all legends relating to Bishop St Henry and Lalli to be fictitious because these stories are preserved in later sources. Once again, I disagree with this nihilistic approach to sources.
21. See a fuller argument regarding these numbers in my *The Age of Hippotoxotai*, MHLR vols1–4 and with the material that I have included on academia.edu. Here it suffices to note that with the claim presented by several modern historians that the barbarian armies which invaded Gaul after 406 consisted only of small numbers of warriors, they would not have been able to take the walled cities of Gaul and Spain. Even the citizen militia of a single sizeable city would have been enough to defeat them. Note for example the successful defence of the city of Arverne against the Visigoths in 471–476. See *MHLR* Vol. 4. The barbarians invaded en masse, with their families, as stated by the period sources. It is a false modern view, ultimately based on the equally false and dated theories of Delbrück, that has led most modern historians to claim the use of small numbers. The usual tendency among modern historians is to claim that when one finds a small figure for an army, this would prove the larger figures in the same or other sources incorrect. This fails to take into account that there existed and still exist small-scale operations and massive military operations, and anything in between, according to the needs.
22. A full ananlysis of the reasoning behind these conclusions can be found from volume 4, covering the fifth century, in the series *Military History of Late Rome*.
23. Clover, p.42ff.

Chapter 4
1. Geoffrey, p.6.9ff., with the sources already mentioned and summarized.
2. Lebedynsky (2011, p.43) amends Olibriones/Briones of Jordanes (formerly said to have been Roman regulars) as Bri[tt]ones, which appears a good guess.
3. What follows is my tentative reconstruction of the likely order of events and their dates, which is based on the information provided by the *Gallic Chronicle* 452, Gildas, Nennius and Geoffrey. The core account in the works of Nennius and Geoffrey is the same, which means that Geoffrey (6.7ff.) used Nennius (36ff.), Nennius' source or a source that had used as his source for the following events.
4. Note, for example, Olympiodorus fr. p.27 (Blockley, ed.).
5. It is unlikely that the Saxons could have shipped all of these to the island, even if the figure of 300,000 as such is a plausible figure for the migration of an entire tribal confederacy as a mass. It is not impossible that 300,000 Saxons (including women and children) could have arrived in stages. This is contrary to my previous view in *MHLR* Vol. 1. On the basis of the extant evidence, it is probable that a great mass of Saxons (including other tribes) migrated to Britain, but what is uncertain is how long this took and when.

6. This same phenomenon can even be seen in modern wars with modern weapons. The Finns are quite familiar with the heroic fighter called Rokka from the novel *Tuntematon Sotilas* (*Unknown Soldier*) by Väinö Linna. His character is based on the war exploits of Villiam Pylkäs, whose actions (number of killed enemies) were so incredible that the author (who knew him personally) lowered the totals for his book. Similar examples of superb individual fighters can be named for the Americans, British, Germans, Russians etc. Their exploits were often such that a single man with his weapon could be the equivalent of a whole combat division.

Chapter 5
1. Based on Geoffrey 6.1ff., with the other sources mentioned previously.
2. The dates have been obtained by dating the events on the basis of the reign of Anthemius. Readers, however, should keep in mind that these dates are only my best educated guesses, based on the very few dates that can be pinpointed.
3. See Syvänne (2004, p.194ff.).
4. See the Introduction with Aelian (Devine 47.1–4/Dain L1–4), Arrian (Technê Taktikê 11) and Syvänne (2nd partially revised version).
5. There exists a problem regarding Pascent. According to one version of Nennius, Vortigern had four sons Vortimer, Cathigirn, Faustus and Pascent – but other sources and manuscripts include variant information. See Halsall (2013, pp.211–12). I have here accepted the version according to which Pascent was the son of Vortigern and not his brother.
6. *Irish Annals*, Charles-Edwards, p.71, n.2.

Chapter 6
1. Geoffrey, 8.18ff.
2. The reference to the location of Dimilioc is based on Thorpe/Geoffrey, p.206, n.1.
3. For a different interpretation of the family tree of Aurelius Ambrosius and Arthur, see Geoffrey Monmouth/Thorpe p.214 n.1.

Chapter 7
1. Geoffrey, 9.1ff.
2. This is my educated guess based on what happened next.
3. The standard tactic was to post groups of four to five men (three to four javelin throwers and one archer) in irregular array in the woods around the army. See Syvänne (2004) for a more detailed discussion of the tactics used in the wooded terrain.
4. My reconstruction of the Battle of Mount Badon is based on Gildas, Nennius, Geoffrey of Monmouth (9.3ff.), the geography of the area near Bath and on A.H. Burne's reconstruction of the battle (pp.16–25). Burne has also adopted the view that Geoffrey of Monmouth's account of the battle should be given greater credit, but I am going even further in the rehabilitation. Bede (1.15–16) stated that the battle under Roman Aurelius Ambrosius took place 44 years after the arrival of the Anglo-Saxons in 449, which would date the battle to the year 493/4. However, this is not the only problem with the text because he also placed the event before his description of the arrival of St. Germanus in Britain in 429. The date 493/4 is too late on the basis of other evidence so this can be discounted. It is very likely that Bede's referral to 44 years comes from Gildas and is placed accidentally in the wrong context.
5. For information regarding the various theories, see Burne and Alcock.

6. In some sources, Prydwen/Pridwen is the name of Arthur's ship. Note that this is the type of shield recommended by the fourth-century *De rebus bellicis*. The reference to the shield can also be found in Gerald of Wales (*De principis instructione* 1.20), according to whom Arthur always went into battle with a shield which had a full-length portrait of Mary/Madonna on it, and that whenever he was about to fight a battle he would always kiss the feet of this image.
7. Could this Avalon be somewhere near the River Avon? My own view, however, is that the island of Avalon must be located somewhere on the shore of Bretagne/Brittany, because it is quite likely that Arthur had been given some sword by King Budicius, who brought up Aurelius Ambrosius Arthur, and it is very likely that this sword would have been forged and made by some local famous Armorican sword-maker. The connection with the Lady of the Lake may be that the sword was forged from iron lifted from the bottom of a lake, as was done for example in Iron-Age Finland. Snyder (p.82) summarizes the information regarding the sword and notes that *Caliburnus* was not the sword drawn from the stone in the legendary version, but a separate sword handed by the Lady of the Lake. According to him, the name comes from the Latin *chalybs* (steel), which means that the word translates as '[*cut*] *from steel*'.
8. The names of Arthur's weapons in the Mabinogion (p.140) are: a sword Caledvwlch (Excalibur, Caliburn, Caliburnus), spear Rhongomynyad (cutting-spear), shield Wynebgwrthucher (face of evening) and knife Carnwennan. His wife's name was Gwenhwyvar (white phantom). See Gantz/Mabinogion.
9. There is actually a superficial similarity in the number of killed in the SHA Aurelian 5.3ff. According to the SHA, before becoming emperor, Aurelian (Aurelianus) killed forty-eight men in a single day, and in the course of several days over 950 enemies, so that the boys composed a song in Aurelian's honour in which it was stated that he killed alone 1,000 enemies. On the basis of this, it would be easy for the traditional 'sober' Classicist to claim that Aurelius/Aurelianus Ambrosius' number of victims in this battle has been invented on the basis of the number killed by Emperor Aurelianus. It should be noted that this whole approach of literary borrowing is a completely false approach to the sources, because in the course of history the same things have happened repeatedly, as a result of which even word-for-word borrowing should not be seen to present suspect evidence. The borrowing in such cases was done for two purposes: firstly, the author quoted the earlier text because it was a particularly good description of what actually happened; secondly, he made this borrowing to demonstrate his learning. This faulty approach followed by the Classicists has resulted in the horrible misunderstandings regarding all extant evidence, and this concerns in particular the analysis of military treatises. Regardless, for the sake of argument I have in this footnote accepted their approach, but only to prove that Nennius and Geoffrey cannot have copied the SHA in this case. There are just too many differences for this to be the case, despite the similarity of the names. Firstly, the SHA states that Aurelian killed forty-eight in a single battle, the remainder of the over 950 being killed in the course of several days. Secondly, both Nennius and Geoffrey state that the victor of the Battle of Badon was Arthur, and not Aurelius or Aurelianus, so there should not have been any reason to bring the emperor Aurelian's figures into the account on the basis of similarity of names – it is my educated guess that we are dealing with two different Aurelianuses. In sum, there are no actual similarities.
10. This translation is in the public domain and I therefore used it. For a better translation, the reader is advised to read Thorpe. Note, however, that for an accurate reading of the

terms, one should really consult the different Latin variants of Geoffrey's text. These are nowadays readily available on the web.
11. Translation of the quote by Giles.

Chapter 8
1. Geoffrey 9.8–9. The loose dating used here shows the problems.

Chapter 9
1. See Appelgren and Appendix 1. Even though Appelgren wrote his study of ancient Finnish hill forts in 1891, it is still the most up-to-date study of its topic because many of the forts then extant have unfortunately now been lost.

Chapter 10
1. Appelgren, pp.xx–xxi; Näsman.
2. Fisher and Davidson also note that there is an inexplicable gap in Saxo's account.

Chapter 11
1. See 'A Bit of Polemics' above (chapter 1) and Ashe (1981, 2013), who names at least one additional supporter of the theory.
2. Ashe (2013, p.58) dates this campaign to have taken place at the same time as Riothamus landed, so that both armies would have cooperated, but in my opinion it is inherently likelier that Paulus' forces were the army with which Riothamus was supposed to unite, but which failed to materialize before Riothamus' defeat. Furthermore, the Romans were commanded by Paulus and not by Syagrius.

Chapter 12
1. For an analysis of whether one should locate *urbs legionis* at Chester or Caerleon, see the discussion in Alcock, p.63; Morris, p.111. I prefer Caerleon.

Chapter 13
1. The tribune in the title usually signified that the person belonged to the imperial bodyguards and had been dispatched as commander of some army or area. Such tribunes were usually members of the *protectores domestici* seconded for duty as commanders of one of the units of the *scholae*, from which such men usually progressed to even greater commands, some of which were temporary while others were permanent. The PLRE2 includes referrals to the orginal sources for each of the historically attested individuals mentioned here.
2. This person is unknown. The PLRE 2 knows Tiberianus (named on a seat in the Flavian amphitheatre at Rome in ca 476/483) and Tiberius (an *illustres* in a poem), but it is impossible to know whether either of these would have been meant. Bidimer served probably in the office of the *MVM per Gallias* in 472, but on the basis of his name he is an unlikely candidate. Consequently, the only guess one may make regarding Lucius is that he was Frollo's unknown successor, and like him he belonged to the imperial bodyguards from which he had been seconded as commander of the Roman forces in the north of Gaul.
3. The exact functions of the office of procurator for this period are not known with certainty, but it is known that one procurator was in charge of collecting rents from the whole of Italy and one in the city of Rome, and others in provinces or large imperial

estates or conglomerations of imperial estates known as *saltus*. For a fuller discussion, see A.H.M Jones (see Index *procuratores*). My own educated guess is that the procurators were officials who had extraordinary temporary powers to collect taxes and rents in the areas assigned to them.
4. The different manuscripts of Geoffrey have slightly different versions. I have here added the *catervae* from Text DE, but it is possible that the *catervae* are a mistake arising from the number 6,000, because in military theory a *caterva* consisted of 6,000 men, or that the strength of 6,000 horsemen is the result arising from the word *catervae* in the original text. If the 6,000 horsemen were deployed as *catervae* as stated by the DE, the meaning would probably be that the horsemen were deployed in small, irregularly organized units which were called *drouggoi* in Romano-Byzantine military theory, the shape of each of which was usually a wedge.
5. The use of two separate forces of cavalry ambushers was to become one of the standard practices during tenth-century Byzantium, but it was not a new invention, as the use of a similar trick by the Goths against the Emperor Decius proves. See Syvänne (2004) and Syvänne, *Decius* (available online at academia.edu).
6. The standard edition states that the Romans were arrayed as a *cuneus*, but the DE has *turmae*. In light of this, it is probable that there has occurred confusion in the transmission of the words and I have amended the text here accordingly. The *cuneus* (wedge) would have been the battle formation that one would expect to have been used by Boso to achieve the breakthrough, which means that it is possible that the attacking formation could have become confused with the defending array. Taken together, the original text could have stated that Boso attacked with a *cuneus*-wedge through the enemy *turmae*. However, since it is also quite well-known that cavalry often used the *cuneus* formation, it is possible that both sides used *cunei* so that Boso would merely have charged through one of the intervals between the *cunei* at the enemy commander. It is also possible that if Boso attacked one of the Roman *cunei* as stated by the standard edition, that the defending Roman *cuneus* just melted away when attacked and thereby opened up a route for Boso's *cuneus* to attack the Roman commander.
7. I agree with William Matthews' assessment that only Saussy would fit the information provided by Geoffrey regarding the locale of the Battle of Siesia.
8. *Porro et illi duodecimo cuneata agmina atque omnia pedestrian fecerunt, quae Romano more ad modum cunei ordinate, sex milia militum cum sescentis sexaginta sex singular omnia continebant.*
9. For a summary of the perimeters of cities in Gaul during the Roman era, see Blanchet. Note, however, that his figures for the Late Roman era are usually too small.
10. This is by far the likeliest explanation for the sudden emergence of the kingdom of Syagrius (destroyed by the king of the Salian Franks, Clovis, in 484) after a period during which other leaders are attested for the north of Gaul. See *MHLR* Vol. 4.

Chapter 14
1. Based mainly on Geoffrey 11.1ff.
2. Mordred had more men than at Camelford and therefore had a longer battle line.
3. Gerald of Wales/Thorpe, p.280ff., with Geoffrey, *Vita Merlini*.

Chapter 15
1. The following is based on Gildas; Geoffrey, *History* 8.1 ff.; ibid. *Vita Merlini*. The dates given in this chapter are uncertain.

254   Britain in the Age of Arthur

2. Gildas writes about the five tyrants of his day as if they would all be contemporary, but in my opinion it is probable that Gildas wrote only figuratively, so there are no real discrepancies between the accounts of Gildas and Geoffrey.
3. These scattered references can be easily found in the index of Thorpe's translation of Gerald.

Chapter 16
1. Historically speaking, southern Sweden was part of Denmark and its inhabitants felt themselves as Danish. Sweden conquered it from Denmark in the seventeenth century and it took a while for the people to accept this change of rule.

Appendix I
1. Among the worst exponents of the ultra-scepticist conservative school of thought (which has its roots in the Classicists school of thought) are the ultra-conservative Finnish historians of the past two generations, who have attempted to deny all credibility for the Medieval sources. These historians claim to know better than the only sources that we have of those centuries. All of the stories, poems, sagas and chronicles that describe events before the fifteenth or sixteenth centuries have supposedly invented their accounts, so that nothing can be trusted. Everything is claimed to be fiction. These same historians even go so far as to deny the existence of different Finnish tribes (Finns/Varsinais-Suomi; Hämäläiset of Häme/Tavastians of Tavastia; Karjalaiset/Carelians of Karjala/Carelia; Pohjalaiset of Pohjanmaa; Savolaiset of Savo/Savolax), which is not only proven by the sources that they dismiss, but also by archaeological evidence, which proves beyond doubt that there were concentrations of population, villages and hill forts in certain areas. It is very odd to deny the existence of Finnish tribes and tribal organizations when there exists very clear evidence for the use of organized labour to build the hill forts!
2. I use Danes here collectively to mean all the different tribes and kingdoms of modern Denmark.
3. These instances of sorcery are not really that different from the intervention of the gods in the narrative histories following the classical tradition. The omens were supposed to present the will of the gods!
4. Appelgren, p.xii ff.; Nicolle.
5. It is not necessary to claim (see Davidson and Fisher, n.80) that Saxo would have invented this name on the basis that, during the campaign of 1171, Esbjern captured a Wendish warrior (Saxo, Book XIV) bearing this name. It is entirely possible that there were several men who had the same name. Note that no one questions the existence of several Eriks, Egils and Haralds for the Vikings!
6. See my *Caracalla: A Military Life* by Pen & Sword for the use of similar tricks.
7. Once again the name Olimar has caused plenty of speculation and ridiculous claims that Saxo invented and modelled it on the basis of the name of the later Slavic leader Otimar (see Davison and Fisher, Vol. 2, pp.81–82). The most convincing one of the speculations would be to equate Olimar with Valamer/Valamir, but on balance there is no specific reason to suspect that there would have also existed a Rutenian king called Olimar.
8. Once again I see no reason to claim that Saxo would have invented these events on the basis of the fighting between Goths and Huns preserved in the Hervavar Saga, or from other sources, as claimed. See the various theories in Davidson and Fisher, Vol. 2, p.82.

9. Once again it is sheer speculation to claim that Uggerus/Ugger would be Yggr, one of the names of Odin. See the speculation in Davidson and Fisher, Vol. 2, p.84. It should also be noted that Odin was not really a god but a man who claimed to be a god, and who was believed by the masses to be a god. See Appendix 3.
10. Saxo has here misplaced the order of events before, during and after the winter, but I have restored those to their right sequence.
11. Davidson and Fisher suggest Volga, Dnieper, Don, but I believe a river route from Lake Ladoga up to the Kiev region would also fit the picture.
12. The –gard would presumably be the – grad/gorod of the Slavs.
13. Appelgren, pp.ix–x; Näsman.
14. Appelgren, pp.vi–x; Kazanski, p.51; Nossov.
15. See my Vol. 2 of *Military History of Late Rome*. It is very strange that historians in general have doubted Jordanes' claims that Hermanaric was a great conqueror, even if this is essentially also confirmed by Ammianus. This smacks of racism. Why is it so difficult to believe that Hermanaric could have forged a vast empire during his own lifetime, when no-one doubts this for the Huns or Mongols? Could it be that, after Hitler, it is very difficult to think that there could have been Germanic conquerors in the past? In truth, to do so is just another form of racism, but this time directed towards the Germanic peoples of the past. It is the historian's job to get past this kind of historical dead weight.
16. The seventh-century destruction was caused by the arrival of the so-called long *kourgan* civilization that betrays strong signs of Finnish culture mixed with Slavic and Baltic ones. The *kourgan* culture that emerged in north-western Russian during the seventh century is usually considered to reflect Finnish culture mixed with Slavic and Baltic ones, so that the Slavic one eventually became the dominant one, or that the Slavs conquered the area and then subjected the locals. The problem with this interpretation is that prior to the seventh century, the cultures in this area were not Finnish, which means that the tribes in question cannot have been Finnish and were probably Slavic. My own interpretation is that the Finns (probably Hämäläiset/Tavastians from Häme/Tavastia) conquered the territory in the seventh century and then became intermixed with the local population, with the result that they eventually adopted the Slavic tongue. This would have been followed by the usual ethnogenesis that can be found in this area. In other words, the Finnish male warriors married the local women, and their descendants became Slavs as the women taught their children the local language. This same phenomenon can be attested with the so-called Rus, who became Slavs within two to three generations. The same phenomenon also concerns modern Finland. DNA studies have demonstrated that most of the Finnish males arrived from Western Europe (from the region of Belgium), while most of the Finnish women arrived from the Urals. This suggests a conquest by some Germanic group, which had forcibly married the local Finnish women, with the natural result that all eventually became Finns. It is not without reason that most peoples call their native language their mother tongue. In male-dominated cultures, women have traditionally been in charge of teaching language skills. The movements of Goths, Heruls and Burgundians from Scandinavia to the east should also stand as further proofs of such movements of people. The Heruls maintained close contacts with Scandinavia, even up to the sixth century. This suggests close networking of peoples along the waterways from Norway and Sweden up to the River Don and Black Sea. Consequently, there were clearly several movements of people from Western Europe, Denmark and Sweden towards the east, but there were also movements of

256   Britain in the Age of Arthur

people from the east to the west. It is in light of this that one should see the account of Odin's conquests in the *Yngliga Saga* (see Snorri and Appendix 3).
17. Appelgren, pp.v–ix.; Nicolle; Kazanski; Nossov.
18. Based on Appelgren, p.xxiff.; Montelius, p.322ff.; Näsman. In the following discussion Finnmark with its Finns probably mean northern sections of Norway, Sweden, Finland, and the Kola Peninsula of Russia because the enemies are Finns and not Lapps and the campaign progressed then against Biarmia.
19. See esp. Näsman.
20. This campaign once again provides a good example of the ultra-conservative Classicists/Medievalist school of interpreting the evidence. According to Davidson and Fisher (2.89), Ludvig Daae had suggested in 1907 that this account is based on the memory of Valdemar's campaign in Norway in 1168. These kinds of claims do not really merit any comments, but I have here still felt it necessary to point out that there were also campaigns in this area during the Iron and Viking Ages, the best evidence of which are the still extant remains of hill forts and boatsheds and works of art.
21. This and the following discussion is based on my interpretation of the evidence presented by Appelgren and Huurre.
22. Could it be that Saxo has failed to distinguish the sailors and ships from each other in Latin?
23. See Vol. 3 of *Military History of Late Rome*.
24. The first time the Huns reached the Rhine region actually took place in about 384/385, when they were campaigning in the region as allies of Bauto, but in that case they did not act as an independent force. However, it is probable that the Huns would have then learnt what route to take there. See *MHLR* Vol. 2.
25. See Vols. 3–4 of *Military History of Late Rome*.
26. The *Nibelungenlied* (4) includes an alternative version. It suggests that the Burgundians conducted a pre-emptive strike under Siegfried/Sigurd against the Saxons and Danes when the Saxon King Liudeger (40,000 warriors) and the king of Denmark, Liudegast, (20,000 warriors) were planning to invade. Liudeger and Liudegast could be interpreted to mean Lyngvi, so that Lyngvi (Frothi or one of his kings?) would have attempted to punish the Burgundians for the protection that they had granted to an outlaw. However, it is still safest to connect the information in the *Saga* with that provided by Saxo, as these clearly contain less legendary material than the *Nibelungenlied*, so that the Burgundians who killed a Danish king were the sons of Gjuki/Gibica rather than Sigurd, and that they had done so as mercenaries/clients of the Huns.
27. The Varangian Guard was formed under Basil II and would therefore be a much later term for an East Roman Guard unit. During the fifth century, the guard units would have consisted primarily of the Scholae and Domestici cavalry units.

Appendix II
1. I have an MA in Finnish History and I do remember that there exist previous studies of this topic, but since this is not the topic of my research now I have chosen not to seek those out.

Appendix III
1. Could it be that Wodan/Woden had also been a mortal who had managed to convince his followers in like manner?
2. Note that the English language came from the Danish Anglo-Saxons!

3. I am purposefully using the 'f' instead of the standard 'ph' in the transliteration because in my opinion it is very strange that when the English language has the letter 'f', that we should still transliterate the Greek 'f' with the 'ph'. For the term, see 'Aelian/Byzantine Interpolation of Aelian' (Devine ed. 38.3, Dain ed. C3).
4. See e.g. SHA Gallieni 13.6ff.; Claudius 6.1ff.; Zosimus 1.40.1ff.
5. See my speculative comments regarding the later Hun Empire in *MHLR* Vol. 1., which are based on probability rather than on narrative evidence.
6. See e.g. SHA Probus 13.5ff.; Eutropius 9.17; Zosimus 1.67.1ff.; with I. Syvänne, *MHLR* Vol. 1, pp.174–75.
7. The use of the Roman salute was appropriate from the point of view of the Italian nationalists and Fascists, as it was part of their national inheritance, but its use by the German Nazis is odd, to say the least, as it was the salutation used by the enemies of the Germanic peoples!
8. The association of the 'far right' with the Nazis and Fascists is one of the greatest hoaxes (perpetuated by Leftist parties) of the twentieth century. In truth, the Nazis and Fascists were extreme versions of Socialist/Leftist movements that adopted the nationalistic ideology. In short, all of the great disasters and massacres of the twentieth century were caused by Leftist parties (Nazis and Communists). The right-wing Conservatives bear no responsibility for those, and neither do the centrist Liberals. Please note, however, that we should make a very clear distinction between the Social Democrats of Europe and the extremist Leftist movements (Nazis and Communists), because the Social Democrats were (and are) in truth their greatest ideological adversaries and therefore forces of good – at least that is my view, despite the fact that I am not a Social Democrat myself. In my opinion, we all owe a great debt of thanks to the job that Social Democrats have done for European societies in the past.
9. The other possibility is that the *caput porcinum* was invented by Septimius Severus or one of his subordinates at the same time as he adopted the unit organization visible in Vegetius and Modestus for his new Parthian legions. It is possible that Severus copied this array from the Germans, thanks to the lessons learned during the Marcomannic Wars, or that the Romans invented it by themselves and it was then copied by Odin during his trek. Another possibility is that the Germans copied the Roman organization for their own use and adopted the system for their *svinfylking* array. See the Introduction for the reasons for these speculations. I have here given my benefit of doubt to the Nordic sources, on the grounds that they credit Odin with the invention and because the infantry rhomboid and its name form no part of the Greco-Roman traditions.
10. Originally a Thessalian array that had been brought to the East by Alexander the Great. See my articles in the academia.edu website and the *Age of Hippotoxotai*.

Appendix IV
1. This chapter is based on my analysis of the sources, the most important of which are St Patrick's own writings (esp. *Confessio* and *Letter to the soldiers of Coroticus*), the *Tirechán's Memoir of St Patrick* and Muirchú's *Life of St Patrick*. My interpretation builds upon the conclusions of J.B. Bury and is therefore indebted to him, even if our interpretations differ greatly. I approach the problem from the viewpoint of military history and military probability, which changes the perspective in a very fundamental way. The references to Muirchú and Tirechan follow the one adopted by the *Royal Irish Academy* (tr. by L. Bieler, www.confessio.ie).

2. Possible candidates for Venta include Venta Silorum (Caerwent) and Venta Belgorum (Winchester). The usual candidates for Bannaventa are towns in the regions of the lower Severn or the three places named Banwen in Glamorgan.
3. The reference to St Patrick's second captivity actually refers to his stay with the crew of the ship (the first being his stay with Miliucc) and not to another capture by some other group.
4. Bury, pp.83–84.
5. It is in fact quite possible that the incident on the ship that took place in St Patrick's youth had resulted from his own sexual preferences, and that these contributed to the willingness of the Irish to rise against him, but it is impossible to know for certain whether something indecent really took place between Patrick and the boys. It is all too easy for us to jump to this conclusion on the basis of the well-publicized behaviour of some modern-day Catholic priests, but at the same time it is quite easy to see why parents back then would have jumped to the same conclusion.

Index

Adelsö, King of, 201
Administration, Administrative, 11–12, 22, 40, 63–4, 120–1, 139–40, 183
Aegidius, Roman general, father of Syagrius, 138
Aella, king, 48
Aesc, son of Horsa, adopted son of Hengist, 47–8
Aesir, people of Odin, 210, 216, 218
Aethion, Duke of Boeotia, 144
Aetius, Roman patrician, general and consul, 35, 37–8, 46, 58, 71–2, 74–7, 83, 135, 209
Agicius, *see* Aetius
Ailill Molt, Irish High-King, 119
Airgialla/Airthir, 235
Ala, alae, 14, 24, 149, 192, 247
Alamanni, Germanic tribal confederacy, 52, 55, 133, 167–8, 220
Alans/Ossetes, Sarmatian tribal confederacy, ix, 51–2, 73–5, 135, 138, 141, 242
see also Sarmatians
Alaric, Gothic king, 52
Albans, *see* St Albans
Albany, 54, 56–8, 61–2, 78, 92, 94–6, 101, 109, 113–15, 119–20, 126, 140–1, 144, 152, 156, 158, 169, 171, 179, 220
see also Scotland
Alclud, town, vii, 97, 109, 111, 113, 115, 118
Aldroenus, King of Bretagne, 58–9
Alexander Severus, emperor (222–235), 265
Alf, Danish King, *see* Aschil/Ascilus

Alf, the son of King Hjalprek of Denmark, 210
Aliduc of Tintagel, 150
Alifantinam/Ali Fatima, king of Spain, 144, 155, 159
Allies, Ally, Alliance, 16, 35, 41, 46, 56, 58, 61–2, 66–7, 78, 96, 105, 109, 115, 120, 123, 131, 133–4, 143–4, 164, 170, 176, 183, 186, 188, 206, 209, 211, 230, 232–3, 236, 238, 256
see also Federates
Allobroges, 143–4, 163–4
see also Burgundians, Burgundy
Aloc, son of Benoc, 49
Alrik, Swedish High-King, 199–200
Alzey, 211
Alvild/Alvila, Gøtar's daughter, 187
Amathorex, bishop, 231
Ambrones, a Celtic people who had joined the Cimbri and Teutones, means probably the Saxons, 56, 67, 76, 78
Ambrosius Aurelius/Aurelianus, *see* Arthur
Ambrosius Merlin, *see* Merlin
Amfippoi, two-horsed cavalry, 218
Amfistomos (double-fronted), 16
Anarauth, Consul of Salisbury, 121
Andecavi, Andegavia, Andegavians, 137, 142, 144
Angenwit, son of Aloc, 49
Angers, 131, 133, 138–9
Angles, 17, 20, 22, 38, 46–7, 57, 130, 186, 206, 221
see also Danes, Hengist, Horsa, Jutes, Saxons
Anglia, East Anglia, Middle Anglia, 47

Anglo-Saxons, Anglo-Saxon, *Anglo-Saxon Chronicle*, vii, xiii, 9, 33–8, 45–8, 58, 61, 70, 75–6, 186, 217, 243–4, 246–7, 256
  see also Angles, Saxons
Annales Cambriae, 35, 178
Annona militaris, 22
Anthemiolus, son of the emperor Anthemius, 145, 151, 168, 170
Anthemius, East Roman Praetorian Prefect, 109
Anthemius, son of Praetorian Prefect Anthemius, West Roman emperor, 35, 119, 122, 131–5, 143, 145, 150–1, 163–4, 168, 170, 182, 250
Antonine Wall, UK, 36–7, 54, 57–8, 120
Antoninus Pius, emperor, 245
Apples, island of, 178–9
  see also Avalon
Aquitania, Aquitanians, 55, 64, 133, 137
  see also Goths
Archers, archery, bow, arrow, vii–viii, 6, 18, 20–1, 23, 31, 87, 107, 141, 145, 149, 197, 202, 210, 237
Arles, 51, 54, 57, 168
Armagh, 240
Armorica, 35, 39, 47, 51–8, 71–2, 74, 77–8, 82–3, 101, 105–106, 131–5, 137, 144, 167, 170, 179, 183
  see also Bretagne
Army, Armies, 13–14, 16–19, 22–4, 30–2, 37, 40, 44, 53–4, 58–9, 65–71, 74, 76, 78–9, 84, 86–8, 90–2, 94–5, 98–9, 101–105, 107, 109–10, 112, 114–15, 118, 123, 126, 131–5, 137–8, 143–8, 150–2, 154–5, 158, 163, 165, 168–71, 173–8, 182–3, 185, 189–97, 202–203, 209, 227, 237, 240, 245, 249–50, 252
Arngrim, Swedish champion, 202
Arthgualchar, Consul of Warwick, 121
Arthur, Ambrosius Aurelius/Aurelianus, Utherpendragon, Riothamus, *Dux Bellorum*, High-King and *Augustus*,

Ambrosius Aurelianus/Aurelius, v, 11, 33, 38–9, 42–5, 47–50, 59–62, 69, 78, 80, 82–97, 99–101, 104, 120, 179, 181–2, 250–1
Utherpendragon, v, 59–61, 82–3, 91–104, 120, 181–2
Arthur, i–iii, v–viii, ix, xii, 6–10, 17, 31–5, 42–5, 47, 50–1, 53, 59, 69, 74, 82–3, 86, 89, 91, 95, 97–101, 104–183, 186, 194–5, 207, 212, 218, 242–4, 246, 248, 250–1
  see also Excalibur, Prydwen, Ron
Arthor, king of Søndmøre and Nordmøre in Norway, 195
Arvandus, Praetorian Prefect of Gaul, 134
Aschil/Ascilus/Aschillius/Aschilus/Alf, King of Dacia/Denmark, 130, 142, 152, 156, 159, 164, 177, 202, 212
Asgarth, capital of Aesir and Odin, 218–19, 228
Assassins, Muslim Hashish eaters, 224
Assassin, Assassins, Assassination, 3, 6, 57, 93, 187, 210
Attila, High-King of the Huns, 38, 46, 75, 77, 196, 207–13
Aube, river, 147–8, 151, 155
Augusel/Auguselus, king of the Scots of Albany, 120, 126, 141, 144, 152, 156, 158, 160, 171–3
Augustine, priest accompanying Palladius, 230
Augustus, title, v, 52–3, 57, 60, 95, 101, 133, 140–1, 144
  emperor Octavian, 101, 223
  see also High-King
Aun, king of Sweden, 212
Aurelianus, see Arthur
Aurelius, see Arthur
Aurelius Conanus, Celtic leader, see Conan
Aurelius Conanus, Briton High-King, 39, 179–80
Autun, x, 147–8, 150–2, 164–5

Index 261

Auxerre/Autissiodorensis/Autessiodurum, 62–3, 66, 69, 230
Auxilia/Auxiliaries, 3, 13, 135, 145
  see also Allies, Federates
Avalon, Isle of, 111, 177–9, 251
  see also Apples
Avaon, subordinate of Conan, 55

Bacaudae/Bagaudae of Armorica, 57–8, 62, 71, 75
Badon, *see* Bath, Battles of
Baldulf, brother of Colgrin, 105
Ballistae, Ballista, 12, 21, 173, 188
Baltic Sea, x, 70, 123–4, 184–5, 187, 191–2, 196, 198, 208, 214, 218–19, 227, 255
  Baltic Crusades, 218
  see also Arthur, Battle of, Frothi, Slavs, Wends
Bambrough, 49
Band of outlaws, 210
Bannaventa/Banavem Taberniae/Bannavem Thaburinde (Ventre/Venta?), 229, 257
Barfleur, Port, 144, 146–7
Bastarnae/Bastarni, mixed tribe, 218
Bath, Badon, ix, 11, 33, 35, 39, 45, 83, 109–11, 115, 142, 151–2, 159, 250
  see also Battle of, Siege of
Battle of
  Agned Cathregonnon/Breguoin/Cat Bregion, mountain of, *see* Mount Damen
  Alclud/Dumbarton/Loch Lomond, ix, 109, 113, 115–19
  Alleluia Victory, *see* Mold
  Andreds-lea, wood of, 48
  Armorica/Bretagne, 54
  Aylesford, Aegels-threp, 47
  Badon/Bath, ix, 33, 35, 39, 45, 83, 109–15, 250–1
  Baltic Sea, x, 184, 191–3
  Bourg-de-Déols/Déols, 133

Caledon Wood, Celidon/Calidonis/Cacoit Celidon, (2 battles), ix, 44, 107–109
Caerleon, City of the Legions (*in urbe Legionis*)/Cair Lion, ix, 44–5, 94–5
  see also Menevia
Camblam River, Camelford, x, 175–8, 253
Carisbrooke/Whit-garas-byrg, 49
Cerdicsford, 49
Cerdics-ore, 48
Conisborough, 88–90, 98
Crayford/Creccanford, 47
Cymenes-ora, 48
Derwent/Derevent, 43, 79
Douglas/Dugas, River, 44, 105
Dumbarton, *see* Alclud
Episford/Epiford/Set thirgabail/Sathenegabail, 43, 79
Field of Maisbeli, 87–8
Gallic Sea, *See* Shore
Glein/Glem, River, 44
Guinnion/Gunnion, castle of, 44, 90
Ireland, Battle with Guillamurius, 122
Ireland, Unknown local associated with Mount Killaraus, 91–2
Lincoln, ix, 106–107
Lomond, Loch, *see* Alclud
Lussas/Bassas, River, *see Lincoln*
Menevia or Caerleaon, 93–5
Mold (Alleluia Victory), ix, 40–1, 44, 63–9, 206, 211, 230
Mont Saint Michel, x, 146–7
Mount Damen, 45, 63, 96–8
Moray, *see* Alclud
Natan-lea/Cerdiesford (Charford), 48–9
Old Sarum/Searo-byrig, 50
Ribroit/Trat Treuroit, River, 45
Saussy/Siesia, x, 34, 147–64, 168, 243, 253
Severn, *see* Badon
'Shore of the Gallic Sea', 43
St Albans, ix, 101–103

Thanet, 113, 115, 170
York/Eboracum, ix, 96–7
Winchester, x, 174–5
Bauto, Roman commander, 256
Bede, historian, 33–5, 61–3, 69–70, 217, 220, 231, 242
Bedvere, cup-bearer, ruler of Normandy/Neustria, 142, 147, 149–50, 152, 158–9, 162
Bekkhild, sister of Attila, 208
Beldeg/Beldegg/Baldrson/Baldr, son of Woden, 221
  see also Odin
Belgium, *Belgica*, 31, 71, 167, 243, 255
Belorussia, 188
Belinus/Benli, tyrannical king, 40–1, 64–6, 69
Belisarius, 6th cent. Roman general, 4
Benedict, priest accompanying Palladius, 230
Benedict, saint, 48–9
Benignus, favourite boy of St Patrick, 240
Benoc, son of Brond, 49
Beowulf, poem, 8, 212
Beowulf/Bodvar Barki, champion, 212
Berbers, Moors, 54, 145
Bernech, kingdom, 45
Berserks, 191, 207, 223–4, 226
  see also Shape Changers
Biarmaland (probably Finnish speaking kingdom), 202–203, 211
Bieda, son of Port, 48
Birka, x, 200–201
Bituriges, 131, 137
Black Ditches of Cavenham, 36
Bloctonius, Briton commander, 152
Boccus, king of the Medes, 144, 157–62
Bodyguards/Bodyguard (word), 14, 61–2, 143, 153, 161–2, 207, 252
  see *Bucellarii, Domestici, Scholae*
Boeotia, 144
Bohuslän, 200

Bononia/Boulogne/Gesoriacum, x, 52, 54–5, 63, 109, 138, 142, 159, 170
Borama-saga, 94
Borellus, Duke of Cenomania, 142, 149–50
Boso, *Dux* of Ridoc/Oxford, 121, 142, 148–9, 152, 156–61, 253
Boulogne, see Bononia
Bourges, ix, 132–3
Boyne, river, 232
Brand, grandson of Odin, 221
Braughing, 67
Brefi, Synod of, 140
Bretagne/Brittany, 9, 11, 20, 33, 35, 38–9, 42, 54–8, 61, 77–8, 101, 131, 133, 139, 162, 170, 251
  see also Armorica
Britaelis, noble in Cornwall, 98
Bron, beloved of St Patrick, 240
Brond, son of Beldeg, 49
Bruning, Saxon leader, 177
Brynhild, sister of Attila, 208, 212
Bucellarii, famuli, late Roman personal retinue of bodyguards, 10, 22, 40, 52, 62, 66, 114, 125, 145, 149, 162, 231
  see also Bodyguards
Budicius, king of Bretagne, 61, 101, 106, 164, 178, 251
Budli, Attila's father, 210–11
Buelt, province of, 44, 94
Burgundians/Burgunds, Germanic tribe, 52, 57, 71–2, 74–5, 134–5, 143, 148, 163–4, 167–8, 170, 208, 210–11, 220, 255–6
  see also Allobroges, Burgundy
Burgundy, province, 74, 123, 133, 135, 143–4, 154, 164
  see also Allobroges, Burgundians
Byzantium, Byzantine, East Roman, 15, 32, 45, 83, 91, 101, 135–6, 145, 160, 167–8, 190, 198, 209, 212, 244, 253, 256
  see also Battle of Saussy

Cabillonum, x, 164, 167
Cador, *Dux* of Cornwall (and King of Cornwall?), 99, 105, 113–15, 120–1, 141, 149–50, 152, 156, 158–60, 170, 177
Cador of Cahors, (same as Cador of Limenich?), 150
Cador Limenich, Briton leader, 177
Cadwallo Laurh/Lewihr, King of the Venedotians, 121, 141
Caerleon, city, ix, 37, 43–5, 58, 90, 94–5, 111, 140, 171, 252
Cair Affrauc, kingdom, 45
Cair-Guorthigirn, city, fort, 43–5, 69
Caius/Gaius the Sewer, Duke of the Andecavi/Andegavia, 142
Caius/Gaius Metellus Cotta, senator, 144
Caius Quintillianus, Lucius Tiberius's nephew, 148
Calpurnius/Cualfarnus, father of St Patrick, 229
Caledonia/Caledonians, 19, 107, 220
  see also Albany, Scotland
Caliburnus *gladius*, *see* Excalibur sword
Camblam River, *see* Battles of
Cambridshire Dykes, Bran Ditch, Brent Ditch, Devil's Ditch, Fleam Dyke, Grim's Dyke/Ditch, 36
Canterbury, 78, 141
Caracalla/Caracallus, Roman emperor (211–217) and monograph by I. Syvänne, 58, 219–20, 247–8, 254
Carelia/Karjala, 203–204, 254
Carisbrooke/With-gaa-byrg, 49
Cassivellanus, Briton leader, 177
Catel Drunluc, 40–1, 65–6
Catellius Bruttius/Brittu, *see* Catel Drunluc
Caterva, Catervae, 74, 102, 148–9, 152, 154, 158–9, 161, 252–3
  see also Cavalry, *Ala*
Cathigirn, son of Vortigern, 44, 250
Cathleus, Map Catel, 142
Cavalry, Horsemen, vii, 6, 13–18, 21, 31–2, 37, 57, 62–3, 65, 68, 71, 74, 86–9, 96, 102, 105, 111, 114, 136, 138, 144, 147–50, 152–63, 171, 173, 175–7, 189–90, 192–3, 195–6, 209–10, 218–19, 226, 237, 245–7, 252–3, 256
  see also *Ala*, Battle of, *Caterva*, Chariot, *Equites*, Siege of, *Turma*, *vexillationes*
Celestius/Celestinus/Celestine, Pope, 46, 63, 69, 230
Cell Raithin, church, 235
Celts/Celtic, 10–11, 53–6, 66, 76, 120–1, 218, 223, 229, 241, 243
Central Asia, 220
Cerdic, Saxon leader and king of the West Saxons, 48–9
Charaton, High-King of the Huns, 208
Chariot (wagon), war chariot, 16, 236–7
Chelric, or Cheldric, Saxon leader, 169–70, 177
  possibly to be identified with Cheldric and/or Cherdic below
Cherdric, mercenary leader, 105, 113, 115, 170
Cheneus, Map Coil, 142
Cherdic, mercenary leader, 78
Cherson/Chersonesus/Chersonites, 207–208
Chester, Deva, ix, 37, 41, 43, 58, 66, 68, 252
Chesterton, G.K., 64,
Childeric, King of the Salian Franks, 132–3, 135, 138
Chinmarchocus, the Duke of Tréguier, 162
Chionatai, probably Hunnic tribe, 220
Christians, Christianity/Christ/Catholic/Orthodox/Jesus Christ, 7–8, 32, 35, 40–1, 52, 63–5, 69–72, 74, 77, 79, 80–1, 88, 91–2, 97, 111, 120, 122, 170–1, 179–81, 183–4, 199, 216, 218, 229–32, 235–8, 240–1, 258
  see also Madonna, Pagan, Pelagians
Cimbri, Germanic people, 56
Cissa, Saxon leader, 48
City of the Legions, *see* Caerleon, Chester
Cirenchester, 107, 115
Clébach, well, 241

Clofaut, Rupmaneton, 142
Colgrin, Saxon leader, 104–105, 113
Coplthi, river, 233
Comes (companion, count, general), 22, 53, 55, 71, 80, 87, 133
Comitatenses/Comitatus, 10, 40, 114, 145
   see also Bodyguards, *Bucellarii*, *Domestici*, *Scholae*
Conaille Muirthemni, coast, 232
Conan/Conanus/Kynan, Celtic/Briton commander, king of Armorica, 54–6, 58, 248
Conanus, *see* Aurelius Conanus
Concessa, mother of St Patrick, 229
Conisborough/Oppidum of Kaerconan/Cunungeburg/Cunegeburc, 88–90, 98
   see also Battles of
Connaught, 233
Constans, brother of Aurelius Ambrosius (Arthur), 59–62, 71, 82
Constans II, son of Constantine III, usurper, 52, 60
Constantine I the Great, emperor (306–337), 13, 52, 54, 58, 60, 93
Constantine III, usurper (407–411), 13, 33, 35–6, 39–40, 51–7, 56–7, 60, 66, 246–8
   see also Maximianus, Maximus
Constantine, king of Damonia, 39
Constantine IV, king of Britain, (ca.417/18–420/428), 58–60, 82
Constantine V, the son of Cador, Duke of Cornwall, cousin of Arthur and his successor, 177–9
Constantinople (Byzantium), city, 253
Constantius I, father of Constantine the Great, emperor (305–306), 55–6
Constantius III, general and emperor (421), 52, 57
Constantius, biographer of St. Germanus, 33, 40, 62–6, 68–9, 72, 74, 180
Coolenni, 232
Cormac mac Art, Irish High-King, 220
Cornovia, Cornovii, 41, 66

Cornwall, iv–v, 11, 36, 55, 76, 82–3, 87, 89, 96, 98–9, 105, 109, 111, 113–15, 120, 140–1, 152, 156, 158–9, 175, 177, 229–30, 242
Coroticus, mercenary commander, 70–1, 257
Council,
   Briton Council (=Round Table), Council (City), Curial class, 10–11, 38, 40–1, 43, 51–3, 58–9, 66, 77, 105, 144, 183
   Council of Advisors (Round Table), 105, 144, 183
   see also Round Table
   Gaul, 51
Cuiful, Map Nogoit, 142
Cuneglasse, ruler of Britons, 39, 180–1
Cuneus, cunei, *see* Wedge
Cursalem/Kursalem, Consul of Caisester/Caistor, 121, 141, 152, 156, 158–60
Cymen, son of Aella, 48
Cynric, son of Cedric and king of the West Saxons, 48–50

Dacia, *see* Jutland
Dag, ruler of Estonia, 193, 196
Dal Riata, Scots, Scotti, 19, 118, 122, 232, 235
Dalmatae, Dalmatia, 54, 91
Dan the Magnificent, king of Denmark, 185, 212
Danaut, Map Papo, 121
Danes, Danish, 20–1, 22, 57, 61–2, 67, 87, 126, 128, 130, 152, 156, 159, 184–6, 188, 190–6, 199, 205–206, 209–10, 212, 217, 242, 244, 254, 256
   see also Angles, Denmark, Frothi III, Jutes, Saxons
Danube, river, 184
David, Arthur's uncle, Archbishop of Caerleon, 140–1
Decurions, cavalry, 15
Dee (Vartry), river, 231
Deira, 57, 78

Demetia, 80, 87, 120, 140–1, 180
Denmark, v, xvii, 21, 57, 61, 123–30, 142, 170, 177, 179, 181, 183, 185, 188, 190–3, 195, 200, 202, 206, 209–10, 212, 217, 219–22, 243, 254–6
   see also Angles, Danes, Frothi III, Jutes, Saxons
Dessi, Irish tribe located in Wales, 229
Deva, see Chester
Devon, 83, 229
Diar, 'gods', priests, judges, 218–19
Dicalydones, 17–18
   see also Picts
Dichu, king of Ulidia, 232–3, 235–6
Dijon, Castrum, x, 151, 154
Dimar, leader in Frothi's forces, 196
Dimilioc, ix, 97–100, 250
   see also Sieges
Dina Emrys, 83–5
   see also Siege of
Diocletian, emperor, 13
Dionotus, king of Cornwall, 55–6
Dnieper, river, 196, 255
Doldavius, King of Gothland, 122, 142
Domangart, son of Ness, 122
Domestici, imperial bodyguards, 55, 145, 252, 256
   see also Bodyguards, *Bucellarii, Scholae*
Don, river, 196, 216, 218–19, 226–8, 255
Dorobernia, 11
Dorchester, 11, 142, 152
Drifa, wife of Vanlandi, 227
Dubricius, Bishop of the City of the Legions, 93, 104, 111, 140
Dubtach-accu-Lugir, 238
Duces, see Dux
Duke/Dukes, see *Dux*
Dumbarton, see also Battles of, Sieges of
Dux (general), v, 10–11, 22, 35, 41, 43–4, 54, 57, 64–6, 80, 82, 87, 89, 96, 98–9, 105, 114, 120, 141, 144–6, 149–50, 152, 154–5, 157, 176–7, 183, 203, 206, 236
Dux Bellorum, title of Arthur, v, 10–11, 44, 82
   see also Arthur

Eastsex, 44, 80
Ebissa, son of Hengist, 42, 78, 122
Eburacum, *see* York
Eddelein, Map Cledauc, 142
Egbrict, Saxon leader, 177
Egther, king of Biarmaland, 202–203
Elaf, Saxon leader, 177
Elafius, Briton noble, 72
Elbe, river, 188, 194
Eldadus, Bishop of Gloucester and brother of Eldol, 90
Eldol, *Dux/Comes* of Gloucester/Claudiocestriae, 80, 87–90
Elephant/Elephants/War Elephants, 16, 207
Eopa/Capa, assassin, 93
Eoppa, son of Esa, 49
Eosa, kinsman of Hengist, 89–90, 96–7, 101–103
Epistrophius, king of the Greeks, 144
Equites, 37, 149
Ercc, the son of Daig, 236–7
Erik, Norwegian leader, 185–9, 191–3, 199–200, 202, 205, 209, 211
Esa, son of Ingwi, 49
Essex, 47
Estonia, 195–7, 202, 210–11
Ethne, daughter of Loegaire, 241
Eudoxius, physician, Bacaudae leader, 75
Euric, King of the Visigoths, 133–4, 168, 170, 182
Evander, Duke of Syria, 144, 149–50
Eventus/Huivenius/Ywain, King of Albany, 171
Everdingus, Roman general, 145
Eylimi, Hunnic leader, 210
Excalibur sword, Caliburnus *gladius*, Caliburn, Arthur's sword, 111, 113–14, 136, 162, 251
Expediti, lightly-equipped infantry, or infantry without baggage train, or both of the above, 68
Exuperantius, Roman general, 57–8

Faeroe Islands, 123
Fafnir/Shilbung, 210
Famuli, *see Bucellarii*
Faustus, son of Vortigern, 42, 44, 69–70, 250
Feast of Tara, 241
  see also Tara
Fecc/Fiacc, Graves of the Men of, 236
Feccol Ferchertni, prophet, 236
Fedelm, daughter of Loegaire, 241
Federates, *foederati*, (treaty-bound allies who were usually located in Roman territory in the fifth century), 10, 14, 31, 36, 46, 48, 53–8, 77, 90, 115, 145, 147, 168, 182–3, 211, 221, 241, 244, 247
  see also Allies
Fiacc, poet and bishop, 238
Fiacc, *see* Fecc
Fianna, military retinues, 220
Finland, Finns, Finnish, 16, 21, 70, 108, 124, 190, 192, 196–203, 203–205, 216, 218, 227–8, 242–3, 249–52, 254–6
Finn, son of Godwulf, 49
Finnmark, (modern meaning north of Norway, the meaning here probably northern Norway, Sweden, Finland and the Kola Peninsula in Russia), 202, 211
Finström in Åland, 204
Fleets (navy, naval, ships, shipping, boathouses, boatshed, keel, amphibious, *chiulis, cyulis, nautae, liburnae, dromones*), vi, x, 10–13, 18–20, 26–32, 36–8, 40, 42–3, 48–9, 56, 61–3, 65, 67, 78–9, 82–3, 89, 91–4, 101–102, 105, 109–10, 112–13, 115–18, 122, 124–6, 128, 132, 135, 138, 147, 149, 168–73, 175, 184–97, 199–200, 202, 205–11, 214–15, 226–7, 229–33, 236, 243–4, 249–50, 256–7
Flintshire, 66
Foederati (Federates), *see* Federates
Fortifications/Fortresses/Forts/Fortified Camps/Walls, Hill Forts, viii–x, 4, 11, 14–16, 18–9, 23, 36–7, 41–2, 49, 57–8, 63, 66–8, 74, 76, 78, 80, 84–6, 96–8, 102, 111–12, 115, 117–18, 120, 125–9, 135, 147–50, 153–5, 162, 165, 168, 173, 184, 186, 188–9, 195–201, 203–205, 208, 236, 242–5, 249, 252, 254, 256
  see also Antonine Wall, Hadrian's Wall
France, *see* Gaul
Francisca, Frankish throwing axe, 20, 31
Franks, Germanic confederacy, 20–2, 31–2, 56, 71, 132–3, 135, 138, 168, 185, 208–10, 213, 220–1, 231, 243, 253
  see also Ripuarian Franks, Salian Franks, Thuringians
Freovin, son of Friodigar, 221
Freovin, son of Odin, 221
Fridlef II, Danish King, 130, 212, 221
Frigg, adulterous wife of Odin, 222
Friodigar/Frodi, son of Brand, 221
Frisian Islands, 8, 42, 78, 124
Frisians, 20, 22, 221
  see also Saxons
Frithleif/Fridlef, 212
Frithowald, son of Frithuwulf, 49
Frithuwulf, son of Finn, 49
Frollo/Flollo/Rollo/Froila/Fronto/Florianus, Florentius, Florus /Floridus, 'Leo's deputy', 131, 133, 135–7
Frothi III the Magnificent, Danish King, vi, 61–2, 65, 70, 130, 142, 184–214, 256
Frothi the Magnificent/Peaceful, possibly to be identified with Frothi III, 212
Frothi IV, 212
Frothi V, 212
Fyn, island, 128, 130, 193, 209, 221

Gallic Chronicles, 32, 38, 46, 62, 72, 74–6, 82–3, 249
Gallic Council, 51
Gallic Sea, coast, 43, 55, 79
Galluc, *Dux* of Roffensis/Rochester, 121
Ganieda, pupil of Merlin, 180
Garthariki, 219
Gascony, 137

Index 267

Gaul, Gauls, Gallic, v, ix, 20, 29, 31–3, 36, 45, 51–6, 63–4, 70–2, 74, 77–8, 82, 86, 91, 104, 109, 122–3, 131–9, 142–68, 170–1, 179, 182–3, 199, 209, 220, 230, 242–3, 245–6, 248–9, 252–3

Gawain (Walvanus, Gwaluanus), nephew of Arthur, 101, 148–9, 152, 158–64, 171–3, 182

Geat, first known ancestor of Woden/Odin, 49

Geoffrey of Monmouth, historian, v, xiii, 8–10, 13–14, 33–5, 39, 43, 51, 53–62, 67, 76, 78–80, 82–7, 91–3, 95, 97–9, 101–106, 109, 111–15, 117, 119–20, 122–3, 125–6, 130–3, 135–7, 139–41, 143–50, 152–5, 157, 159–65, 169–71, 173–83, 212, 241–4, 248–53

Gerald of Wales, historian, 39, 69, 140, 178, 180, 242–3, 250, 253

Gerin (Gerinus) of Chartres, 142, 148, 152, 156, 158–60

Germania, provinces Superior, Prima, 45, 57, 71

Germans, Germanic peoples, Germany, 8, 21–25, 32, 46, 54, 56, 78–9, 88, 93, 96, 101, 104–106, 108, 131, 141, 147, 152, 169, 177, 180, 188, 199, 201, 208–11, 216, 218–20, 223–8, 246–7, 250, 255, 257
  see also Alamanni, Berserks, Franks, Germania, Goths, Marcomanni, Odin, Quadi, Saxons, Scandinavia, Suevi/Suebi, Vandals

Germanus, see St. Germanus

Gerontius, Roman commander, 53, 56–7

Gesoriacum, see Bononia

Gestiblind, King of Götaland, 199

Gewis/Gavir, son of Wigg, 221

Gewis, Odin's descendant, 221

Gewissei, tribe, 60, 80, 90

Giants' Ring of Mount Killaraus, 91–2

Giant, Giants, Giant stones, 86, 91, 146–7
  see also Retho

Gibica, Burgundian, 210–11, 256

Gildas, historian, xiii, 32–9, 45, 51, 53, 57–8, 61–3, 69, 76, 83, 107, 109, 179–81, 242, 248–50, 253

Gillarvus, Irish *dux*, 177

Gillasel, Irish *dux*, 177

Gillomanius, Irish High King, 92–4

Gillpatrick, Irish *dux*, 177

Gjuki/Gibica, 210, 256

Glaslyn, river, 85

Glastonbury, 178, 243

Globus, globi (independently operating cavalry or infantry unit/units), 22, 24–5, 246

Glomer, pirate, 194, 196

Gloucester, 11, 80, 87, 90, 105, 110, 112, 115, 141, 152

Goar, Alan king, 74

Godwulf, son of Geat, 49

Gold, 95, 108, 111, 152, 157, 159, 210, 217, 231

Gorangonus, earl, *regulus* (minor king), 78

Gorboriam, Map Goit, 142

Gorlois, *Dux* of Cornwall/*Cornubiae*, 89, 96–100, 103, 149

Gosact, son of Miliucc, 235

Gøtar, king of Norway, 185–8, 191, 209

Gothland/Götaland, 'Land of the Goths' in mainland Sweden (can also mean Gotland), v, 122–3, 126, 142, 144, 181, 199, 205
  see also Gotland, Västergötaland, Östergötaland

Gotland, island, (can also mean Gothland), 126, 144, 181, 199–200, 203, 205
  see also Gothland, Visigoths

Goths, Visigoths, Germanic tribal confederacy, 4, 35, 45, 52, 55, 64, 71–2, 123, 126, 130–1, 133–5, 137, 143, 145, 147–8, 167–8, 170, 184–5, 196, 208, 219–20, 227–8, 249, 253–5
  see also Gothland, Gotland

Gracianus (Gratianus?), the Freedman, general of Constantine III, usurper, (it is

possible that he should be identified with the usurper Gratian), 56
Granard, 235
Graves of the Men of Fecc/Fiacc, 236
Gratian/Gratianus, Roman emperor, 45, 54–5
Gratian/Gratianus, (it is possible that he should be identified with Gracianus), British usurper, 51, 56–7
Gregory of Tours, historian, 32–3, 48, 131, 138, 165, 182, 242
Greek, Greeks, people, sources, theory, 8, 13, 22, 25, 56, 88, 187, 218, 245, 256
Greeks (East Romans), 134, 163
Greek Fire, 101
Grellach Dabaill by the side of Cass in Mag Lifi, 94
Gual, Wall of (probably Hadrian's Wall), 42, 78
Guallauc of Salisbury, 139, 160
Guanius, mercenary leader, 56
Gudme, town, 128
Gueneri in the Kingdom of Dimetae, 43
Guerinus Carnotensis/Gerin of Chatres, 142, 144
Guernsey, island, 55–6
Guillamurius, Irish High-King, 122, 142
Guinevere/Guanhumara/Gwenhwyfar, wife of Arthur, 120, 146, 169, 171, 178, 186, 243
Guitard, *Dux* of the Pictones/Pictavians, 137, 142, 150, 152, 158–9, 162
Guithelinus, Archbishop of London, 58–9, 61
Gundaharius/Gunnar/Gunther, Burgundian king, 208, 210
Gundioc, Burgundian *MVM* and king, 133, 135, 143, 145
Gundobad, Burgundian *MVM* and king, 143, 164, 168
Gunfacius, King of the Orkneys, 122, 142
Gunthiof, son of Alrik, king of Värmland and Solör, 199

Gunnar, *see* Gundaharius
Gunvara, sister of Frothi, 186–7
Guorthegirnaim, province of, 44, 94
Guttorm (possibly Gislaharius, Gisleher), 210
Gwenddolen, King of Scotland, 180
Gwenhyvar, wife of Arthur (probably Guinevere), 120
Gylfi, king of Sweden, 221–2

Hadrian's Wall, UK, 18, 35–7, 54, 57–8, 76, 78, 242
Halfdan, 212
Halogaland, 202, 211
Hälsingland, Hälsings, province, 195–6, 200, 202
Halland, 200
Hämäläiset (Tavastians), 254–5
Hämeenlinna (Castle of Häme/Tavastia), city and castle, 204
Hanunda, Hunnic princess, wife of Frothi, 130, 185–7, 191, 208
Hebrides, Islands, xiv–xv
Hedmark, 202, 211
Heimir, Frankish leader, 208, 210
Helena, Hoel's niece, 146–7
Helgi, Danish king, 212
Heliogabalus, Roman emperor, 247
Hengist/Hengest, Saxon leader and king, 38, 40, 42–4, 46–8, 61–2, 69, 78–80, 82, 86–90, 169, 217–19, 221, 247
Henry IV, king of France, 97
Hephthalites, White Huns, 220
Her/Er, son of Hider/Hyder, 150
Hermanaric, '3rd century Gothic Alexander the Great', 198, 255
Hermianus, Roman general, 145
Heruli/Heruls, Germanic tribe, 20, 22, 32, 52, 55, 147, 168, 219–20, 222, 227, 255 *see also* Saxons
High-King, title, v, 10–11, 18–19, 44, 52, 70, 92, 119, 122–3, 127, 131, 140–1, 182–3, 185, 199, 208, 220, 230, 232, 236 *see also* Arthur, Riothamus, Vortigern

Hild, daughter of Høgin, 194
Hill Forts, *see* Fortifications
Hippolutus, Duke of Crete, 144
Hippotoxotai, The Age of, 1, 244–6, 249, 257
Hirtacius, king of the Parthians, 144, 155–6
Hithin, one of the kings of Norway, 194, 196, 199, 211
Hjalprek, king of Denmark, 210
Hoel, King of Brittany, 101, 106, 109, 111, 113–15, 117, 137, 142, 144, 146–7, 152, 158–62, 170
Høgin, a *regulus* in Jutland, 194–6, 199, 211
Hogni (Gernot?), Burgundian leader?, 210
Holdin, king of the Ruteni, 142, 152, 158–60, 162
Homosexual/Gays, 6, 181, 240
Honorius, emperor (395–423), 36, 45, 51–2, 56–7
Horsa, Saxon leader and king, 38, 40, 42–3, 46–7, 61–2, 78–9, 82, 169, 218, 221, 247
Hleithrar (Leire), 221
Hroar, king of Northumberland, 212
Hrolf, king of Denmark, 212
Humber, 78, 87, 104, 169
Hun, king of the Huns, 196
Huns, Hun leaders/kings, 38, 46, 56, 71–2, 75, 77, 82, 130, 184–5, 187–8, 191–9, 206–13, 218, 220, 254–6
  see also Aetius, Attila, Frothi III, Hanunda, Hun, Litorius, Wanius, Xiognu
Hyderus, the son of Nu, 148
Hyrelgas of Periron/Hireglas de Perirut, Bedevere's nephew, 150, 159–61

Iaginvius of Bodloan, Briton commander, 162
Iceland, island, kingdom, v, 122–4, 142, 144, 170, 181
Icknield Way, 36
Ida, son of Eoppa, Northumbrian king, 45, 49, 221
Illus, East Roman Magister Militum and rebel, 91, 101

Imbaltus, Roman commander in Gaul, 54
Imperator, 10, 95
Infantry, footmen, vii, 13–19, 21–4, 31–2, 57, 67, 86–9, 96, 102, 105, 114, 144, 148–9, 152–63, 165, 171, 173, 176–7, 189, 226–7, 236, 245–6, 257
Ingwi, son of Angenwit, 49
Inis Patrick/Isles of the Children of Cor, 232
Inis, plain, 235
Intelligence gathering, information gathering, scouts, scouting, spying, spies, reconnaissance (words), 4, 11–12, 15–16, 30, 32, 61, 87, 95, 102, 105, 122, 147–51, 154, 186–8, 191–3, 205
Inverness, 115
Ireland, island, v–vi, x, 9, 17, 19, 41, 45, 57–8, 69–71, 91–5, 98, 115, 118, 122–3, 129–30, 142, 144, 164, 169, 179, 181, 183, 205–206, 211, 220, 229–41, 243, 248
Irish/Scots/Scotti, 17–20, 33, 35, 37, 39–42, 46, 51, 56–8, 66, 70–1, 76, 82, 87, 91–5, 105, 109, 111, 113, 115, 118–20, 122, 126, 164, 169–70, 177, 206, 211, 220, 229–44, 246, 248–50, 257–8
  see also Ireland

Jämtland, Jämts, province, 195–6, 200
Jarnbers, province, 196
Jersey, island, 55–6
Jesus, *see* Christians
Jews, 7, 236
John Lydus, 14, 154
Jonathel, *Dux* of Dorchester, 121, 142, 152, 160
Jordan, noble in Cornwall, 98
Jordanes, historian, 32, 131, 133, 182, 242, 249, 255
Jugein, Consul of Leicester, 121, 141, 152, 160
Julian/Julianus, son of Constantine III, usurper, 52, 60
Julius the Martyr, Church of, 171

Julius Caesar, Roman dictator, 101, 143
Jutes, 17, 20, 22, 38, 46–7, 57, 123, 130, 186, 206, 221
  see also Angles, Denmark, Frothi III, Jutland, Saxons
Jutland, Jylland, Dacia/Dania, v, 124–8, 130, 142, 144, 185, 189, 193–6, 199, 206, 209, 211, 221
  see also Danes, Denmark, Frothi, Jutes, Saxons

Kaicester, 11, 141
Kambria, 93, 95
Katigern/Catigirn, son of Vortigern, 43, 79
Kay/Kai, Senechal, ruler of Anjou, 111, 139, 142, 147, 152, 158–9, 162
Kent, Kentish-men, 42, 44, 46–7, 78–9, 169
Keredic, Briton king, 181
Kervillus/Kervil, Irish leader, 204
Kharkov, 197
Kidarite Huns, 220
Kiev, 197
Kildare in Leinster, 92
Killaraus, *see* Giants, Mount
Kimbelim, Map Trunat, 142
Kimmare, 142
Kincar, Map Began, 142
Kinlich, Map Neton, 142
Kolotchin Civilization, xvii
Kurland, Kurlanders, 195, 210
Kursalem, *see* Cursalem
Kursk, 197
Kynniarc/Kinmare, *Dux* of Durobernia/Canterbury, 121, 141

Laesø, island, 186
Ladoga, Laatokka, lake, 191, 197, 204, 228, 255
Langobards/Lombards, 210
Langres, x, 150–2, 154–5, 164–5
Lapland, Lapplands, Lapps, two provinces, 196, 202–3
Lapps, people, 202–203, 205

Legions, legionaries, City of Legions (Caerleon), 3, 13–15, 17, 25, 36–7, 43, 45, 47, 56–8, 63, 65, 90, 93, 95, 104, 111, 140–1, 144–5, 149, 152–4, 157, 171, 252, 257
  see also Caerleon, Chester
Leicester/Legecester, 11, 141, 152
Leinster, Leinstermen, 92, 94–5, 230, 232–3, 235–6, 241
Lelius/Laelius Hostiensis, Roman commander, 157
Leo, East Roman emperor, 144–5, 163, 170, 178, 182
Leodegarius, consul of Bolonia, probably to be identified as Leodegrance, 142, 159–60
Leodegrance, King of Cameliard, 120
Limitanei, frontier troops, 3
Lindum, *see* Lincoln
Lincoln, ix, 80, 106–7
Linnamäki, linnanmäki, linnapää, loss mägi, linna mägi, hill forts, 197
Lithuania, Lithuanian, viii, 188, 197
Litorius, Roman general, 71–2
Lochru, magician, 237
Loegaire/Loigaire, Irish High-King, 70, 92, 94–5, 230, 232, 236–8, 240–1
Logistics, *see* Supply
Loire, river, 132–3, 137, 168
London, Londinium, ix, 47, 56, 58, 60–2, 64, 66, 80, 90, 97, 103, 105–107, 119, 141, 178–9, 224, 242–4
Lone, place and boatshed, ix, 125
Longiones, 220
Loth of Lodonesia/de Lendeseia, *Dux*/*Consul* of Lothia, nephew of Sichelm, King of Norway, 101–103, 120–1, 123, 125–6, 142, 152, 158–9, 164, 171, 177, 182, 194, 212
Lothian, 120
Lovat, river, 196
Lucetmael, magician, 238
Lucius Catellus, senator, 144

Index

Lucius Hiberius/Hiberus/Tiberius, Roman general/tribune, Procurator of the Republic, 34, 143–63, 252
Lugdunensis, province in Gaul, 167
Lugus, Celtic god, 218
Lunius/Linnius, region, 44, 105
Lyngvi, Nordic king, 210, 256
Lyon/Lugdunum, 54, 180

Mabinogion, Welch tale, 13, 16, 53, 55, 111, 123, 139, 163, 243, 251
Macc Cuil moccu Greccae, king of Ulaid, 240
Mace Dregin, Irish father 240
Madonna, 44, 90, 122, 250
  see also Christians
Maegla, son of Port, 48
Maeldinus, pupil of Merlin, 180
Maglocune, Malgo, King of Kings, ruler of Britons, 39, 181
Mainz, city, 31–2
Majorian/Maiorianus, subordinate of Aetius, emperor, 75
Mälären, lake, region, 200–201, 203, 222, 228
Malvasius, king of Iceland, 142
Man, Isle of, 240
Marcellinus, *Magister Militum* in Dalmatia, 91, 101, 113
Marcian (Marcianus), emperor (450–457), 46
Marcomanni, Germanic tribe, Marcomannic War, 25, 219, 247, 257
Marcus, British usurper, 51–2
Marius Lepidus, senator, 144, 156–9
Martianus, *see Marcian*
Maurice/Mauricius Cador of Cahors/Cadorcanensem, 150, 157
Mauron, Consul of Worcester, 121
Maximianus, emperor (285–305), note the confusion between Constantine III (407–411), Maximus (408–411) and Maxiamianus emperor (285–305), 39–40, 53–4, 56–7, 248
  see also Constantine III
Maximus, Maxen, usurper (408–411), note the confusion with Maximianus and Constantine III, 13, 33, 35, 39–42, 53–4, 56, 66, 247
  see also Constantine III, Maximianus
Maximus, usurper and emperor (383–388), 25, 39, 45, 247
Meath, 232–3
Melga, king of the Picts, mercenary commander, 56–7
Menevia in Kambria, 93–5
Mercia, 47
Merlin, Ambrosius, sorcerer, philosopher, architect, *dux*, 34, 42–4, 80–2, 85, 90–3, 98, 100–101, 140, 178–80, 253
Merlin Silvester (Celidonius), 180
Meros (pl. *mere*, military division, roughly the equivalent of legion 6,000–7,000 men), 15, 17, 56
Metz, 211
Mevil/Maevill, Nordic leader, 194
Micipsa, king of Babylon, 144, 159
Middlesex, 44, 80
Militia, paramilitary forces, 10, 37, 68–9, 84, 87, 107, 165, 183, 249
Miliucc in Ulidia, Irish chieftain, 229, 232, 235, 257
Moel Fenli, hill fort, 41, 66
Moira (pl. *moirai*, military division/regiment), 17
Monesan, daughter of unknown king, 241
Mont Saint Michel, x, 147
  see also Battle of, Siege of
Moors, *see Berbers*
Moray, 115, 120, 126, 140–1
Mordred, son of Loth and Anna but likely to be son of Budicius and Anna, brother of Gawain, 'Arthur's nephew', vi, 101, 146, 164, 169–78, 253
Mordred's sons, 178

Morgan, sorceress, Arthur's cousin, 178–9
Morvid, Consul of Gloucester, 121, 141, 152, 162–3
Moschino Civilization, xvii, 228
Moscow, 197–8
Mount Ambrius (= Mount Arvaius/Snowdon?), 80, 90, 93
Mount Killaraus, 91–2
  see also Giants
Mount Mis, 232–5
Mount Snowdon/Mount Erith/Mount Arvaius, 80, 86
Muirchú, historian, 230, 232, 235–42, 244, 257
Munster, 233

Nakolinna, 204
Nanna/Nana, 218
Narbonne/Narbo, city, 72
Natan-leod, Briton king, 48
National Socialist Party, Nazis, 226
Naval Tactics, see Fleets
Navy, see Fleets
Nennius, historian, xiii, 33–5, 39–45, 61–6, 69, 78–80, 83, 86, 90, 93–5, 97, 105, 107, 113, 122, 217, 230, 242, 247, 249–51
Netherlands, 31, 147
Niall, Irish mercenary king, 70, 94
Nibelungenlied, 8, 210–11, 244, 256
Normandy/Neustria, 139, 142
Normans, 84, 178, 245
Northern Europe, see Norway, Denmark, Sweden, Finland, Estonia, Russia
Northumbria, 49
Norway, Norwegians, v, 20–2, 29, 57–8, 61–2, 78, 87, 105, 120, 122–7, 129–30, 142, 144, 152, 159, 170, 177, 179, 181, 183, 185–8, 191, 194–5, 199–200, 202–203, 206–207, 212, 216–17, 222, 244, 255–6
Numeri (*arithmos, arithmoi, katalogoi*), national *numeri*, irregular unit, 14

Octar, see Ottar
Octha, Octa, son of Hengist, king of the Saxons of Kent, 42, 44, 78, 89–90, 94–7, 101–103, 122

Odbrict, king of Norway, 177
Oddi, Danish leader, 185–6
Odin, military leader and king who came to be identified with the Germanic god Woden, vi, x, 25, 49, 191, 210, 216–28, 247, 254–5, 257
  see also Woden
Odovacar/Adovacrius, mercenary commander, later King of Italy, 133, 138, 168, 182
Offa's Dyke, 36, 40, 63, 120
  see also Fortifications
Ofura, daughter of Frothi, 130, 202, 212
Öland, Ölanders, 192, 195, 200
Olcan, follower of St Patrick, 240
Old-Saxons, 38, 47
Olimar, 'king of the East/Ruthenia/Rutenia', 191, 193–6, 199, 202, 211–12, 254
Ømi/Aumum, Harbour near Stavanger, 187
Onager/Onagri (one-armed stone-thrower), 12, 15
  see also *Ballistae*, Stone Thrower
Ønef, Nordic king, 194, 196
Orkneys, islands, v, 42, 78, 122–3, 142, 144, 170, 179, 181, 194–6, 206
Orleans, 142, 148–9
Osla Big Knife, Saxon leader, 111
Östergötaland, 'East Gothic Land', 200
  see also Gothland, Västergötaland
Osterøy, see Lone
Ottar/Octar/Uptaros, king of the Huns, 208, 211
Ouse, river, 105
Oxford, Ridoc, 8, 11, 34, 142, 148, 152, 169, 243–4

Paedophile, Pederastry, 6, 240, 245
  see also Homosexual
Pagan, pagans, god, gods, goddess, 7, 11, 30, 41–2, 44, 52, 70–1, 79–81, 82, 88, 90–1, 101, 113, 118, 169–71, 188, 216–19, 223, 225, 227–30, 236, 238, 240–1, 249, 254
  see also Christians, *Diar*, Franks, Ireland, Loegaire, Marcellinus, Merlin, Odin,

Saxons, St Germanus, St Patrick, Vortigern, Vortimer
Palace, 187, 238
Palladius, bishop, 41, 46, 69–70, 230–2, 247
Pamprepius, Neo-Platonist soothsayer, 91, 101
Pandrasus, king of Egypt, 144, 157, 160
Pannonia, 208
Paramilitary forces, *see* Militia
Paris, ix, 54, 135–6, 139, 149
Pascent/Paschent/Pascentius, son of Vortigern, 44, 93–6, 250
Patrick, Saint, *see* St. Patrick
Paulus, *Comes* (and *MVM?*), 133, 135, 252
Pelagians, 40, 62–5, 69, 72, 74, 140, 230
 see also Christians
Peredur, Map Eridur, King of North Welch, 142, 179–80
Petreius, senator, 148–9
Pictones, people of Poitou, 137, 142
Picts, Pictish, vii, ix, 17–20, 35–42, 46, 51, 56–9, 61–3, 65–7, 71–2, 76–8, 82, 87, 105, 109, 111, 113, 115, 119, 170, 177, 205–206, 211, 220, 230–2, 240, 242, 244
 see also Saxons
Pohjanmaa (area), Pohjalaiset (people of Pohjanmaa), 200, 203–205, 254
Poitou, Poitevins, 137, 142, 150, 152
 see also Pictones
Poland, 191
Polytetes, Duke of Bithynia, 144
Port, Saxon leader, 48
Portsmouth, 48
Potitus, grandfather of St Patrick, 229
Powys, 40–1, 65–6
Prefect, *Praefectus* (various different positions), 11, 41, 65, 91, 133, 207
Princeps (various different), 10–11, 14, 40, 52
Procopius, historian, 4, 7, 222
Provisions *see* Supply
Prydwen/Pridwen *clipeus*, Arthur's round shield, 111, 122, 250
Prydwen (Fair-face), Arthur's ship, 122, 250

Punta formation, 247
 see also Wedge
Pyramus, Archbishop of York, 120

Quintus Carucius, senator, 144, 149, 157
Quintus Milvius Catulus, senator, 144, 157–8

Rafn, Danish leader, 185
Reconnaissance, *see* Intelligence Gathering
Regin, Map Claut, 142, 210
Regin/Nibelung, 210
 see also Regin, Map Claut
Reidgotaland, 221
Reidgotaland, 221
Renis, river, (Rhine?), 69
Rennes, 54
Rennesøy, island near Stavanger, 191
Renwein, daughter of Hengist, 78–9
Rerir, grandson of Odin, 221
Retho, giant duellist, 86
 see also Giant
Revil/Raefill, Nordic leader, 194, 196
Rhine, river, 31–2, 55, 185, 196, 208, 211, 256
Rhombus, rhomboid, 13, 15, 22, 24–5, 88, 226–7, 247, 257
 see also *Globus*, *Punta*, Wedge
Rhydderch, king of the Cumbrians, 180
Richborough, x, 169–71, 173
 see also Battle of
Richerius, Briton leader, 149–50
Ricimer, barbarian *patricius* in the West, 133, 135, 143, 145, 148, 154, 164, 168, 170
Riculf, King of Norway, 125–7
Riddomarcus, Briton commander, 162
Riocatus, nephew of Faustus, 70
Riothamus, Riotimus, High-King, 10, 35, 70, 91, 123, 131–5, 164, 182, 252
 see also Arthur, High-King, Vortigern
Ripuarian Franks, 31, 185, 208–209
 see also Franks, Salian Franks, Thuringians
Rochester, Roffensis, 141

Roller, Erik's brother, 186–7, 191, 194–5
Rome, city, Italy, Roman Empire, 4, 11, 17, 31, 35, 38, 45–6, 51–2, 54, 57, 62, 69, 72, 74, 77, 80, 83, 91, 106, 122, 140–1, 143–5, 163–4, 168, 170, 176, 178, 182–3, 209, 216, 220, 230, 245, 252
Ron lancea, Arthur's spear/lance, 111
Round Table, 10, 43, 51, 53, 77, 120
 see also Council
Ruga, King of the Huns, 208
Russia, Ruscia, Saxo's medieval Russia, 113, 130, 191, 195–9, 201–202, 207, 211–12, 219, 228, 243, 250, 255
Ruthenia, Rutenia, Ruthenians, 191
Rutupiae, *see* Richborough

Saaremaa, island, 197
Saeming, son of Odin, 222
Saga, Sagas, 94, 185, 207–208, 210, 212, 216–19, 223–4, 227, 244, 254–6
Saga of King Hrolf Kraki, 212, 244
Saga of the Volsungs, 208, 210, 212, 221, 244
Saga of the Ynglings, 212, 222–3
Salian Franks, Salii, 31, 138, 221, 253
 see Franks, Ripuarian Franks, Thuringians
Salisbury/Kaercaradduc, 11, 80, 90, 141, 159
Sallustius of Emesa, Cynic philosopher, 91, 101
Saltvik in Åland, 204
Samsø, island, 205
Samson, Bishop of York, 93
Sarmatians, 131, 218
 see also Alans, Goths, Dacia
Saussy, *see* Battle of
Savoy/Sapaudia, 75
Saxland, *see* Saxony
Saxo Grammaticus, historian, 22–5, 29, 33, 61–2, 124, 126, 130, 184–5, 187–97, 199, 202–203, 205–207, 209–12, 214, 216–17, 222, 226, 242, 244, 247, 252, 254, 256
Saxon Port, 43, 79

Saxon Shore, 37
Saxons, Germanic confederacy, v, vii, ix, xiii, 9, 11, 17, 20–52, 55–7, 61–2, 64–7, 70–2, 76–80, 82–4, 86–90, 93–7, 101–15, 122–3, 130, 133, 135, 138–9, 144, 164, 169–70, 173, 175–80, 183, 186, 206, 210–11, 217, 220–1, 230, 242–4, 246–7, 249, 256
 see also Angles, Arthur, Danes, Franks, Hengist, Heruls, Horsa, Jutes, Vortigern, Vortimer
Saxony, 196, 219–21
Scandinavia, Scandinavians, viii, ix, 22–3, 25, 27–8, 32, 88, 123–4, 147, 152, 158–9, 187–8, 194, 197–200, 202, 206, 209–10, 212, 214, 216–18, 223–4, 226, 243, 246, 255
 see also Germans, Saxons, Denmark, Norway, Sweden
Scholae, 145, 252, 256
Sciri, Germanic tribe, 168
Scotland, 11, 17, 19, 56, 61, 78, 90, 92–4, 97, 104–105, 107, 109, 115, 120, 129, 141, 169, 171, 180, 206, 220
 see also Albany, Irish, Picts, Saxons
Scots, Scotti *see* Irish
Seax, Scramasax, a short sword which gave its name to the Saxons, vii, 20–1, 31, 132
Segitius, priest accompanying St Patrick, 231
Seine, river, 55, 74, 135, 138, 148–9
Semnones, 220
 see also Suevi, Alamanni
Septimius Severus. L. emperor (193–211) and father of Caracalla, 13, 25, 220, 257
Serses, king of the Itureans, 144, 157, 160
Sertorius, king of Libya, 144, 149, 157–9, 161–2
Severn/Havren, river, 109, 111, 257
Shape changer, 147, 206–207, 223, 227
 see also Berserks
Shetland Islands, 123, 179
Ships, *see* Fleets

Sichelin, king of Norway, uncle of Loth, 123
Sidonius, Bishop of Clermont, 70, 132, 134–5, 164, 182
Siege Warfare, 4, 14–15, 20–1, 31, 39, 43, 48, 69, 72, 79, 83–6, 89–91, 96–101, 105–11, 113, 115–19, 127, 129, 135–7, 167–8, 174, 200
  see also Ballistae, Onager, Fleets
Siege of,
  Andredscester, 48, 66
  Angers, 133
  Bath/Badon, 39, 109–15
  Caledon Wood, 107–109
  Clermond, 167 (*see MHLR* Vol 5 for details)
  Dimilioc and Tintagel, 96–101
  Dina Emrys, 83–6
  Dumbarton, Alclud, Loch Lomond, ix, 109, 111, 113, 115–19
  Lincoln, ix, 106–107
  Narbonne, 72
  Paris, 135–7
  Rome (5th cent., *see MHLR* Vol.5 for details), 168
  Rome (6th cent., *see MHLR* Vol.6 for details), 4
  St Albans, 102
  Thanet, 79
  Vortimer besieges Saxons, 79
  York (several), 90–1, 96, 105
  see also Battle of
Siesia, *see* Battle of
Sigar, son of Vitrgils, 221
Sigmund, king of Hunland, 210
Sigtunir, close to Sigtuna, 222
Sigurd/Siegfried the Dragon-Slayer, 210, 256
Silchester, ix, 59, 104, 115
Silver, 108, 199, 231
Sjaelland, 128, 130, 186, 192–3, 209, 221
Skalk of Scania, 199, 202
Skåne, 200

Skioldungs, 221
Skítblathnir, Odin's ship, 227
Skjold, son of Odin, 221
Slan/Slain, stream, 232
Slaves, 18, 38, 71, 92, 191, 229, 235–6
Slavs, 187–91, 196–9, 209, 211, 218, 254–5
  see also Wends
Sleipnir, Odin's horse, 218–19
Småland, 200
Snaer, mother of the wife of Vanladi, 227
Snorri, Icelandic historian, 212, 216–18, 220–2, 242, 244, 255
Snowdon, *see* Mt. Snowdon
Snowdonia, 84–5
Soissons, x, 135, 138, 167
Söleyjar, i.e. Solör in Norway, 199
Somerset, 87, 109, 229
Southampton, 106, 146, 171, 175
South-humbrians, 47
Southsex, 44, 80
Spain, Spaniards, 52, 72, 144–7, 155–6, 158–9, 168, 199, 245, 247, 249
Spying, *see* Intelligence Gathering
Squire, Squires, Servants, 15, 147
St Albans, city, ix, 64, 101–103
St Amphibalus, Church of, 59, 179
St Ambrius, monastery, 80, 90, 93
St Germanus, Bishop of Auxerre and general, 33, 37, 40–4, 46, 53, 61–70, 72–6, 79, 86, 91, 180, 206, 211, 230–1, 247–8
St Germanus of Man, Garmon, 66
St Patrick, bishop, vi, x, 41, 45–6, 69–71, 91–2, 229–42, 244, 247, 257–8
Stater, King of the Demetians, 121
Stenby, x, 201
Stevns, town, 128
Stilicho, Roman patrician and general, 36, 51–3, 55
Stone Thrower, 12, 21, 69, 86, 147
  see also Ballista, Onager, Siege of
Strangford, lake, 232

Stratagems, ruses, 44, 79, 95, 98, 100, 103, 190
Strategikon (military treatise), 107, 150, 176
Strategy/Diplomacy (goals and strategies very broadly conceived), 37–8, 57, 63, 74, 83, 98, 111, 144–5, 148, 190–1, 193, 209, 235
  see also Battle of, Stratagem
Strumik, Slavic king, 190
Suevi/Suebi, Germanic confederacy, 51–2, 72, 147, 199
Sulpicius Subuculus, Roman commander, 157
Supply, Logistics, Supply Depots/Hubs/Bases, Food, Provisions, 3, 16, 54, 56, 112, 143, 148–9, 165, 186, 194, 200
  see also Annona
Sussex, 47
Svedbegg/Svipdag, son of Vitta, 221
Sveigthir, 4th successor of Odin, 227
Svitjoth, land of the Swedes, 218, 227
Sweden, Swedish, vi, viii, 21–3, 32, 123, 126–7, 130, 142, 183, 188, 190, 194–6, 199–205, 210–12, 214–15, 217–18, 221–2, 227–8, 243–4, 254–5
Syagrius, Roman King, 133, 138, 167–8, 252–3

Taliesin, pupil of Merlin, 180
Tana Fork, 218, 228
  see also Vana
Tara, x, 233, 236–9, 241
Taxes, tax, taxpayers, donative, 22, 37, 58, 64, 78, 95, 104, 120, 143, 194, 199, 202–203, 205, 211, 249, 252
  see also Annona
Teucer, Duke of Phrygia, 144, 157
Teutones, Germanic people, 56
Thames, river, 56
Thanet, 79, 113, 115, 169–70, 173
  see also Battle of, Siege of
Thengil, king of Finnmark, 202
Theodosius I, emperor (379–395), 56

Theodosius II, emperor (402/408–450), 45, 56, 207
Thor, Odin's son, 217, 223
Thorias the Tall, the king of Jämtland and Hälsingland in Sweden, 195
Thorisarius, Roman general, 145
Thuringians, 31, 208
  see also Franks, Ripurian Franks, Salian Franks
Tibatto, *bacaudae* leader, 62, 71, 74–5
  see also Armorica, Bretagne
Tintagel, ix, 97–100, 150
Tirechan, historian, 230–1, 238–42, 244, 257
Tiurinlinna, x, 204
Tivis, river, 43
Torcilingi/Turcilingi, 168
Torquay, ix, 84
Torslunda, 223
Tosterön Island, 201
Totnes, ix, 58, 83–4, 98, 109–10, 115
Touchemlya Culture, 198
Tractus Armoricani, Dux, 54, 57, 64
Trade, 1, 11, 13, 201, 246
Tremorius, Archbishop of the City of the Legions (Caerleon), 90
Treves, see Trier
Tribune (various), 11, 14, 24–5, 64, 131, 133, 143, 252
Trier, 54, 72
Trinovantum, 79
Troilus, philosopher, 91
Troy, 218
Troyes/Tricasses/Trecassina/Augustobona, 9, 63, 69
Tuath, 19
Turma,
  Turma, division/legion/*meros* of the battle line, 24, 176
  Turma, a cohort or larger unit usually meaning infantry, 24, 89, 96–7, 102, 247
  Turma, unspecified cavalry unit, 150, 253

Turma (unit of 500/512 horsemen), 14
Turma (unit of 32–36 horsemen), 13
Tuulos, 204
Twrch Trwyth, Saxon leader, 111

Ugger/Uggerus, seer of Hunnic king, 193, 254
Ulfin of Ridcaradoch, familiar of Utherpendragon (i.e. Arthur), 98
Ulaid, 233, 235, 240
Ulidia, kingdom, 229, 231–2
Ulster, 233, 242–3, 249
Urgennius/Urbgennius, *Dux* of Bath, 121, 142
Urian, king of Moray/Mureif, 120–1, 141, 171
Utherpendragon, *see* Arthur

Valens, emperor, 17
Valentinian/Valentinianus I, emperor, 17, 247
Valentinian III (Valentianus), emperor (423–455), 45–6, 247
Valentius, *see* Valentinian III
Valhalla, 223–6
Valsgärde helmet, vii–viii
Vana/Vanha (various forms), 218, 227–8
Vana, wife of Sveigthir, 227–8
Vanlandi, son of Vana and Sveigthir, 227
Vandals, Germanic confederacy, 51–2, 147, 220
Västergötaland, 'West Gothic Land', 200
  see also Gothland
Veggdegg, son of Odin, 221
Vendel, A Place and Historical Period in Sweden, vii–viii, 32, 190, 206–207, 219, 224, 242
Vegetius, military theorist, 14–15, 24–5, 153, 227, 247, 257
Venedotia, 87, 120, 140–1
Verturiones, *see* Picts
Verulamium, *see* St Albans
Vexillum, Vexilla, Vexillationes, flag, military unit, 14, 192

Vicar/*Vicarius*, 25
Victor, son of Maximianus/Maximus, 39
Vienne, 53
Vigiles, guards, 96
Vik, 202, 211
Visbur, son of Vanlandi and Drifa, 227
Visigoths, *see* Goths
Vitrgils, son of Veggdegg, 221
Vitta, father of Hengist, 221
Volga, river, 196, 228, 255
Volkhov, river, 196
Vortimer, son of Vortigern, 11, 42–4, 47, 79, 82, 250
Vortigern, High-King, v, 10–11, 38, 40–4, 46–7, 51, 59–62, 65–6, 69–71, 76–86, 91, 93, 95, 180, 206, 221, 247, 250
Vortipore/Vortiporius, ruler of Britons, 39, 42, 69, 180
Vulteius Catellus, Roman commander, 149–50

Wagon, *see* Chariot
Wales, Welsh, 9, 11, 18–19, 33–4, 36, 39, 41, 43, 47–8, 53, 57–8, 66, 69, 76, 80, 83–4, 87, 92–5, 97, 103, 120, 123, 140–1, 178–82, 206, 229–30, 241–3, 246, 250, 253
  see also Venedotia, Kambria, Demetia, Caerleon, Merlin, Vortigern, St. Germanus
Wanius, king of the Huns, mercenary leader, 56–7
Wansdyke, Woden's Dyke, 36, 120, 243
Warwick/Warguit/Carguiet, 11, 141
Wat's Dyke, 36, 63, 120
Wecta, king, 47
Wedge, *cuneus, caput porci/porcinum, Svinfylking*, vii, 13, 15–17, 21–7, 87–9, 111, 114, 148–9, 153–6, 160, 174, 176, 226–7, 246–7, 253, 257
  see also Battle of, *cuneus, Punta, Rhombus*
Wends, Slavic people, x, 187–9, 191, 193, 209, 254
  see also Slavs

Wessex, 47
West-Saxons, 46, 49
Whitsun, feast, 93, 140
Wicklow, 232–3
Wihtgar, king, 49
Wihtgils, king, 47
Wigg, son of Freovin, 221
Wightwarians, Wight, 46, 49
Winchester/Gwintonia urbe, x, 59, 80, 90, 93, 95, 171, 174–5, 178–9, 257
  see also Battle of
Wippidsfleet, shore of, 38, 46–7
Wipped, thane, 47
Wise King of the East, Xiognu/Hun term, 218
Wise King of the West, Xiognu/Hun term, 218
Witta, king, 47
Woden, Germanic god meaning here Odin the Man, son of Frithowald, 47, 49, 223, 225–6, 256
  see also Odin
Worcester, 11, 141
Worms, viii, 211
Wroxeter, 41, 66

Xanten, 210
Xiognu/Hun, 218
  see also Huns

Ygerna, wife of Gorlois, 'mother', i.e. wife of Arthur, 97–101, 120, 149
Yngvi, Ynglings, 212, 222–3
York/Eboracum, city, x, 80, 84, 87, 89–90, 93, 96–7, 105, 120, 141, 171

Zosimus, historian, 51–2, 54, 184, 256–7